March 29, 2005

Dear Mr. Speaker:

Pursuant to Section 406 of Public Law 101-246, amended by Public Law 108-447, I am transmitting herewith the annual report for 2004 on Voting Practices at the United Nations.

This report assesses the voting practices of the governments of UN member states in the General Assembly and Security Council for 2004, and evaluates the actions and responsiveness of those governments to U.S. policy on issues of special importance to the United States.

We are sending a copy of this report to each U.S. diplomatic mission abroad so that they will be fully informed about the extent to which the government to which they are accredited supports U.S. priorities at the United Nations.

Sincerely,

Condoleezza Rice

Enclosure:
    Annual Voting Report for 2004.

The Honorable
    J. Dennis Hastert,
        Speaker of the House of Representatives.

THE SECRETARY OF STATE

WASHINGTON

March 29, 2005

Dear Mr. Chairman:

Pursuant to Section 406 of Public Law 101-246, amended by Public Law 108-447, I am transmitting herewith the annual report for 2004 on Voting Practices at the United Nations.

This report assesses the voting practices of the governments of UN member states in the General Assembly and Security Council for 2004, and evaluates the actions and responsiveness of those governments to U.S. policy on issues of special importance to the United States.

We are sending a copy of this report to each U.S. diplomatic mission abroad so that they will be fully informed about the extent to which the government to which they are accredited supports U.S. priorities at the United Nations.

Sincerely,

Condoleezza Rice

Enclosure:
Annual Voting Report for 2004.

The Honorable
    Richard G. Lugar, Chairman,
        Committee on Foreign Relations
        United States Senate.

I – INTRODUCTION

This publication is the 22nd annual Report to the Congress on Voting Practices at the United Nations. It is submitted in compliance with Section 406 of Public Law 101-246. This law provides, in relevant part:

"The Secretary of State shall transmit to the Speaker of the House of Representatives and the chairman of the Committee on Foreign Relations of the Senate a full and complete annual report which assesses for the preceding calendar year, with respect to each foreign country member of the United Nations, the voting practices of the governments of such countries at the United Nations, and which evaluates General Assembly and Security Council actions and the responsiveness of those governments to United States policy on issues of special importance to the United States."

The fiscal year 2005 Consolidated Appropriations Act (Public Law 108-447) called for expanded treatment by the report of Middle East issues, requiring "a separate listing of all plenary votes cast by member countries of the United Nations in the General Assembly on resolutions specifically related to Israel that are opposed by the United States." This information appears in a new Annex at the end of this report.

This report reviews voting practices in the UN Security Council and General Assembly (UNGA) in calendar year 2004 and presents data in a variety of formats. All Security Council resolutions for the entire year are described, and voting on them is tabulated (Section II). The report also statistically measures the overall voting of UN member states at the 59th General Assembly in fall 2004 in comparison with the U.S. voting record (Section III). In addition to an alphabetical listing of all countries, the report presents the voting record in a rank-ordered listing by voting coincidence percentage and geographic regions, by selected bloc groupings, and in a side-by-side comparison with the amount of U.S. aid given to each country in fiscal year 2004. It also lists and describes UNGA resolutions selected as important to U.S. interests, again with tables for regional and political groupings (Section IV). In Section V it presents all data by country. Finally, this year's report includes an Annex on General Assembly resolutions on Israel opposed by the United States.

The Security Council and the General Assembly deal with a full spectrum of issues—including threats to peace and security, terrorism, disarmament, economic and social development, humanitarian relief, and human rights—that are considered critical to U.S. interests. A country's behavior at the United Nations is always relevant to its bilateral relationship with the United States, a point the Secretary of State routinely makes in letters of instruction to new U.S. Ambassadors. Nevertheless, a country's voting record in the United Nations is only one dimension of its relations with the United States. Bilateral economic, strategic, and political issues are at times more directly important to U.S. interests.

1

SECURITY COUNCIL

The Security Council held 216 meetings in 2004 and adopted 59 out of 62 resolutions that were considered. It also issued 48 presidential statements, consensus documents issued by the Council president on behalf of the members. Voting coincidence percentages for Security Council members were high, with most resolutions (93.2 percent) adopted unanimously.

Russia and the United States were the only permanent members of the Security Council to exercise their veto power. Russia vetoed a draft resolution on Cyprus that the United States and the United Kingdom had submitted, and the United States vetoed two draft resolutions on the Middle East. Germany, Romania, and the United Kingdom abstained on the two draft resolutions the United States vetoed. The United States abstained on one resolution on the Middle East which was adopted. Algeria, China, and Pakistan abstained on two U.S.-cosponsored resolutions on Sudan; Algeria, Brazil, China, Pakistan, Philippines, and Russia abstained on a U.S.-cosponsored resolution on the elections in Lebanon. See Section II for vote descriptions and tables of voting summaries.

GENERAL ASSEMBLY

The General Assembly opened its 59th session on September 14, 2004, and held 76 Plenary sessions before recessing on December 23, 2004. It adopted 282 resolutions, more than in the past few years, but still below the 332 of 1990. The subject matter of the resolutions covered the full gamut of UN concerns: security, arms control, economic, social and humanitarian issues, human rights, budget and financial matters, and legal concerns. The resolutions that were the subject of recorded votes continued primarily to address arms control, the Middle East, and human rights.

Of the 282 resolutions adopted in Plenary, 213 (75.5 percent) were adopted by consensus. This figure and similar ones in recent years (78 percent in 2003, 82 percent in 2002 and 2001, 76 percent in 2000, 76.9 percent in 1999, 78 percent in 1998, 75.2 percent in 1997, 72.9 percent in 1996, 76.6 percent in 1995, and 77.4 percent in 1994) illustrate the high rate of consensus in the work of the General Assembly.

VOTING COINCIDENCE WITH THE UNITED STATES

On non-consensus issues, i.e., those on which a vote was taken, the average overall General Assembly voting coincidence of all UN members with the United States in 2004 was 23.3 percent, down from 31.2 percent in 2002, and reflecting the general downward trend since 1995, when voting coincidence reached 50.6 percent. This decline in voting coincidence with the United States on non-consensus issues in the years since 1995 reverses the steady and dramatic increase in the years immediately following the end of the Cold War. The 50.6 percent figure in 1995 was the first time the coincidence figure had exceeded 50 percent since 1978, while the 23.3 percent figure in 2004 is still considerably higher than the low point of 15.4 percent in 1988.

The following table illustrates the gradual decrease in overall voting coincidence with the United States since the post-Cold War high of 50.6 percent in 1995. This decrease is reflected in the steady drop in coincidence on human rights votes. On human rights issues, the 2004 voting coincidence percentage was up from the previous three years. On arms control votes, the trend has been generally upward; however, that trend began to reverse itself in 2001 and continued in 2003 and 2004. Since 1995, the trend on Middle East issues has been generally downward, except in 2001 and 2002, years in which the coincidence increased. Coincidence dropped significantly in 2004.

Year	Arms Control	Middle East	Human Rights	Overall Votes
2004	17.9%	9.8%	44.9%	23.3%
2003	30.7%	16.5%	34.3%	25.5%
2002	41.9%	32.4%	23.7%	31.2%
2001	50.4%	29.0%	33.9%	31.7%
2000	66.1%	11.9%	55.7%	43.0%
1999	57.9%	22.7%	52.5%	41.8%
1998	64.0%	22.5%	62.8%	44.2%
1997	65.8%	26.2%	61.9%	46.7%
1996	62.3%	28.3%	68.3%	49.4%
1995	60.9%	35.2%	81.0%	50.6%

When consensus resolutions are factored in as votes identical to those of the United States, a much higher measure of agreement with U.S. positions can be seen. This figure (81.2 percent), which more accurately reflects the work of the General Assembly, is slightly below the 85–88 percent range recorded since the statistic was first included in this report in 1993. It was 80.7 percent in 2003, 83 percent in 2002, 85 percent in 2001, 87.6 percent in 2000, 86.4 percent in 1999, 88.3 percent in 1998, 87.3 percent in 1997, 87.3 percent also in 1996, 88.2 percent in 1995, 88.8 percent in 1994, and 88.3 percent in 1993. (See Section III—General Assembly—Overall Votes for additional comparisons.)

The coincidence figure on votes considered important to U.S. interests (35 percent) is significantly higher than the percentage registered on overall votes (23.3 percent). (See Section IV—Important Votes, for a side-by-side comparison of important and overall votes for each UN member.)

As in past years, Israel (93.2 percent), Palau (98.5 percent), and Micronesia (78 percent) were among the highest in voting coincidence with the United States. Marshall Islands, Australia, the United Kingdom, France,

Albania, Canada, and Spain were also among the top 10 countries, with Latvia, Monaco, and Iceland close behind.

In general, however, 2004 saw declining voting coincidences with the United States, even among friends and allies. Most members of the Western European and Others Group (WEOG) continued to score higher than average coincidence levels with the United States; the average was 45.9 percent, which is down from 46.1 percent in 2003, 49.9 percent in 2002, 54.4 percent in 2001, 61.5 percent in 2000, 67.1 percent in 1999, 65.2 percent in 1998, and 70.9 percent in 1997. There has been a growing divergence between the United States and the European Union, which at 44.3 percent is down from 45.5 percent in 2003, 49.5 percent in 2002, 53.5 percent in 2001, 62.5 percent in 2000, 68.5 percent in 1999, 66.7 percent in 1998, and 73 percent in 1997. The Eastern European Group was also down in 2004, at an average of 38 percent, which is down from 38.7 percent in 2003, 43.7 percent in 2002, 48.8 percent in 2001, 58 percent in 2000, 61.7 percent in 1999 and 1998, and 68.6 percent in 1997 and 1996. After the latter group's meteoric rise in coincidence with the United States immediately following the dissolution of the Soviet bloc, it largely matched the coincidence level of the Western European countries before its decline in the past six years. The NATO and Nordic countries also decreased in voting coincidence with the United States, continuing to reverse the upward trend of the late 1990s. The African and Asian groups, the Islamic Conference, the Non-Aligned Movement, and the Latin American and Caribbean group all declined in voting coincidence with the United States.

The following five bar graphs depict voting trends since the end of the Cold War. Voting coincidence with the United States, in terms of both overall and important votes, is broken down by year for issues, geographic groups, and political groups.

OVERALL PLENARY VOTES

By Issues by Year

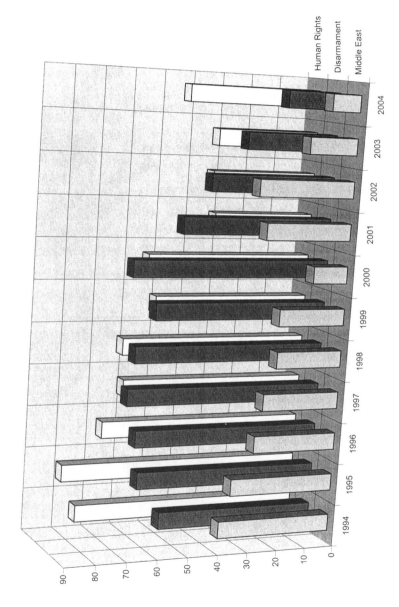

Human Rights
Disarmament
Middle East

Percent of Voting Coincidence with the United States

OVERALL PLENARY VOTES

Geographic Groups

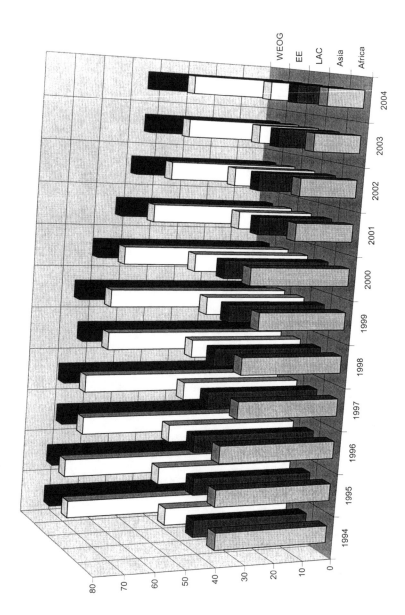

Percent of Voting Coincidence with the United States

OVERALL PLENARY VOTES

Political Groups

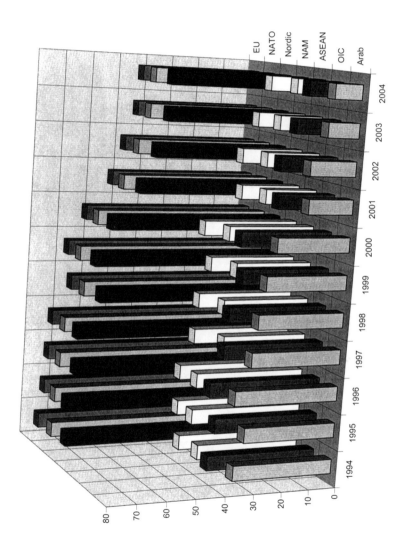

Percent of Voting Coincidence with the United States

IMPORTANT VOTES

Geographic Groups

WEOG
EE
LAC
Africa
Asia

90 80 70 60 50 40 30 20 10 0

1994 1995 1996 1997 1998 1999 2000 2001 2002 2003 2004

Percent of Voting Coincidence with the United States

IMPORTANT VOTES

Political Groups

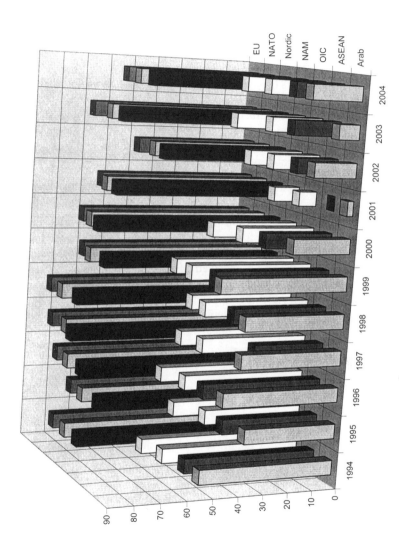

Percent of Voting Coincidence with the United States

REALIZATION OF U.S. PRIORITIES

The United States set forth five major objectives for the 59th General Assembly: (1) advancing economic freedom as a route to freedom and prosperity, especially in developing countries; (2) ending child sex tourism; (3) promoting democracy and increasing cooperation among democratic countries in the United Nations; (4) banning human cloning through an international convention against human cloning; and (5) bringing balance to Middle East resolutions to support the Roadmap to Middle East Peace.

The United States made modest gains in each of these five areas during the session. The United States succeeded in adding important references to free market policies to resolutions on development, and in adding language addressing sex tourism to a resolution on the trafficking of women and girls. Cooperation among members of the UN democracy caucus continued to gain momentum, with passage of a resolution encouraging the work of intergovernmental and nongovernmental organizations in promoting and consolidating democracy. With regard to cloning, although a U.S.-cosponsored resolution calling for the negotiation of a convention to ban all forms of human cloning was not adopted, the General Assembly did adopt a proposal to form a working group to draft a Declaration urging all member states to prohibit any attempts to create human life through the process of cloning. Finally, the United States made progress in increasing the number of "no" votes and abstentions on one-sided Middle East resolutions, although it did not succeed in reducing the number of such resolutions. The United States believes that General Assembly resolutions dealing with the Middle East should be consistent with the principles of the performance-based Roadmap and the Madrid Peace Conference of 1991.

In the First Committee [Disarmament and International Security], the United States joined consensus on a resolution that followed up on last year's U.S.-introduced resolution to initiate a process to modernize the Committee. While not the U.S. version, this resolution preserved key U.S. recommendations. The United States joined consensus on a resolution on bilateral strategic nuclear arms reductions. However, the United States voted nearly alone in the First Committee and in the Plenary of the General Assembly on resolutions on elimination of nuclear weapons and the risk of nuclear proliferation in the Middle East.

The United States achieved several positive outcomes on economic and development issues in the Second Committee. These included a follow-up resolution on Financing for Development and changes to a resolution on economic integration which ultimately included U.S.-supported references to good governance, rule of law, and free market policies. The General Assembly for the first time graduated two countries, the Maldives and Cape Verde, from Least Developed Country (LDC) status, and adopted a resolution providing further momentum for other countries' graduation.

10

On human rights issues, the United States was disappointed to see a phenomenon seen in the UN Commission on Human Rights take hold in the Third Committee—the growing support for no-action motions which prevented consideration of resolutions on country human rights situations. Majorities in the Third Committee voted for no-action motions to avoid dealing with resolutions on Belarus (a U.S. resolution), Sudan, and Zimbabwe. The United States was encouraged, however, by the steps taken by the UN democracy caucus, including its support for a Romanian-sponsored resolution to encourage the work of intergovernmental and nongovernmental organizations in promoting and consolidating democracy. The resolution passed with no votes opposed. Passage of a resolution condemning religious intolerance with no votes against it was also a victory. The United States welcomed the passage of resolutions condemning the human rights situations in the Democratic Republic of the Congo, Iran, Myanmar (by consensus), and Turkmenistan. Finally, the United States succeeded in adding references addressing sex tourism and sexual exploitation to a resolution on trafficking of women and girls.

In the Fifth [Budget] Committee, the United States pressed for several measures to strengthen the Office of Internal Oversight Services (OIOS), and achieved passage of a resolution providing for member state access to any OIOS report upon request. The Fifth Committee also adopted a revised biennial budget for 2004–2005 which provided funds for greatly enhanced worldwide security for UN personnel, including a new Department of Safety and Security, which the United States strongly supported. The United States also joined consensus on the proposed outline of a biennial budget for 2006–2007.

Two legal issues of great importance to the United States continued to receive attention in the Sixth Committee. The United States cosponsored a Costa Rican resolution calling for the negotiation of a convention to ban all forms of human cloning. This resolution was not adopted; the Committee instead adopted a proposal to form a working group to draft a Declaration urging all member states to prohibit any attempts to create human life through the process of cloning. The General Assembly adopted a resolution calling upon states to ratify or accede to the Rome Statute of the International Criminal Court. The United States has long-standing concerns about the ICC, and disassociated from consensus on this resolution.

FORMAT AND METHODOLOGY

The format and presentation of this report are consistent with provisions of Public Law 101-246 as amended by Public Law 108-447, and the methodology employed is the same as that used since the report's inception.

The tables in this report provide a measurement of the voting coincidence of UN member countries with the United States. However, readers are cautioned about interpreting voting coincidence percentages. In

Section III (General Assembly Overall Votes), Section IV (General Assembly Important Votes and Consensus Actions), and the Annex, the percentages in the last column of the tables, under "votes only," are calculated using only votes on which both the United States and the other country in question voted Yes or No; not included are those instances when either state abstained or was absent. Abstentions and absences are often difficult to interpret, but they make a mathematical difference, sometimes significant, in the percentage results. The inclusion of the number of abstentions and absences in the tables of this report enables the reader to consider them in calculating voting coincidence percentages.

The percentages in the second to the last column of the tables, under "including consensus," offer another perspective on General Assembly activity. These figures, by presenting the percentage of voting coincidence with the United States after including consensus resolutions as additional identical votes, more accurately reflect the extent of cooperation and agreement in the General Assembly. Since not all states are equally active at the United Nations, the report credits to each country a portion of the 213 consensus resolutions based on its participation in the 89 recorded Plenary votes, plus one in the Third Committee. Each country's participation rate was calculated by dividing the number of Yes/No/Abstain votes it cast in the Plenary and on the one counted vote in the Third Committee (i.e., the number of times it was not absent) by the total number of Plenary votes (plus the one vote in the Third Committee). However, this calculation assumes, for want of an attendance record, that all countries were present or absent for consensus resolutions in the same ratio as for recorded votes.

Moreover, the content of resolutions should be considered in interpreting the figures in either of the aforementioned columns. There may be overwhelming agreement with the U.S. position on a matter of less importance to the United States and less support for a resolution it considers more important. These differences are difficult to quantify and to present in two coincidence figures.

Questions about this report may be directed to the Bureau of International Organization Affairs in the Department of State.

II – SECURITY COUNCIL

The Security Council's membership in 2004 consisted of the five permanent members—China, France, Russia, the United Kingdom, and the United States—and 10 non-permanent members: Algeria, Angola, Benin, Brazil, Chile, Germany, Pakistan, Philippines, Romania, and Spain. The following table summarizes the activity of the Security Council for the year and compares it with the previous 15 years.

YEAR	MEETINGS	RESOLUTIONS CONSIDERED	RESOLUTIONS ADOPTED	U.S. VETOES	PRESIDENTIAL STATEMENTS
2004	216	62	59	2	48
2003	208	69	67	2	30
2002	238	70	68	2	42
2001	192	54	52	2	39
2000	167	52	50	0	41
1999	124	67	65	0	34
1998	116	73	73	0	38
1997	117	57	54	2	57
1996	114	59	57	1	49
1995	130	67	66	1	63
1994	160	78	77	0	82
1993	171	95	93	0	88
1992	129	74	74	0	94
1991	53	42	42	0	21
1990	69	40	37	2	14
1989	69	25	20	5	17

In 2004, the Security Council considered 62 draft resolutions and adopted 59. Russia and the United States were the only permanent members of the Council to exercise their veto. Russia vetoed a draft resolution on Cyprus, while the United States vetoed two draft resolutions on the Middle East. The Council was again heavily engaged in efforts to resolve conflicts and to give direction to UN peacekeeping missions. Much of the Council's attention was focused on the following issues: Africa (28 resolutions); the Middle East (six resolutions and two draft resolutions); Iraq (three resolutions); Haiti (three resolutions); non-proliferation of weapons of mass destruction (one resolution); and counter-terrorism (four resolutions). The Council also adopted resolutions on Afghanistan, Bosnia and Herzegovina, Cyprus, East Timor, Georgia, children and armed conflict, international criminal tribunals, and the International Court of Justice.

RESOLUTIONS

Substantive resolutions formally addressed by the Security Council during the year are listed and described below. They are organized alphabetically by topic, and within each topic, by date. Each listing provides the number of the resolution, date of the vote, voting results (Yes-No-Abstain), including an indication of the U.S. vote, and a summary description. The full texts of resolutions adopted by the Security Council in 2004 are available online at http://www.un.org/Docs/sc/unsc_resolutions04.html. The U.S. position at the time the resolution was adopted and additional background information, as needed, follow each description.

COUNTRY RESOLUTIONS

AFGHANISTAN

S/Res/1536   March 26   15(US)-0-0

Decides to extend the UN Assistance Mission in Afghanistan (UNAMA) for an additional period of 12 months. Encourages Afghan authorities to enable an electoral process that provides for voter participation that is representative of the national demographics, including women and refugees and calls upon all eligible Afghans to fully participate in the registration and electoral process. Welcomes the progress made since the commencement of the disarmament, demobilization, and reintegration (DDR) process in October 2003 and the contribution of the International Observer Group; stresses that Afghan efforts to achieve further progress on DDR are critical, particularly for the creation of an environment more conducive to the conduct of free and fair elections. Welcomes the efforts to date of the Afghan authorities to implement their National Drug Control Strategy adopted in May 2003. Stresses that tackling the drug trade cannot be separated from creating a strong economy and a secure environment in Afghanistan and notes with concern the assessment made by the UN Office on Drugs and Crime in its last Afghan opium survey.

Requests UNAMA, with the support of the Office of the UN High Commissioner for Human Rights, to continue to assist the Afghan Independent Human Rights Commission in the full implementation of the human rights provisions of the new Afghan constitution, particularly those regarding the full enjoyment of women of their human rights. Welcomes the progress made by the International Security Assistance Force in expanding its presence outside of Kabul. Welcomes the development of the new Afghan National Army and Afghan National Police as important steps towards the goal of Afghan security forces providing security and ensuring the rule of law throughout the country.

Background: The Secretary-General reported to the Security Council on March 19, 2003, that insecurity in Afghanistan continued, that the newly created Afghan security institutions required further strengthening, and that trafficking in illegal narcotics was a threat to the success of Afghanistan's state-building. However, many areas showed improvement, such as training of the Afghan National Army; voluntary DDR of ex-soldiers or officers; and strengthening of the justice system.

In January, a Constitutional Loya Jirga adopted a new constitution, which created the framework for establishing rule of law, a necessary precondition for the success of political, security, and reconstruction efforts. This constitution called for every effort to be made to hold presidential and legislative elections, requiring a massive voter registration effort, and by March 15, 1.46 million voters out of an estimated total of 2.5 million eligible voters had registered (approximately 27 percent of these were women). Afghanistan held its first national democratic Presidential elections on October 9, and Hamid Karzai was announced as the official winner on November 3 and inaugurated on December 7. Parliamentary and local elections are planned for spring 2005.

U.S. Position: The United States drafted and introduced this resolution, which was adopted unanimously. The United States led several programs in Afghanistan in the areas of police training, drug eradication, deployment of national police forces and the Afghan National Army, supporting UNAMA in local conflict resolution, supporting voter registration and DDR efforts, and supporting local security task forces.

S/Res/1563   September 17   15(US)-0-0

Acting under Chapter VII of the UN Charter, extends the authorization of the International Security Assistance Force (ISAF), as defined in Resolutions 1386 (2001) and 1510 (2003), for a period of 12 months beyond October 13, 2004. Recognizes the need to strengthen the ISAF, and calls upon member states to contribute personnel, equipment, and other resources to the ISAF, and to make contributions to the Trust Fund established pursuant to Resolution 1386 (2001). Calls upon the ISAF to continue to work in close consultation with the Afghan Transitional Administration and its successors, the Special Representative of the Secretary-General, and the Operation Enduring Freedom Coalition in the implementation of the force mandate.

Background: Resolution 1386 (2001) initially authorized the ISAF to provide security in Kabul for six months beginning in December 2001. That authorization had been extended regularly until the adoption of Resolution 1510 (2003), which expanded the scope and geographic range of ISAF's mandate and set a precedent for annual renewal. In August, Eurocorps, a multinational army comprised of forces from Belgium, France, Germany, Luxembourg, and Spain, took over the command of ISAF from Canada.

U.S. Position: The United States joined other Council members in unanimously adopting this resolution to extend the mandate of ISAF.

BOSNIA AND HERZEGOVINA

S/Res/1551   July 9   15(US)-0-0

Acting under Chapter VII of the UN Charter, reminds the parties that, in accordance with the Dayton Peace Agreement [of 1995], they have committed themselves to cooperate fully with all entities involved in the implementation of this peace settlement, or which are otherwise authorized by the Security Council, including the International Criminal Tribunal for the

Former Yugoslavia. Underlines that full cooperation with the International Tribunal includes the surrender for trial of all persons indicted by the Tribunal and provision of information to assist in Tribunal investigations. Authorizes the member states to continue for a further planned period of six months the multinational stabilization force (SFOR) as established in accordance with Resolution 1088 (1996) under unified NATO command and control in order to fulfill the role specified in the Peace Agreement, and expresses its intention to review the situation with a view to extending this authorization further as necessary.

Welcomes NATO's decision to conclude its current SFOR operation in Bosnia and Herzegovina by the end of 2004 and further welcomes the European Union's (EU) intention to launch an EU mission, including a military component, to Bosnia and Herzegovina from December 2004. Authorizes the member states [acting under the SFOR authorization] to take all necessary measures to effect the implementation of and to ensure compliance with the Peace Agreement; authorizes member states to take all necessary measures to assist SFOR, and recognizes the right of the force to take all necessary measures to defend itself from attack or threat of attack. Decides that the status of forces agreements currently contained in the Peace Agreement shall apply provisionally to the proposed EU mission; and invites all states to continue to provide appropriate support and facilities for member states acting under the SFOR operation or the EU mission.

Background: A multinational implementation force, IFOR, was sent to Bosnia and Herzegovina in December 1995 to maintain peace and stability after the 1992–1995 conflict. In December 1996, the Security Council endorsed a NATO-led SFOR in Bosnia and Herzegovina as the successor to the NATO-led IFOR to help ensure compliance with the military provisions of the Peace Agreement. SFOR exercises a wide range of functions in support of civilian efforts related to law enforcement activities, police reform, humanitarian relief and refugees, demining, human rights, elections, rehabilitation of infrastructure, and economic reconstruction. In June 2004, NATO decided to terminate its leadership of the multinational stabilization force by the end of the year. At the same time, the EU announced its intention to establish a follow-on mission to SFOR.

U.S. Position: The United States cosponsored this resolution with France, Germany, Italy, Romania, Russia, Spain, and the United Kingdom. The United States added language to endorse the transition from NATO's force to the EU follow-on mission, welcoming the change as an indication of growing stability in the region.

S/Res/1575   November 22   15(US)-0-0

Acting under Chapter VII of the UN Charter, reminds the parties that, in accordance with the Dayton Peace Agreement [of 1995], they have committed themselves to cooperate fully with all entities involved in the implementation of this peace settlement, including the International Tribunal for the Former Yugoslavia, as it carries out its responsibilities for dispensing justice impartially, and underlines that full cooperation by states and entities with the International Tribunal includes the surrender for trial of all persons indicted by the Tribunal and provision of information to assist the Tribunal investigations.

Acknowledges the support of the authorities of Bosnia and Herzegovina for the European Union (EU) force and the continued NATO presence and their confirmation that both are the legal successors to the multinational stabilization force (SFOR) and can take such actions as are required, including the use of force, to ensure compliance with the Peace Agreement and relevant UN Security Council resolutions. Welcomes the EU's intention to launch an EU military operation in Bosnia and Herzegovina from December 2004. Authorizes establishment for an initial planned period of 12 months of a multinational stabilization force (EUFOR) as a legal successor to SFOR under unified command and control. Welcomes NATO's decision to conclude the SFOR operation in Bosnia and Herzegovina by the end of 2004, and to maintain a NATO Headquarters in Bosnia and Herzegovina to continue to assist in implementing the Peace Agreement in conjunction with EUFOR and authorizes establishment of a NATO Headquarters as a legal successor to SFOR. Recognizes that the Peace Agreement and the provisions of its previous relevant resolutions shall apply to and in respect of both EUFOR and the NATO presence as they have applied to and in respect of SFOR.

Authorizes the member states acting under above paragraphs to take all necessary measures to effect the implementation of and to ensure compliance with the annexes of the Peace Agreement. Authorizes member states to take all necessary measures in defense of the EUFOR or NATO presence and to assist both organizations in carrying out their missions, and recognizes the right of both the EUFOR and the NATO presence to take all necessary measures to defend themselves from attack or threat of attack.

Background: In Resolution 1551, the Security Council endorsed NATO's decision to conclude its current SFOR operation in Bosnia and Herzegovina by the end of 2004, the EU's intention to launch a mission, including a military component, from December 2004, and the establishment of a NATO headquarters to carry out certain operational tasks. Preparing for this transition, the Netherlands, in its role as EU President, and Germany (transmitting a letter from the NATO Secretary-General) each sent a letter on November 19 to the Security Council's President setting out the roles of NATO and the EU. The Government of Bosnia-Herzegovina also wrote to the Council expressing its endorsement for the new arrangements.

U.S. Position: The United States cosponsored this resolution with Romania.

BURUNDI

S/Res/1545   May 21   15(US)-0-0

Acting under Chapter VII of the UN Charter, decides to authorize, for an initial period of six months from June 1, 2004, with the intention to renew it for further periods, the deployment of a peacekeeping operation in Burundi entitled UN Operation in Burundi (ONUB) in order to support and help to implement the efforts undertaken by Burundians to restore lasting peace and bring about national reconciliation, as provided under the Arusha Agreement. Decides that ONUB will be headed by the Special Representative of the Secretary-General, and will initially be composed of existing African Mission in Burundi (AMIB) forces, and requests the Secretary-General, acting in liaison with the African Union, to ensure the transfer of authority over AMIB, with ONUB's framework, to his Special Representative for Burundi. Decides further that ONUB shall consist of a maximum of 5,650 military personnel, including 200 observers and 125 staff officers, up to 120 civilian police personnel, as well as the appropriate civilian personnel.

Authorizes ONUB to use all necessary means to carry out the following mandate: ensure the respect of ceasefire agreements; promote the re-establishment of confidence between all Burundian forces; carry out the disarmament and demobilization portions of the national program of disarmament, demobilization, and reintegration (DDR) of combatants; monitor the illegal flow of arms across the national borders in cooperation with the UN Mission in the Democratic Republic of Congo (MONUC); contribute to the creation of the necessary security conditions for the provision of humanitarian assistance, and facilitate the voluntary return of refugees and internally displaced persons; contribute to the successful completion of the electoral process stipulated in the Arusha Agreement by ensuring a secure environment; and without prejudice to the responsibility of the transitional Government of Burundi, protect civilians under threat of physical violence.

Decides that ONUB shall provide advice and the following assistance to the transitional Government and authorities to contribute to their efforts: monitor Burundi's borders, with special attention to refugees as well as to movements of combatants; carry out institutional reforms and the constitution of integrated national defense and internal security forces and training and monitoring of the police; proceed with electoral activities; complete implementation of reform of the judiciary and correction system; and ensure the promotion and protection of human rights, with particular attention to women, children, and vulnerable persons, and investigate human rights violations to put an end to impunity. Decides further that ONUB shall cooperate with the Government and authorities of Burundi, as well as other international partners, to ensure the coherence of their work in extending state authority and utilities throughout the territory; and in carrying out the national program of DDR of combatants and members of their families.

Reaffirms the obligation of all parties to comply fully with international humanitarian law related to the protection of humanitarian and related UN personnel, and urges unimpeded access by humanitarian personnel to all people in need of assistance. Requests all parties and concerned states to facilitate the voluntary, safe, and sustainable return of refugees and internally displaced persons, and to cooperate fully to this end with ONUB and the relevant international organizations.

Background: Rebel factions have fought Burundian government forces since 1993. Burundian political parties signed the Arusha Agreement on Peace and Reconciliation in Burundi in 2000, but the Agreement did not include a ceasefire agreement and Hutu rebel groups did not participate in the process. Although rebel groups and government forces continued to fight sporadically, Burundi was able to continue its implementation of the Arusha Agreement to restore peace and bring about national reconciliation. A Transitional Government was inaugurated in November 2001 and Burundi's National Assembly and Transitional Senate opened in January and February 2002. One of the rebel groups later signed a ceasefire agreement and joined the transitional government. Key provisions of the Agreement have still not been implemented and the Secretary-General recommended in his March 16, 2004, report that the Security Council authorize a multidimensional peacekeeping operation comprising military and civilian components. This operation would help Burundi implement security sector and judicial reform, adoption of legal instruments, and organization of elections.

U.S. Position: The United States voted for this resolution, believing that this show of international support will strengthen Burundian parties' efforts to implement their ceasefire and peace agreements.

S/Res/1577   December 1   15(US)-0-0

Acting under Chapter VII of the UN Charter, decides to extend the mandate of the UN Operation in Burundi (ONUB) to June 1, 2005. Urges the governments and parties concerned in the region to denounce the use and incitement of violence, and to unequivocally condemn human rights and international humanitarian law violations; and to actively cooperate with ONUB and UN Organization Mission in the Democratic Republic of the Congo (MONUC) and with efforts aimed at ending the impunity of those who commit human rights violations. Calls upon the Governments of the Democratic Republic of the Congo and of Rwanda to cooperate unreservedly with the Government of Burundi to ensure that the investigation into the Gatumba massacre is completed and that those responsible are brought to justice, and requests ONUB and MONUC to provide assistance to the Burundian and Congolese authorities to facilitate completion of the investigation and strengthen security of vulnerable populations. Expresses its intention to consider appropriate actions against those individuals who threaten the peace and national reconciliation process in Burundi.

Background: ONUB was established by Resolution 1545, adopted on May 21, 2004. A report by the Secretary-General to the Security Council on November 15 called for a six-month renewal of the mandate set forth in Security Council Resolution 1545. The Secretary-General reported that while progress was being made towards political reconciliation, human rights violations (such as the Gatumba massacre on August 13) continued and highlighted the importance of a continued UN presence in the region.

U.S. Position: The United States voted for this resolution, along with all other Council members. The United States supported this resolution with the understanding that the resolution in no way directs, encourages, or authorizes ONUB to cooperate with or support the International Criminal Court. Furthermore, the United States supported this resolution based on the understanding that the resolution does not change the existing mandate of ONUB regarding the investigation of violations of international humanitarian law.

COTE D'IVOIRE

S/Res/1527   February 4   15(US)-0-0

Acting under Chapter VII of the UN Charter, decides that the mandate of the UN Mission in Cote d'Ivoire, MINUCI, shall be extended until February 27, 2004. Decides to renew until February 27, 2004, the authorization given to member states participating in ECOWAS [Economic Community of West African States] forces together with French forces supporting them. Calls on the signatories of the Linas-Marcoussis Agreement to carry out expeditiously their responsibilities under the Linas-Marcoussis Agreement and to take the steps called for by the Secretary-General in paragraph 86 of his report, and expresses its readiness to help them to achieve lasting peace and stability. Requests the Secretary-General, pending a decision by the Security Council on the reinforcement of the UN presence in Cote d'Ivoire, to prepare the deployment of a possible peacekeeping operation within five weeks after such decision by the Council.

Background: The Secretary-General's January 6 report stated that hard-line elements among the Ivorian parties were determined to undermine the peace process and to seek a military solution to the crisis. The Secretary-General recommended that, should the Ivorian parties make sufficient progress in implementing the Linas-Marcoussis agreements by February 4, the Security Council consider authorizing the deployment of a multi-dimensional UN peacekeeping operation to support the peace process in Cote d'Ivoire.

U.S. Position: The United States voted to support this technical rollover of MINUCI's mandate, allowing more time for the Security Council to consider the recommendations in the Secretary-General's January 6 report regarding a possible UN peacekeeping mission in Cote d'Ivoire. The United States wanted to ensure that, should a new mission be created, it would have a clear mandate, an appropriate size and a clear exit strategy.

S/Res/1528   February 27   15(US)-0-0

Acting under Chapter VII of the UN Charter, decides to establish the UN Operation in Cote d'Ivoire (UNOCI) for an initial period of 12 months from April 4, 2004, and requests the Secretary-General to transfer authority from MINUCI (UN Mission in Cote d'Ivoire) and the ECOWAS forces to UNOCI on that date, and decides therefore to renew the mandate of the UN Mission in Cote d'Ivoire until April 4, 2004. Decides that UNOCI will comprise, in addition to the appropriate civilian, judiciary and corrections component, a military strength of a maximum of 6,240 personnel, including 200 military observers and 120 staff officers, and up to 350 civilian police officers. Reaffirms its strong support for the Secretary-General's Special Representative and approves his full authority for the coordination and conduct of all the activities of the UN system in Cote d'Ivoire.

Decides that the mandate of UNOCI, in coordination with the French forces authorized below, shall include observing and monitoring the implementation of the comprehensive ceasefire agreement of May 3, 2003; assisting the Government of National Reconciliation in monitoring the borders; assisting in disarmament, demobilization, reintegration of the combatants; coordinating implementation of a voluntary repatriation and resettlement program for ex-combatants; protecting UN personnel, installations and equipment, and protecting civilians under threat of imminent violence; facilitating the free flow of people, goods, and humanitarian assistance; providing support for implementation of the peace process; and assisting in the field of human rights, public information and law and order. Authorizes UNOCI to use all necessary means to carry out its mandate, within its capabilities and its areas of deployment. Decides to renew until April 4, 2004, the authorization given to the French forces and ECOWAS forces through its Resolution 1527 (2004); and authorizes for a period of 12 months from April 4, 2004, the French forces to use all necessary means in order to support UNOCI in accordance with the agreement to be reached between UNOCI and the French authorities.

Background: In the Secretary-General's January 6 report on the situation in Cote d'Ivoire, he had recommended the deployment of a UN peacekeeping operation. On February 4, the Security Council adopted a technical rollover of MINUCI, before deciding to accept the Secretary-General's recommendation.

U.S. Position: The United States voted for this resolution because it believed the new UN mission has an important role to play in restoring peace and stability not only to Cote d'Ivoire, but also to the whole of West Africa. The United States believed that the presence of UN peacekeepers in Cote d'Ivoire, Sierra Leone, and Liberia, and coordination of their efforts, would help promote an end to conflict and restore democracy and economic activity in the region. The United States continued to urge the Ivorian government,

President Gbagbo, and the Forces nouvelles to meet their commitments to the Linas-Marcoussis Agreement.

S/Res/1572   November 15   15(US)-0-0

Acting under Chapter VII of the UN Charter, condemns the air strikes committed by the national armed forces of Cote d'Ivoire which constitute flagrant violations of the ceasefire agreement of May 3, 2003, and demands that all Ivoirian parties to the conflict, the Government of Cote d'Ivoire, as well as Forces nouvelles, fully comply with the ceasefire. Reiterates its full support for the action undertaken by the UN Operation in Cote d'Ivoire (UNOCI) and French forces in accordance with their mandate under Resolution 1528 (2004). Emphasizes that there can be no military solution to the crisis and that the full implementation of the Linas-Marcoussis and Accra III Agreements remains the only way to resolve the crisis persisting in the country. Urges the President of the Republic of Cote d'Ivoire, the heads of all the Ivoirian political parties, and the leaders of the Forces nouvelles immediately to begin implementing all the commitments they have made under these agreements. Encourages the Secretary-General, African Union, and the Economic Community of West African States (ECOWAS) to continue their efforts to relaunch the peace process. Demands that the Ivoirian authorities stop all radio and television broadcasting inciting hatred, intolerance, and violence, requests UNOCI to strengthen its monitoring role in this regard, and urges the Government of Cote d'Ivoire and the Forces nouvelles to take all necessary measures to ensure the security and the safety of civilian persons, including foreign nationals and their property.

Decides that all states shall, for a period of 13 months from the date of adoption of this resolution, take the necessary measures to prevent the direct or indirect supply, sale, or transfer to Cote d'Ivoire, of arms or any related materiel, with certain exceptions, including for UNOCI and the French forces who support them. Decides that all states shall take the necessary measures, for a period of 12 months, to prevent the entry into or transit through their territories of all persons who constitute a threat to the peace and national reconciliation process in Cote d'Ivoire, in particular those who block the implementation of the Linas-Marcoussis and Accra III Agreements, any other person determined as responsible for serious violations of human rights and international humanitarian law in Cote d'Ivoire, any other person who incites publicly hatred and violence, and any other person determined by the Committee to be in violation of the arms embargo, provided that nothing in this paragraph shall oblige a state to refuse entry into its territory to its own nationals.

Decides that all states shall, for a period of 12 months, freeze immediately all financial assets and economic resources which are on their territories at the date of adoption of this resolution or at any time thereafter, owned or controlled directly or indirectly by the persons designated by the Committee or that are held by entities owned or controlled directly or indirectly by any persons acting on their behalf or at their direction, as designated by the Committee, and decides further that all states shall ensure that any funds, financial assets, or economic resources are prevented from being made available by their nationals or by any persons within their territories, to or for the benefit of such persons or entities.

Decides to establish a Committee of the Security Council consisting of all the members of the Council to undertake tasks including to designate the individuals and entities subject to the measures, and update this list regularly; and seek from all states concerned, particularly those in the region, information regarding actions taken to implement the measures. Requests all states concerned, particularly those in the region, to report to the Committee, within 90 days from the date of adoption of this resolution, on the actions they have taken to implement the measures, and authorizes the Committee to request whatever further information it may consider necessary. Decides that the travel ban and assets freeze shall enter into force on December 15, 2004, unless the Security Council shall determine before then that the signatories of the Linas-Marcoussis and Accra III Agreements have implemented all their commitments under the Accra III Agreement and are embarked towards full implementation of the Linas-Marcoussis Agreement.

Background: Since the 2003 Linas-Marcoussis accord halted fighting in Cote d'Ivoire between the Government of President Laurent Gbagbo and the rebels, full implementation of the ceasefire agreement has not been achieved. In July 2004, the parties, in a high-level meeting in the Ghanian capital that included officials from the United Nations and the African Union, reached another agreement known as Accra III, which sought to resolve disputed parts of the 2003 accord and offered a new framework for resolution of the conflict.

The peace process continues to be plagued by obstacles and resistance. Both parties to the conflict have not abided by the timetable set by Accra III. Parliament failed to meet the deadline for political reforms set for September 29, 2004. The ex-rebels ignored the deadline for disarmament set for October 15 and even withdrew from the unity government on October 28. Government aircraft violated the peace accords and began air strikes in November, killing nine French peacekeepers. France retaliated by destroying the tiny Ivorian air force. An angry exchange of words between France and Cote d'Ivoire ensued, as President Gbagbo's supporters rioted against foreigners in Abidjan, the country's largest city. France subsequently introduced this resolution in the Security Council.

U.S. Position: The United States, along with Chile, Germany, Romania, Spain, and the United Kingdom, joined France as cosponsors of the resolution. The United States believed the resolution would urge the Government and rebels of Cote d'Ivoire to fulfill their obligations under the peace accords. The United States further welcomed efforts by the African Union, ECOWAS, and the Secretary-General to help resolve the crisis.

CYPRUS

Not adopted   April 21   14(US)-1(Russia)-0

Decides to terminate the mandate of the UN Peacekeeping Force in Cyprus and maintain a UN operation in Cyprus, which shall be known as the UN Settlement Implementation Mission in Cyprus. Acting under Chapter VII of the UN Charter, decides that all states shall take the necessary measures to prevent the promotion or the direct or indirect sale, supply, or transfer to Cyprus by their nationals of arms and any related material, and the provision of any technical assistance, advice, or training, financing, or financial assistance related to military activities to Cyprus. Decides that these measures shall remain in place until the Security Council decides otherwise based on a request from the federal government of the United Cyprus Republic, and confirmation from the Secretary-General that the continued application of the arms embargo is no longer necessary for the maintenance of international peace and security. Decides further to establish a committee of the Security Council consisting of all the members of the Council to gather information on the sale, supply, or transfer of arms and related material; consider information concerning violations of these measures; and draft guidelines to facilitate implementation of the embargo.

Background: In February, the Secretary-General resumed negotiations with the Cypriot leaders to achieve a comprehensive settlement of the question of Cyprus. Despite a series of meetings, deadlock persisted on key issues. On March 31, the Secretary-General finalized the "Comprehensive Settlement of the Cyprus Problem," and submitted it to the leadership on each side. The Settlement outlined an arms embargo and the replacement of the UN Peacekeeping Force in Cyprus, whose main task was to maintain a *de facto* ceasefire, with a new operation that would have a more substantive political role and would work actively to promote the implementation of the Settlement. Cyprus would vote on the Settlement plan in an April 24 referendum. The Secretary-General requested that the Security Council adopt this resolution before the referendum in order to provide assurances to Greek Cypriots that the security structures provided for in the Settlement would be in place before they voted on April 24.

U.S. Position: The United States cosponsored this resolution with the United Kingdom. Russia's veto prevented the Security Council from providing assurances on security structures to the Greek Cypriots prior to the referendum on adopting the Settlement.

S/Res/1548   June 11   15(US)-0-0

Welcomes the Secretary-General's intention to complete a review within three months of the UN Peacekeeping Force in Cyprus' (UNFICYP) mandate, force levels, and concept of operations. Decides to extend the UNFICYP mandate for a further period ending December 15, 2004, and to consider the recommendations of the Secretary-General in his review of

UNFICYP and to act upon them within one month. Urges the Turkish Cypriot side and the Turkish forces to rescind without delay all remaining restrictions on UNFICYP, and calls upon them to restore in Strovilia the military status quo which existed there prior to June 30, 2000.

Background: The "Comprehensive Settlement of the Cyprus Problem was approved by the Turkish Cypriot electorate but rejected by the Greek Cypriot electorate, and did not enter into force. As a result, the Secretary-General recommended the continuance of UNFICYP to maintain the ceasefire but noted his intention to review the mission's mandate, force levels, and concept of operations.

U.S. Position: The United States voted for this resolution. In its explanation of vote, the United States noted that significant developments, including the results of the referenda and Cyprus' entry into the European Union, had fundamentally changed the situation in Cyprus and necessitated a critical examination of UNFICYP. The United States welcomed the Secretary-General's commitment to provide recommendations on UNFICYP.

S/Res/1568   October 22   15(US)-0-0

Welcomes the Secretary-General's intention to conduct a further review of the UN Peacekeeping Operation in Cyprus' (UNFICYP's) mandate, force levels, and concept of operation. Endorses the Secretary-General's recommendations for the amendment of the concept of operations and force level of the UNFICYP, as outlined in his report of September 24, 2004. Decides to extend UNFICYP's mandate for a further period ending June 15, 2005. Urges the Turkish Cypriot side and the Turkish forces to rescind without delay all remaining restrictions on UNFICYP, and calls upon them to restore in Strovilia the military status quo which existed there prior to June 30, 2000.

Background: Resolution 1548 (2004) welcomed the Secretary-General's intention to review UNFICYP's mandate, force levels, and concept of operations. The Secretary-General's review team noted decreasing incidents at crossing points and an improved security situation and recommended an increase in the number of civilian police and a 30 percent decrease in the number of military personnel.

U.S. Position: The United States voted for this resolution, and reaffirmed its support for the Secretary-General's Good Offices Mission report of May 28, 2004. The United States appreciated the Secretary-General's examination of UNFICYP and recommendation to reduce force levels by 30 percent. The United States also welcomed the further review of UNFICYP to take place before the next mandate renewal in June 2005.

DEMOCRATIC REPUBLIC OF THE CONGO

S/Res/1522   January 15   15(US)-0-0

Encouraged by the progress achieved in the peace process in the Democratic Republic of the Congo (DROC) since the conclusion of the Global and All Inclusive Agreement signed in Pretoria on December 17, 2002, and the subsequent establishment of the Government of National Unity and Transition, welcomes the efforts currently undertaken to set up the first integrated and unified brigade in Kisangani as a step toward the elaboration and implementation of a comprehensive program for the formulation of a Congolese integrated national army. Decides that, since the Government of National Unity and Transition has been established and is in place, its demand for the demilitarization of Kisangani and its surroundings laid down in Resolution 1304 (2000) shall not apply to the restructured and integrated forces of the DROC and to the armed forces included in the comprehensive program for the formation of an integrated and restructured national army. Urges the Government of National Unity and Transition to take the appropriate measures for the restructuring and integration of the armed forces of the DROC, in accordance with the Global and All Inclusive Agreement, including setting up a Supreme Defense Council and the elaboration of a national plan for disarmament, demobilization, and reintegration, as well as the necessary legislative framework. Calls upon the international community to provide further assistance for the integration and restructuring of the armed forces of the DROC.

Background: In Resolution 1304 (2000), the Council demanded that Ugandan and Rwandan forces, as well as forces of the Congolese armed opposition and other armed groups, completely withdraw from Kisangani, and called on all parties to the Lusaka Cease-fire Agreement to respect the demilitarization of the city and its surroundings. Due to the efforts under way to set up the first integrated and unified brigade in Kisangani, this earlier demand was adjusted in order to allow the brigade to operate in that city.

U.S. Position: The United States joined all other Security Council members in adopting this resolution.

S/Res/1533   March 12   15(US)-0-0

Acting under Chapter VII of the UN Charter, requests the UN Organization Mission in the Democratic Republic of the Congo (MONUC) to continue to report on the position of armed groups, arms supplies, and the presence of foreign military and to inspect, without notice as it deems it necessary, the cargo of aircraft and of any transport vehicle; and authorizes MONUC to seize or collect, as appropriate, the arms and any related materiel whose presence in the territory of the Democratic Republic of the Congo (DROC) violates the arms embargo imposed by Resolution 1493, and to dispose of such arms and related materiel as appropriate.

Decides to establish a Committee of the Security Council consisting of all members of the Council (the Committee) to, among other things, seek information from all states, particularly those in the region, regarding their actions to implement the provisions from Resolution 1493 regarding the arms embargo, the ban on assistance, especially military or financial assistance, to armed groups in DROC, and the urging of Rwanda and Uganda to exercise a positive influence on armed groups in DROC under their influence, and thereafter to request from them whatever further information it may consider useful; and to present reports with recommendations on strengthening the measures from Resolution 1493. Requests all states, in particular those in the region, to report to the Committee, within 60 days, on actions taken to implement the arms embargo in Resolution 1493, and authorizes the Committee thereafter to request from member states whatever further information it may consider necessary. Requests the Secretary-General to create, for a period expiring on July 28, 2004, a group of experts consisting of no more than four members, to examine and analyze information gathered by MONUC in the context of its monitoring mandate; recommend ways of improving the capabilities of states interested, in particular those of the region, to ensure the arms embargo is effectively implemented; and provide the Committee with regular reports that include a list, with supporting evidence, of those found to have violated the arms embargo and their supporters for possible future measures by the Council.

Background:　The Secretary-General reported in November 2003 that while progress had been made, much remained to be achieved, with Rwandan military personnel allegedly still present in the eastern DROC. He also noted the incessant flow of arms into DROC, which violated the embargoes required by previous Council resolutions.

U.S. Position:　The United States joined all other Council members in adopting this resolution.　In the U.S. view, the resolution's adoption represented a critical step forward in the Security Council's collective effort to reduce the illegal flow of weapons into the DROC. The United States believed the new sanctions committee could bring international pressure to bear against those who continued to ship arms to the DROC contrary to existing multilateral restrictions that member states were obligated to implement.

S/Res/1552　　　　July 27　　　　15(US)-0-0

Acting under Chapter VII of the UN Charter, reaffirms the demands in Resolution 1493 (2003) regarding freedom of movement of UN personnel, assistance to armed groups in the Democratic Republic of the Congo, and access to the UN Mission in the Democratic Republic of the Congo (MONUC).　Decides to renew until July 31, 2005, the arms embargo in Resolution 1493 and all provisions of Resolution 1533, which established a sanctions committee and a group of experts to monitor cooperation with the sanctions.

Background: After cross-border violence in Rwanda and the Democratic Republic of the Congo (DROC) in May, the Security Council issued a Presidential Statement, which noted and condemned Rwandan military activities that impeded MONUC's freedom of movement. After a month of volatility in the DROC, the Security Council issued another Presidential Statement in June that warned all parties against violations of the embargo imposed by Resolution 1493. Specifically, the Council urged Rwanda to not provide any practical or political support to armed groups in the DROC.

U.S. Position: The United States voted for this resolution in support of the peace process in the Democratic Republic of the Congo.

S/Res/1555   July 29   15(US)-0-0

Decides to extend the mandate of the UN Mission in the Democratic Republic of the Congo (MONUC), as contained in Resolutions 1493 (2003) and 1533 (2004), both adopted under Chapter VII of the UN Charter, until October 1, 2004. Requests the Secretary-General to submit a report to the Council before August 16 on the execution by MONUC of its mandate.

Background: Resolution 1493 (2003) established an arms embargo, increased the troop ceiling, and bolstered MONUC's mandate by authorizing the mission to use all necessary means to fulfill its mandate in Ituri and North and South Kivu where fighting had occurred in 2003. Resolution 1533 (2004) established a committee to monitor the embargo against all armed groups operating in the eastern Democratic Republic of the Congo that was established by Resolution 1493.

U.S. Position: The United States joined the other Council members in adopting this resolution unanimously.

S/Res/1565   October 1   15(US)-0-0

Acting under Chapter VII of the UN Charter, decides to extend the deployment of the UN Mission in the Democratic Republic of the Congo (MONUC) until March 31, 2005. Requests the Secretary-General to arrange the rapid deployment of additional military capabilities for MONUC in accordance with the recommendation contained in his letter dated September 3, 2004, to deploy as soon as possible in the provinces of North and South Kivu all the brigades and appropriate force enablers. Authorizes the increase of MONUC's strength by 5,900 personnel, including up to 351 civilian police personnel, as well as the deployment of appropriate civilian personnel, appropriate and proportionate air mobility assets and other force enablers, and expresses its determination to keep MONUC's strength and structure under regular review. Requests the Secretary-General to report to the Council within one month on reforms necessary to improve the structures of command and control and the management of military information within MONUC, and to rationalize the civilian and police components to MONUC.

Decides that MONUC will have a mandate to deploy and maintain a presence in the key areas of potential volatility; discourage violence, in particular by deterring the use of force to threaten the political process; allow UN personnel to operate freely, particularly in the eastern part of the Democratic Republic of the Congo; establish the necessary operational links with the UN Operation in Burundi, and with the Governments of the Democratic Republic of the Congo (DROC) and Burundi; discourage cross-border movements of combatants; monitor the implementation of the arms embargo in Resolution 1493, including by inspecting, as it deems it necessary and without notice, the cargo of aircraft and of any transport vehicle using the ports, airports, airfields, military bases, and border crossings in North and South Kivu and in Ituri; and seize and dispose of as appropriate, arms and any related materiel violating the arms embargo. Decides that MONUC's mandate, in support of the Government of National Unity and Transition, will also include support operations to disarm foreign combatants led by the Armed Forces of the DROC; facilitation of the demobilization and voluntary repatriation of the disarmed foreign combatants and their dependents; contribution to the disarmament of Congolese combatants; and assistance in the establishment of a secure environment for free, transparent, and peaceful elections to take place. Decides that MONUC will also have the mandate to provide advice and assistance to the transitional government and authorities to contribute to their efforts to take forward essential legislation, including the future constitution, security sector reform, and the electoral process.

Stresses the need for the Government of National Unity and Transition to carry out the process provided for by the Global and All Inclusive Agreement, and to implement the recommendations regarding restoring security, territorial reunification of the country, and preparation for elections in the Secretary-General's third special report. Calls upon the Government of National Unity and Transition to cooperate closely with MONUC in establishing three joint commissions on essential legislation, security sector reform, and elections, and in implementing the security sector reform. Urges the Government of National Unity and Transition to develop without further delay a plan for the disarmament of foreign combatants, and to entrust its implementation to the Armed Forces of the DROC, with MONUC's support.

Urges each of the Governments of the DROC, Burundi, Rwanda, and Uganda to ensure that its territory is not used to infringe the sovereignty of the others; to normalize bilateral relations; and to cooperate in assuring border security. Urges in particular the Governments of the DROC and Rwanda to work together and with MONUC and the African Union to remove the threat posed by foreign armed groups. Calls upon the Government of National Unity and Transition to prevent the use of the media to incite hatred or tensions among communities. Strongly condemns violence and other violations of international humanitarian law and human rights. Demands that all parties cooperate fully with the operations of MONUC and ensure the safety and unhindered access for UN and associated personnel in carrying out their mandate, throughout the territory of the DROC.

Expresses grave concern at the allegations of sexual exploitation and misconduct by civilian and military personnel of MONUC and requests the Secretary-General to continue to fully investigate these allegations to take appropriate action, and further encourages MONUC to conduct training for personnel, and urges troop-contributing countries to take appropriate disciplinary action on their personnel.

Background: In the Secretary-General's August 16, 2004, report, he noted that while the Transitional Government and MONUC had made progress in restoring peace and achieving unity in the DROC, the country was still unsettled, with tensions occasionally erupting into violence. Reiterating the need for a political settlement in DROC, the Secretary-General laid out the core tasks the Transitional Government must accomplish. The Secretary-General stated that MONUC lacked capacity to contribute to the peace process and the mandated tasks were not specific enough, recommending specific tasks that MONUC would accomplish, as well as an increase of 5,900 military personnel.

U.S. Position: The United States joined other Council members in adopting this resolution. The United States shared the Secretary-General's concerns about MONUC's challenges. The United States issued a Statement of Position supporting the resolution with the understanding that the resolution "...does not direct MONUC to cooperate with the International Criminal Court." U.S. policy ensures "...that members of the [U.S.] Armed Forces participating in UN peace operations are protected from criminal prosecution or other assertion of jurisdiction by the International Criminal Court." The resolution does not mention the International Criminal Court.

ETHIOPIA/ERITREA

S/Res/1531   March 12   15(US)-0-0

Decides to extend the UN Mission in Ethiopia and Eritrea's (UNMEE) mandate until September 15, 2004. Requests the Secretary-General to monitor the situation closely and to keep under review the mission's effectiveness, and to adjust and streamline the mission's operations as needed. Calls on the parties to cooperate fully and promptly with the Boundary Commission and to create the necessary conditions for demarcation to proceed expeditiously, including through the unequivocal restating of Ethiopia's acceptance of the Boundary Commission's decision, Ethiopia's appointment of field liaison officers, and the payment of its dues to the Boundary Commission. Reaffirms the crucial importance of a political dialogue between the two countries for the completion of the peace process and the consolidation of progress achieved so far.

Reiterates its support for the Secretary-General's initiative to exercise his good offices by appointing a Special Envoy for Ethiopia and Eritrea, Lloyd Axworthy (Canada) in order to facilitate the implementation of the Algiers Agreements, the Boundary Commission's decision, and the relevant Security Council resolutions and decisions; and to encourage the normalization of diplomatic relations between the two countries. Emphasizes that this appointment does not constitute an alternative mechanism. Stresses that the Special Envoy enjoys the unanimous support of the witnesses to the Algiers Agreements, namely the United Nations, the United States, Algeria, the African Union, and the European Union; and urges both parties, particularly the Government of Eritrea, to engage constructively and without further delay with the Special Envoy.

Background: The Secretary-General reported in March that the parties' overall cooperation showed signs of gradual deterioration over the previous few months. He appointed Lloyd Axworthy as his Special Envoy for Ethiopia and Eritrea to explore with those governments how best to overcome the impasse in the implementation of the Algiers Agreement (cessation of hostilities agreements signed in 2000). The Secretary-General also reported that, since his December report, the parties had made no progress in the demarcation of the border.

The Security Council established UNMEE in July 2000 through Resolution 1312, following two years of fighting between Ethiopia and Eritrea over a border dispute and expanded it through Resolution 1320 in September 2000 to include the monitoring of cessation of hostilities. The Boundary Commission is an independent body of international legal experts established in 2001, charged with recommending a demarcation of the disputed border.

U.S. Position: The United States voted for this resolution. The United States was concerned about the political impasse between Ethiopia and Eritrea and emphasized the need to re-evaluate UNMEE's mandate and streamline the mission if demarcation could not go forward.

S/Res/1560   September 14   15(US)-0-0

Decides to extend the mandate of the UN Mission in Ethiopia and Eritrea (UNMEE) until March 15, 2005, and approves the adjustments to UNMEE, as recommended by the Secretary-General in his report. Calls upon Eritrea and Ethiopia to cooperate fully and expeditiously with UNMEE in the implementation of its mandate, to ensure the security of all UNMEE staff, and to remove all restrictions on the work and movement of UNMEE and its staff.

Stresses that Ethiopia and Eritrea have the primary responsibility for the implementation of the Algiers Agreement and of the Boundary Commission's decision and calls upon both parties to show political leadership to normalize their relationship. Calls on the parties to cooperate fully and promptly with the Boundary Commission and to create the necessary conditions for demarcation to proceed expeditiously, including through the payment of Ethiopia's dues to the Boundary Commission and the appointment of field liaison officers. Urges Ethiopia to show the political will to reaffirm unequivocally its acceptance of the Boundary Commission's decision, and take the necessary steps to enable the Commission to demarcate the border without further delay. Calls on Eritrea to enter into dialogue and cooperation with the Secretary-General's Special Envoy for Ethiopia and Eritrea. Reiterates full support for the Secretary-General's Special Envoy for Ethiopia and Eritrea, Lloyd Axworthy (Canada), in his efforts to facilitate the implementation of the Algiers Agreements, the decision of the Boundary Commission and normalization of diplomatic relations between the two countries through his good offices.

Background: Although the parties entrusted the Boundary Commission with post-war border demarcation, the Commission has been unable to proceed with its task. Ethiopia has rejected significant parts of the Boundary Commission's final and binding decision of April 13, 2002. Eritrea has insisted that dialogue is not possible before the completion of the demarcation process and therefore has refused to engage with the Secretary-General's Special Envoy on the peace process.

In his September 2, 2004, report, the Secretary-General reported no major incidents between Ethiopia and Eritrea, but expressed concern over whether continued military stability could be guaranteed without progress in the political process. In his report, the Secretary-General recommended adjustments to and streamlining of UNMEE's operations.

U.S. Position: The United States voted for this resolution, and renewed its commitment to provide seven U.S. military observers for the Mission.

GEORGIA

S/Res/1524   January 30   15(US)-0-0

Decides to extend mandate of the UN Observer Mission in Georgia (UNOMIG) for a new period terminating on July 31, 2004, subject to a review as appropriate of its mandate by the Council in the event of changes in the mandate of the Commonwealth of Independent States (CIS) peacekeeping force.

Reaffirms the commitment of all member states to the sovereignty, independence, and territorial integrity of Georgia within its internationally recognized borders, and the necessity to define the status of Abkhazia within the state of Georgia in strict accordance with these principles. Strongly supports the sustained efforts of the Secretary-General and his Special Representative, Russia, the Group of Friends of the Secretary-General, and the Organization for Security and Cooperation in Europe, to promote the stabilization of the situation and the achievement of a comprehensive political settlement. Deeply regrets the continued refusal of the Abkhaz side to agree to a discussion on the substance of the document entitled "Basic Principles for the Distribution of Competences between Tbilisi and Sukhumi" and its transmittal letter, and urges both parties to give them full and open consideration, and to engage in constructive negotiations on their substance.

Welcomes the start of the deployment of a civilian police component of UNOMIG and calls on the parties to cooperate and actively support the police component. Calls on the Georgian side to continue to improve security for joint UNOMIG and CIS peacekeeping force patrols in the Kodori Valley. Underlines that it is the primary responsibility of both sides to provide appropriate security and to ensure the freedom of movement of UNOMIG, the CIS peacekeeping force, and other international personnel.

Background: UNOMIG was established in August 1993 to verify compliance with the ceasefire agreement between the Government of Georgia and the Abkhaz authorities in Georgia. UNOMIG also observes the operation of the CIS peacekeeping force in the region. Resolution 1494, adopted by the Council in July 2003, authorized a civilian police component to be added to UNOMIG. Because of the critical role that UNOMIG plays in maintaining stability in the area, the Secretary-General recommended a further six-month extension of the Mission's mandate. The Group of Friends of the Secretary-General on Georgia is comprised of France, Germany, Romania, Russia, the United Kingdom, and the United States.

U.S. Position: The United States introduced this resolution along with the other members of the Group of Friends of the Secretary-General on Georgia.

S/Res/1554   July 29   15(US)-0-0

Decides to extend the mandate of the UN Observer Mission in Georgia (UNOMIG) for a new period terminating on January 31, 2005, subject to a review as appropriate of its mandate by the Council in the event of changes in the mandate of the Commonwealth of Independent States (CIS) peacekeeping force. Reaffirms the commitment of all member states to the sovereignty, independence, and territorial integrity of Georgia within its internationally recognized borders, and the necessity to define the status of Abkhazia within the state of Georgia. Deeply regrets the continued refusal of the Abkhaz side to agree to a discussion on the substance of the document entitled "Basic Principles for the Distribution of Competences between Tbilisi and Sukhumi" and again strongly urges the Abkhaz side to receive the document in its transmittal letter. Urges both parties thereafter to give the document full and open consideration, and to engage in constructive negotiations on its substance.

Regrets also the lack of progress on political status negotiations. Reminds all concerned to refrain from any action that might impede the peace process. Expresses concern that despite the start of the deployment of a civilian police component as part of UNOMIG, as agreed by the parties, the deployment of the remaining officers in the Gali sector is still outstanding, and calls upon the Abkhaz side to allow for a swift deployment of the police component in this region. Underlines that it is the primary responsibility of both sides to provide appropriate security and to ensure the freedom of movement of UNOMIG, the CIS peacekeeping force, and other international personnel; strongly condemns the repeated abductions of personnel of those missions in the past, deeply deplores that none of the perpetrators has been brought to justice, and reiterates that it is the responsibility of the parties to end this impunity.

Background: The Secretary-General reported in July 2004 on the unstable situation in Abkhazia. Despite incremental progress on specific issues related to the conflict, the parties still have not had a substantive dialogue on the key issues of the conflict. In the absence of a political settlement, the area will continue to be unsettled. The presence of UNOMIG prevents the resumption of hostilities while the parties pursue a lasting solution. The Secretary-General therefore recommended that the Council extend the mandate of UNOMIG for further period of six months.

U.S. Position: The United States introduced this resolution along with other members of the Group of Friends of the Secretary-General on Georgia.

GUINEA-BISSAU

S/Res/1580   December 22   15(US)-0-0

Decides to extend the mandate of the UN Peace-Building Support Office in Guinea-Bissau (UNGOBIS), as a special political mission, for one year. Decides also to revise UNOGBIS's mandate to include support efforts to enhance political dialogue; promotion of national reconciliation and respect for the rule of law and human rights; support to all national stakeholders to ensure the full restoration of constitutional normalcy and assist with free and transparent presidential elections; assistance in strengthening conflict prevention; support of national efforts to reform the security sector, including the development of stable civil-military relations; encouragement of the government to fully implement the UN Program of Action on illicit trade in small arms; and assistance to the United Nations to mobilize international financial assistance to the Government to actively support efforts of the UN system and Guinea-Bissau's partners toward strengthening state institutions and structure to enable them to uphold the rule of law, respect of human rights, and unimpeded and independent functioning of the executive, legislative, and judicial branches of government.

Encourages the authorities of Guinea-Bissau to enhance political dialogue and pursue constructive civil-military relations, as a way forward towards the peaceful completion of the political transition, including the holding of presidential elections as envisaged in the Political Transitional Charter. Calls upon the National Assembly of Guinea-Bissau, while addressing the issue of granting an amnesty for all those involved in military interventions since 1980, to take account of the principles of justice and fight against impunity. Strongly urges the government, together with military authorities to agree on a national plan for the reform of the security sector, in particular military reform. Invites the Secretary-General to establish an Emergency Fund, to be administered by the UN Development Program, to support efforts related to the planning and implementation of military reform.

Background: The Secretary-General's December report to the Security Council noted Guinea-Bissau's progress since the 1998–1999 conflict and encouraged the authorities to continue their efforts to complete the political transition peacefully. Most important among these efforts included holding presidential elections by May 2005. To that end, he stated that essential political dialogue be enhanced and more constructive civil/military relations be promoted.

U.S. Position: The United States voted for this resolution, which was adopted unanimously.

HAITI

S/Res/1529	February 29	15(US)-0-0

Acting under Chapter VII of the UN Charter, calls on member states to support the constitutional succession and political process now under way in Haiti and the promotion of a peaceful and lasting solution to the current crisis; and authorizes the immediate deployment of a Multinational Interim Force (MIF) for a period of not more than three months. The force's mandate includes contributing to a secure and stable environment; facilitating the provision of humanitarian assistance; and facilitating the provision of international assistance to the Haitian police and Coast Guard to establish and maintain public safety and protect human rights.

Declares its readiness to establish a follow-on UN stabilization force to support continuation of a peaceful and constitutional political process and the maintenance of a secure environment, and requests the Secretary-General, in consultation with the Organization of American States, to submit recommendations for the size, structure and mandate of such a force. Welcomes the Secretary-General's appointment of a Special Adviser for Haiti, and requests the Secretary-General to elaborate a program of action for the United Nations. Authorizes the member states participating in the MIF in Haiti to take all necessary measures to fulfill its mandate.

Background: This resolution followed the resignation of President Jean-Bertrand Aristide and his departure from the country on February 29, 2004. Boniface Alexandre, head of Haiti's Supreme Court, was subsequently sworn in as acting President, in accordance with Haiti's Constitution. Haiti's political situation had become volatile after flawed elections in May 2000, and in recent months, confrontations became violent as the positions of the government and opposition hardened.

U.S. Position: The United States introduced this resolution on behalf of Friends of Haiti Group (Brazil, Canada, Chile, France, and the United States) as a basis for restoring stability and for a peaceful and constitutional transition in Haiti. The United States welcomed the quick and unified response of the Security Council to address the crisis in Haiti and support international efforts to help the Haitian people.

S/Res/1542   April 30   15(US)-0-0

Decides to establish the UN Stabilization Mission in Haiti (MINUSTAH), the stabilization force called for in Resolution 1529 (2004), for an initial period of six months, with the intention to renew for further periods; and requests that authority be transferred from the MIF (Multinational Interim Force) to MINUSTAH on June 1, 2004. Requests the Secretary-General to appoint a Special Representative in Haiti who will have overall authority on the ground for the coordination and conduct of all the activities of the UN agencies, funds, and programs in Haiti. Decides that MINUSTAH will consist of a civilian and a military component in accordance with the Secretary-General's report on Haiti; a civilian component to include a maximum of 1,622 civilian police and a military component to include up to 6,700 troops of all ranks.

Acting under Chapter VII of the UN Charter, decides that MINUSTAH shall have the mandate in support of the Transitional Government to ensure a secure and stable environment within which the constitutional and political process can take place; assist the Transitional Government in monitoring, restructuring and reforming the Haitian National Police; and assist the Transitional Government with comprehensive and sustainable disarmament, demobilization, and reintegration programs, among other things. Authorizes the Secretary-General to take all necessary steps to facilitate and support the early deployment of MINUSTAH in advance of the UN assumption of responsibilities from the MIF.

Background: The Secretary-General's April 16 report proposed to send UN military and police forces to Port-au-Prince as the vanguard of a UN stabilization mission, to be composed of up to 6,700 troops and 1,622 civilian police, that would take over from the U.S.-led MIF (to which the United States had contributed 1,800 military personnel) on June 1, 2004. The report welcomed the recent Consensus on the Political Transition Pact that allowed Haitian sectoral leaders to design a way forward in the transitional period, although the pact did not include the support of Fanni Lavalas, the political party of former President Jean-Bertrand Aristide. Most Haitian stakeholders have agreed that municipal, parliamentary and presidential elections will be held before the end of 2005, with an elected President to be sworn in on February 7, 2006.

U.S. Position: The United States voted for this resolution. The United States and its MIF partners were committed to ensuring a smooth transition from the U.S.-led interim force to the UN mission. The United States will continue to work closely with its partners, including the United Nations and the Organization of American States, to ensure the success of this mission.

S/Res/1576	November 29	15(US)-0-0

Acting under Chapter VII of the UN Charter, decides to extend the mandate of the UN Stabilization Mission in Haiti (MINUSTAH) until June 1, 2005, with the intention to renew for further periods. Welcomes the Secretary-General's report of November 18, 2004, on MINUSTAH and endorses his recommendations. Encourages the Transitional Government to continue to explore actively all possible ways to include in the democratic and electoral process those who currently remain outside the transition process but have rejected violence. Urges relevant international financial institutions and donor countries to disburse promptly the funds pledged at the International Donors Conference on Haiti held July 19–20.

Background: Pursuant to Resolution 1542 (2004), authority was transferred from the multinational interim force to MINUSTAH on June 1, 2004. On November 18, the Secretary-General reported on MINUSTAH's deployment progress and the mission's activities recommending modifications to MINUSTAH's structure to add, for an interim period, a formed police unit within its authorized strength and to augment MINUSTAH's capacity to implement disarmament, demobilization, and reintegration projects in the community. He also recommended an 18-month extension of the mission's mandate.

U.S. Position: The United States joined other Council members in adopting this resolution.

IRAQ

S/Res/1546	June 8	15(US)-0-0

Acting under Chapter VII of the UN Charter, endorses the formation of a sovereign Interim Government of Iraq, as presented on June 1, 2004, which will assume full responsibility and authority by June 30, 2004, for governing Iraq while refraining from taking any actions affecting Iraq's destiny beyond the limited interim period until an elected Transitional Government of Iraq assumes office. Welcomes that, also by June 30, 2004, the occupation will end and the Coalition Provisional Authority will cease to exist, and that Iraq will reassert its full sovereignty. Reaffirms the right of the Iraqi people freely to determine their own political future and to exercise full authority and control over their financial and natural resources.

Notes that, upon dissolution of the Coalition Provisional Authority, the funds in the Development Fund for Iraq shall be disbursed solely at the discretion of the Government of Iraq. Decides that the Development Fund for Iraq shall be utilized in a transparent and equitable manner and through the Iraqi budget including to satisfy outstanding obligations against the Development Fund for Iraq; that arrangements for the depositing of proceeds from export sales of petroleum, petroleum products, and natural gas established in Resolution 1483 (2003) shall continue to apply; and that the International Advisory and Monitoring Board shall continue its activities in monitoring the Development Fund for Iraq and shall include as an additional full voting member a duly qualified individual designated by the Government of Iraq. Decides that, in connection with the dissolution of the Coalition Provisional Authority, the Interim Government of Iraq and its successors shall assume the rights, responsibilities, and obligations relating to the Oil-for-Food Program that were transferred to the Authority. Further decides that, following a 120-day transition period from the date of adoption of this resolution, the Interim Government of Iraq and its successors shall assume responsibility for certifying delivery of goods under previously prioritized contracts.

Endorses the proposed timetable for Iraq's political transition to democratic government, including holding of direct democratic elections by December 31, 2004, if possible, and in no case later than January 31, 2005, to select a Transitional National Assembly which will form a Transitional Government of Iraq and draft a permanent constitution for Iraq leading to a constitutionally elected government by December 31, 2005. Decides that in implementing their mandate to assist the Iraqi people and government, the Special Representative of the Secretary-General and the UN Assistance Mission for Iraq (UNAMI), as requested by the Government of Iraq, shall play a leading role to assist in the convening, during the month of July 2004, of a national conference to select a Consultative Council; advise and support the Independent Electoral Commission of Iraq, as well as the Interim Government of Iraq and the Transitional National Assembly, on the process for holding elections; and promote national dialogue and consensus-building on the drafting of a national constitution by the people of Iraq. Decides that the Special Representative of the Secretary-General and the UNAMI shall also advise the Government of Iraq in the development of effective civil and social services; contribute to the coordination and delivery of reconstruction, development, and humanitarian assistance; promote the protection of human rights, national reconciliation, and judicial and legal reform in order to strengthen the rule of law in Iraq; and advise and assist the Government of Iraq on initial planning for the eventual conduct of a comprehensive census.

Notes that the presence of the multinational force in Iraq is at the request of the incoming Interim Government of Iraq and therefore reaffirms the authorization for the multinational force under unified command established under Resolution 1511 (2003), having regard for letters from U.S. Secretary of State Colin Powell and Dr. Ayad Allawi annexed to the resolution. Decides that the multinational force shall have the authority to take all necessary measures to contribute to the maintenance of security and stability in Iraq in accordance with the annexed letters expressing, among other things, the Iraqi request for the continued presence of the multinational force and setting out its tasks, including preventing and deterring terrorism, so that the United Nations can fulfill its role in assisting the Iraqi people and the Iraqi people can implement freely and without intimidation the timetable and program for the political process and benefit from reconstruction and rehabilitation activities. Welcomes, in this regard, that arrangements are being put in place to establish a security partnership between the sovereign Government of Iraq and the multinational force and to ensure coordination between the two, and notes also in this regard that Iraqi security forces are responsible to appropriate Iraqi ministers; and that the Government of Iraq has authority to commit Iraqi security forces to the multinational force to engage in operations with it, and that security structures described in the annexed letters will serve as the fora for the Government of Iraq and the multinational force to reach agreement on the full range of fundamental security and policy issues, including policy on sensitive offensive operations, and will ensure full partnership between Iraqi security forces and the multinational force, through close coordination and consultation. Decides further that the mandate for the multinational force shall be reviewed at the request of the Government of Iraq or 12 months from the date of this resolution, and that this mandate shall expire upon the completion of the political process outline. Declares that it will terminate this mandate earlier if requested by the Government of Iraq. Notes the intention to create a distinct entity under unified command of the multinational force with a dedicated mission to provide security for the UN presence in Iraq; recognizes that the implementation of measures to provide security for staff members of the UN system working in Iraq would require significant resources; and calls upon member states and relevant organizations to provide such resources, including contributions to that entity.

Reaffirms its intention to revisit the mandates of the UN Monitoring, Verification, and Inspection Commission, and the International Atomic Energy Agency. Requests member states and international and regional organizations to contribute assistance to the multinational force, including military forces, as agreed with the Government of Iraq, to help meet the needs of the Iraqi people for security and stability, humanitarian, and reconstruction assistance, and to support UNAMI efforts. Welcomes efforts by member states and international organizations to respond in support of requests by the Interim Government of Iraq to provide technical and expert assistance while Iraq is rebuilding its administrative capacity. Reiterates its request that member states, international financial institutions, and other organizations strengthen their efforts to assist the people of Iraq in the reconstruction and development of the Iraqi economy, including by providing international experts and necessary resources through a coordinated program of donor assistance.

Background: Resolution 1483 (2003) supported the formation of an Iraqi interim administration during the temporary administration of Iraq by the

United States and the United Kingdom, furthered efforts to restore and establish institutions for representative governance, authorized efforts to promote economic reconstruction and basic civilian administration, and created the Development Fund for Iraq (DFI). It also reaffirmed that Iraq must meet its disarmament obligations and underlined the Security Council's intention to revisit the mandates of the UN Monitoring, Verification, and Inspection Commission, and the International Atomic Energy Agency. Resolution 1511 (2003) acknowledged the creation of an Iraqi interim administration, called for a timetable and program to draft a constitution and hold elections, and authorized a multinational force to take all necessary steps to contribute to the maintenance of security and stability in Iraq. That timetable and program were discussed in an Agreement on November 15, 2003, between the Iraqi Governing Council and the Coalition Provisional Authority (CPA), including the drafting of a fundamental law to govern Iraq until a permanent constitution could be drafted and approved by the Iraqi people.

Resolution 1500 (2003) established UNAMI to support the Secretary-General in fulfilling the UN mandate under Resolution 1483, and subsequent resolutions, and in accordance with the structure and responsibilities set out in the Secretary-General's July 2003 report, for an initial period of 12 months. UNAMI began operations in Iraq in 2003 to assist the people of Iraq, but after the August 19, 2003, terrorist bombings of its headquarters in Baghdad and subsequent attacks, the Secretary-General evacuated all international UN personnel. UNAMI continued limited operations from outside Iraq until the United Nations re-established a small presence in Baghdad in August 2004. The United Nations led the process to establish the Independent Electoral Commission of Iraq; the Interim Iraqi Government, which assumed full responsibility and authority for governing Iraq in June; and the National Conference, which was convened in August.

U.S. Position: The United States cosponsored this resolution with the United Kingdom and Romania as part of its plan to restore self-government to the people of Iraq. The U.S. key objectives with this resolution were to mark the progress in the political transition in Iraq, including the nearing end of the CPA's temporary administration of Iraq, provide for a leading UN role, confirm the mandate of the multinational force, describe the security partnership between Iraq and the multinational force, and transition the DFI to Iraqi control. In explaining its vote, the United States noted that this resolution "...makes clear that Iraq's sovereignty will be undiluted, and that the Government of Iraq will have the sovereign authority to request and to decline assistance, including in the security sector. The Government of Iraq will have the final say on the presence of the multinational force. The resolution also addresses the current security reality, and affirms the security structures and mechanisms warranted at this time."

S/Res/1557   August 12   15(US)-0-0

Decides to extend the mandate of the UN Assistance Mission for Iraq (UNAMI) for a period of 12 months. Expresses its intention to review the mandate of UNAMI in 12 months or sooner if requested by the Government of Iraq.

Background: The Secretary-General reported on August 5, 2004, that much remained to be done for the Iraqis to succeed in rebuilding their country and recommended that UNAMI's mandate be extended. The United Nations re-established a small presence in Iraq in mid-August 2004, after having withdrawn all international personnel in the aftermath of the August 19, 2003, terrorist attack against UN Headquarters in Baghdad.

U.S. Position: The United States and United Kingdom co-drafted the resolution, which was adopted unanimously.

IRAQ/KUWAIT

S/Res/1538   April 21   15(US)-0-0

Expressing the desire to see a full and fair investigation of efforts by the former Government of Iraq to evade the provisions of Resolution 661 (1990), and subsequent relevant resolutions; concerned by public news reports and commentaries that have called into question the administration and management of the Oil-for-Food (OFF) Program established pursuant to Resolution 986 (1995), and subsequent relevant resolutions; and affirming the letter of the Security Council President of March 31, 2004, welcoming the Secretary-General's decision to create an independent, high-level inquiry to investigate the administration and management of the OFF Program; welcomes the appointment of the independent high-level inquiry and calls upon the Coalition Provisional Authority (CPA), Iraq, and all other member states, including their national regulatory authorities, to cooperate fully by all appropriate means with the inquiry.

Background: Security Council Resolution 661 (1990) imposed sanctions on Iraq in response to its invasion of Kuwait. Due to concerns about deteriorating nutritional and health conditions in Iraq, the Security Council adopted Resolution 986 (1995) that established the OFF Program, which allowed Iraq to export limited quantities of oil to finance the purchase of supplies meeting humanitarian needs and various mandated UN activities concerning Iraq. A press article appearing in the Iraqi newspaper *Al Mada* in January 2004 listed 270 individuals and companies that were alleged to have been the recipients of illegal commissions associated with oil vouchers from the former regime. Included in this list was Benon Sevan, former Executive Director of the UN Office of the Iraq Program, which was charged with the administration of the OFF program.

In response to public speculation over this list, the Secretary-General authorized an internal investigation on the matter through the UN Office of

Internal Oversight Services. In order to ensure that the investigation was wholly independent of the United Nations, the Secretary-General proposed an independent, high-level inquiry, called the Independent Inquiry Committee (IIC), which the Council welcomed in Resolution 1538. The IIC is chaired by Paul A. Volcker, former Chairman of the Federal Reserve, and includes Justice Richard Goldstone (South Africa), former Chief Prosecutor of the UN International Criminal Tribunals for the former Yugoslavia and Rwanda, and Mark Pieth (Switzerland), a Professor of Criminal Law and Criminology at the University of Basel.

U.S. Position: The United States cosponsored this resolution, which was adopted by consensus. In addition, in a letter from the Security Council President to the Secretary-General dated March 31, 2004, the United States joined other Council members commending the Secretary-General's decision to establish this inquiry panel. The United States expressed its intent to cooperate with the inquiry. Separately, the CPA, in coordination with Iraqi officials, authorized and funded a comprehensive Baghdad-based investigation, to be administered by the Iraqi Board of Supreme Audit (BSA). The CPA, BSA, and the IIC soon thereafter agreed to a Memorandum of Understanding designed to promote cooperation and coordination between the two investigations.

LIBERIA

S/Res/1532   March 12   15(US)-0-0

Acting under Chapter VII of the UN Charter, decides that, to prevent former Liberian President Charles Taylor, his immediate family members, senior officials of the former Taylor regime, or other close allies or associates as designated by the Committee established by Resolution 1521 (2003) from using misappropriated funds and property to interfere in the restoration of peace and stability in Liberia and the sub-region, all states in which there are funds or assets owned or controlled directly or indirectly by Charles Taylor, Jewell Howard Taylor, and Charles Taylor, Jr. and/or those other individuals designated by the Committee shall freeze without delay all such funds and assets, and shall ensure that neither these nor any other funds or assets are made available to or for the benefit of such persons. Further decides that the Committee shall identify, maintain and regularly update and review every six months the list of those individuals and entities identified by the Committee as being subject to these measures, and seek from all states information regarding the actions taken by them to trace and freeze such funds and assets.

Decides to review these measures at least once a year, the first review taking place by December 22, 2004, in conjunction with the review of the measures imposed by Resolution 1521 (2003). Expresses its intention to consider whether and how to make available the frozen funds or assets to the Government of Liberia once it has established transparent accounting and auditing mechanisms to ensure the responsible use of government revenue.

Background: Under Resolution 1521 (2003), the Security Council agreed to extend UN sanctions on Liberia originally imposed in 2001 under Resolution 1343. In a 2003 report to the Security Council's sanctions committee, a UN panel of experts recommended an assets freeze. At U.S. insistence, former President Charles Taylor resigned in August 2003 after months of bloody clashes between rebels and government militia wrecked the Liberian capital, Monrovia. His resignation paved the way for the signing of a comprehensive peace agreement and establishment of a national transitional government. Taylor also faces a number of charges by the Special Court for Sierra Leone relating to serious violations of international law for atrocities allegedly committed during Sierra Leone's decade-long civil war in the 1990s. The United States has provided critical military and logistical support to West African and subsequently UN peacekeepers, who helped to restore stability.

U.S. Position: The United States introduced this resolution as a leading advocate in the United Nations of using multilateral sanctions to address instability in Liberia and the sub-region.

S/Res/1549   June 17   15(US)-0-0

Decides to re-establish the Panel of Experts appointed pursuant to Resolution 1521 (2003) for a further period to commence no later than June 30 until December 21, 2004, with the mandate to conduct a follow-up assessment mission to Liberia and neighboring states, in order to investigate and compile a report on the implementation and any ongoing violations of the arms embargo, travel ban, and embargo of rough diamonds, round logs, and timber products, including violations involving rebel movements and financing for the illicit trade of arms; assess the progress made towards the goals of maintaining and respecting the ceasefire and establishing and maintaining stability in Liberia and the sub-region; and monitor the implementation and enforcement of the freezing of funds and economic resources of former Liberian President Charles Taylor and his family. Further requests the Panel to provide a mid-term report to the Council for its review, through the Committee, no later than September 30, 2004, and also requests that the Panel present a final report to the Council no later than December 10, 2004. Requests the Secretary-General to appoint by June 30, 2004, no more than five experts to fulfill the Panel's mandate.

Background: The Secretary-General's May 26 report on Liberia detailed progress made towards the goals prescribed in Resolution 1521 (2003), in order for the Council to consider lifting sanctions imposed on Liberia. The report stated that while the Liberian Government had made encouraging progress towards these goals, much remained to be done to rigorously apply and implement recommendations for reform of the timber and diamond sectors and that international smuggling networks remained in place and could be reactivated at any time.

U.S. Position: The United States joined other Council members in unanimously adopting this resolution. The United States believed that the time had come, as Resolution 1521 stated, for the National Transitional

Government to establish transparent accounting and auditing mechanisms to ensure that all government revenues are not used to fuel conflict, but rather to improve the lives of all Liberians. The United States believed that former President Charles Taylor should be held accountable for his actions in Sierra Leone and should appear before the Sierra Leone Special Court.

S/Res/1561   September 17   15(US)-0-0

Decides to extend the mandate of UN Mission in Liberia (UNMIL) until September 19, 2005. Calls on all Liberian parties to demonstrate their full commitment to the peace process and to work together to ensure that free, fair, and transparent elections take place as planned no later than October 2005. Calls on the international community to respond to the continuing need for funds for the critically important rehabilitation and reintegration phase and to fulfill pledges made at the International Reconstruction Conference on Liberia held in February 2004.

Background: Created on September 19, 2003, UNMIL is responsible for supporting, observing, and monitoring the implementation of the Comprehensive Peace Agreement of August 18, 2003, in Liberia in the aftermath of the resignation and departure of former President Charles Taylor. One year after UNMIL's creation, the Secretary-General reported that by disarming some estimated 90,000 former combatants and deploying troops across the country to maintain security, UNMIL had improved the security situation, which facilitated the delivery of humanitarian aid and restoration of state authority. However, he reported that serious challenges remained, including ongoing factionalism that had recently deteriorated briefly into violence, continued ongoing systemic corruption, lack of transparency and failure by the transitional government to deliver public services, and need for significant reform of the security services and justice system. Other major donors must begin to deliver promptly on their pledges of assistance.

U.S. Position: The United States voted for this resolution.

S/Res/1579   December 21   15(US)-0-0

Acting under Chapter VII of the UN Charter, decides to renew the measures on arms, travel, and timber imposed by Resolution 1521 (2003) for a further period of 12 months with a review after six months, and to renew the measures on diamonds in Resolution 1521 (2003) for a further period of six months with a review after three months. Further decides to re-establish the Panel of Experts appointed pursuant to Resolution 1549 (2004) until June 21, 2005, to conduct a follow-up assessment mission to Liberia and neighboring states in order to investigate and compile a report on the implementation, and any violations, of the measures imposed by this resolution; assess the impact and effectiveness of the measures imposed by Resolution 1532 (2004); assess the progress made towards meeting the established conditions; assess the humanitarian and socio-economic impact of the measures imposed by Resolution 1521 (2003); report to the Council through the Committee by June

7, 2005, on all issues listed above; and provide a preliminary report to the Council through the Committee by March 21, 2005, on progress towards meeting the conditions for lifting the measures on diamonds imposed by Resolution 1521 (2003).

Background: Upon review of progress made by the National Transitional Government towards achieving the conditions set forth in the above mentioned Resolutions, and upon examination of reports (dated September 24, 2004, and December 6, 2004) submitted by the UN Panel of Experts on Liberia to the Security Council, the Council unanimously adopted this resolution to renew the previously imposed measures.

U.S. Position: The United States voted for this resolution. The United States recognizes the need to quickly restore Liberia's timber industry as a source of legitimate and much needed revenue for the National Transitional Government. This vote reflects the U.S. call for security, transparency, and accountability within all sectors of the Liberian economy to ensure that economic revenues support legitimate developmental and governmental agendas rather than fuel conflict in Liberia and West Africa.

MIDDLE EAST

S/Res/1525   January 30   15(US)-0-0

Endorses the report of the Secretary-General on UNIFIL [UN Interim Force in Lebanon] of January 20, 2004, and in particular its recommendation to renew the mandate of UNIFIL for a further period of six months. Decides to extend the present mandate until July 31, 2004. Reaffirms strong support for the territorial integrity, sovereignty, and political independence of Lebanon within internationally recognized boundaries. Encourages the Government of Lebanon to continue efforts to ensure the return of its effective authority throughout the south, including the deployment of Lebanese armed forces, and stresses the importance of the Government of Lebanon continuing to extend these measures and calls on it to do its utmost to ensure a calm environment throughout the south, including along the Blue Line. Condemns all acts of violence; expresses great concern about the serious breaches and the sea, land, and continuing air violations of the withdrawal line; and urges the parties to put an end to these violations, to refrain from any act or provocation that could further escalate the tension, and to abide scrupulously by their obligation to respect the safety of UNIFIL and other UN personnel. Stresses the importance of, and the need to achieve, a comprehensive, just and lasting peace in the Middle East.

Background: The Security Council established UNIFIL with Resolution 425 (1978) in the wake of the 1978 Israeli invasion of southern Lebanon. UNIFIL's mandate include confirming the withdrawal of the Israeli Army from southern Lebanon, assisting the Lebanese Government in restoring its authority in the south, and restoring international peace and security in the region. Following the July 2000 withdrawal of Israeli forces from Lebanon, the UN Secretary-General declared that UNIFIL had completed the first two parts of its mandate, and that the mission was now focused on the third element, restoring peace and security in the region.

In the Secretary-General's January 20 report on UNIFIL, he expressed concern over recent breaches of the line of withdrawal, or Blue Line, by both Israel and Hizballah that led to the deaths of six Israeli and Lebanese individuals. In his view, the fragile stability of southern Lebanon was under threat after an upsurge in violent incidents during the past six months. In light of prevailing conditions in the area, the Secretary-General recommended that UNIFIL's mandate be extended for another six months.

U.S. Position: The United States joined all other Council member in adopting this resolution.

Not adopted   March 24   11-1(US)-3 (UK,
                                           Germany, Romania)

Condemns the most recent extrajudicial execution committed by Israel, the occupying Power, that killed Sheikh Ahmed Yassin along with six other Palestinians outside a mosque in Gaza City and calls for a complete cessation of extrajudicial executions; condemns also all terrorist attacks against any civilians as well as all acts of violence and destruction. Calls on all sides to immediately undertake an unconditional cessation of acts of violence, including all acts of terrorism, provocation, incitement, and destruction. Calls on both parties to fulfill their obligations under the Roadmap endorsed by Security Council Resolution 1515 (2003) and to work with the Quartet to implement it in order to achieve the vision of the two states living side-by-side in peace and security.

Background: Algeria and Libya introduced this resolution in the Security Council in response to the killing of Hamas leader Sheikh Ahmcd Yassin on March 22.

U.S. Position: The United States vetoed this resolution. In explaining its vote, the United States noted that the draft resolution did not refer to the terrorist attack by Hamas committed the previous week, which left 10 Israelis dead. This resolution did not condemn that attack, nor did it condemn those responsible despite Council members specifically requesting inclusion of these references. This one-sided resolution also would not further peace and security in the region.

S/Res/1544   May 19   14-0-1(US)

Calls on Israel to respect its obligations under international humanitarian law, and insists, in particular, on its obligation not to undertake demolition of homes contrary to that law. Expresses grave concern regarding the humanitarian situation of Palestinians made homeless in the Rafah area and calls for the provision of emergency assistance to them. Calls for the cessation of violence and for respect of and adherence to legal obligations, including those under international humanitarian law. Calls on both parties to immediately implement their obligations under the Roadmap.

Background: On May 19, 2004, an attack by the Israeli occupying forces in the Rafah camp resulted in the deaths of Palestinian civilians. Earlier that week, the UN Relief and Works Agency for Palestine Refugees in the Near East reported that nearly 2,200 people had been left without shelter and 191 homes had been demolished throughout Gaza since the beginning of May.

U.S. Position: The United States abstained on this resolution. The United States expressed "deep regret [for] the loss of life of innocent Palestinian civilians in Gaza" on May 19. In the U.S. view, although Israel has the right to act to defend itself and its citizens, its operations in Gaza in recent days did not serve the purposes of peace and security, and did not enhance Israel's security. Rather, they worsened the humanitarian situation and resulted in confrontations between Israeli forces and Palestinians. For its part, the United States had urged the Israeli Government to exercise maximum restraint. The United States did not vote in favor of this resolution because it did not believe that the resolution sufficiently addressed the context of the recent events in Gaza. The resolution also did not address issues such as Palestinian terrorists smuggling weapons into Gaza and the Palestinian Authority's obligation under the Roadmap to act against terror.

S/Res/1550   June 29   15(US)-0-0

Decides to renew the mandate of the UN Disengagement Observer Force (UNDOF) for a period of six months, until December 31, 2004. Requests the Secretary-General to submit, at the end of this period, a report on the developments in the situation and the measures taken to implement Resolution 338 (1973).

Background: UNDOF was established in 1974 to supervise and maintain the ceasefire between Israeli and Syrian forces in the Golan Heights. In the Secretary-General's June 21 report on UNDOF, he recommended an extension of the mandate for a further six months, although the area of operations of UNDOF remained generally quiet. While urging both parties to respect international law and to exercise restraint, he stated in the report that the situation in the Middle East was likely to remain tense until a comprehensive settlement covering all aspects of the Middle East problem was reached.

U.S. Position: The United States voted for this routine extension of UNDOF.

S/Res/1553   July 29   15(US)-0-0

Endorses the Secretary-General's July 21, 2004 report on the UN Interim Force in Lebanon (UNIFIL), and in particular its recommendation to renew UNIFIL's mandate for a further period of six months. Decides to extend the present mandate until January 31, 2005. Reiterates strong support for the territorial integrity, sovereignty, and political independence of Lebanon within internationally recognized boundaries. Encourages the Government of Lebanon to continue efforts to ensure the return of its effective authority throughout the south, including the deployment of Lebanese armed forces, stresses the importance of the Government of Lebanon continuing to extend these measures, and calls on the Government of Lebanon to do its utmost to ensure a calm environment throughout the south, including along the Blue Line. Calls upon the parties to ensure UNIFIL is accorded full freedom of movement in the discharge of its mandate throughout its area of operation. Supports the continued efforts of UNIFIL to maintain the ceasefire along the withdrawal line through mobile patrols and observation from fixed positions and through close contacts with the parties to correct violations, resolve incidents, and prevent their escalation.

Background: The Secretary-General submitted a report on July 21 describing numerous armed encounters across the Blue Line over the previous six months, the majority of which were between Hizballah and the Israel Defense Forces. None of these events spiraled out of control, but the risk remained that while the parties continued to ignore their obligations under the relevant Security Council resolutions, hostilities could escalate. The Secretary-General recommended a six-month extension of UNIFIL's mandate to continue maintaining peace and security

U.S. Position: The United States voted for this resolution.

S/Res/1559	September 2	9(US)-0-6(Algeria, Brazil, China, Pakistan, Philippines, and Russia)

Reaffirms its call for the strict respect of the sovereignty, territorial integrity, unity, and political independence of Lebanon under the sole and exclusive authority of the Government of Lebanon throughout Lebanon. Calls upon all remaining foreign forces to withdraw from Lebanon, and calls for the disbanding and disarmament of all Lebanese and non-Lebanese militias. Supports the extension of the control of the Government of Lebanon over all Lebanese territory. Declares its support for a free and fair electoral process in Lebanon's upcoming presidential election conducted according to Lebanese constitutional rules devised without foreign interference or influence.

Background: At the time of the resolution, the Lebanese constitution banned a president from serving two consecutive terms, but under pressure from Syria, the Lebanese Parliament was expected to amend the constitution to extend the term of the current pro-Syrian president by three years. Syria has maintained forces in Lebanon since 1976, when the former responded to the latter's civil war by sending in troops.

U.S. Position: This resolution was introduced by the United States and France, and cosponsored by Germany and the United Kingdom. The United States believes that Lebanon should be allowed to determine its own future and assume control of its own territory. Therefore, the Lebanese Parliament and the Lebanese Cabinet should express the will of the Lebanese people through a free and fair presidential electoral process, unhindered by the pressures of Syria and its agents. The Government of Lebanon should also extend control over all Lebanese territory, as called for by the Security Council over the past four years. The United States believes that the continued presence of armed Hizballah militia elements, as well as the presence of the Syrian military and Iranian forces in the region, thwarts that goal.

Not adopted   October 5   11-1(US)-3(Germany, Romania, UK)

Demands the immediate cessation of all military operations in the area of Northern Gaza and the withdrawal of the Israeli occupying forces from that area. Calls on Israel, the occupying power, to ensure the unfettered access and safety of UN personnel and all medical and humanitarian aid workers to provide emergency assistance to the civilian population, and calls for the respect of the inviolability of the facilities of the UN agencies in the field, including the UN Relief and Works Agency for Palestine Refugees in the Near East. Calls on both parties to immediately implement their obligations under the Roadmap and with this goal in mind closely cooperate with the Quartet of international intermediaries.

Background: Algeria, Pakistan, and Tunisia introduced this resolution to the Security Council in response to Israeli military operations in the northern Gaza Strip in late September conducted in response to Palestinian rocket attacks on Israeli civilians.

U.S. Position: The United States vetoed this resolution, stating that it was unbalanced because the text failed to refer to Palestinian attacks on Israel. In its explanation of vote, the United States reminded the Council that both sides need to renounce violence and recommit to the Roadmap. The United States believed that the Security Council "should reverse the incessant stream of one anti-Israel resolution after another, and apply pressure even-handedly, on both sides, to return to the road of peace."

S/Res/1578   December 15   15(US)-0-0

Having considered the report of the Secretary-General on the UN Disengagement Force (UNDOF) of December 7, 2004, and also reaffirming its Resolution 1308 (2000) of July 17, 2000, decides to renew the mandate of UNDOF for a period of six months.

Background: The Secretary-General's December 7 report on UNDOF recommended an extension of the mandate for a further six-month period. Although the area of operations of UNDOF [Israel-Syria sector] remained generally quiet, the report recommended an extension due to the very tense nature of the situation in the Middle East.

U.S. Position: The United States supported this resolution, which was adopted unanimously.

SIERRA LEONE

S/Res/1537   March 30   15(US)-0-0

Decides that the mandate of the UN Mission in Sierra Leone (UNAMSIL) shall be extended for a period of six months until September 30, 2004. Welcomes the Secretary-General's intention to adjust the timetable for UNAMSIL's drawdown during 2004, in order to ensure a more gradual reduction in its military strength. Urges the Government of Sierra Leone to intensify its efforts to develop an effective and sustainable police force, army, penal system, and independent judiciary, so that the government can rapidly take over from UNAMSIL full responsibility for maintaining law and order throughout Sierra Leone, and encourages donors and UNAMSIL to continue to assist the government in this regard. Decides that a residual UNAMSIL presence will remain in Sierra Leone for an initial period of six months from January 1, 2005, reduced from the December 2004 level of 5,000 troops by February 28, 2005, to a new ceiling of 3,250 troops, 141 military observers, and 80 UN civilian police personnel; and requests the Secretary-General to proceed with planning on the basis of the recommendations in his report, in order to ensure a seamless transition from the current configuration of UNAMSIL to the residual presence. Requests UNAMSIL to share its experience with the UN Mission in Liberia and the UN Operation in Cote d'Ivoire and to carry out its mandate in close liaison with them, especially in the prevention of movements of arms and combatants across borders and in the implementation of disarmament, demobilization, and reintegration programs.

Background: The Secretary-General noted in his March 19 report that while the Government of Sierra Leone had made substantial progress in extending its authority throughout the country, it still required assistance. The national police force was not fully capable of handling widespread public disturbances. There was also a risk that supporters of Sierra Leone Special Court indictees might cause trouble as the trials got underway. Violence against women, including sexual exploitation, as well as discrimination against women in law and in practice, remained to be addressed. The Secretary-General recommended keeping a residual post-UNAMSIL peacekeeping presence to provide continued support for the training of the Sierra Leone police and capacity-building support for national human rights organizations.

U.S. Position: The United States voted for this resolution. The United States had hoped that the Sierra Leonean government would have made more progress in assuming full responsibility for governance, so that UNAMSIL could keep the original drawdown schedule, but agreed that it still required support from UNAMSIL, particularly in the security sector. The United States favored extending UNAMSIL, rather than closing it and replacing it with a new mission, as the Secretary-General had recommended, since it was administratively simpler and less costly. Others on the Security Council agreed with the United States.

S/Res/1562   September 17   15(US)-0-0

Acting under Chapter VII of the UN Charter, decides that the mandate of UN Mission in Sierra Leone (UNAMSIL) shall be extended until June 30, 2005. Decides further that the tasks of the residual UNAMSIL presence, which shall remain in Sierra Leone for an initial period of six months from January 1, 2005, as set out in Resolution 1537 (2004), shall be to monitor the overall security situation and support the Sierra Leone armed forces and police in patrolling the border and diamond-mining areas and in maintaining internal security, including for the Special Court for Sierra Leone; assist the Sierra Leone police with its program of recruitment, training, and mentoring; protect UN personnel, installations, and equipment and ensure the security and freedom of movement of UN personnel; monitor the repatriation, reception, resettlement, and reintegration of Sierra Leonean ex-combatants from abroad; monitor, investigate, report, and promote the observance of human rights; disseminate information on UNAMSIL's mandate and publicize the government's primary responsibility for national security; and monitor progress towards consolidation of state authority throughout the country. Authorizes the residual UNAMSIL to use all necessary means to carry out its mandate.

Urges the Government of Sierra Leone to intensify its efforts to develop an effective and sustainable police force, armed forces, penal system, and independent judiciary, so that the government can take over from UNAMSIL as soon as possible full responsibility for maintaining law and order throughout Sierra Leone, including in the sensitive diamond-producing areas. Encourages donors and UNAMSIL, in accordance with its mandate, to continue to assist the government in this regard, as well as to assist the government in restoring public services throughout the country.

Background: Sierra Leone continued to make gradual progress toward the consolidation of peace, and this progress allowed UNAMSIL to continue reducing its forces from 17,500 to 9,000 by September. However, security in the border areas remained volatile, with arms allegedly being smuggled into Liberia from Sierra Leone.

U.S. Position: The United States joined other Council members in unanimously adopting this resolution.

SOMALIA

S/Res/1558   August 17   15(US)-0-0

Acting under Chapter VII of the UN Charter, stresses the obligation of all states to comply fully with the embargo on delivery of weapons and military equipment in Resolution 733 (1992). Requests the Secretary-General, in consultation with the Committee established pursuant to Resolution 751

(1992), to re-establish for a period of six months the Monitoring Group with the following mandate: continue the tasks outlined in Resolution 1519; continue updating information on the draft list of those who continue to violate the arms embargo inside and outside Somalia; continue making recommendations based on its investigations, on the previous reports of the Panel of Experts appointed pursuant to Resolutions 1425 (2002) and 1474 (2003), and on the Monitoring Group's first report; work closely with the Committee on specific recommendations for additional measures to improve overall compliance with the arms embargo; and provide the Council, through the Committee, a midterm report and a final report covering all the tasks set out here. Reaffirms the need for implementation of the actions set out in Resolution 1519. Expects the Committee to recommend to the Council appropriate measures in response to violations of the arms embargo by developing, in close consultation with the Monitoring Group, specific proposals to improve compliance.

Background: In 1992, the Security Council adopted Resolution 733, which established an arms embargo in Somalia to combat weapons and ammunition supplies fueling conflict that beset Somalia for 13 years. In 2003, Resolution 1519 called for the Secretary-General to establish a monitoring group composed of four experts for a period of six months. The Monitoring Group traveled throughout the region in 2004 and found evidence of continued violations of the embargo, which threatened the Somali peace process. In its August 11, 2004, report, the Group recommended continued monitoring of arms embargo violations.

U.S. Position: The United States joined other Council members adopting this resolution.

SUDAN

S/Res/1547	June 11	15(US)-0-0

Welcoming the signature of the Declaration on June 5, 2004, in Nairobi, Kenya, in which the parties confirmed their agreement to the six protocols signed between the Government of Sudan and the Sudan People's Liberation Movement/Army; condemning all acts of violence and violations of human rights and international humanitarian law by all parties; and urging the two parties involved to conclude speedily a Comprehensive Peace agreement, welcomes the Secretary-General's proposal to establish, for an initial period of three months and under the authority of a Special Representative of the Secretary-General, a UN advance team in Sudan as a special political mission, dedicated to prepare for the introduction of a peace support operation following the signing of the Comprehensive Peace Agreement. Declares its readiness to consider establishing a UN peace support operation to support the implementation of a Comprehensive Peace Agreement. Calls upon the parties to use their influence to bring an immediate halt to the fighting in the Darfur region, in the Upper Nile, and elsewhere; urges the parties to the Ndjamena

Cease-fire Agreement of April 8 to conclude a political agreement without delay; welcomes African Union efforts to that end; and calls on the international community to be prepared for constant engagement, including extensive funding in support of peace in Sudan.

Background: In response to an October 2003 request from the Security Council for a plan for UN support for the implementation of a comprehensive peace agreement, the Secretary-General established a task force and issued a report on June 7, 2004, concluding that because of Sudan's violent history (it has been engulfed in civil conflict for all but 11 of the 48 years since its independence in 1956), enormous size, and lack of infrastructure, peace negotiations will require an extensive and carefully coordinated response from the international community. As a first step, the Secretary-General proposed to deploy an advance team for an initial period of three months to begin practical preparations for a future UN peace operation. The Secretary-General also urged the parties to the Darfur conflict to conclude a political agreement without a delay, an action that the report deemed fundamental to the success of a future UN role in the Sudan.

The two-year Naivasha peace process resulted in several separate agreements that were designed to end to a 21-year civil war between the Muslim government and Christian and animist rebels. The Darfur conflict began when African Muslims in the western Darfur region rebelled against the Arab Muslim government, which has since struck back by supporting local militias collectively known as the Janjaweed to counter the rebels.

U.S. Position: The United States, along with the United Kingdom, took the lead in pushing for adoption of this resolution. The United States also drew attention to a Group of Eight statement dated June 10 in which the countries pledged their assistance in ending the conflicts in Sudan and in providing humanitarian assistance, called on all parties to commit themselves to respecting the right of all Sudanese to live in peace and dignity, and looked to the United Nations to lead an international effort to avert a major disaster and to work together to achieve that end.

| **S/Res/1556** | July 30 | 13(US)-0-2(China, Pakistan) |

Acting under Chapter VII of the UN Charter, calls on the Government of Sudan to fulfill immediately all of the commitments it made in the July 3, 2004, Communique, including particularly by facilitating international relief for the humanitarian disaster and by means of a moratorium on all restrictions that might hinder the provision of humanitarian assistance and access to the affected populations, by advancing independent investigation in cooperation with the United Nations of violations of human rights and international humanitarian law, by the establishment of credible security conditions for the protection of the civilian population and humanitarian actors, and by the resumption of political talks with dissident groups from the Darfur region. Endorses the deployment of international monitors, including the protection force envisioned by the African Union (AU), to the Darfur region under the leadership of the AU and urges the international community to continue to support these efforts. Stresses the need for the Government of Sudan and all involved parties to facilitate the work of the monitors. Urges member states to reinforce the international monitoring team, led by the AU, including the protection force, by providing personnel and other assistance. Welcomes the contributions already made by the European Union and the United States to support the AU-led operation.

Demands that the Government of Sudan fulfill its commitments to disarm the Janjaweed militias and apprehend and bring to justice Janjaweed leaders and their associates who have incited and carried out human rights and international humanitarian law violations and other atrocities. Further requests the Secretary-General to report in 30 days, and monthly thereafter, to the Council on the progress or lack thereof by the Government of Sudan on this matter and expresses its intention to consider further actions, including measures as provided for in Article 41 of the UN Charter on the Government of Sudan, in the event of non-compliance.

Decides that all states shall take the necessary measures to prevent the sale or supply to all nongovernmental entities and individuals, including the Janjaweed, operating in the states of North Darfur, South Darfur, and West Darfur, of arms and related material or provision of arms-related assistance. Urges the international community to make available assistance to mitigate the humanitarian catastrophe now unfolding in the Darfur region and calls upon member states to honor pledges that have been made against needs in Darfur and Chad and underscoring the need to contribute generously towards fulfilling the unmet portion of the UN consolidated appeals. Encourages the Secretary-General's Special Representative for Sudan and the independent expert of the Commission on Human Rights to work closely with the Government of Sudan in supporting independent investigation of violations of human rights and international humanitarian law in the Darfur region.

Background: The Darfur conflict began when African Muslims in the western Darfur region rebelled against the Arab Muslim government, which struck back by supporting local militias known as the Janjaweed to counter the rebels. During this conflict, both sides have violated human rights and humanitarian law. However, on April 8, 2004, Sudan signed a ceasefire with the rebels. Secretary-General Annan visited Sudan in July to observe the situation. Before he left, the United Nations and Sudan issued a Joint Communique, in which Khartoum promised to disarm the militias, provide unhindered humanitarian access, and bring perpetrators of human rights abuses to justice. The Secretary-General urged the Security Council to pressure Sudan to act on its commitments.

U.S. Position: The United States drafted this resolution and presented it to the Security Council with Chile, France, Germany, Romania, Spain, and the United Kingdom as cosponsors. The United States believed that the international community needed to send a strong message to Sudan that it must act and fulfill its commitments or face consequences. Because Sudan had not taken action on its promises, the resolution requested the Secretary-General to report every 30 days on Sudan's progress in upholding its commitments. Almost a month had passed from the time Sudan and the United Nations signed the Joint Communique when this resolution was adopted. The United States believed that this was enough time for Sudan to have made a start on upholding its pledges.

S/Res/1564   September 18   11(US)-0-4 (Algeria,
                                                 China, Pakistan, Russia)

Acting under Chapter VII of the UN Charter, declares its grave concern that the Government of Sudan has not fully met its obligations to improve the security of the civilian population of Darfur and deplores the recent ceasefire violations by all parties, in particular the reports by the Cease-Fire Commission of Government of Sudan helicopter assaults and Janjaweed attacks on three villages on August 26. Welcomes and supports the intention of the African Union (AU) to enhance its monitoring mission in Darfur. Urges member states to support the AU by providing all equipment, logistical, financial, material, and other resources. Calls upon the Government of Sudan and the rebel groups to work together under the AU to reach a political solution in the Abuja negotiations under the leadership of President Obasanjo, urges the parties to sign and implement the humanitarian agreement immediately, and to conclude a protocol on security issues as soon as possible. Urges the Government of Sudan and the Sudan People's Liberation Movement to conclude a comprehensive peace accord expeditiously.

Reiterates its call for the Government of Sudan to end the climate of impunity in Darfur by identifying and bringing to justice all those responsible, including members of popular defense forces and Janjaweed militias, for the widespread human rights abuses, and insists that the Government of Sudan stop all violence and atrocities. Demands that the Government of Sudan submit to the AU Mission for verification the names of Janjaweed militiamen disarmed and arrested for human rights abuses. Demands all armed groups cease all violence, cooperate with humanitarian relief and monitoring efforts, and facilitate the safety and security of humanitarian staff.

Requests that the Secretary-General establish an international commission of inquiry to investigate reports of violations of international humanitarian law and human rights law in Darfur, to determine whether or not acts of genocide have occurred and to identify the perpetrators of such violations with a view to ensuring that those responsible are held accountable, and further requests the Secretary-General to increase the number of human rights monitors in Darfur. Calls on member states to provide contributions to humanitarian efforts in Darfur and Chad to address the shortfall in response to continued UN appeals. Declares that if the Government of Sudan fails to comply fully with Resolution 1556 (2004) or this resolution, the Council shall consider taking additional measures as contemplated in Article 41 of the UN Charter, such as actions to affect Sudan's petroleum sector and the Government of Sudan or its individual members.

Background: The Secretary-General's Special Representative for Sudan, Jan Pronk (Netherlands), reported to the Security Council on September 2 that the Government of Sudan had not fully complied with Resolution 1556 and was failing to meet its obligations to ensure the protection of its own civilian population. The Government of Sudan had failed to disarm the Janjaweed militias or stop their attacks on civilians, although it had ceased military attacks in areas with high numbers of internally displaced persons (IDPs), deployed extra police, removed restrictions on humanitarian relief, and started negotiations with Darfur's two rebel groups. Pronk also called for the mission of the AU to be expanded in size and mandate, to intensify its monitoring of the ceasefire agreement, to play a larger role in protecting IDPs and other civilians in Darfur, and to encourage greater humanitarian access.

U.S. Position: The United States introduced and led the push for adoption of this resolution, which was cosponsored by Germany, Romania, Spain, and the United Kingdom. The resolution advanced the U.S. objective of passing a strong resolution with broad support urging the international community to fulfill its pledges of humanitarian assistance, providing international support for an expanded and proactive AU role in Darfur, and making it clear to the Sudanese government and the Darfur rebels that they must act to comply fully with Resolution 1556 and the new resolution. With the Secretary of State having declared on September 9 that the United States had concluded that atrocities in Darfur amounted to genocide, the establishment of a commission of inquiry to act quickly was a high priority. This resolution also called for completion on an urgent basis of the North-South and Abuja negotiations as essential to creating a peaceful and united Sudan, declared that the Council would consider additional measures if Sudan failed to comply, and requested an international commission of inquiry to investigate reports of violations of international humanitarian and human rights law in Darfur and to determine whether or not acts of genocide had occurred.

S/Res/1569   October 26   15(US)-0-0

Decides to hold meetings in Nairobi on November 18–19, 2004, and that the agenda for these meetings will be "The Reports of the Secretary-General on Sudan." Decides also to discuss Sudan with representatives of the African Union (AU) and the Intergovernmental Authority on Development at the meetings, and to take the opportunity of the Security Council presence in Nairobi to discuss other peace efforts in the region with both the AU and the Intergovernmental Authority on Development.

Background: The Government of Sudan and the Sudan People's Liberation Movement have engaged in peace talks for over two years aimed at ending a 21-year civil war. The latest round finished on October 30.

U.S. Position: This was a U.S.-initiated resolution. The United States proposed holding this Security Council meeting in Nairobi to emphasize the importance of a rapid conclusion to the peace talks. The United States joined Council members in adopting this resolution unanimously.

S/Res/1574   November 19   15(US)-0-0

Declares its strong support for the efforts of the Government of Sudan and the Sudan People's Liberation Movement/Army to reach a Comprehensive Peace Agreement, encourages the parties to redouble their efforts, and welcomes the signing of the Memorandum of Understanding in Nairobi on November 19, 2004, attached to this resolution, and the agreement that the six protocols referred to in the Nairobi Declaration of June 5, 2004, constitute and form the core Peace Agreement. Strongly endorses the parties' commitment to reach a final comprehensive agreement by December 31, 2004, and expects that it will be fully and transparently implemented.

Declares its commitment, upon conclusion of a Comprehensive Peace Agreement, to assist the people of Sudan in their efforts to establish a peaceful, united, and prosperous nation, on the understanding that the parties are fulfilling all their commitments. Urges continuation of efforts to prepare for delivery of an assistance package for the reconstruction and economic development of Sudan to be implemented once a Comprehensive Peace Agreement has been signed and its implementation begins, and welcomes the initiative of Norway to convene a donors' conference.

Welcomes the operations of the Joint Military Commission, the Civilian Protection Monitoring Team, and the Verification and Monitoring Team in anticipation of the implementation of a Comprehensive Peace Agreement and the establishment of a UN peace support operation. Reiterates its readiness, upon the signature of a Comprehensive Peace Agreement, to consider establishing a UN peace support operation to support the implementation of that agreement, and its request to the Secretary-General to submit to the Council recommendations for the size, structure, and mandate of such an operation. Welcomes the preparatory work carried out by the UN Advance Mission in Sudan and extends its mandate to March 10, 2005.

Underlines the importance of progress in peace talks in Abuja towards resolving the crisis in Darfur. Insists that all parties to the Abuja peace talks negotiate in good faith to reach agreement speedily. Welcomes the signature of the Humanitarian and Security Protocols on November 9, 2004, urges the parties to implement these rapidly, and looks forward to the early signature of a Declaration of Principles with a view to a political settlement. Demands that government and rebel forces cease all violence and attacks; refrain from forcible relocation of civilians; cooperate with international humanitarian relief and monitoring efforts; ensure that their members comply with international humanitarian law; facilitate the safety and security of humanitarian staff; and allow unhindered access and passage by humanitarian agencies. In accordance with its previous resolutions on Sudan, decides to take appropriate action against any party failing to fulfill its commitments. Strongly supports the African Union (AU) decisions to increase its mission in Darfur to 3,320 personnel and to enhance its mandate, and urges member states to provide the required resources, and urges the Government of Sudan and all rebel groups to cooperate fully with the AU.

Background: The United States was President of the Security Council during November 2004 and took the Security Council to Nairobi, Kenya, for two days of meetings to demonstrate international support for a peace deal in Sudan. This was only the fourth time since 1952 that the Security Council met away from UN headquarters in New York. The United States had worked intensively with the parties for over three years to complete the North-South peace talks, and viewed the Nairobi meeting as an opportunity to show parties involved in the Naivasha negotiations that the international community was engaged in seeking a peaceful future for Sudan, and making clear that the international community would remain committed to helping the country move forward upon signing of a peace agreement.

U.S. Position: The United States provided strong leadership in achieving this resolution, which was authored by the United Kingdom. In a statement, the United States urged the leaders of Sudan and the Sudan Liberation Movement/Army to meet their commitment to sign a peace agreement by the end of 2004, and reiterated that the violence and atrocities in Darfur must end.

TIMOR-LESTE

S/Res/1543   May 14   15(US)-0-0

Decides to extend the mandate of the UN Mission of Support in Timor-Leste (UNMISET) for a period of six months, with a view to subsequently extending the mandate for a final six months. Decides to reduce UNMISET's size and revise its tasks, in accordance with the Secretary-General's recommendations in his April 29 report. Decides accordingly that UNMISET's mandate shall consist of support for the public administration and justice system of East Timor and for justice in the area of serious crimes; support to the development of law enforcement in East Timor; and support for East Timor's security and stability. Decides that UNMISET will include up to 58 civilian advisors, 157 civilian police advisors, 42 military liaison officers, 310 formed troops, and a 125-person International Response Unit. Decides that internationally accepted human rights principles shall continue to form an integral part of training and capacity building carried out by UNMISET. Requests the Secretary-General to report regularly to the Security Council on implementation of the resolution with recommendations for any modifications to UNMISET, with a view to completing its mandate by May 20, 2005.

Emphasizes that the Serious Crimes Unit should complete all investigations by November 2004, and should conclude trials and other activities as soon as possible and no later than May 20, 2005.

Background: Resolution 1410 (2002) had established UNMISET as a successor mission of the UN Transitional Administration in East Timor for a period of two years, to assist in building a critical core administrative structure, provide interim law enforcement and public security, and contribute to the maintenance of the country's external and internal security. According to Resolution 1410, UNMISET's downsizing should proceed as quickly as possible. In 2004, the Secretary-General recommended the extension of UNMISET for a further year, at a reduced size and with a modified mandate.

U.S. Position: The United States voted for this resolution. The United States agreed with the Secretary-General that the security situation in East Timor was still fragile and warranted continuing UNMISET, although on a much-reduced scale. The United States included language in the resolution that called for the Secretary-General to develop a transitional plan for UNMISET and to report regularly on the progress of the handover that the United States expects to occur in May 2005.

S/Res/1573   November 16   15(US)-0-0

Decides to extend the mandate of the UN Mission of Support in Timor-Leste (UNMISET) for a final period of six months until May 20, 2005. Decides also to maintain UNMISET's current tasks, configuration, and size in order to allow the mission to complete key tasks of its mandate and consolidate gains made thus far. Requests UNMISET to focus increasingly on implementing its exit strategy, particularly with a view to ensure increasing involvement and ownership of the Timorese in the mission's three program areas. Urges, in particular, UN development and humanitarian agencies and multilateral financial institutions to start immediately planning for a smooth transition in East Timor to a sustainable development assistance framework. Reaffirms the need to fight against impunity and, in this regard, takes note of the Secretary-General's intention to continue to explore possible ways to address this issue with a view to making proposals as appropriate.

Background: A technical assistance mission that visited Timor-Leste in early October concluded that Timor-Leste still had not reached the critical threshold of self-sufficiency. Based on the mission's conclusions, the Secretary-General recommended another six-month renewal of UNMISET's mandate, with a view to terminating operations in May 2005. At the same time, he noted that UNMISET would need to complete its exit strategy within the six-month timeframe.

U.S. Position: The United States voted for this resolution.

WESTERN SAHARA

S/Res/1523   January 30   15(US)-0-0

Decides to extend the mandate of the UN Mission for the Referendum in Western Sahara (MINURSO) until April 30, 2004. Requests that the

Secretary-General provide a report on the situation before the end of the present mandate.

Background: MINURSO has been in place since April 1991 when Morocco and the POLISARIO Front agreed to a ceasefire in their long-running dispute over the status of Western Sahara. The Secretary-General's latest report on MINURSO recommended the mission be extended for another three months to give Morocco more time to respond to a peace plan for the disputed area. The peace plan, submitted in 2003 by the Secretary-General's Personal Envoy James Baker (United States), called for a referendum on the permanent future status of Western Sahara within four or five years. Resolution 1495 (2003) supported the Baker plan and called upon the parties to work towards acceptance of the peace plan.   It was accepted by the POLISARIO Front in July 2003.

U.S. Position: The United States introduced this resolution on behalf of the Group of Friends of Western Sahara (France, Russia, Spain, the United Kingdom, and the United States).

S/Res/1541   April 29   15(US)-0-0

Reaffirms its support for the Peace Plan for the Self-Determination of the People of Western Sahara as an optimum political solution on the basis of agreement between the two parties. Calls upon all the parties and the states of the region to cooperate fully with the Secretary-General and his Special Envoy. Decides to extend the mandate of the UN Mission for the Referendum in Western Sahara (MINURSO) until October 31, 2004. Requests that the Secretary-General provide a report on the situation before the end of the present mandate and to include an evaluation of the mission size necessary for MINURSO to carry out its mandated tasks, with a view towards its possible reduction.

Background: The POLISARIO Front officially accepted the Baker peace plan in July 2003 but Morocco rejected essential elements of the peace plan in April 2004, leading the Secretary-General to recommend an extension of MINURSO's mandate, providing more time to work for acceptance of the peace plan.

U.S. Position: The United States introduced this resolution on behalf of the Group of Friends of Western Sahara. The United States believed the Baker plan provided a fair and balanced basis on which to move forward toward resolving the longstanding dispute of nearly 30 years, and urged the parties and neighboring states to seize the opportunity presented by the plan to move the process forward.

S/Res/1570   October 28   15(US)-0-0

Decides to extend the mandate of the UN Mission for the Referendum in Western Sahara (MINURSO) until April 30, 2005. Requests the Secretary-General to provide a report on the situation before the end of the mandate period and an interim report, within three months from adoption of the resolution, on the evolution of the situation and on the mission's size and concept of operation, with further detail on the options discussed in the Secretary-General's report of October 20, 2004, on the possible reduction of MINURSO staff, including civilian and administrative personnel.

Background: The Secretary-General's October 20 report noted that Morocco continued to object to essential elements of the Peace Plan for Self-Determination. The report proposed either maintaining the current military observer force level or reducing the force level by 16 percent, and the Council agreed to demonstrate the UN's continued commitment to the mission's mandate for an additional six-month period.

U.S. Position: The United States introduced this resolution on behalf of the Group of Friends of Western Sahara. The United States looked forward to receiving the Secretary-General's report on the evolution of the situation in the Western Sahara and on the mission's size and concept of operation, with recommendations for possible reductions in MINURSO's civilian and administrative staff.

THEMATIC RESOLUTIONS

CHILDREN AND ARMED CONFLICT

S/Res/1539   April 22   15(US)-0-0

Strongly condemns the recruitment and use of child soldiers by parties to armed conflict in violation of international obligations, killing and maiming of children, rape and other sexual violence mostly committed against girls, abduction and forced displacement, denial of humanitarian access to children, attacks against schools and hospitals, as well as trafficking, forced labor, and all forms of slavery, and all other violations and abuses committed against children affected by armed conflict. Expresses its intention to take appropriate measures to curb linkages between illicit trade in natural and other resources, illicit trafficking in small arms and light weapons, cross-border abduction and recruitment, and armed conflict, which can prolong armed conflict and intensify its impact on children. Requests the Secretary-General to propose effective measures to control this illicit trade and trafficking.

Takes note with deep concern of the continued recruitment and use of children by parties mentioned in the Secretary-General's report in situations of armed conflict and requests the Secretary-General to ensure that compliance by these parties is reviewed regularly. Requests the Secretary-General to devise, preferably within three months, an action plan for a systematic and comprehensive monitoring and reporting mechanism to provide timely, objective, accurate, and reliable information on the recruitment and use of child soldiers. Decides to continue the inclusion of specific provisions for the protection of children in the mandates of UN peacekeeping operations. Notes with concern all the cases of sexual exploitation and abuse of women and children, especially girls, in humanitarian crises. Requests contributing countries to incorporate the Six Core Principles of the Inter-Agency Standing Committee on Emergencies into pertinent codes of conduct for peacekeeping personnel and to develop appropriate disciplinary and accountability mechanisms. Reiterates its request to the Secretary-General to ensure that in all his reports on country-specific situations, the protection of children is included as a specific aspect of the report.

Background: The Secretary-General issued a report on children and armed conflict on November 10, 2003. Despite some gains, the general situation remained precarious for children in armed conflict situations. Parties to conflict continued to violate children's rights, causing terror, deprivation, and vulnerability to children in eastern Democratic Republic of the Congo, Iraq, Liberia, and the occupied Palestinian territories. Children have been killed, made orphans, maimed, abducted, deprived of education and health care, and left with deep emotional scars. Children have also been recruited as soldiers. Despite some progress, parties to conflict in Afghanistan, Burma, Burundi, Chechnya, Colombia, the Cote d'Ivoire, the Democratic Republic of the Congo, Liberia, Nepal, the Philippines, Somalia, Sri Lanka, the Sudan, and Uganda continued to recruit and use child soldiers. The Secretary-General listed in annexes to his report the specific groups that recruited child soldiers.

U.S. Position: The United States voted for this resolution. During the Security Council debate on this topic, the United States recognized the terrible consequences to children during conflicts. The United States supported the Secretary-General listing all governments and groups that illegally recruit and use child soldiers so that UN teams and the Security Council could actively monitor these groups.

INTERNATIONAL COURT OF JUSTICE

S/Res/1571   November 4   Adopted Without Vote

Noting with regret the resignation of Judge Gilbert Guillaume, taking effect on February 11, 2005, decides that the election to fill the vacancy shall take place on February 15, 2005, at a meeting of the Security Council and at a meeting of the General Assembly at its 59th session.

Background: On October 11, 2004, Judge Gilbert Guillaume notified the President of the Court of his resignation, effective February 11, 2005.

U.S. Position: The United States agreed with the rest of the Council to adopt this resolution without a vote.

INTERNATIONAL CRIMINAL TRIBUNALS

S/Res/1534   March 26   15(US)-0-0

Acting under Chapter VII of the UN Charter, reaffirms the necessity of trial of persons indicted by the International Criminal Tribunal for the former Yugoslavia (ICTY) and the International Criminal Tribunal for Rwanda (ICTR) and reiterates its call on all states to intensify cooperation with and render all necessary assistance to the tribunals, particularly to bring Radovan Karadzic, Ratko Mladic, and Ante Gotovina to the ICTY. Emphasizes the importance of fully implementing the Completion Strategies, as set out in Resolution 1503 (2003), that call on the ICTY and ICTR to take all possible measures to complete investigations by the end of 2004, to complete all trial activities at first instance by the end of 2008, and to complete all work in 2010; urges each tribunal to plan and act accordingly.

Background: The Security Council created the ICTR (1994) and ICTY (1993) to try those senior leaders most responsible for serious violations of international humanitarian law. The ICTY has convicted over 40 persons. The ICTR has convicted 18 persons, including the former Rwanda Prime Minister Jean Kambanda.

U.S. Position: The United States voted for this resolution.

S/Res/1567   October 14   15(US)-0-0

Having considered the nominations for Permanent Judges of the International Tribunal for the Former Yugoslavia received by the Secretary-General, forwards the following nominations to the General Assembly in accordance with the Statute of the International Tribunal: Mr. Carmel A. Agius (Malta), Mr. Jean-Claude Antonetti (France), Mr. Iain Bonomy (United Kingdom), Mr. Liu Daqun (China), Mr. Mohammed Amin El-Abbassi El Mahdi (Egypt), Mr. Elhagi Abdulkader Emberesh (Libyan Arab Jamahiriya), Mr. Rigoberto Espinal Irias (Honduras), Mr. O-gon Kwon (Republic of Korea), Mr. Theodor Meron (United States), Mr. Bakone Melema Moloto (South Africa), Ms. Prisca Matimba Nyambe (Zambia), Mr. Alphonsus Martinus Maria Orie (Netherlands), Mr. Kevin Horace Parker (Australia), Mr. Fausto Pocar (Italy), Mr. Yenyi Olungu (Democratic Republic of the Congo), Mr. Sharada Prasad Pandit (Nepal), Ms. Vonimbolana Rasoazanany (Madagascar), Mr. Patrick Lipton Robinson (Jamaica), Mr. Wolfgang Schomburg (Germany), Mr. Mohamed Shahabuddeen (Guyana), Ms. Christine Van den Wyngaert (Belgium), Mr. Volodymyr A. Vassylenko (Ukraine).

Background: The International Criminal Tribunal for the former Yugoslavia (ICTY) was established by Security Council Resolution 827 in 1993 in the face of serious violations of international humanitarian law committed in the territory of the former Yugoslavia since 1991, and as a response to the threat to international peace and security posed by those serious violations. The ICTY Chambers consist of 16 permanent judges and a maximum of nine temporary judges. The 16 permanent judges are elected by the General Assembly from a list of nominees forwarded by the Security Council. Permanent judges serve for four years and may be re-elected.

U.S. Position: The United States voted for this resolution. The list included an American judge, Theodor Meron, who has served on the Tribunal since March 2001 and is currently serving as President of the Tribunal.

NON-PROLIFERATION

S/Res/1540   April 28   15(US)-0-0

Acting under Chapter VII of the UN Charter, decides that all states shall refrain from providing any form of support to non-state actors that attempt to develop, acquire, manufacture, possess, transport, transfer or use nuclear, chemical, or biological weapons and their means of delivery. Decides also that all states, in accordance with their national procedures, shall adopt and enforce appropriate effective laws which prohibit any non-state actor to manufacture, acquire, possess, develop, transport, transfer, or use nuclear, chemical, or biological weapons and their means of delivery, particularly for terrorist purposes, as well as attempts to engage in any of the foregoing activities, participate in them as an accomplice, assist, or finance them.

Decides also that all states shall take and enforce effective measures to establish domestic controls to prevent the proliferation of nuclear, chemical, or biological weapons and their means of delivery, including by establishing appropriate controls over related materials, and shall develop and maintain appropriate, effective measures to account for and secure such items in production, use, storage, or transport; develop and maintain appropriate, effective physical protection measures; develop and maintain appropriate, effective border controls and law enforcement efforts to detect, deter, prevent, and combat, including through international cooperation when necessary, the illicit trafficking and brokering in such items in accordance with their national legal authorities and legislation and consistent with international law; establish, develop, review, and maintain appropriate, effective national export and trans-shipment controls over such items, including appropriate laws and regulations to control export, transit, trans-shipment, and re-export, and controls on providing funds and services related to such export and trans-shipment such as financing, and transporting that would contribute to proliferation, as well as establishing end-user controls; and establishing and enforcing appropriate criminal or civil penalties for violations of such export control laws and regulations. Recognizes the utility in implementing this resolution of effective national control lists and calls upon all member states to pursue at the earliest opportunity the development of such lists.

Decides that none of the obligations set forth in this resolution shall be interpreted to conflict with or alter the rights and obligations of state parties to the Nuclear Non-Proliferation Treaty, the Chemical Weapons Convention, and the Biological and Toxin Weapons Convention, or alter the responsibilities of the International Atomic Energy Agency (IAEA) or the Organization for the Prohibition of Chemical Weapons (OPCW).

Calls upon all states to promote the universal adoption, implementation, and strengthening of multilateral proliferation treaties to which they are parties; adopt national rules and regulations to ensure compliance with their commitments under the key multilateral non-proliferation treaties; renew and fulfill their commitments to multilateral cooperation, in particular within the framework of the IAEA, OPCW, and the Biological and Toxin Weapons Convention, as important means of pursuing and achieving their common objectives in the area of non-proliferation and of promoting international cooperation for peaceful purposes; develop appropriate ways to work with and inform industry and the public regarding their obligations under such laws; promote dialogue and cooperation on nonproliferation so as to address the threat posed by proliferation of nuclear, chemical, or biological weapons, and their means of delivery; and take cooperative action to prevent illicit trafficking in nuclear, chemical, or biological weapons, their means of delivery, and related materials. Recognizes that some states may require assistance in implementing the provisions of this resolution within their territories and invites states in a position to do so to offer assistance in response to specific requests to the states lacking the legal and regulatory infrastructure, implementation experience, and/or resources for fulfilling the provisions of this resolution.

Decides to establish for a period of no longer than two years a Security Council Committee consisting of all members of the Council, which will report to the Security Council on the implementation of this resolution, and to this end calls upon states to present a first report no later than six months from the adoption of this resolution to the Committee on steps they have taken or intend to take to implement this resolution.

Background: In his September 2003 address to the General Assembly, President Bush called attention to the threat posed by rogue states and terrorists acquiring weapons of mass destruction and their means of delivery. He asked the Security Council to adopt a resolution that would criminalize "...proliferation of weapons of mass destruction, enact strict export controls consistent with international standards, and secure sensitive materials within their borders."

The proliferation of weapons of mass destruction has been recognized as a threat to national and international security. International treaties and regimes, most importantly the Nuclear Non-Proliferation Treaty, Chemical Weapons Convention, and Biological Weapons Convention, have established solid global norms against proliferation. However, proliferators—state and non-state actors—employ increasingly aggressive measures to obtain weapons of mass destruction, their delivery systems, and related materials, equipment, and technology. Against this backdrop, efforts to address illicit trafficking and defeat proliferators needed to be stepped up. In response, supplier countries—

individually and collectively—have worked to put in place more stringent export controls and enforcement measures and to promulgate such efforts, and focus has turned to adopting additional measures to make it harder and more costly for proliferators to ply their deadly trade. In early 2004, the revelation of the global network of Dr. A.Q. Khan provided a stark illustration of the problem, and reinforced the urgency of President Bush's call for a UN resolution. For many years Dr. Khan's network sold equipment and expertise related to weapons of mass destruction to outlaw regimes on the black market.

U.S. Position: The United States, as the lead sponsor of this resolution, ensured that the resolution responded to the President's call for member states to criminalize the proliferation of weapons of mass destruction, to enact strict export controls consistent with international standards, and to secure any and all sensitive materials within their own borders. The United States worked with the other four permanent members of the Security Council to develop a unified position to accomplish these objectives, which was then adopted with minor amendment by the full Security Council.

Through this resolution, the UN Security Council for the first time acknowledged under Chapter VII the threat to international peace and security posed by the proliferation of weapons of mass destruction. It imposed a baseline requirement that all states respond to the growing threat of states and non-state actors acquiring weapons of mass destruction, their delivery systems, and related materials by drafting and implementing laws to 1) secure items within their borders, 2) ensure that their entities are not involved in networks supplying proliferators, and 3) ensure that their territories are not used to in any way to assist state or non-state actors of proliferation concern. Finally, the resolution affirmed the Council's support for cooperative efforts such as the Prolifersation Security Initiative.

TERRORISM

S/Res/1526	January 30	15(US)-0-0

Acting under Chapter VII of the UN Charter, decides to improve the implementation of the measures imposed by Resolutions 1267 (1999), 1333 (2000), 1390 (2000), and 1455 (2003) with respect to individuals, groups, undertakings and entities associated with Osama bin Laden, or members of the Al Qaida organization or the Taliban. All member states are obligated to impose asset freezes, travel bans, and arms embargoes, against such individuals, groups, undertakings and entities as designated by the 1267 Sanctions Committee established by Resolution 1267 (1999). Decides to strengthen the mandate of the Committee to include, in addition to the oversight of states' implementation of the measures referred to above, a central role in assessing information for the Council's review regarding effective implementation of the measures, as well as in recommending improvements to the measures. Decides that the measures referred to above will be further improved in 18 months, or sooner if necessary.

Decides, in order to assist the Committee in the fulfillment of its mandate, to establish for a period of 18 months a New York-based Analytical Support and Sanctions Monitoring Team under the direction of the Committee. Requests the Secretary-General to appoint no more than eight members of the Monitoring Team; and further requests the Monitoring Team to submit three comprehensive, independent reports to the Committee.

Background: In 1999, the Security Council established the Sanctions Committee by Resolution 1267.

U.S. Position: The United States cosponsored this resolution as part of an effort to institutionalize stronger counter-terrorism measures in the United Nations.

S/Res/1530   March 11   15(US)-0-0

Condemns in the strongest terms the bomb attacks in Madrid, Spain, perpetrated by the terrorist group ETA on March 11, 2004, and regards such act, like any act of terrorism, as a threat to peace and security. Expresses its deepest sympathy and condolences to the people and Government of Spain and to the victims of the terrorist attacks and their families. Urges all states, in accordance with their obligations under Resolution 1373 (2001), to cooperate actively in efforts to find and bring to justice the perpetrators, organizers and sponsors of this terrorist attack. Expresses its reinforced determination to combat all forms of terrorism, in accordance with its responsibilities under the UN Charter.

Background: The Spanish Ambassador to the United Nations, Inocencio Arias, subsequently wrote a letter of explanation (dated March 15) to the Security Council President explaining Spain's imputation of guilt to ETA, later revealed to be inaccurate.

U.S. Position: The United States voted for this resolution.

S/Res/1535   March 26   15(US)-0-0

Endorses the report of the Counter-Terrorism Committee (CTC) on its revitalization. Decides that the revitalized CTC will consist of the Plenary—composed of the Security Council member states—and the Bureau, composed of the Chair and the Vice-Chairs, assisted by the Counter-Terrorism Committee Executive Directorate (CTED) to be established as a special political mission, under the policy guidance of the Plenary, for an initial period ending December 31, 2007, and subject to a comprehensive review by the Security Council by December 31, 2005, to enhance the CTC's ability to monitor the implementation of Resolution 1373 (2001) and effectively continue its capacity-building work. Requests the Secretary-General to appoint within 45 days, after consultation with and subject to the approval of the Council, an Executive Director of the CTED who will take up office as soon as possible.

Background: The CTC was authorized by Resolution 1373 (2001), adopted shortly after the September 11 terrorist attacks, in order to monitor efforts by states to implement a wide range of counter-terrorism measures required by the resolution.   Through its capacity-building and global coordination initiatives, the CTC has become a significant element in the worldwide campaign against terrorism.   The CTC's mandate set forth in Resolution 1373 was not changed by this new resolution.

Taking into consideration the CTC Chair's report (November 14, 2003) on the problems encountered both by member states and the CTC itself in the implementation of Resolution 1373, Resolution 1535 reorganized and consolidated the CTC's support staff under the new CTED, so that the CTC might be able to respond more quickly and flexibly to requests for assistance from states and international organizations and to better facilitate the exchange of counter-terrorism information.   The CTED would be responsible for the following tasks, among others: supporting and advising the plenary and the chairperson; ensuring the comprehensive follow-up of all of the Committee's decisions; facilitating the provision of assistance to states in order to further their implementation of Resolution 1373; and supervising the collection of all relevant information in following up implementation.   This measure followed the adoption in January 2004 of Resolution 1526, which strengthened the ability of the 1267 Sanctions Committee to carry out its work with the support of a new monitoring team.   Taken together, these UN Security Council resolutions were practical yet innovative steps that demonstrated the international community's determination to actively cooperate in the ongoing campaign against terrorism.

U.S. Position: The United States voted for this resolution.   The United States is committed to working through the UN system and with other member states to build upon and refine existing counter-terrorism capacities and practices, including in the financial, law enforcement and information-sharing areas.   By revamping and restructuring key UN mechanisms, the United States is working to ensure that they are more responsive, accountable, and better equipped to address the terrorist threat.

S/Res/1566   October 8   15(US)-0-0

Acting under Chapter VII of the UN Charter, condemns in the strongest terms all acts of terrorism irrespective of their motivation, whenever and by whomsoever committed, as one of the most serious threats to peace and security. Calls upon all states to cooperate fully in the fight against terrorism, especially with those states where or against whose citizens terrorist acts are committed, in accordance with their obligations under international law, in order to find, deny safe haven, and bring to justice, on the basis of the principle to extradite or prosecute, any person who supports, facilitates, participates, or attempts to participate in the financing, planning, preparation, or commission of terrorist acts or provides safe havens. Recalls that criminal acts committed with the intent to cause death or serious bodily injury, or taking of hostages, with the purpose to provoke a state of terror in the general public or in a group of persons or particular persons, intimidate a population or compel a government or an international organization to do or to abstain from doing any act, which constitute offences within the scope of and as defined in the international conventions and protocols relating to terrorism, are under no circumstances justifiable by considerations of a political, philosophical, ideological, racial, ethnic, religious, or other similar nature, and calls upon all states to prevent such acts and, if not prevented, to ensure that such acts are punished by penalties consistent with their grave nature.

Calls upon all states to become party, as a matter of urgency, to the relevant international conventions and protocols. Calls upon relevant organizations to strengthen international cooperation in the fight against terrorism and to intensify their interactions with the United Nations and the Counter-Terrorism Committee (CTC) with a view to facilitating full and timely implementation of Resolution 1373. Requests the CTC to develop a set of best practices to assist states in implementing the provisions of Resolution 1373 related to the financing of terrorism. Directs the CTC to start visits to states, with the consent of the states concerned, in order to enhance the monitoring of the implementation of Resolution 1373 and facilitate the provision of technical and other assistance for such implementation.

Decides to establish a working group consisting of all members of the Security Council to consider and submit recommendations to the Council on practical measures to be imposed upon individuals, groups, or entities involved in or associated with terrorist activities, other than those designated by the Al Qaida/Taliban Sanctions Committee. Requests further the working group to consider the possibility of establishing an international fund to compensate victims of terrorist acts and their families, which might be financed through voluntary contributions, which could consist in part of assets seized from terrorist organizations, their members, and sponsors, and submit its recommendations to the Council.

Background: In September, terrorists seized a school in Beslan, Russia, in which more than 300 people, mostly children, were killed. In response to this event, Russia drafted this resolution to address terrorism committed against civilians.

U.S. Position: The United States voted for adoption of this resolution. In its Explanation of Vote, the U.S. representative said "...the deliberate massacre of innocents is never justifiable in any cause."

VOTING SUMMARIES

The table below lists the votes of Security Council members on the 62 draft resolutions introduced in 2004. Resolutions on which a Security Council member voted No or abstained are identified by the resolution number (if the resolution was adopted) in parentheses or in a footnote. The United States vetoed two draft resolutions and abstained on one, all on the Middle East.

COUNTRY	YES	NO	ABSTAIN
United States	59	2*	1 (1544)
Algeria	60	0	2 (1559, 1564)
Angola	62	0	0
Benin	62	0	0
Brazil	61	0	1 (1559)
Chile	62	0	0
China	59	0	3 (1556, 1559, 1564)
France	62	0	0
Germany	60	0	2*
Pakistan	59	0	3 (1556, 1559, 1564)
Philippines	61	0	1 (1559)
Romania	60	0	2*
Russia	59	1	2 (1559, 1564)
Spain	62	0	0
United Kingdom	60	0	2*

*The United States vetoed two draft resolutions on the Middle East; Germany, Romania, and the United Kingdom abstained on both of those draft resolutions.

In the following table, the 61 Security Council votes on which the United States voted Yes or No are tabulated on the same basis as overall votes for the General Assembly in this report (Sections III and IV). Voting coincidence percentages are calculated accordingly. Resolutions adopted without a vote are included as Yes votes. Security Council members are ranked by voting coincidence with the United States. When the percentage is the same, members are ranked by the number of identical votes. When the number of votes is the same, members are ranked alphabetically. Because abstentions reduce the number of identical votes, they lower the rank order of those countries that abstain. It should be noted that group dynamics in the Security Council, whose 15 members frequently consult closely on issues before resolutions are presented for adoption, are quite different from those in the General Assembly.

COUNTRY	IDENTICAL VOTES	OPPOSITE VOTES	ABSTEN-TIONS	VOTING COINCIDENCE
Germany	59	0	2	100%
Romania	59	0	2	100%
United Kingdom	59	0	2	100%
Angola	59	2	0	96.7%
Benin	59	2	0	96.7%
Chile	59	2	0	96.7%
France	59	2	0	96.7%
Spain	59	2	0	96.7%
Brazil	58	2	1	96.7%
Philippines	58	2	1	96.7%
Algeria	57	2	2	96.6%
China	56	2	3	96.6%
Pakistan	56	2	3	96.6%
Russia	56	3	2	94.9%
Average	58.1	1.6	1.1	97.3%

III—GENERAL ASSEMBLY—OVERALL VOTES

Eighty-nine Plenary votes plus one important Third Committee vote were recorded at the 59th session of the UN General Assembly (UNGA). Of the total 90 votes, the United States voted Yes 17 times and No 62 times; it abstained on 11 votes.

COMPARISON WITH U.S. VOTE

The tables that follow are based on the 79 instances the United States voted either Yes or No in Plenary or on the motion in the Third Committee. Columns show the number of times the United States and the pertinent country cast identical (Yes/Yes or No/No) and opposite (Yes/No or No/Yes) votes, as well as the number of times a country abstained or was absent for these 79 votes. Voting coincidence percentages are derived by dividing the number of identical votes by the total of identical and opposite votes, the same method used in all previous editions of this report. The column headed "Voting Coincidence (Including Consensus)" presents the percentage of voting coincidence with the United States after factoring in consensus resolutions as additional identical votes. Extent of participation was also factored in (see Introduction: Format and Methodology).

Section III contains five parts: (1) lists of UN member states alphabetically and in rank order by voting coincidence percentage; (2) lists of countries by UN regional group, in rank order by voting coincidence percentage; (3) lists of countries by other groupings, again in rank order; (4) a comparison of 2004 voting coincidence percentages with those of the preceding five years; and (5) a side-by-side comparison of each country's voting coincidence with the United States and a calculation of the amount of bilateral U.S. assistance provided to that country in fiscal year 2004 (from the Foreign Operations, Export Financing, Related Programs Act and P.L. 480 funds).

All members voted during the session. The United States again voted No in Plenary more often than any other UN member (25 percent of U.S. No votes coincided with those of three or fewer countries), voting No alone on only two occasions, which was much lower than last year. The United States voted No with only one other country 10 times (five times with Palau, and once each with Israel, the Marshall Islands, and the United Kingdom). On several other occasions, the United States was joined in a No vote by Israel and one or two other countries (usually France, India, Marshall Islands, Micronesia, Pakistan, Palau, or the United Kingdom).

U.S. votes in isolation were on a resolution concerning the Comprehensive Test Ban Treaty and on a paragraph vote on promoting an integrated management approach to the Caribbean Sea. Votes with Israel and Palau were on issues regarding arms control, racism, travel, decolonization, development, and the U.S. embargo of Cuba. Marshall Islands voted with the United States on rights of the child and the U.S. embargo of Cuba. The United

Kingdom voted with the United States on resolutions on decolonization and arms control. France, India, Micronesia, and Pakistan voted with the United States on resolutions concerning arms control.

The Palestinian Authority is not a UN member and does not have voting privileges.

All Countries (Alphabetical)

COUNTRY	IDENTICAL VOTES	OPPOSITE VOTES	ABSTEN-TIONS	ABSENCES	VOTING COINCIDENCE INCLUDING CONSENSUS	VOTES ONLY
Afghanistan	5	52	0	22	75.6%	8.8%
Albania	29	29	15	6	88.6%	50.0%
Algeria	7	63	8	1	77.6%	10.0%
Andorra	29	40	9	1	85.7%	42.0%
Angola	9	43	7	20	79.8%	17.3%
Antigua-Barbuda	6	50	12	11	79.4%	10.7%
Argentina	17	51	11	0	81.9%	25.0%
Armenia	18	49	11	1	82.4%	26.9%
Australia	34	26	17	2	90.3%	56.7%
Austria	29	39	11	0	86.1%	42.6%
Azerbaijan	8	56	8	7	78.5%	12.5%
Bahamas	7	57	10	5	78.3%	10.9%
Bahrain	6	62	8	3	77.4%	8.8%
Bangladesh	6	64	9	0	77.4%	8.6%
Barbados	6	57	11	5	78.4%	9.5%
Belarus	5	57	12	5	78.1%	8.1%
Belgium	29	37	11	2	86.5%	43.9%
Belize	8	61	8	2	77.8%	11.6%
Benin	10	57	6	6	78.6%	14.9%
Bhutan	3	39	19	18	80.6%	7.1%
Bolivia	18	60	1	0	79.4%	23.1%
Bosnia/Herzegovina	29	39	11	0	86.1%	42.6%
Botswana	8	56	5	10	77.3%	12.5%
Brazil	10	57	12	0	79.6%	14.9%
Brunei Darussalam	6	63	10	0	77.7%	8.7%
Bulgaria	30	38	11	0	86.5%	44.1%
Burkina Faso	10	60	6	3	78.3%	14.3%
Burundi	6	55	9	9	78.2%	9.8%
Cambodia	8	60	7	4	77.7%	11.8%
Cameroon	12	44	20	3	83.2%	21.4%
Canada	32	32	13	2	88.2%	50.0%
Cape Verde	5	57	5	12	76.7%	8.1%
Central African Rep.	10	52	4	13	78.1%	16.1%
Chad	5	17	1	56	78.4%	22.7%
Chile	20	54	4	1	80.9%	27.0%
China	6	62	10	1	77.6%	8.8%
Colombia	7	59	13	0	78.9%	10.6%
Comoros	5	57	4	13	76.7%	8.1%
Congo	3	43	1	32	75.9%	6.5%
Costa Rica	15	56	5	3	79.8%	21.1%

All Countries (Alphabetical) (Cont'd)

COUNTRY	IDENTICAL VOTES	OPPOSITE VOTES	ABSTEN-TIONS	ABSENCES	VOTING COINCIDENCE INCLUDING CONSENSUS	VOTES ONLY
Cote d'Ivoire	11	50	11	7	80.4%	18.0%
Croatia	29	39	11	0	86.1%	42.6%
Cuba	5	63	8	3	76.8%	7.4%
Cyprus	29	43	7	0	84.9%	40.3%
Czech Republic	30	37	10	2	86.6%	44.8%
DPR of Korea	2	59	8	10	75.7%	3.3%
Dem. Rep. Congo	9	24	2	44	80.6%	27.3%
Denmark	31	38	10	0	86.5%	44.9%
Djibouti	9	62	6	2	77.6%	12.7%
Dominica	6	57	10	6	78.0%	9.5%
Dominican Republic	16	52	10	1	81.2%	23.5%
Ecuador	11	59	8	1	79.0%	15.7%
Egypt	6	65	6	2	76.7%	8.5%
El Salvador	18	56	4	1	80.3%	24.3%
Equatorial Guinea	11	43	7	18	80.6%	20.4%
Eritrea	7	59	7	6	77.3%	10.6%
Estonia	27	38	12	2	86.1%	41.5%
Ethiopia	8	50	11	10	79.8%	13.8%
Fiji	12	53	9	5	79.7%	18.5%
Finland	30	39	10	0	86.2%	43.5%
France	33	28	17	1	89.7%	54.1%
Gabon	7	51	1	20	76.7%	12.1%
Gambia	6	44	1	28	76.2%	12.0%
Georgia	22	38	15	4	85.0%	36.7%
Germany	30	37	11	1	86.6%	44.8%
Ghana	10	59	8	2	78.5%	14.5%
Greece	30	39	9	1	86.1%	43.5%
Grenada	19	46	10	4	82.7%	29.2%
Guatemala	17	54	8	0	81.0%	23.9%
Guinea	8	38	2	31	77.8%	17.4%
Guinea-Bissau	14	52	1	12	79.1%	21.2%
Guyana	9	60	8	2	78.4%	13.0%
Haiti	8	36	23	12	83.9%	18.2%
Honduras	14	45	11	9	82.1%	23.7%
Hungary	29	38	11	1	86.3%	43.3%
Iceland	30	36	12	1	87.0%	45.5%
India	13	52	14	0	81.3%	20.0%
Indonesia	6	66	7	0	76.8%	8.3%
Iran	6	65	8	0	76.9%	8.5%
Iraq	3	51	3	22	74.6%	5.6%

All Countries (Alphabetical) (Cont'd)

COUNTRY	IDENTICAL VOTES	OPPOSITE VOTES	ABSTEN-TIONS	ABSENCES	VOTING COINCIDENCE INCLUDING CONSENSUS	VOTES ONLY
Ireland	28	40	11	0	85.8%	41.2%
Israel	55	4	14	6	98.4%	93.2%
Italy	30	39	10	0	86.1%	43.5%
Jamaica	8	56	9	6	78.7%	12.5%
Japan	27	36	16	0	87.0%	42.9%
Jordan	12	63	2	2	77.8%	16.0%
Kazakhstan	7	57	8	7	77.7%	10.9%
Kenya	8	56	15	0	79.8%	12.5%
Kiribati	1	1	0	77	85.1%	50.0%
Kuwait	7	63	7	2	77.2%	10.0%
Kyrgyzstan	8	52	6	13	78.5%	13.3%
Laos	3	57	9	10	76.7%	5.0%
Latvia	32	36	9	2	86.9%	47.1%
Lebanon	6	63	5	5	76.5%	8.7%
Lesotho	6	61	6	6	76.8%	9.0%
Liberia	8	51	9	11	78.9%	13.6%
Libya	7	65	6	1	76.8%	9.7%
Liechtenstein	28	39	12	0	86.1%	41.8%
Lithuania	30	39	10	0	86.2%	43.5%
Luxembourg	29	38	10	2	86.2%	43.3%
Madagascar	9	62	5	3	77.4%	12.7%
Malawi	9	31	10	29	81.8%	22.5%
Malaysia	6	64	9	0	77.4%	8.6%
Maldives	7	62	3	7	76.6%	10.1%
Mali	10	61	3	5	77.2%	14.1%
Malta	28	42	8	1	85.0%	40.0%
Marshall Islands	44	28	3	4	89.7%	61.1%
Mauritania	3	32	5	39	77.8%	8.6%
Mauritius	8	59	11	1	78.7%	11.9%
Mexico	17	57	5	0	80.1%	23.0%
Micronesia	46	13	4	16	94.4%	78.0%
Monaco	29	33	8	9	86.7%	46.8%
Mongolia	10	58	7	4	78.5%	14.7%
Morocco	8	62	5	4	77.3%	11.4%
Mozambique	6	54	3	16	76.8%	10.0%
Myanmar (Burma)	8	60	10	i	78.5%	11.8%
Namibia	11	62	5	1	78.1%	15.1%
Nauru	21	32	16	10	86.5%	39.6%
Nepal	9	62	7	1	77.8%	12.7%
Netherlands	30	40	9	0	85.9%	42.9%

All Countries (Alphabetical) (Cont'd)

COUNTRY	IDENTICAL VOTES	OPPOSITE VOTES	ABSTEN- TIONS	ABSENCES	VOTING COINCIDENCE INCLUDING CONSENSUS	VOTES ONLY
New Zealand	28	41	10	0	85.5%	40.6%
Nicaragua	18	51	7	3	81.4%	26.1%
Niger	9	52	2	16	76.8%	14.8%
Nigeria	11	63	5	0	77.9%	14.9%
Norway	29	39	10	1	86.0%	42.6%
Oman	7	64	7	1	77.1%	9.9%
Pakistan	6	56	15	2	79.3%	9.7%
Palau	67	1	0	11	99.6%	98.5%
Panama	18	59	1	1	79.5%	23.4%
Papua New Guinea	11	40	21	7	83.4%	21.6%
Paraguay	18	55	5	1	80.3%	24.7%
Peru	18	54	7	0	81.1%	25.0%
Philippines	9	60	9	1	78.5%	13.0%
Poland	32	38	9	0	86.6%	45.7%
Portugal	30	39	10	0	86.2%	43.5%
Qatar	7	63	7	2	77.2%	10.0%
Republic of Korea	24	37	18	0	86.4%	39.3%
Republic of Moldova	22	38	16	3	85.7%	36.7%
Romania	30	38	11	0	86.5%	44.1%
Russia	11	48	20	0	82.4%	18.6%
Rwanda	6	47	3	23	77.0%	11.3%
St. Kitts and Nevis	1	5	0	73	79.9%	16.7%
Saint Lucia	9	58	7	5	78.2%	13.4%
St.Vincent/Grenadines	9	58	8	4	78.6%	13.4%
Samoa	17	40	12	10	83.6%	29.8%
San Marino	28	40	11	0	85.8%	41.2%
Sao Tome/Principe	5	49	4	21	77.5%	9.3%
Saudi Arabia	5	64	8	2	76.7%	7.2%
Senegal	10	65	4	0	77.2%	13.3%
Serbia/Montenegro	29	39	11	0	86.1%	42.6%
Seychelles	7	40	0	32	77.1%	14.9%
Sierra Leone	8	58	10	3	78.7%	12.1%
Singapore	9	57	12	1	79.4%	13.6%
Slovak Republic	30	39	10	0	86.2%	43.5%
Slovenia	30	38	11	0	86.5%	44.1%
Solomon Islands	12	41	13	13	82.2%	22.6%
Somalia	6	62	6	5	77.0%	8.8%
South Africa	8	62	8	1	77.7%	11.4%
Spain	30	36	13	0	87.1%	45.5%
Sri Lanka	9	61	9	0	78.4%	12.9%

All Countries (Alphabetical) (Cont'd)

COUNTRY	IDENTICAL VOTES	OPPOSITE VOTES	ABSTEN-TIONS	ABSENCES	VOTING COINCIDENCE INCLUDING CONSENSUS	VOTES ONLY
Sudan	10	65	4	0	77.2%	13.3%
Suriname	6	63	9	1	77.5%	8.7%
Swaziland	7	43	7	22	78.7%	14.0%
Sweden	29	39	11	0	86.1%	42.6%
Switzerland	28	38	12	1	86.3%	42.4%
Syria	7	62	6	4	76.8%	10.1%
Tajikistan	6	49	5	19	77.3%	10.9%
Thailand	10	57	12	0	79.6%	14.9%
TFYR Macedonia	28	38	11	2	86.1%	42.4%
Timor-Leste	18	55	0	6	79.8%	24.7%
Togo	8	64	5	2	77.0%	11.1%
Tonga	3	35	15	26	81.1%	7.9%
Trinidad and Tobago	11	57	6	5	78.6%	16.2%
Tunisia	7	63	7	2	77.0%	10.0%
Turkey	24	45	5	5	83.3%	34.8%
Turkmenistan	3	49	7	20	77.0%	5.8%
Tuvalu	7	39	15	18	81.6%	15.2%
Uganda	5	55	16	3	78.9%	8.3%
Ukraine	18	45	14	2	83.4%	28.6%
United Arab Emirates	5	62	10	2	77.5%	7.5%
United Kingdom	38	29	12	0	89.6%	56.7%
UR Tanzania	8	59	9	3	78.4%	11.9%
Uruguay	14	54	10	1	80.5%	20.6%
Uzbekistan	5	35	18	21	81.9%	12.5%
Vanuatu	4	29	21	25	84.1%	12.1%
Venezuela	8	65	6	0	77.3%	11.0%
Vietnam	4	63	2	10	75.2%	6.0%
Yemen	6	64	9	0	77.4%	8.6%
Zambia	9	62	7	1	77.8%	12.7%
Zimbabwe	5	64	7	3	76.5%	7.2%
Average	14.8	48.8	8.6	6.8	81.2%	23.3%

All Countries (By Voting Coincidence Including Consensus)

COUNTRY	IDENTICAL VOTES	OPPOSITE VOTES	ABSTEN-TIONS	ABSENCES	VOTING COINCIDENCE INCLUDING CONSENSUS	VOTES ONLY
Palau	67	1	0	11	99.6%	98.5%
Israel	55	4	14	6	98.4%	93.2%
Micronesia	46	13	4	16	94.4%	78.0%
Australia	34	26	17	2	90.3%	56.7%
France	33	28	17	1	89.7%	54.1%
Marshall Islands	44	28	3	4	89.7%	61.1%
United Kingdom	38	29	12	0	89.6%	56.7%
Albania	29	29	15	6	88.6%	50.0%
Canada	32	32	13	2	88.2%	50.0%
Spain	30	36	13	0	87.1%	45.5%
Iceland	30	36	12	1	87.0%	45.5%
Japan	27	36	16	0	87.0%	42.9%
Latvia	32	36	9	2	86.9%	47.1%
Monaco	29	33	8	9	86.7%	46.8%
Czech Republic	30	37	10	2	86.6%	44.8%
Germany	30	37	11	1	86.6%	44.8%
Poland	32	38	9	0	86.6%	45.7%
Belgium	29	37	11	2	86.5%	43.9%
Bulgaria	30	38	11	0	86.5%	44.1%
Denmark	31	38	10	0	86.5%	44.9%
Nauru	21	32	16	10	86.5%	39.6%
Romania	30	38	11	0	86.5%	44.1%
Slovenia	30	38	11	0	86.5%	44.1%
Republic of Korea	24	37	18	0	86.4%	39.3%
Hungary	29	38	11	1	86.3%	43.3%
Switzerland	28	38	12	1	86.3%	42.4%
Finland	30	39	10	0	86.2%	43.5%
Lithuania	30	39	10	0	86.2%	43.5%
Luxembourg	29	38	10	2	86.2%	43.3%
Portugal	30	39	10	0	86.2%	43.5%
Slovak Republic	30	39	10	0	86.2%	43.5%
Austria	29	39	11	0	86.1%	42.6%
Bosnia/Herzegovina	29	39	11	0	86.1%	42.6%
Croatia	29	39	11	0	86.1%	42.6%
Estonia	27	38	12	2	86.1%	41.5%
Greece	30	39	9	1	86.1%	43.5%
Italy	30	39	10	0	86.1%	43.5%
Liechtenstein	28	39	12	0	86.1%	41.8%
Serbia/Montenegro	29	39	11	0	86.1%	42.6%
Sweden	29	39	11	0	86.1%	42.6%

All Countries (By Voting Coincidence Including Consensus) (Cont'd)

COUNTRY	IDENTICAL VOTES	OPPOSITE VOTES	ABSTEN-TIONS	ABSENCES	VOTING COINCIDENCE INCLUDING CONSENSUS	VOTES ONLY
TFYR Macedonia	28	38	11	2	86.1%	42.4%
Norway	29	39	10	1	86.0%	42.6%
Netherlands	30	40	9	0	85.9%	42.9%
Ireland	28	40	11	0	85.8%	41.2%
San Marino	28	40	11	0	85.8%	41.2%
Andorra	29	40	9	1	85.7%	42.0%
Republic of Moldova	22	38	16	3	85.7%	36.7%
New Zealand	28	41	10	0	85.5%	40.6%
Kiribati	1	1	0	77	85.1%	50.0%
Georgia	22	38	15	4	85.0%	36.7%
Malta	28	42	8	1	85.0%	40.0%
Cyprus	29	43	7	0	84.9%	40.3%
Vanuatu	4	29	21	25	84.1%	12.1%
Haiti	8	36	23	12	83.9%	18.2%
Samoa	17	40	12	10	83.6%	29.8%
Papua New Guinea	11	40	21	7	83.4%	21.6%
Ukraine	18	45	14	2	83.4%	28.6%
Turkey	24	45	5	5	83.3%	34.8%
Cameroon	12	44	20	3	83.2%	21.4%
Grenada	19	46	10	4	82.7%	29.2%
Armenia	18	49	11	1	82.4%	26.9%
Russia	11	48	20	0	82.4%	18.6%
Solomon Islands	12	41	13	13	82.2%	22.6%
Honduras	14	45	11	9	82.1%	23.7%
Argentina	17	51	11	0	81.9%	25.0%
Uzbekistan	5	35	18	21	81.9%	12.5%
Malawi	9	31	10	29	81.8%	22.5%
Tuvalu	7	39	15	18	81.6%	15.2%
Nicaragua	18	51	7	3	81.4%	26.1%
India	13	52	14	0	81.3%	20.0%
Dominican Republic	16	52	10	1	81.2%	23.5%
Peru	18	54	7	0	81.1%	25.0%
Tonga	3	35	15	26	81.1%	7.9%
Guatemala	17	54	8	0	81.0%	23.9%
Chile	20	54	4	1	80.9%	27.0%
Dem. Rep. Congo	9	24	2	44	80.8%	27.3%
Bhutan	3	39	19	18	80.6%	7.1%
Equatorial Guinea	11	43	7	18	80.6%	20.4%
Uruguay	14	54	10	1	80.5%	20.6%
Cote d'Ivoire	11	50	11	7	80.4%	18.0%

All Countries (By Voting Coincidence Including Consensus) (Cont'd)

COUNTRY	IDENTICAL VOTES	OPPOSITE VOTES	ABSTEN-TIONS	ABSENCES	VOTING COINCIDENCE INCLUDING CONSENSUS	VOTES ONLY
El Salvador	18	56	4	1	80.3%	24.3%
Paraguay	18	55	5	1	80.3%	24.7%
Mexico	17	57	5	0	80.1%	23.0%
St. Kitts and Nevis	1	5	0	73	79.9%	16.7%
Angola	9	43	7	20	79.8%	17.3%
Costa Rica	15	56	5	3	79.8%	21.1%
Ethiopia	8	50	11	10	79.8%	13.8%
Kenya	8	56	15	0	79.8%	12.5%
Timor-Leste	18	55	0	6	79.8%	24.7%
Fiji	12	53	9	5	79.7%	18.5%
Brazil	10	57	12	0	79.6%	14.9%
Thailand	10	57	12	0	79.6%	14.9
Panama	18	59	1	1	79.5%	23.4%
Antigua-Barbuda	6	50	12	11	79.4%	10.7%
Bolivia	18	60	1	0	79.4%	23.1%
Singapore	9	57	12	1	79.4%	13.6%
Pakistan	6	56	15	2	79.3%	9.7%
Guinea-Bissau	14	52	1	12	79.1%	21.2%
Ecuador	11	59	8	1	79.0%	15.7%
Colombia	7	59	13	0	78.9%	10.6%
Liberia	8	51	9	11	78.9%	13.6%
Uganda	5	55	16	3	78.9%	8.3%
Jamaica	8	56	9	6	78.7%	12.5%
Mauritius	8	59	11	1	78.7%	11.9%
Sierra Leone	8	58	10	3	78.7%	12.1%
Swaziland	7	43	7	22	78.7%	14.0%
Benin	10	57	6	6	78.6%	14.9%
St.Vincent/Grenadines	9	58	8	4	78.6%	13.4%
Trinidad/Tobago	11	57	6	5	78.6%	16.2%
Azerbaijan	8	56	8	7	78.5%	12.5%
Ghana	10	59	8	2	78.5%	14.5%
Kyrgyzstan	8	52	6	13	78.5%	13.3%
Mongolia	10	58	7	4	78.5%	14.7%
Myanmar (Burma)	8	60	10	1	78.5%	11.8%
Philippines	9	60	9	1	78.5%	13.0%
Barbados	6	57	11	5	78.4%	9.5%
Chad	5	17	1	56	78.4%	22.7%
Guyana	9	60	8	2	78.4%	13.0%
Sri Lanka	9	61	9	0	78.4%	12.9%
UR Tanzania	8	59	9	3	78.4%	11.9%

All Countries (By Voting Coincidence Including Consensus) (Cont'd)

COUNTRY	IDENTICAL VOTES	OPPOSITE VOTES	ABSTEN- TIONS	ABSENCES	VOTING COINCIDENCE INCLUDING CONSENSUS	VOTES ONLY
Bahamas	7	57	10	5	78.3%	10.9%
Burkina Faso	10	60	6	3	78.3%	14.3%
Burundi	6	55	9	9	78.2%	9.8%
Saint Lucia	9	58	7	5	78.2%	13.4%
Belarus	5	57	12	5	78.1%	8.1%
Central African Rep.	10	52	4	13	78.1%	16.1%
Namibia	11	62	5	1	78.1%	15.1%
Dominica	6	57	10	6	78.0%	9.5%
Nigeria	11	63	5	0	77.9%	14.9%
Belize	8	61	8	2	77.8%	11.6%
Guinea	8	38	2	31	77.8%	17.4%
Jordan	12	63	2	2	77.8%	16.0%
Mauritania	3	32	5	39	77.8%	8.6%
Nepal	9	62	7	1	77.8%	12.7%
Zambia	9	62	7	1	77.8%	12.7%
Brunei Darussalam	6	63	10	0	77.7%	8.7%
Cambodia	8	60	7	4	77.7%	11.8%
Kazakhstan	7	57	8	7	77.7%	10.9%
South Africa	8	62	8	1	77.7%	11.4%
Algeria	7	63	8	1	77.6%	10.0%
China	6	62	10	1	77.6%	8.8%
Djibouti	9	62	6	2	77.6%	12.7%
Sao Tome/Principe	5	49	4	21	77.5%	9.3%
Suriname	6	63	9	1	77.5%	8.7%
United Arab Emirates	5	62	10	2	77.5%	7.5%
Bahrain	6	62	8	3	77.4%	8.8%
Bangladesh	6	64	9	0	77.4%	8.6%
Madagascar	9	62	5	3	77.4%	12.7%
Malaysia	6	64	9	0	77.4%	8.6%
Yemen	6	64	9	0	77.4%	8.6%
Botswana	8	56	5	10	77.3%	12.5%
Eritrea	7	59	7	6	77.3%	10.6%
Morocco	8	62	5	4	77.3%	11.4%
Tajikistan	6	49	5	19	77.3%	10.9%
Venezuela	8	65	6	0	77.3%	11.0%
Kuwait	7	63	7	2	77.2%	10.0%
Mali	10	61	3	5	77.2%	14.1%
Qatar	7	63	7	2	77.2%	10.0%
Senegal	10	65	4	0	77.2%	13.3%
Sudan	10	65	4	0	77.2%	13.3%

All Countries (By Voting Coincidence Including Consensus) (Cont'd)

COUNTRY	IDENTICAL VOTES	OPPOSITE VOTES	ABSTEN-TIONS	ABSENCES	VOTING COINCIDENCE INCLUDING CONSENSUS	VOTES ONLY
Oman	7	64	7	1	77.1%	9.9%
Seychelles	7	40	0	32	77.1%	14.9%
Rwanda	6	47	3	23	77.0%	11.3%
Somalia	6	62	6	5	77.0%	8.8%
Togo	8	64	5	2	77.0%	11.1%
Tunisia	7	63	7	2	77.0%	10.0%
Turkmenistan	3	49	7	20	77.0%	5.8%
Iran	6	65	8	0	76.9%	8.5%
Cuba	5	63	8	3	76.8%	7.4%
Indonesia	6	66	7	0	76.8%	8.3%
Lesotho	6	61	6	6	76.8%	9.0%
Libya	7	65	6	1	76.8%	9.7%
Mozambique	6	54	3	16	76.8%	10.0%
Niger	9	52	2	16	76.8%	14.8%
Syria	7	62	6	4	76.8%	10.1%
Cape Verde	5	57	5	12	76.7%	8.1%
Comoros	5	57	4	13	76.7%	8.1%
Egypt	6	65	6	2	76.7%	8.5%
Gabon	7	51	1	20	76.7%	12.1%
Laos	3	57	9	10	76.7%	5.0%
Saudi Arabia	5	64	8	2	76.7%	7.2%
Maldives	7	62	3	7	76.6%	10.1%
Lebanon	6	63	5	5	76.5%	8.7%
Zimbabwe	5	64	7	3	76.5%	7.2%
Gambia	6	44	1	28	76.2%	12.0%
Congo	3	43	1	32	75.9%	6.5%
DPR Korea	2	59	8	10	75.7%	3.3%
Afghanistan	5	52	0	22	75.6%	8.8%
Vietnam	4	63	2	10	75.2%	6.0%
Iraq	3	51	3	22	74.6%	5.6%
Average	14.8	48.8	8.6	6.8	81.2%	23.3%

UN REGIONAL GROUPS

The following tables show the percentage of voting coincidence with U.S. votes in Plenary. They list UN member states by UN regional grouping, in rank order by voting coincidence percentage.

African Group

COUNTRY	IDENTICAL VOTES	OPPOSITE VOTES	ABSTEN-TIONS	ABSENCES	VOTING COINCIDENCE INCLUDING CONSENSUS	VOTES ONLY
Dem. Rep. Congo	9	24	2	44	80.8%	27.3%
Chad	5	17	1	56	78.4%	22.7%
Malawi	9	31	10	29	81.8%	22.5%
Cameroon	12	44	20	3	83.2%	21.4%
Guinea-Bissau	14	52	1	12	79.1%	21.2%
Equatorial Guinea	11	43	7	18	80.6%	20.4%
Cote d'Ivoire	11	50	11	7	80.4%	18.0%
Guinea	8	38	2	31	77.8%	17.4%
Angola	9	43	7	20	79.8%	17.3%
Central African Rep.	10	52	4	13	78.1%	16.1%
Namibia	11	62	5	1	78.1%	15.1%
Benin	10	57	6	6	78.6%	14.9%
Nigeria	11	63	5	0	77.9%	14.9%
Seychelles	7	40	0	32	77.1%	14.9%
Niger	9	52	2	16	76.8%	14.8%
Ghana	10	59	8	2	78.5%	14.5%
Burkina Faso	10	60	6	3	78.3%	14.3%
Mali	10	61	3	5	77.2%	14.1%
Swaziland	7	43	7	22	78.7%	14.0%
Ethiopia	8	50	11	10	79.8%	13.8%
Liberia	8	51	9	11	78.9%	13.6%
Senegal	10	65	4	0	77.2%	13.3%
Sudan	10	65	4	0	77.2%	13.3%
Djibouti	9	62	6	2	77.6%	12.7%
Madagascar	9	62	5	3	77.4%	12.7%
Zambia	9	62	7	1	77.8%	12.7%
Botswana	8	56	5	10	77.3%	12.5%
Kenya	8	56	15	0	79.8%	12.5%
Gabon	7	51	1	20	76.7%	12.1%
Sierra Leone	8	58	10	3	78.7%	12.1%
Gambia	6	44	1	28	76.2%	12.0%
Mauritius	8	59	11	1	78.7%	11.9%
UR Tanzania	8	59	9	3	78.4%	11.9%
Morocco	8	62	5	4	77.3%	11.4%

African Group (Cont'd)

COUNTRY	IDENTICAL VOTES	OPPOSITE VOTES	ABSTEN-TIONS	ABSENCES	VOTING COINCIDENCE INCLUDING CONSENSUS	VOTES ONLY
South Africa	8	62	8	1	77.7%	11.4%
Rwanda	6	47	3	23	77.0%	11.3%
Togo	8	64	5	2	77.0%	11.1%
Eritrea	7	59	7	6	77.3%	10.6%
Algeria	7	63	8	1	77.6%	10.0%
Mozambique	6	54	3	16	76.8%	10.0%
Tunisia	7	63	7	2	77.0%	10.0%
Burundi	6	55	9	9	78.2%	9.8%
Libya	7	65	6	1	76.8%	9.7%
Sao Tome/Principe	5	49	4	21	77.5%	9.3%
Lesotho	6	61	6	6	76.8%	9.0%
Somalia	6	62	6	5	77.0%	8.8%
Mauritania	3	32	5	39	77.8%	8.6%
Egypt	6	65	6	2	76.7%	8.5%
Uganda	5	55	16	3	78.9%	8.3%
Cape Verde	5	57	5	12	76.7%	8.1%
Comoros	5	57	4	13	76.7%	8.1%
Zimbabwe	5	64	7	3	76.5%	7.2%
Congo	3	43	1	32	75.9%	6.5%
Average	7.9	53.4	6.2	11.6	78.0%	12.9%

Asian Group

COUNTRY	IDENTICAL VOTES	OPPOSITE VOTES	ABSTEN-TIONS	ABSENCES	VOTING COINCIDENCE INCLUDING CONSENSUS	VOTES ONLY
Micronesia	46	13	4	16	94.4%	78.0%
Marshall Islands	44	28	3	4	89.7%	61.1%
Japan	27	36	16	0	87.0%	42.9%
Cyprus	29	43	7	0	84.9%	40.3%
Nauru	21	32	16	10	86.5%	39.6%
Republic of Korea	24	37	18	0	86.4%	39.3%
Samoa	17	40	12	10	83.6%	29.8%
Timor-Leste	18	55	0	6	79.8%	24.7%
Solomon Islands	12	41	13	13	82.2%	22.6%
Papua New Guinea	11	40	21	7	83.4%	21.6%
India	13	52	14	0	81.3%	20.0%
Fiji	12	53	9	5	79.7%	18.5%
Jordan	12	63	2	2	77.8%	16.0%
Tuvalu	7	39	15	18	81.6%	15.2%

Asian Group (Cont'd)

COUNTRY	IDENTICAL VOTES	OPPOSITE VOTES	ABSTEN-TIONS	ABSENCES	VOTING COINCIDENCE INCLUDING CONSENSUS	VOTES ONLY
Thailand	10	57	12	0	79.6%	14.9%
Mongolia	10	58	7	4	78.5%	14.7%
Singapore	9	57	12	1	79.4%	13.6%
Kyrgyzstan	8	52	6	13	78.5%	13.3%
Philippines	9	60	9	1	78.5%	13.0%
Sri Lanka	9	61	9	0	78.4%	12.9%
Nepal	9	62	7	1	77.8%	12.7%
Uzbekistan	5	35	18	21	81.9%	12.5%
Vanuatu	4	29	21	25	84.1%	12.1%
Cambodia	8	60	7	4	77.7%	11.8%
Myanmar (Burma)	8	60	10	1	78.5%	11.8%
Kazakhstan	7	57	8	7	77.7%	10.9%
Tajikistan	6	49	5	19	77.3%	10.9%
Maldives	7	62	3	7	76.6%	10.1%
Syria	7	62	6	4	76.8%	10.1%
Kuwait	7	63	7	2	77.2%	10.0%
Qatar	7	63	7	2	77.2%	10.0%
Oman	7	64	7	1	77.1%	9.9%
Pakistan	6	56	15	2	79.3%	9.7%
Afghanistan	5	52	0	22	75.6%	8.8%
Bahrain	6	62	8	3	77.4%	8.8%
China	6	62	10	1	77.6%	8.8%
Brunei Darussalam	6	63	10	0	77.7%	8.7%
Lebanon	6	63	5	5	76.5%	8.7%
Bangladesh	6	64	9	0	77.4%	8.6%
Malaysia	6	64	9	0	77.4%	8.6%
Yemen	6	64	9	0	77.4%	8.6%
Iran	6	65	8	0	76.9%	8.5%
Indonesia	6	66	7	0	76.8%	8.3%
Tonga	3	35	15	26	81.1%	7.9%
United Arab Emirates	5	62	10	2	77.5%	7.5%
Saudi Arabia	5	64	8	2	76.7%	7.2%
Bhutan	3	39	19	18	80.6%	7.1%
Vietnam	4	63	2	10	75.2%	6.0%
Turkmenistan	3	49	7	20	77.0%	5.8%
Iraq	3	51	3	22	74.6%	5.6%
Laos	3	57	9	10	76.7%	5.0%
DPR of Korea	2	59	8	10	75.7%	3.3%
Average	10.1	52.8	9.3	6.9	79.5%	16.1%

Latin American and Caribbean Group (LAC)

COUNTRY	IDENTICAL VOTES	OPPOSITE VOTES	ABSTEN-TIONS	ABSENCES	VOTING COINCIDENCE INCLUDING CONSENSUS	VOTES ONLY
Grenada	19	46	10	4	82.7%	29.2%
Chile	20	54	4	1	80.9%	27.0%
Nicaragua	18	51	7	3	81.4%	26.1%
Argentina	17	51	11	0	81.9%	25.0%
Peru	18	54	7	0	81.1%	25.0%
Paraguay	18	55	5	1	80.3%	24.7%
El Salvador	18	56	4	1	80.3%	24.3%
Guatemala	17	54	8	0	81.0%	23.9%
Honduras	14	45	11	9	82.1%	23.7%
Dominican Republic	16	52	10	1	81.2%	23.5%
Panama	18	59	1	1	79.5%	23.4%
Bolivia	18	60	1	0	79.4%	23.1%
Mexico	17	57	5	0	80.1%	23.0%
Costa Rica	15	56	5	3	79.8%	21.1%
Uruguay	14	54	10	1	80.5%	20.6%
Haiti	8	36	23	12	83.9%	18.2%
St. Kitts and Nevis	1	5	0	73	79.9%	16.7%
Trinidad/Tobago	11	57	6	5	78.6%	16.2%
Ecuador	11	59	8	1	79.0%	15.7%
Brazil	10	57	12	0	79.6%	14.9%
Saint Lucia	9	58	7	5	78.2%	13.4%
St.Vincent/Grenadines	9	58	8	4	78.6%	13.4%
Guyana	9	60	8	2	78.4%	13.0%
Jamaica	8	56	9	6	78.7%	12.5%
Belize	8	61	8	2	77.8%	11.6%
Venezuela	8	65	6	0	77.3%	11.0%
Bahamas	7	57	10	5	78.3%	10.9%
Antigua-Barbuda	6	50	12	11	79.4%	10.7%
Colombia	7	59	13	0	78.9%	10.6%
Barbados	6	57	11	5	78.4%	9.5%
Dominica	6	57	10	6	78.0%	9.5%
Suriname	6	63	9	1	77.5%	8.7%
Cuba	5	63	8	3	76.8%	7.4%
Average	11.9	54.0	8.1	5.0	79.6%	18.0%

Western European and Others Group (WEOG)

COUNTRY	IDENTICAL VOTES	OPPOSITE VOTES	ABSTEN- TIONS	ABSENCES	VOTING COINCIDENCE INCLUDING CONSENSUS	VOTES ONLY
Israel	55	4	14	6	98.4%	93.2%
Australia	34	26	17	2	90.3%	56.7%
United Kingdom	38	29	12	0	89.6%	56.7%
France	33	28	17	1	89.7%	54.1%
Canada	32	32	13	2	88.2%	50.0%
Monaco	29	33	8	9	86.7%	46.8%
Iceland	30	36	12	1	87.0%	45.5%
Spain	30	36	13	0	87.1%	45.5%
Denmark	31	38	10	0	86.5%	44.9%
Germany	30	37	11	1	86.6%	44.8%
Belgium	29	37	11	2	86.5%	43.9%
Finland	30	39	10	0	86.2%	43.5%
Greece	30	39	9	1	86.1%	43.5%
Italy	30	39	10	0	86.1%	43.5%
Portugal	30	39	10	0	86.2%	43.5%
Luxembourg	29	38	10	2	86.2%	43.3%
Netherlands	30	40	9	0	85.9%	42.9%
Austria	29	39	11	0	86.1%	42.6%
Norway	29	39	10	1	86.0%	42.6%
Sweden	29	39	11	0	86.1%	42.6%
Switzerland	28	38	12	1	86.3%	42.4%
Andorra	29	40	9	1	85.7%	42.0%
Liechtenstein	28	39	12	0	86.1%	41.8%
Ireland	28	40	11	0	85.8%	41.2%
San Marino	28	40	11	0	85.8%	41.2%
New Zealand	28	41	10	0	85.5%	40.6%
Malta	28	42	8	1	85.0%	40.0%
Turkey	24	45	5	5	83.3%	34.8%
Average	30.6	36.1	10.9	1.3	86.9%	45.9%

Eastern European Group (EE)

COUNTRY	IDENTICAL VOTES	OPPOSITE VOTES	ABSTEN- TIONS	ABSENCES	VOTING COINCIDENCE INCLUDING CONSENSUS	VOTES ONLY
Albania	29	29	15	6	88.6%	50.0%
Latvia	32	36	9	2	86.9%	47.1%
Poland	32	38	9	0	86.6%	45.7%
Czech Republic	30	37	10	2	86.6%	44.8%

Eastern European Group (EE) (Cont'd)

COUNTRY	IDENTICAL VOTES	OPPOSITE VOTES	ABSTEN-TIONS	ABSENCES	VOTING COINCIDENCE INCLUDING CONSENSUS	VOTES ONLY
Bulgaria	30	38	11	0	86.5%	44.1%
Romania	30	38	11	0	86.5%	44.1%
Slovenia	30	38	11	0	86.5%	44.1%
Lithuania	30	39	10	0	86.2%	43.5%
Slovak Republic	30	39	10	0	86.2%	43.5%
Hungary	29	38	11	1	86.3%	43.3%
Bosnia-Herzegovina	29	39	11	0	86.1%	42.6%
Croatia	29	39	11	0	86.1%	42.6%
Serbia/Montenegro	29	39	11	0	86.1%	42.6%
TFYR Macedonia	28	38	11	2	86.1%	42.4%
Estonia	27	38	12	2	86.1%	41.5%
Georgia	22	38	15	4	85.0%	36.7%
Republic of Moldova	22	38	16	3	85.7%	36.7%
Ukraine	18	45	14	2	83.4%	28.6%
Armenia	18	49	11	1	82.4%	26.9%
Russia	11	48	20	0	82.4%	18.6%
Azerbaijan	8	56	8	7	78.5%	12.5%
Belarus	5	57	12	5	78.1%	8.1%
Average	24.9	40.6	11.8	1.7	85.2%	38.0%

OTHER GROUPINGS

The following tables show the voting coincidence percentage with U.S. votes in Plenary. They list UN member states by other groupings inside and outside of the UN system, in rank order by voting coincidence percentage.

Arab Group

COUNTRY	IDENTICAL VOTES	OPPOSITE VOTES	ABSTEN- TIONS	ABSENCES	VOTING COINCIDENCE INCLUDING CONSENSUS	VOTES ONLY
Jordan	12	63	2	2	77.8%	16.0%
Sudan	10	65	4	0	77.2%	13.3%
Djibouti	9	62	6	2	77.6%	12.7%
Morocco	8	62	5	4	77.3%	11.4%
Syria	7	62	6	4	76.8%	10.1%
Algeria	7	63	8	1	77.6%	10.0%
Kuwait	7	63	7	2	77.2%	10.0%
Qatar	7	63	7	2	77.2%	10.0%
Tunisia	7	63	7	2	77.0%	10.0%
Oman	7	64	7	1	77.1%	9.9%
Libya	7	65	6	1	76.8%	9.7%
Bahrain	6	62	8	3	77.4%	8.8%
Somalia	6	62	6	5	77.0%	8.8%
Lebanon	6	63	5	5	76.5%	8.7%
Mauritania	3	32	5	39	77.8%	8.6%
Yemen	6	64	9	0	77.4%	8.6%
Egypt	6	65	6	2	76.7%	8.5%
United Arab Emirates	5	62	10	2	77.5%	7.5%
Saudi Arabia	5	64	8	2	76.7%	7.2%
Iraq	3	51	3	22	74.6%	5.6%
Average	6.7	61.0	6.3	5.1	77.1%	9.9%

Association of Southeast Asian Nations (ASEAN)

COUNTRY	IDENTICAL VOTES	OPPOSITE VOTES	ABSTEN- TIONS	ABSENCES	VOTING COINCIDENCE INCLUDING CONSENSUS	VOTES ONLY
Thailand	10	57	12	0	79.6%	14.9%
Singapore	9	57	12	1	79.4%	13.6%
Philippines	9	60	9	1	78.5%	13.0%
Cambodia	8	60	7	4	77.7%	11.8%
Myanmar (Burma)	8	60	10	1	78.5%	11.8%
Brunei Darussalam	6	63	10	0	77.7%	8.7%

91

Association of Southeast Asian Nations (ASEAN) (Cont'd)

COUNTRY	IDENTICAL VOTES	OPPOSITE VOTES	ABSTEN-TIONS	ABSENCES	VOTING COINCIDENCE INCLUDING CONSENSUS	VOTES ONLY
Malaysia	6	64	9	0	77.4%	8.6%
Indonesia	6	66	7	0	76.8%	8.3%
Vietnam	4	63	2	10	75.2%	6.0%
Laos	3	57	9	10	76.7%	5.0%
Average	6.9	60.7	8.7	2.7	77.8%	10.2%

European Union (EU)

COUNTRY	IDENTICAL VOTES	OPPOSITE VOTES	ABSTEN-TIONS	ABSENCES	VOTING COINCIDENCE INCLUDING CONSENSUS	VOTES ONLY
United Kingdom	38	29	12	0	89.6%	56.7%
France	33	28	17	1	89.7%	54.1%
Latvia	32	36	9	2	86.9%	47.1%
Poland	32	38	9	0	86.6%	45.7%
Spain	30	36	13	0	87.1%	45.5%
Denmark	31	38	10	0	86.5%	44.9%
Czech Republic	30	37	10	2	86.6%	44.8%
Germany	30	37	11	1	86.6%	44.8%
Slovenia	30	38	11	0	86.5%	44.1%
Belgium	29	37	11	2	86.5%	43.9%
Finland	30	39	10	0	86.2%	43.5%
Greece	30	39	9	1	86.1%	43.5%
Italy	30	39	10	0	86.1%	43.5%
Lithuania	30	39	10	0	86.2%	43.5%
Portugal	30	39	10	0	86.2%	43.5%
Slovak Republic	30	39	10	0	86.2%	43.5%
Hungary	29	38	11	1	86.3%	43.3%
Luxembourg	29	38	10	2	86.2%	43.3%
Netherlands	30	40	9	0	85.9%	42.9%
Austria	29	39	11	0	86.1%	42.6%
Sweden	29	39	11	0	86.1%	42.6%
Estonia	27	38	12	2	86.1%	41.5%
Ireland	28	40	11	0	85.8%	41.2%
Cyprus	29	43	7	0	84.9%	40.3%
Malta	28	42	8	1	85.0%	40.0%
Average	30.1	37.8	10.5	0.6	86.5%	44.3%

Islamic Conference (OIC)

COUNTRY	IDENTICAL VOTES	OPPOSITE VOTES	ABSTEN-TIONS	ABSENCES	VOTING COINCIDENCE INCLUDING CONSENSUS	VOTES ONLY
Albania	29	29	15	6	88.6%	50.0%
Turkey	24	45	5	5	83.3%	34.8%
Chad	5	17	1	56	78.4%	22.7%
Cameroon	12	44	20	3	83.2%	21.4%
Guinea-Bissau	14	52	1	12	79.1%	21.2%
Cote d'Ivoire	11	50	11	7	80.4%	18.0%
Guinea	8	38	2	31	77.8%	17.4%
Jordan	12	63	2	2	77.8%	16.0%
Benin	10	57	6	6	78.6%	14.9%
Nigeria	11	63	5	0	77.9%	14.9%
Niger	9	52	2	16	76.8%	14.8%
Burkina Faso	10	60	6	3	78.3%	14.3%
Mali	10	61	3	5	77.2%	14.1%
Kyrgyzstan	8	52	6	13	78.5%	13.3%
Senegal	10	65	4	0	77.2%	13.3%
Sudan	10	65	4	0	77.2%	13.3%
Guyana	9	60	8	2	78.4%	13.0%
Djibouti	9	62	6	2	77.6%	12.7%
Azerbaijan	8	56	8	7	78.5%	12.5%
Uzbekistan	5	35	18	21	81.9%	12.5%
Gabon	7	51	1	20	76.7%	12.1%
Sierra Leone	8	58	10	3	78.7%	12.1%
Gambia	6	44	1	28	76.2%	12.0%
Morocco	8	62	5	4	77.3%	11.4%
Togo	8	64	5	2	77.0%	11.1%
Kazakhstan	7	57	8	7	77.7%	10.9%
Tajikistan	6	49	5	19	77.3%	10.9%
Maldives	7	62	3	7	76.6%	10.1%
Syria	7	62	6	4	76.8%	10.1%
Algeria	7	63	8	1	77.6%	10.0%
Kuwait	7	63	7	2	77.2%	10.0%
Mozambique	6	54	3	16	76.8%	10.0%
Qatar	7	63	7	2	77.2%	10.0%
Tunisia	7	63	7	2	77.0%	10.0%
Oman	7	64	7	1	77.1%	9.9%
Libya	7	65	6	1	76.8%	9.7%
Pakistan	6	56	15	2	79.3%	9.7%
Afghanistan	5	52	0	22	75.6%	8.8%
Bahrain	6	62	8	3	77.4%	8.8%

Islamic Conference (OIC) (Cont'd)

COUNTRY	IDENTICAL VOTES	OPPOSITE VOTES	ABSTEN-TIONS	ABSENCES	VOTING COINCIDENCE INCLUDING CONSENSUS	VOTES ONLY
Somalia	6	62	6	5	77.0%	8.8%
Brunei Darussalam	6	63	10	0	77.7%	8.7%
Lebanon	6	63	5	5	76.5%	8.7%
Suriname	6	63	9	1	77.5%	8.7%
Bangladesh	6	64	9	0	77.4%	8.6%
Malaysia	6	64	9	0	77.4%	8.6%
Mauritania	3	32	5	39	77.8%	8.6%
Yemen	6	64	9	0	77.4%	8.6%
Egypt	6	65	6	2	76.7%	8.5%
Iran	6	65	8	0	76.9%	8.5%
Indonesia	6	66	7	0	76.8%	8.3%
Uganda	5	55	16	3	78.9%	8.3%
Comoros	5	57	4	13	76.7%	8.1%
United Arab Emirates	5	62	10	2	77.5%	7.5%
Saudi Arabia	5	64	8	2	76.7%	7.2%
Turkmenistan	3	49	7	20	77.0%	5.8%
Iraq	3	51	3	22	74.6%	5.6%
Average	7.9	56.2	6.7	8.2	77.9%	12.3%

Non-Aligned Movement (NAM)

COUNTRY	IDENTICAL VOTES	OPPOSITE VOTES	ABSTEN-TIONS	ABSENCES	VOTING COINCIDENCE INCLUDING CONSENSUS	VOTES ONLY
Cyprus	29	43	7	0	84.9%	40.3%
Malta	28	42	8	1	85.0%	40.0%
Grenada	19	46	10	4	82.7%	29.2%
Dem. Rep. Congo	9	24	2	44	80.8%	27.3%
Chile	20	54	4	1	80.9%	27.0%
Nicaragua	18	51	7	3	81.4%	26.1%
Peru	18	54	7	0	81.1%	25.0%
Guatemala	17	54	8	0	81.0%	23.9%
Honduras	14	55	11	9	82.1%	23.7%
Dominican Republic	16	52	10	1	81.2%	23.5%
Panama	18	59	1	1	79.5%	23.4%
Bolivia	18	60	1	0	79.4%	23.1%
Chad	5	17	1	56	78.4%	22.7%
Malawi	9	31	10	29	81.8%	22.5%
Papua New Guinea	11	40	21	7	83.4%	21.6%

Non-Aligned Movement (NAM) (Cont'd)

COUNTRY	IDENTICAL VOTES	OPPOSITE VOTES	ABSTEN-TIONS	ABSENCES	VOTING COINCIDENCE INCLUDING CONSENSUS	VOTES ONLY
Cameroon	12	44	20	3	83.2%	21.4%
Guinea-Bissau	14	52	1	12	79.1%	21.2%
Equatorial Guinea	11	43	7	18	80.6%	20.4%
India	13	52	14	0	81.3%	20.0%
Cote d'Ivoire	11	50	11	7	80.4%	18.0%
Guinea	8	38	2	31	77.8%	17.4%
Angola	9	43	7	20	79.8%	17.3%
Trinidad/Tobago	11	57	6	5	78.6%	16.2%
Central African Rep.	10	52	4	13	78.1%	16.1%
Jordan	12	63	2	2	77.8%	16.0%
Ecuador	11	59	8	1	79.0%	15.7%
Namibia	11	62	5	1	78.1%	15.1%
Benin	10	57	6	6	78.6%	14.9%
Nigeria	11	63	5	0	77.9%	14.9%
Seychelles	7	40	0	32	77.1%	14.9%
Thailand	10	57	12	0	79.6%	14.9%
Niger	9	52	2	16	76.8%	14.8%
Mongolia	10	58	7	4	78.5%	14.7%
Ghana	10	59	8	2	78.5%	14.5%
Burkina Faso	10	60	6	3	78.3%	14.3%
Mali	10	61	3	5	77.2%	14.1%
Swaziland	7	43	7	22	78.7%	14.0%
Ethiopia	8	50	11	10	79.8%	13.8%
Liberia	8	51	9	11	78.9%	13.6%
Singapore	9	57	12	1	79.4%	13.6%
Saint Lucia	9	58	7	5	78.2%	13.4%
Senegal	10	65	4	0	77.2%	13.3%
Sudan	10	65	4	0	77.2%	13.3%
Guyana	9	60	8	2	78.4%	13.0%
Philippines	9	60	9	1	78.5%	13.0%
Sri Lanka	9	61	9	0	78.4%	12.9%
Djibouti	9	62	6	2	77.6%	12.7%
Madagascar	9	62	5	3	77.4%	12.7%
Nepal	9	62	7	1	77.8%	12.7%
Zambia	9	62	7	1	77.8%	12.7%
Botswana	8	56	5	10	77.3%	12.5%
Jamaica	8	56	9	6	78.7%	12.5%
Kenya	8	56	15	0	79.8%	12.5%
Uzbekistan	5	35	18	21	81.9%	12.5%

Non-Aligned Movement (NAM) (Cont'd)

COUNTRY	IDENTICAL VOTES	OPPOSITE VOTES	ABSTEN-TIONS	ABSENCES	VOTING COINCIDENCE INCLUDING CONSENSUS	VOTES ONLY
Gabon	7	51	1	20	76.7%	12.1%
Sierra Leone	8	58	10	3	78.7%	12.1%
Vanuatu	4	29	21	25	84.1%	12.1%
Gambia	6	44	1	28	76.2%	12.0%
Mauritius	8	59	11	1	78.7%	11.9%
UR Tanzania	8	59	9	3	78.4%	11.9%
Cambodia	8	60	7	4	77.7%	11.8%
Myanmar (Burma)	8	60	10	1	78.5%	11.8%
Belize	8	61	8	2	77.8%	11.6%
Morocco	8	62	5	4	77.3%	11.4%
South Africa	8	62	8	1	77.7%	11.4%
Rwanda	6	47	3	23	77.0%	11.3%
Togo	8	64	5	2	77.0%	11.1%
Venezuela	8	65	6	0	77.3%	11.0%
Bahamas	7	57	10	5	78.3%	10.9%
Colombia	7	59	13	0	78.9%	10.6%
Eritrea	7	59	7	6	77.3%	10.6%
Maldives	7	62	3	7	76.6%	10.1%
Syria	7	62	6	4	76.8%	10.1%
Algeria	7	63	8	1	77.6%	10.0%
Kuwait	7	63	7	2	77.2%	10.0%
Mozambique	6	54	3	16	76.8%	10.0%
Qatar	7	63	7	2	77.2%	10.0%
Tunisia	7	63	7	2	77.0%	10.0%
Oman	7	64	7	1	77.1%	9.9%
Burundi	6	55	9	9	78.2%	9.8%
Libya	7	65	6	1	76.8%	9.7%
Pakistan	6	56	15	2	79.3%	9.7%
Barbados	6	57	11	5	78.4%	9.5%
Sao Tome/Principe	5	49	4	21	77.5%	9.3%
Lesotho	6	61	6	6	76.8%	9.0%
Afghanistan	5	52	0	22	75.6%	8.8%
Bahrain	6	62	8	3	77.4%	8.8%
Somalia	6	62	6	5	77.0%	8.8%
Brunei Darussalam	6	63	10	0	77.7%	8.7%
Lebanon	6	63	5	5	76.5%	8.7%
Suriname	6	63	9	1	77.5%	8.7%
Bangladesh	6	64	9	0	77.4%	8.6%
Malaysia	6	64	9	0	77.4%	8.6%

Non-Aligned Movement (NAM) (Cont'd)

COUNTRY	IDENTICAL VOTES	OPPOSITE VOTES	ABSTEN-TIONS	ABSENCES	VOTING COINCIDENCE INCLUDING CONSENSUS	VOTES ONLY
Mauritania	3	32	5	39	77.8%	8.6%
Yemen	6	64	9	0	77.4%	8.6%
Egypt	6	65	6	2	76.7%	8.5%
Iran	6	65	8	0	76.9%	8.5%
Indonesia	6	66	7	0	76.8%	8.3%
Uganda	5	55	16	3	78.9%	8.3%
Belarus	5	57	12	5	78.1%	8.1%
Cape Verde	5	57	5	12	76.7%	8.1%
Comoros	5	57	4	13	76.7%	8.1%
United Arab Emirates	5	62	10	2	77.5%	7.5%
Cuba	5	63	8	3	76.8%	7.4%
Saudi Arabia	5	64	8	2	76.7%	7.2%
Zimbabwe	5	64	7	3	76.5%	7.2%
Bhutan	3	39	19	18	80.6%	7.1%
Congo	3	43	1	32	75.9%	6.5%
Vietnam	4	63	2	10	75.2%	6.0%
Turkmenistan	3	49	7	20	77.0%	5.8%
Iraq	3	51	3	22	74.6%	5.6%
Laos	3	57	9	10	76.7%	5.0%
DPR of Korea	2	59	8	10	75.7%	3.3%
Average	8.6	55.2	7.4	7.8	78.4%	13.5%

Nordic Group

COUNTRY	IDENTICAL VOTES	OPPOSITE VOTES	ABSTEN-TIONS	ABSENCES	VOTING COINCIDENCE INCLUDING CONSENSUS	VOTES ONLY
Iceland	30	36	12	1	87.0%	45.5%
Denmark	31	38	10	0	86.5%	44.9%
Finland	30	39	10	0	86.2%	43.5%
Norway	29	39	10	1	86.0%	42.6%
Sweden	29	39	11	0	86.1%	42.6%
Average	29.8	38.2	10.6	0.4	86.4%	43.8%

North Atlantic Treaty Organization (NATO)

COUNTRY	IDENTICAL VOTES	OPPOSITE VOTES	ABSTEN- TIONS	ABSENCES	VOTING COINCIDENCE INCLUDING CONSENSUS	VOTES ONLY
United Kingdom	38	29	12	0	89.6%	56.7%
France	33	28	17	1	89.7%	54.1%
Canada	32	32	13	2	88.2%	50.0%
Latvia	32	36	9	2	86.9%	47.1%
Poland	32	38	9	0	86.6%	45.7%
Iceland	30	36	12	1	87.0%	45.5%
Spain	30	36	13	0	87.1%	45.5%
Denmark	31	38	10	0	86.5%	44.9%
Czech Republic	30	37	10	2	86.6%	44.8%
Germany	30	37	11	1	86.6%	44.8%
Bulgaria	30	38	11	0	86.5%	44.1%
Romania	30	38	11	0	86.5%	44.1%
Slovenia	30	38	11	0	86.5%	44.1%
Belgium	29	37	11	2	86.5%	43.9%
Greece	30	39	9	1	86.1%	43.5%
Italy	30	39	10	0	86.1%	43.5%
Lithuania	30	39	10	0	86.2%	43.5%
Portugal	30	39	10	0	86.2%	43.5%
Slovak Republic	30	39	10	0	86.2%	43.5%
Hungary	29	38	11	1	86.3%	43.3%
Luxembourg	29	38	10	2	86.2%	43.3%
Netherlands	30	40	9	0	85.9%	42.9%
Norway	29	39	10	1	86.0%	42.6%
Estonia	27	38	12	2	86.1%	41.5%
Turkey	24	45	5	5	83.3%	34.8%
Average	30.2	37.2	10.6	0.9	86.6%	44.8%

HISTORICAL COMPARISON

The following table shows the percentage of voting coincidence with the United States in Plenary for each UN member in the 59th UNGA and each of the previous five years.

COUNTRY	59TH 2004	58TH 2003	57TH 2002	56TH 2001	55TH 2000	54TH 1999
Afghanistan	8.8%	17.7%	21.4%	19.5%	25.9%	25.8%
Albania	50.0%	49.2%	48.4%	68.3%	85.3%	68.8%
Algeria	10.0%	11.7%	12.9%	16.9%	25.5%	27.9%
Andorra	42.0%	41.2%	46.8%	51.7%	61.1%	67.2%
Angola	17.3%	22.5%	17.4%	25.5%	47.9%	28.6%

Historical Comparison (Cont'd)

COUNTRY	59TH 2004	58TH 2003	57TH 2002	56TH 2001	55TH 2000	54TH 1999
Antigua and Barbuda	10.7%	17.9%	26.3%	10.3%	35.7%	30.4%
Argentina	25.0%	24.3%	34.2%	32.8%	44.2%	44.4%
Armenia	26.9%	22.9%	29.3%	31.3%	43.4%	46.9%
Australia	56.7%	58.1%	52.1%	55.6%	63.5%	66.7%
Austria	42.6%	42.0%	46.8%	50.9%	60.4%	65.6%
Azerbaijan	12.5%	15.7%	21.5%	20.0%	39.6%	41.2%
Bahamas	10.9%	23.0%	27.3%	25.5%	39.0%	34.3%
Bahrain	8.8%	10.5%	18.7%	19.0%	26.4%	30.9%
Bangladesh	8.6%	16.3%	21.3%	22.7%	33.9%	31.5%
Barbados	9.5%	15.9%	31.3%	21.1%	38.1%	37.3%
Belarus	8.1%	16.7%	18.9%	23.2%	34.4%	32.8%
Belgium	43.9%	46.3%	50.0%	53.4%	63.0%	69.2%
Belize	11.6%	18.8%	22.7%	15.4%	41.4%	32.3%
Benin	14.9%	17.6%	18.8%	19.6%	38.2%	28.8%
Bhutan	7.1%	17.0%	16.0%	20.4%	29.2%	25.8%
Bolivia	23.1%	22.2%	29.2%	25.4%	38.1%	37.1%
Bosnia/Herzegovina	42.6%	43.3%	50.7%	66.7%	70.6%	76.2%
Botswana	12.5%	16.9%	16.4%	26.4%	32.2%	33.8%
Brazil	14.9%	20.8%	31.0%	29.0%	39.7%	38.9%
Brunei Darussalam	8.7%	15.0%	21.3%	22.4%	32.2%	31.0%
Bulgaria	44.1%	45.6%	49.3%	54.5%	61.1%	68.8%
Burkina Faso	14.3%	12.2%	21.1%	18.8%	33.3%	29.0%
Burundi	9.8%	18.8%	25.8%	15.1%	32.7%	**
Cambodia	11.8%	16.3%	19.4%	19.0%	35.6%	21.0%
Cameroon	21.4%	18.2%	27.7%	22.2%	40.0%	28.3%
Canada	50.0%	48.4%	49.3%	57.1%	66.0%	69.2%
Cape Verde	8.1%	14.5%	19.2%	15.5%	34.5%	29.0%
Central African Rep	16.1%	20.0%	**	**	**	**
Chad	22.7%	0.0%	9.7%	5.6%	13.9%	25.0%
Chile	27.0%	24.1%	30.7%	32.8%	41.9%	40.3%
China	8.8%	13.2%	17.6%	17.2%	25.0%	21.1%
Colombia	10.6%	20.0%	28.6%	25.4%	37.7%	34.7%
Comoros	8.1%	10.7%	16.1%	19.6%	13.2%	16.0%
Congo	6.5%	18.5%	18.7%	12.2%	30.8%	27.4%
Costa Rica	21.1%	26.8%	31.0%	28.6%	44.4%	42.4%
Cote d'Ivoire	18.0%	13.5%	16.4%	17.3%	40.7%	29.4%
Croatia	42.6%	43.1%	46.7%	49.1%	61.2%	56.7%
Cuba	7.4%	8.2%	16.2%	10.2%	21.2%	17.7%
Cyprus	40.3%	36.1%	41.0%	43.5%	50.9%	57.6%
Czech Republic	44.8%	46.2%	48.1%	54.2%	63.0%	67.2%
Dem. Rep. of the Congo	27.3%	32.1%	5.6%	14.3%	16.7%	16.7%
DPR of Korea	3.3%	9.2%	10.9%	2.1%	4.7%	4.1%

99

Historical Comparison (Cont'd)

COUNTRY	59TH 2004	58TH 2003	57TH 2002	56TH 2001	55TH 2000	54TH 1999
Denmark	44.9%	44.9%	48.7%	54.2%	63.0%	68.7%
Djibouti	12.7%	11.7%	20.5%	17.7%	33.9%	31.0%
Dominica	9.5%	22.9%	28.9%	25.0%	50.0%	31.3%
Dominican Republic	23.5%	25.0%	28.9%	26.2%	38.6%	39.6%
Ecuador	15.7%	20.7%	29.2%	25.4%	37.5%	35.5%
Egypt	8.5%	12.8%	20.0%	15.9%	21.1%	28.6%
El Salvador	24.3%	27.9%	32.5%	30.0%	41.1%	38.6%
Equatorial Guinea	20.4%	15.4%	8.7%	16.7%	60.0%	37.5%
Eritrea	10.6%	18.7%	23.1%	22.6%	36.8%	27.7%
Estonia	41.5%	43.9%	48.0%	55.8%	65.3%	71.4%
Ethiopia	13.8%	19.5%	19.7%	24.2%	37.3%	31.9%
Fiji	18.5%	22.9%	31.1%	27.1%	41.1%	28.1%
Finland	43.5%	44.1%	48.0%	52.6%	62.3%	67.2%
France	54.1%	50.7%	56.0%	59.6%	64.6%	73.4%
Gabon	12.1%	17.4%	11.4%	22.6%	31.6%	16.7%
Gambia	12.0%	19.1%	21.7%	8.3%	42.2%	13.3%
Georgia	36.7%	47.1%	45.1%	50.0%	61.4%	68.6%
Germany	44.8%	47.0%	49.3%	55.2%	64.8%	70.1%
Ghana	14.5%	17.1%	19.4%	24.2%	35.0%	30.0%
Greece	43.5%	42.0%	48.1%	52.6%	61.1%	67.7%
Grenada	29.2%	19.0%	27.8%	23.2%	39.3%	33.3%
Guatemala	23.9%	24.3%	35.6%	30.5%	42.6%	41.5%
Guinea	17.4%	16.4%	17.1%	17.4%	34.5%	26.2%
Guinea-Bissau	21.2%	13.4%	0.0%	**	**	35.8%
Guyana	13.0%	18.8%	25.3%	22.2%	35.9%	33.8%
Haiti	18.2%	14.7%	17.1%	19.0%	41.1%	33.8%
Honduras	23.7%	26.7%	30.1%	28.3%	35.1%	34.6%
Hungary	43.3%	44.8%	49.3%	55.4%	64.2%	70.1%
Iceland	45.5%	44.8%	48.7%	54.4%	63.0%	68.7%
India	20.0%	19.7%	21.2%	18.0%	21.8%	21.9%
Indonesia	8.3%	16.9%	22.1%	20.9%	32.8%	30.0%
Iran	8.5%	11.7%	19.7%	19.7%	30.4%	27.1%
Iraq	5.6%	**	**	**	**	**
Ireland	41.2%	39.4%	44.7%	48.3%	56.4%	63.1%
Israel	93.2%	89.7%	92.6%	91.7%	96.2%	90.0%
Italy	43.5%	45.1%	50.0%	52.6%	62.3%	67.7%
Jamaica	12.5%	17.9%	25.3%	25.0%	40.4%	32.9%
Japan	42.9%	39.4%	48.6%	48.3%	58.8%	63.3%
Jordan	16.0%	11.5%	13.5%	15.9%	28.6%	29.7%
Kazakhstan	10.9%	22.4%	28.6%	32.7%	54.8%	55.3%
Kenya	12.5%	14.7%	23.0%	24.6%	36.2%	27.0%
Kiribati	50.0%	0.0%	0.0%	100.0%	0.0%	**

Historical Comparison (Cont'd)

COUNTRY	59TH 2004	58TH 2003	57TH 2002	56TH 2001	55TH 2000	54TH 1999
Kuwait	10.0%	13.2%	26.5%	22.6%	32.8%	34.2%
Kyrgyzstan	13.3%	19.4%	22.0%	**	40.8%	**
Laos	5.0%	13.9%	5.4%	7.3%	21.2%	16.1%
Latvia	47.1%	44.1%	49.3%	55.8%	66.0%	67.2%
Lebanon	8.7%	10.7%	12.9%	16.9%	20.4%	23.4%
Lesotho	9.0%	17.5%	20.3%	30.0%	50.0%	20.0%
Liberia	13.6%	**	**	**	**	**
Libya	9.7%	10.7%	17.7%	14.1%	23.6%	26.1%
Liechtenstein	41.8%	40.3%	45.5%	50.9%	60.4%	66.2%
Lithuania	43.5%	45.6%	48.6%	54.5%	64.7%	68.8%
Luxembourg	43.3%	45.6%	48.7%	53.4%	63.0%	69.2%
Madagascar	12.7%	17.1%	24.1%	21.7%	32.8%	32.7%
Malawi	22.5%	18.5%	19.7%	18.8%	50.0%	48.1%
Malaysia	8.6%	17.1%	22.4%	19.7%	33.3%	32.4%
Maldives	10.1%	17.5%	27.3%	25.4%	36.2%	35.6%
Mali	14.1%	17.1%	18.4%	19.7%	33.9%	29.9%
Malta	40.0%	39.7%	42.9%	47.5%	54.2%	60.0%
Marshall Islands	61.1%	78.7%	97.9%	91.9%	73.9%	74.5%
Mauritania	8.6%	9.2%	10.8%	11.1%	12.9%	**
Mauritius	11.9%	16.9%	27.8%	32.1%	36.7%	35.6%
Mexico	23.0%	20.7%	27.1%	22.7%	34.4%	30.0%
Micronesia	78.0%	82.0%	89.8%	93.2%	100.0%	100.0%
Monaco	46.8%	46.3%	52.1%	59.3%	60.4%	72.6%
Mongolia	14.7%	18.9%	27.4%	26.6%	39.3%	32.4%
Morocco	11.4%	10.5%	14.7%	18.6%	30.6%	30.8%
Mozambique	10.0%	16.5%	19.0%	25.8%	33.3%	30.4%
Myanmar (Burma)	11.8%	12.2%	15.9%	12.1%	22.6%	21.0%
Namibia	15.1%	16.5%	18.5%	17.2%	34.5%	29.0%
Nauru	39.6%	38.5%	42.6%	51.4%	48.0%	**
Nepal	12.7%	17.7%	22.7%	22.7%	33.3%	30.0%
Netherlands	42.9%	44.9%	50.0%	54.4%	64.2%	69.7%
New Zealand	40.6%	38.6%	44.0%	50.8%	59.3%	62.1%
Nicaragua	26.1%	25.7%	32.5%	38.0%	40.7%	38.3%
Niger	14.8%	15.2%	**	**	**	**
Nigeria	14.9%	19.8%	26.5%	21.2%	33.3%	35.2%
Norway	42.6%	46.3%	48.7%	55.2%	63.6%	68.8%
Oman	9.9%	11.7%	19.7%	17.2%	25.5%	30.9%
Pakistan	9.7%	17.9%	19.4%	13.2%	15.7%	25.0%
Palau	98.5%	97.1%	100.0%	50.0%	100.0%	**
Panama	23.4%	20.7%	28.7%	28.4%	37.1%	32.4%
Papua New Guinea	21.6%	28.8%	32.2%	31.0%	40.0%	26.9%
Paraguay	24.7%	23.1%	30.2%	33.3%	41.1%	39.4%

Historical Comparison (Cont'd)

COUNTRY	59TH 2004	58TH 2003	57TH 2002	56TH 2001	55TH 2000	54TH 1999
Peru	25.0%	23.0%	32.9%	27.9%	40.4%	35.7%
Philippines	13.0%	17.7%	24.1%	24.6%	35.0%	31.9%
Poland	45.7%	50.0%	50.0%	54.2%	63.0%	68.2%
Portugal	43.5%	46.3%	49.3%	51.7%	60.0%	67.7%
Qatar	10.0%	11.5%	20.0%	16.9%	32.2%	31.4%
Republic of Korea	39.3%	38.3%	45.7%	45.3%	52.2%	61.4%
Republic of Moldova	36.7%	35.7%	50.0%	50.9%	41.5%	66.1%
Romania	44.1%	41.8%	48.7%	53.6%	62.3%	68.2%
Russia	18.6%	26.4%	30.4%	34.5%	44.4%	46.0%
Rwanda	11.3%	18.2%	28.9%	6.3%	30.8%	10.0%
St. Kitts and Nevis	16.7%	33.3%	39.1%	23.1%	48.3%	41.7%
Saint Lucia	13.4%	16.5%	18.1%	18.9%	35.6%	25.8%
St. Vincent/Grenadines	13.4%	17.5%	30.0%	0.0%	54.3%	28.6%
Samoa	29.8%	24.6%	30.9%	47.5%	47.1%	40.6%
San Marino	41.2%	41.2%	47.4%	50.0%	59.6%	60.6%
Sao Tome and Principe	9.3%	50.0%	16.2%	**	38.5%	**
Saudi Arabia	7.2%	9.5%	14.5%	15.8%	26.4%	30.9%
Senegal	13.3%	18.5%	23.2%	23.1%	36.5%	35.1%
Serbia/Montenegro (1)	42.6%	41.8%	47.4%	48.3%	36.4%	**
Seychelles	14.9%	16.3%	14.3%	20.0%	**	26.8%
Sierra Leone	12.1%	23.1%	25.4%	22.0%	39.2%	33.3%
Singapore	13.6%	19.7%	23.9%	23.8%	36.8%	31.7%
Slovak Republic	43.5%	44.8%	48.1%	51.7%	62.3%	67.7%
Slovenia	44.1%	42.6%	48.6%	53.6%	62.3%	67.7%
Solomon Islands	22.6%	26.0%	35.5%	30.8%	40.4%	38.2%
Somalia	8.8%	14.5%	6.7%	**	**	**
South Africa	11.4%	14.9%	20.8%	23.6%	40.0%	39.7%
Spain	45.5%	45.5%	49.4%	52.6%	61.1%	67.7%
Sri Lanka	12.9%	18.3%	19.7%	21.2%	33.9%	32.4%
Sudan	13.3%	13.2%	17.1%	14.3%	25.0%	26.8%
Suriname	8.7%	18.4%	11.4%	37.9%	54.8%	25.0%
Swaziland	14.0%	15.7%	32.1%	18.4%	32.2%	30.8%
Sweden	42.6%	42.0%	46.1%	48.3%	60.4%	65.2%
Switzerland	42.4%	43.1%	47.3%	*	*	*
Syria	10.1%	9.6%	13.2%	14.3%	15.4%	20.3%
Tajikistan	10.9%	24.6%	22.7%	**	57.6%	38.2%
Thailand	14.9%	17.6%	24.7%	24.2%	36.2%	33.8%
TFYR Macedonia (2)	42.4%	43.1%	47.4%	52.9%	60.8%	55.7%
Timor-Leste	24.7%	20.8%	32.4%	*	*	*
Togo	11.1%	15.4%	21.1%	22.7%	33.9%	29.9%
Tonga	7.9%	24.5%	39.5%	35.3%	50.0%	**
Trinidad and Tobago	16.2%	18.4%	31.0%	24.1%	50.0%	34.7%

Historical Comparison (Cont'd)

COUNTRY	59TH 2004	58TH 2003	57TH 2002	56TH 2001	55TH 2000	54TH 1999
Tunisia	10.0%	10.7%	14.3%	15.9%	28.6%	31.0%
Turkey	34.8%	32.4%	42.9%	42.4%	52.6%	56.1%
Turkmenistan	5.8%	13.2%	15.8%	21.1%	52.9%	44.8%
Tuvalu	15.2%	26.7%	7.7%	81.3%	100.0%	*
Uganda	8.3%	22.2%	22.2%	21.4%	36.1%	35.0%
Ukraine	28.6%	28.4%	38.8%	40.4%	50.9%	50.0%
United Arab Emirates	7.5%	10.8%	17.6%	12.7%	30.0%	32.9%
United Kingdom	56.7%	57.1%	57.1%	63.2%	71.7%	75.8%
UR Tanzania	11.9%	20.0%	23.4%	22.4%	33.9%	23.1%
Uruguay	20.6%	22.5%	31.3%	29.0%	41.1%	36.4%
Uzbekistan	12.5%	38.2%	50.0%	**	81.8%	80.8%
Vanuatu	12.1%	28.0%	18.8%	37.5%	40.8%	**
Venezuela	11.0%	18.5%	22.2%	20.9%	35.5%	32.4%
Vietnam	6.0%	8.2%	9.0%	9.3%	22.6%	15.3%
Yemen	8.6%	11.5%	17.6%	12.1%	25.9%	24.2%
Zambia	12.7%	17.7%	22.4%	20.3%	34.4%	32.9%
Zimbabwe	7.2%	17.3%	14.3%	22.2%	34.5%	28.6%
Average	23.3%	25.5%	31.2%	31.7%	43.0%	41.8%

* Not yet a UN member.
** Non-participating UN member.
(1) Formerly Yugoslavia. Yugoslavia was not permitted to participate in the 47th –54th sessions of UNGA. Readmitted 10/31/2000.
(2) Listed alphabetically as "the Former Yugoslav Republic of Macedonia."

Countries Receiving U.S. Assistance (U.S. Dollars in Thousands)

COUNTRY	AMOUNT	VOTING COINCIDENCE INCLUDING CONSENSUS	VOTES ONLY
Afghanistan	1,798,746	75.6%	8.8%
Albania	36,534	88.6%	50.0%
Algeria	1,653	77.6%	10.0%
Andorra		85.7%	42.0%
Angola	91,745	79.8%	17.3%
Antigua and Barbuda		79.4%	10.7%
Argentina	1,087	81.9%	25.0%
Armenia	79,816	82.4%	26.9%
Australia		90.3%	56.7%
Austria		86.1%	42.6%
Azerbaijan	49,628	78.5%	12.5%
Bahamas	1,264	78.3%	10.9%
Bahrain	25,250	77.4%	8.8%
Bangladesh	94,550	77.4%	8.6%
Barbados		78.4%	9.5%
Belarus	8,055	78.1%	8.1%
Belgium		86.5%	43.9%
Belize	2,082	77.8%	11.6%
Benin	23,082	78.6%	14.9%
Bhutan		80.6%	7.1%
Bolivia	155,345	79.4%	23.1%
Bosnia/Herzegovina	64,726	86.1%	42.6%
Botswana	11,658	77.3%	12.5%
Brazil	28,243	79.6%	14.9%
Brunei Darussalam		77.7%	8.7%
Bulgaria	42,962	86.5%	44.1%
Burkina Faso	11,646	78.3%	14.3%
Burundi	26,330	78.2%	9.8%
Cambodia	53,629	77.7%	11.8%
Cameroon	3,503	83.2%	21.4%
Canada		88.2%	50.0%
Cape Verde	6,081	76.7%	8.1%
Central African Republic	996	78.1%	16.1%
Chad	21,196	78.4%	22.7%
Chile	947	80.9%	27.0%
China	863	77.6%	8.8%
Colombia	574,026	78.9%	10.6%
Comoros	121	76.7%	8.1%
Congo	27	75.9%	6.5%
Costa Rica	1,395	79.8%	21.1%
Cote d'Ivoire	15,155	80.4%	18.0%

Countries Receiving U.S. Assistance (U.S. Dollars in Thousands) (Cont'd)

COUNTRY	AMOUNT	VOTING COINCIDENCE INCLUDING CONSENSUS	VOTES ONLY
Croatia	25,703	86.1%	42.6%
Cuba	21,369	76.8%	7.4%
Cyprus	38,820	84.9%	40.3%
Czech Republic	10,145	86.6%	44.8%
DPR of Korea	45,704	75.7%	3.3%
Dem. Rep. of the Congo	71,219	80.6%	27.3%
Denmark		86.5%	44.9%
Djibouti	8,049	77.6%	12.7%
Dominica		78.0%	9.5%
Dominican Republic	33,968	81.2%	23.5%
Ecuador	55,536	79.0%	15.7%
Egypt	1,867,652	76.7%	8.5%
El Salvador	43,573	80.3%	24.3%
Equatorial Guinea		80.6%	20.4%
Eritrea	72,817	77.3%	10.6%
Estonia	8,382	86.1%	41.5%
Ethiopia	345,274	79.8%	13.8%
Fiji	1,668	79.7%	18.5%
Finland		86.2%	43.5%
France		89.7%	54.1%
Gabon	2,655	76.7%	12.1%
Gambia	2,604	76.2%	12.0%
Georgia	90,954	85.0%	36.7%
Germany		86.6%	44.8%
Ghana	59,131	78.5%	14.5%
Greece	568	86.1%	43.5%
Grenada		82.7%	29.2%
Guatemala	50,561	81.0%	23.9%
Guinea	32,568	77.8%	17.4%
Guinea-Bissau		79.1%	21.2%
Guyana	11,590	78.4%	13.0%
Haiti	132,324	83.9%	18.2%
Honduras	50,771	82.1%	23.7%
Hungary	8,982	86.3%	43.3%
Iceland		87.0%	45.5%
India	128,171	81.3%	20.0%
Indonesia	125,908	76.8%	8.3%
Iran		76.9%	8.5%
Iraq	500	74.6%	5.6%
Ireland	21,870	85.8%	41.2%
Israel	2,624,424	98.4%	93.2%
Italy		86.1%	43.5%

Countries Receiving U.S. Assistance (U.S. Dollars in Thousands) (Cont'd)

COUNTRY	AMOUNT	VOTING COINCIDENCE INCLUDING CONSENSUS	VOTES ONLY
Jamaica	24,186	78.7%	12.5%
Japan		87.0%	42.9%
Jordan	559,833	77.8%	16.0%
Kazakhstan	41,867	77.7%	10.9%
Kenya	142,502	79.8%	12.5%
Kiribati	1,322	85.1%	50.0%
Kuwait		77.2%	10.0%
Kyrgyzstan	43,529	78.5%	13.3%
Laos	3,412	76.7%	5.0%
Latvia	10,018	86.9%	47.1%
Lebanon	36,794	76.5%	8.7%
Lesotho	3,621	76.8%	9.0%
Liberia	224,511	78.9%	13.6%
Libya		76.8%	9.7%
Liechtenstein		86.1%	41.8%
Lithuania	8,572	86.2%	43.5%
Luxembourg		86.2%	43.3%
Madagascar	35,756	77.4%	12.7%
Malawi	41,551	81.8%	22.5%
Malaysia	1,169	77.4%	8.6%
Maldives	181	76.6%	10.1%
Mali	43,040	77.2%	14.1%
Malta	250	85.0%	40.0%
Marshall Islands		89.7%	61.1%
Mauritania	10,560	77.8%	8.6%
Mauritius	144	78.7%	11.9%
Mexico	71,676	80.1%	23.0%
Micronesia	1,963	94.4%	78.0%
Monaco		86.7%	46.8%
Mongolia	14,454	78.5%	14.7%
Morocco	20,797	77.3%	11.4%
Mozambique	79,613	76.8%	10.0%
Myanmar (Burma)	12,923	78.5%	11.8%
Namibia	26,835	78.1%	15.1%
Nauru		86.5%	39.6%
Nepal	45,314	77.8%	12.7%
Netherlands		85.9%	42.9%
New Zealand		85.5%	40.6%
Nicaragua	45,004	81.4%	26.1%
Niger	10,895	76.8%	14.8%
Nigeria	80,240	77.9%	14.9%
Norway		86.0%	42.6%

Countries Receiving U.S. Assistance (U.S. Dollars in Thousands) (Cont'd)

COUNTRY	AMOUNT	VOTING COINCIDENCE INCLUDING CONSENSUS	VOTES ONLY
Oman	26,075	77.1%	9.9%
Pakistan	400,441	79.3%	9.7%
Palau		99.6%	98.5%
Panama	18,185	79.5%	23.4%
Papua New Guinea	292	83.4%	21.6%
Paraguay	12,467	80.3%	24.7%
Peru	180,581	81.1%	25.0%
Philippines	111,167	78.5%	13.0%
Poland	34,783	86.6%	45.7%
Portugal	752	86.2%	43.5%
Qatar		77.2%	10.0%
Republic of Korea		86.4%	39.3%
Republic of Moldova	27,651	85.7%	36.7%
Romania	42,170	86.5%	44.1%
Russia	107,049	82.4%	18.6%
Rwanda	50,430	77.0%	11.3%
St. Kitts and Nevis		79.9%	16.7%
Saint Lucia		78.2%	13.4%
St. Vincent/Grenadines		78.6%	13.4%
Samoa	1,293	83.6%	29.8%
San Marino		85.8%	41.2%
Sao Tome and Principe	238	77.5%	9.3%
Saudi Arabia	24	76.7%	7.2%
Senegal	34,331	77.2%	13.3%
Serbia/Montenegro	134,553	86.1%	42.6%
Seychelles	98	77.1%	14.9%
Sierra Leone	22,125	78.7%	12.1%
Singapore	430	79.4%	13.6%
Slovak Republic	7,983	86.2%	43.5%
Slovenia	3,289	86.5%	44.1%
Solomon Islands	72	82.2%	22.6%
Somalia	23,835	77.0%	8.8%
South Africa	99,085	77.7%	11.4%
Spain		87.1%	45.5%
Sri Lanka	25,992	78.4%	12.9%
Sudan	435,930	77.2%	13.3%
Suriname	1,471	77.5%	8.7%
Swaziland	1,705	78.7%	14.0%
Sweden		86.1%	42.6%
Switzerland		86.3%	42.4%
Syria		76.8%	10.1%
Tajikistan	34,106	77.3%	10.9%

Countries Receiving U.S. Assistance (U.S. Dollars in Thousands) (Cont'd)

COUNTRY	AMOUNT	VOTING COINCIDENCE INCLUDING CONSENSUS	VOTES ONLY
Thailand................................	9,173	79.6%	14.9%
TFYR Macedonia...............	49,670	86.1%	42.4%
Timor-Leste........................	27,985	79.8%	24.7%
Togo	2,693	77.0%	11.1%
Tonga..................................	1,729	81.1%	7.9%
Trinidad and Tobago		78.6%	16.2%
Tunisia................................	11,726	77.0%	10.0%
Turkey................................	50,600	83.3%	34.8%
Turkmenistan......................	8,398	77.0%	5.8%
Tuvalu		81.6%	15.2%
Uganda	182,720	78.9%	8.3%
Ukraine...............................	113,013	83.4%	28.6%
United Arab Emirates.........	250	77.5%	7.5%
United Kingdom.................		89.6%	56.7%
UR Tanzania.......................	77,128	78.4%	11.9%
Uruguay..............................		80.5%	20.6%
Uzbekistan..........................	38,442	81.9%	12.5%
Vanuatu	1,878	84.1%	12.1%
Venezuela	6,497	77.3%	11.0%
Vietnam..............................	22,314	75.2%	6.0%
Yemen	33,471	77.4%	8.6%
Zambia................................	85,187	77.8%	12.7%
Zimbabwe...........................	15,457	76.5%	7.2%
Total Bilateral....................	13,445,267		
Plus Regional Programs: ..			
Africa..................................	740,690		
East Asia and Pacific.........	85,508		
Europe and Eurasia............	348,580		
Near East	356,165		
South Asia	82,253		
Western Hemisphere	205,185		
Total Bilateral and Geographic Regional...	15,263,648		
Global Programs.................	5,804,610		
Grand Total, FY 2003 Foreign Operations and Public Law 480 Funds.	21,068,258		

IV—GENERAL ASSEMBLY—IMPORTANT VOTES AND CONSENSUS ACTIONS

Public Law 101-246 calls for analysis and discussion of "votes on issues which directly affected United States interests and on which the United States lobbied extensively." An important basis for identifying important issues is consistency with the State Department's Strategic Goals. For the 59th UN General Assembly (UNGA) in 2004, 10 votes and 16 consensus resolutions were identified for inclusion in this section.

Section IV contains five parts: (1) a listing and description of the 10 important votes at the 59th UNGA (nine votes in the Plenary and one in the Third Committee); (2) a listing and description of the 16 important consensus resolutions at the 59th UNGA; (3) voting coincidence percentages with the United States on these important actions that were adopted by votes, arranged both alphabetically by country and in rank order of agreed votes; (4) voting coincidence percentages by UN regional groups and other important groups; and (5) a comparison of voting coincidence percentages on important votes with those on overall votes from Section III. An additional column in the tables of important votes (parts three and four above) presents the percentage of voting coincidence with the United States after including the 16 important consensus resolutions as additional identical votes. Since not all states are equally active at the United Nations, these coincidence percentages were refined to reflect a country's rate of participation in all UN voting overall. The participation rate was calculated by dividing the number of Yes-No-Abstain votes cast by a UN member in Plenary (i.e., the number of times it was not absent) by the total number of Plenary votes, plus one vote from the Third Committee (90).

IMPORTANT VOTES

The following 10 important votes are identified by a short title, document number, date of vote, and results (Yes-No-Abstain), with the U.S. vote noted. The first paragraph gives a summary description of the resolution or decision using language from the document ("General Assembly" is the subject of the verbs in the first paragraph), and the subsequent paragraphs provide background, if pertinent, and explain the U.S. position. The resolutions/decisions are listed in order by the date adopted, and then in numerical order.

1. U.S. Embargo Against Cuba

A/Res/59/11   October 28   179-4(US)-1

Calls on all states to refrain from promulgating and applying laws and measures such as the "Helms-Burton Act," whose extra-territorial consequences allegedly affect the sovereignty of other states and the legitimate interests of entities or persons under their jurisdiction and the freedom of trade and navigation; urges states to repeal such laws.

Background: In 1960, the United States imposed a trade and financial transaction embargo on Cuba because of Castro's repressive policies and expropriation of U.S. property without compensation. The United States strengthened the embargo in 1962, 1992, and 1996. A resolution condemning this embargo has been adopted by the General Assembly since 1992.

U.S. Position: The United States again voted against this resolution, emphasizing the trade embargo is a bilateral issue that is not an appropriate subject for UN consideration. This resolution constituted an attempt by Cuba to divert attention from its government's failings. The measures imposed by the United States do not constitute a blockade, as the embargo does not affect Cuba's trade with other nations. Cuba remains free to trade with any other country in the world, and indeed does so. Moreover, U.S. law permits the sale of food and medicine. Israel, the Marshall Islands, and Palau also voted No; Micronesia abstained.

2. Situation of Human Rights in Sudan

No-action motion   November 24   91-74(US)-11

Welcomes the leadership role and the engagement of the African Union in addressing the situation in Darfur. Expresses grave concern at the widespread and grave violations of human rights and international humanitarian law in Darfur and the continuous violations of human rights throughout the Sudan. Calls upon the Government of the Sudan to take all measures necessary to actively promote and protect human rights and international humanitarian law, to immediately take all steps necessary to stop all violence and atrocities, and to end the climate of impunity in Darfur by identifying and bringing to justice all those responsible for the widespread abuses of human rights and violations of international humanitarian law. Urges the Government of the Sudan, the Sudan Liberation Movement, and the Justice and Equality Movement to respect and fully implement in Darfur the ceasefire agreement signed at N'Djamena on April 8, 2004, and calls upon the international community to expand its support for activities aimed at improving respect for human rights and humanitarian law in the Sudan.

Background: The draft resolution's sponsors and cosponsors were deeply concerned about the continuing gross human rights violations committed by the government against the people of Darfur, despite increased international scrutiny. Additionally, the United States remained disappointed by the adoption of a weak Sudan resolution in the Commission on Human Rights in April 2004 and supported a stronger resolution in the Third Committee. It worked closely with the European Union (EU) to support an EU text at least as strong as resolutions considered in the Security Council. South Africa, on behalf of the African group and with the support of the Organization of Islamic Conference, introduced a procedural no-action motion, to block consideration of the resolution in Third Committee. The motion was adopted by a vote of 91-74(US)-11; thus consideration of the draft resolution was ended before a vote on the resolution itself could take place.

U.S. Position: The United States cosponsored this European Union-sponsored resolution and spoke on the floor against the procedural motion. The U.S. Government is deeply disappointed that the Third Committee of the General Assembly passed the no-action motion on this resolution, and on two other resolutions concerning human rights country situations (no-action motions also were passed in November 2004 against resolutions addressing the human rights situations in Belarus and Zimbabwe). The United States is concerned that the UN General Assembly Third Committee dismissed consideration of gross violations of human rights in the Sudan.

3. Committee on the Exercise of the Inalienable Rights of the Palestinian People

A/Res/59/28   December 1   104-7(US)-63

Requests the Committee to continue to exert all efforts to promote the realization of the inalienable rights of the Palestinian people, to support the Middle East peace process, and to mobilize international support for and assistance to the Palestinian people. Authorizes the Committee to make such adjustments in its approved program of work as it may consider appropriate and necessary in the light of developments and to report thereon to the General Assembly at its 60th session and thereafter.

Background: The General Assembly established the Committee by Resolution 3376 in 1975 and renews its support of the Committee annually.

U.S. Position: The United States believes that the continuation of this Committee that embodies institutional discrimination against Israel is inconsistent with UN support for the efforts of the Quartet to achieve a just and durable solution. (The Quartet is a group comprised of the United States, the United Nations, the European Union, and Russia.) The United States believes this Committee should be abolished and actively lobbies other countries to withdraw their support for the annual resolution renewing the Committee's mandate.

4. Division for Palestinian Rights of the Secretariat

A/Res/59/29   December 1   103-8(US)-64

Requests the Secretary-General to continue to provide the Division with the necessary resources and to ensure that it continues to carry out its program of work as detailed in relevant earlier resolutions, in consultation with the committee on the Exercise of the Inalienable Rights of the Palestinian People and under its guidance. Requests the Secretary-General to ensure the continued cooperation of the Department of Public Information and other units of the Secretariat in enabling the Division to perform its tasks. Also requests the Committee on Palestinian Rights and the Division to continue to organize an annual exhibit on Palestinian rights or a cultural event, in observance of the International Day of Solidarity with the Palestinian People.

Background: The General Assembly established the Division for Palestinian Rights by Resolution 32/40 in 1977.

U.S. Position: The United States believes that the continuation of the division, which embodies institutional discrimination against Israel, is inconsistent with UN support for the efforts of the Quartet to achieve a just and durable solution. The United States believes this division should be abolished and actively lobbies other countries to withdraw their support for the annual resolution renewing the division's mandate.

5. Fissile Material Cutoff Treaty (FMCT)

A/Res/59/81   December 3   179-2(US)-2

Recalls the decision of the Conference on Disarmament to establish an *ad hoc* committee which shall negotiate a non-discriminatory, multilateral, and internationally and effectively verifiable treaty banning the production of fissile material for nuclear weapons or other nuclear explosive devices. Urges the Conference on Disarmament to agree on a program of work that includes the immediate commencement of negotiations on such a treaty.

Background: Since 1999, the Conference on Disarmament (CD) has been unable to establish an *ad hoc* committee to negotiate an FMCT. This 65-nation body operates by consensus, and competing priorities among the political groups therein have resulted in a failure by the CD to adopt a program of work over the past eight years. As the result of an internal policy review, the United States in July 2004 reaffirmed at the CD its continued support for the negotiation of an FMCT. The United States at that time also announced its concern that such a treaty could not be effectively verified.

U.S. Position: The text of the resolution, which is a decade or more old, calls for the negotiation of an "internationally and effectively verifiable treaty." Since the United States no longer believes that an FMCT can be effectively verified, the United States voted against this resolution both in the First Committee, where the United States delivered an Explanation of Vote laying out its position, and in the Plenary.

6. Work of the Special Committee to Investigate Israeli Practices Affecting the Human Rights of the Palestinian People and Other Arabs of the Occupied Territories

A/Res/59/121   December 10   84-9(US)-80

Commends the efforts of the Special Committee in performing the tasks assigned to it by the General Assembly. Deplores those policies and practices of Israel that violate the human rights of the Palestinian people and other Arabs of the occupied territories, expresses grave concern about the situation in the Occupied Palestinian Territory, including East Jerusalem, and requests the Special Committee to continue to investigate Israeli policies and practices. Requests the Secretary-General to provide the Special Committee with all necessary facilities and to continue to make available such staff as may be necessary so that the Special Committee may continue its work.

Background: The General Assembly established the Special Committee by Resolution 2443 in 1968.

U.S. Position: The United States believes that the continuation of this Committee that embodies institutional discrimination against Israel is inconsistent with UN support for the efforts of the Quartet to achieve a just and durable solution. The United States believes this Committee should be abolished and actively lobbies other countries to withdraw their support for the annual resolution that renews the Committee's mandate.

7. Elimination of All Forms of Religious Intolerance

A/Res/59/199   December 20   186(US)-0-0

Reaffirms that freedom of thought, conscience, religion, or belief is a human right derived from the inherent dignity of the human person and guaranteed to all without discrimination. Urges states to ensure that no one within their jurisdiction is, because of their religion or belief, deprived of the right to life, liberty, and security of person; the right to freedom of expression; the right not to be subjected to torture or other cruel, inhuman, or degrading treatment or punishment, and the right not to be arbitrarily arrested or detained; and to protect their physical integrity and bring to justice all perpetrators of violations of these rights.

Urges states to devote particular attention to combating all practices motivated by religion or belief which lead, directly or indirectly, to human rights violations and to discrimination against women. Recognizes that legislation alone is not enough to prevent violations of human rights, including the right to freedom of religion or belief, and that the exercise of tolerance and nondiscrimination by persons and groups is necessary for the full realization of the aims of the Declaration on the Elimination of All Forms of Intolerance and of Discrimination Based on Religion or Belief, and in this regard invites states, religious bodies, and civil society to undertake dialog at all levels to promote greater tolerance, respect, and understanding of freedom of religion or belief and to encourage and promote, through the educational system and by other means, understanding, tolerance, and respect in matters relating to freedom of religion or belief.

Recognizes with deep concern the overall rise in instances of intolerance and violence directed against members of many religious communities in various parts of the world, including cases motivated by Islamophobia, anti-Semitism, and Christianophobia.

Urges states to exert their utmost efforts, in accordance with their national legislation and in conformity with international human rights standards, to ensure that religious places, sites, and shrines are fully respected and protected, and to take additional measures in cases where they are vulnerable to desecration or destruction.

Background: The General Assembly adopted the Declaration on the Elimination of All Forms of Intolerance and of Discrimination Based on Religion or Belief in 1981, which spelled out the UN Charter provision to promote and encourage universal respect for and observance of human rights and fundamental freedoms for all without distinction as to religion. The General Assembly has been adopting this resolution every year since 1981; for the first time, it has references to Islamophobia, anti-Semitism, and Christianophobia.

U.S. Position: Religious freedom is a principal cornerstone for the United States. Immigrants settled in the United States seeking freedom from religious discrimination; freedom to practice religion is the first amendment to the U.S. Constitution. The United States believes that laws prohibiting religious discrimination reduce or eliminate other fears which divide people along ethnic, racial, and national lines. One of the U.S. goals at this year's General Assembly was for the Assembly to adopt a resolution which addressed the problem of anti-Semitism. The United States was one of more than 50 cosponsors of this resolution.

8. Enhancing the Role of Regional, Subregional, and Other Organizations and Arrangements in Promoting and Consolidating Democracy

A/Res/59/201   December 20   172(US)-0-15

Declares that the essential elements of democracy include respect for human rights and fundamental freedoms, including the freedom of association and assembly, the freedom of expression, the right to take part in the conduct of public affairs, the right to vote in genuine periodic free elections by universal and equal suffrage, as well as a pluralistic system of political parties and organizations, respect for the rule of law, the separation of powers, transparency and accountability in public administration, and a free, independent, and pluralistic media.

Acknowledges that democracy contributes to the realization of all human rights, and that democracy contributes substantially to preventing violent conflict, and to accelerating reconciliation and reconstruction in post-conflict peace-building. Reaffirms that the promotion and protection of all human rights is a basic prerequisite for the existence of a democratic society.

Recognizes the importance of actions taken at the regional and subregional levels aimed at developing and consolidating democratic institutions. Invites intergovernmental, regional, sub-regional, and other organizations, as well as relevant nongovernmental organizations, to work towards the promotion and consolidation of democracy by identifying and disseminating best practices and experiences in promoting and protecting democratic processes; establishing and supporting civic education programs that provide access to information on democratic governance; encouraging the study of democracy, human rights, and good governance in schools and universities; and working with the Office of the High Commissioner of Human Rights (OHCHR) focal point for democracy.

Welcomes the adoption by various organizations of institutional rules designed to prevent situations that threaten democratic institutions. Encourages member states and intergovernmental, regional, and cross-regional organizations to initiate networks and partnerships with a view to assisting the governments and civil society in their respective regions in disseminating knowledge and information about the role of democratic institutions and mechanisms in meeting the political, economic, social, and cultural challenges in their respective societies. Invites the UN system to identify, develop, and coordinate effective policies of assistance in the field of democracy, and to support programs of technical assistance to states, upon their request, aimed at developing an independent judiciary, strengthening political party systems and independent media, and fostering a democratic culture.

Finally, calls upon the OHCHR to stimulate dialogue and interaction within the United Nations and between the United Nations and interested organizations on the ways and means of promoting democratic values and principles.

Background: Several members of the UN democracy caucus put this resolution forward, and many of these delegations cosponsored the resolution. It followed up on a 2004 resolution at the 60th session of the Commission on Human Rights establishing a "focal point" for democracy in the OHCHR which was co-tabled by the United States, East Timor, Peru, and Romania for the democracy caucus.

U.S. Position: The United States supported and cosponsored this resolution because of its commitment to strengthening and spreading democracy throughout the world. The United States believes that increasing the number of democracies worldwide and strengthening fragile democracies will promote the observance of internationally accepted human rights standards and democratic principles and send strong signals to those who violate these standards.

9. Situation of Human Rights in the Islamic Republic of Iran

A/Res/59/205   December 20   71(US)-54-55

Expresses its serious concern at the continuing violations of human rights in the Islamic Republic of Iran; the worsening situation with regard to freedom of opinion and expression and freedom of the media, including arbitrary arrest and detention without charge or trial; the disqualifications of prospective candidates in the Majlis elections and the intimidation of opposition activists before the February 2004 elections; the continuing executions in the absence of respect for internationally recognized safeguards, and in particular deplores the execution of persons below 18 years of age, contrary to Iran's obligations under the Convention on the Rights of the Child and the International Covenant on Civil and Political Rights, as well as public executions; the use of torture and other forms of cruel, inhuman, and degrading punishment; the continued restrictions on free assembly and forcible dissolution of political parties; the systemic discrimination against women and girls in law and in practice; the continuing discrimination against persons belonging to minorities, including Christians, Jews, and Sunnis, and the increased discrimination against the Baha'is; the continuing persecution of human rights defenders, political opponents, religious dissenters, and reformists.

Calls upon the Government of Iran to abide by its obligations freely undertaken under the International Covenants on Human Right and other international human rights instruments; to implement fully the ban on torture, announced in April 2004 by the head of the judiciary, and the related parliamentary legislation of May 2004; to expedite judicial reform, to guarantee the dignity of the individual and to ensure the full application of due process of law and fair and transparent procedures by an independent and impartial judiciary, and in this context to ensure respect for the rights of the defense and the equity of verdicts in all instances, including for members of religious minority groups, officially recognized or otherwise; to eliminate all forms of discrimination based on religious grounds or against persons belonging to minorities, including the Baha'is, Christians, Jews, and Sunnis, and to address this matter in an open manner, with the full participation of the minorities themselves, and to ensure respect for the freedom of religion or belief of all persons; to end amputation and flogging and all other forms of punishment that are cruel, inhuman, or degrading; and to abolish the punishment of execution by stoning and, in the meantime, to end the practice of stoning as recommended by the head of the judiciary.

Background: The Government of Iraq disqualified large numbers of prospective candidates from the February 2004 parliamentary elections. The government also continued its practices of summary executions in absence of internationally recognized safeguards; use of torture; discriminatory treatment towards women and girls; and persecution of minorities, journalists, students, academics, and clerics.

U.S. Position: The United States cosponsored this Canadian-sponsored resolution and lobbied other delegations to vote in favor of the text. The United States believes that this resolution demonstrated the international community's concern over the human rights situation in Iran and the desire to hold the government accountable for its human rights abuses.

10. International Trade and Development

A/Res/59/221   December 22   166-2(US)-6

Recognizes that a universal multilateral trading system can substantially stimulate development worldwide, benefiting countries at all stages of development, thereby promoting economic growth and sustainable development that is necessary to achieve the internationally agreed development goals. Reaffirms the value of multilateralism to the global trading system while ensuring balance and parallel progress within and between areas under negotiation, bearing in mind the needs and concerns of developing countries. Emphasizes that bilateral trade arrangements should complement the goals of the multilateral trading system and expresses its concern about the adoption of a number of unilateral actions that are not consistent with the rules of the World Trade Organization (WTO). Invites the UN Conference on Trade and Development to monitor and assess the evolution of the international trading system.

Background: Debated heavily in the Second Committee, this proposal from the Group of 77 and China deals with, among others, the topics of how to increase coherence between the external economic environment and national efforts, and in that context how to ensure that the monetary and financial system, as well as the trade system, reinforce rather than undermine each other.

U.S. Position: The United States voted against this resolution. Although the United States endorses many of the principles enunciated in the resolution and remains fully committed to the Doha Development Agenda (2001), it strongly believes that the United Nations should not pronounce on issues under negotiation in the WTO. The United States believes that the declarations and decisions of the WTO are carefully balanced compromises and efforts by outside parties to distort those decisions or to prejudge issues under negotiation in the WTO can only hamper the current negotiations.

IMPORTANT CONSENSUS ACTIONS

The 16 important consensus resolutions are listed and described below. For each resolution, the listing provides a short title, the document number, and date adopted. The first paragraph gives the summary description of the resolution, using language from the resolution ("General Assembly" is the subject of the verbs). Subsequent paragraphs provide background and explain the U.S. position. The resolutions are listed in order by dated and then in numerical order.

1. International Convention Against the Reproductive Cloning of Human Beings

Proposal adopted   November 19

Background: The Sixth (Legal) Committee considered two draft resolutions concerning a possible international convention against human cloning. Costa Rica introduced a resolution, which the United States cosponsored, that called for negotiation of a convention to ban all forms of human cloning. Belgium introduced a draft resolution that sought to ban reproductive cloning only, which would have left the door open for states to allow so-called "research," "therapeutic," or "experimental" cloning. In the final days of negotiation, Italy introduced a draft Declaration that urged all member states to prohibit any attempts to create human life through the process of cloning. In an effort to build an international consensus, the Sixth Committee agreed by consensus to form a Working Group to meet in February 2005 using the Italian proposal as the basis for its work.

U.S. Position: The United States has consistently held the position that all human cloning—for reproduction and research alike—should be banned. The United States supported the Costa Rican proposal to negotiate a convention banning all human cloning. When this proposal was withdrawn, the United States joined consensus to form the Working Group to draft a Declaration urging all member states to prohibit cloning. The U.S. goal is a strong UN statement that all human cloning should be prohibited. The formation of a Working Group will provide further opportunity for the United Nations to agree on this position.

2. International Criminal Court

A/Res/59/43   December 2

Calls upon all states that are not yet parties to the Rome Statute of the International Criminal Court (ICC) to consider ratifying or acceding to it without delay, and encourages efforts aimed at promoting awareness of the results of the UN Diplomatic Conference of Plenipotentiaries on the Establishment of an International Court, held in Rome from June 15–July 17, 1998. Calls upon all states to consider becoming parties on the Agreement on Privileges and Immunities of the International Criminal Court without delay.

Welcomes the holding of the third session of the Assembly of States Parties to the Rome Statute in The Hague from September 6–10, 2004; also welcomes the election of the new President of the Assembly of States Parties, new members to the Committee on Budget and Finance, and the second Deputy-Prosecutor, and the Assembly of States Parties' adoption of a number of decisions and resolutions. Recalls the Assembly of States Parties' establishment of a Special Working Group on the Crime of Aggression, open to all states on an equal footing.

Recalls that pursuant to the Relationship Agreement, the ICC may attend and participate in work of the General Assembly in the capacity of observer, and also that the Court may submit reports on its activities to the 59th and following sessions of the General Assembly.

Background: Following the General Assembly's adoption of this resolution, the United States made a short statement disassociating itself from consensus and the Netherlands made a longer statement on behalf of the European Union.

U.S. Position: The United States dissociated itself from consensus on this resolution in light of its long-standing concerns about the ICC. These concerns include the ICC's claimed authority to investigate and prosecute persons who are nationals of countries that are not parties to the Rome Statute, including U.S. citizens, and the lack of provision in the Rome Statute for UN Security Council oversight of the ICC's activities.

3. Bilateral Strategic Nuclear Arms Reductions and the New Strategic Framework

A/Res/59/94   December 3

Welcomes the entry into force of the Treaty on Strategic Offensive Reductions (the Moscow Treaty) on June 1, 2003, under which the United States and Russia are committed to reducing and limiting their strategic nuclear warheads so that by December 31, 2012, the aggregate number of such warheads does not exceed 1,700 to 2,200 for each party. Recognizes that the Moscow Treaty is an important result of the new bilateral strategic relationship, which will help establish more favorable conditions for actively promoting security and cooperation, and enhancing international stability.

Supports the continued commitment of the United States and Russia to cooperative efforts in strategic offensive reductions. Acknowledges the contribution that the United States and Russia have made to nuclear disarmament by reducing their deployed strategic warheads by about half since the end of the cold war.

Recognizes the importance of the Treaty on the Reduction and Limitation of Strategic Offensive Arms (START), which is still in force, and of its provisions, which will lay the foundation for ensuring confidence, transparency, and predictability in further reductions. Also recognizes that, since the end of the cold war, the United States has reduced the number of START-accountable deployed strategic warheads from over 10,000 to less than 6,000, and has also eliminated 1,032 launchers for intercontinental ballistic missiles and submarine-launched ballistic missiles, 350 heavy bombers, and 28 ballistic missile submarines, and removed four additional ballistic missile submarines from strategic service. Further recognizes that, in the same time period, Russia has reduced the number of START-accountable deployed strategic warheads to less than 5,000, and has also eliminated 1,250 launchers for intercontinental ballistic missiles and submarine-launched ballistic missiles, 43 ballistic missile submarines, and 65 heavy bombers.

Notes with approval that, since the end of the cold war, the United States and Russia have halted the production of fissile material for nuclear weapons and have committed themselves to eliminating excess fissile material resulting from the dismantlement of weapons no longer needed for national security. Also welcomes the independent action taken by the United States to dispose of 174 metric tons of excess highly enriched uranium from its nuclear weapons program, of which 50 metric tons have already been downblended for use as reactor fuel. Supports continued efforts by the United States and Russia to implement the 1997 Agreement concerning Cooperation regarding Plutonium Production Reactors and the 2000 Agreement concerning the Management and Disposition of Plutonium Designated as No Longer Required for Defense Purposes and Related Cooperation.

Background: The United States and Russia signed a treaty on strategic offensive reductions and issued a joint declaration on the new strategic relationship between Russia and the United States on May 24, 2002. The treaty entered into force on June 1, 2003.

U.S. Position: The United States recognized that new global challenges required a new foundation for strategic relations with Russia based on mutual security, trust, openness, cooperation, and predictability. The mutual determination of Russia and the United States to work towards these goals deserve the endorsement of the world community.

4. Improving the Effectiveness of the Methods of Work of the First Committee

A/Res/59/95   December 3

Invites member states to consider the biennialization or triennialization of the agenda items discussed in the First Committee, on a voluntary basis, and particularly when no specific action is required for the implementation of relevant resolutions. Further invites member states to submit draft resolutions in a more concise, focused, and action-oriented manner and, where practical, to consider the possibility of submitting draft decisions.

Reiterates that the Secretary-General shall keep all committees, including the First Committee, informed of the detailed estimated cost of all resolutions and decisions that have been recommended by the committees for approval by the Assembly. Requests the First Committee, in the light of the growing interconnectedness of issues before the General Assembly, to explore the forms of mutual cooperation with other main committees.

Background: This resolution follows up on the U.S. Improvement Initiative in the 2003 First Committee. In 2004, the United States submitted a draft resolution in the First Committee that merged with a competing draft resolution on reform from the Non-Aligned Movement after extensive negotiations. The resulting joint measure was approved by consensus. On a separate track, and in accordance with Resolution 58/316, efforts related to this resolution resulted in the First Committee Chair (Mexico) forwarding consensus recommendations to the General Assembly's General Committee on reorganizing the First Committee's agenda.

U.S. Position: This resolution preserved all key U.S. recommendations, including a call on the Secretariat to improve its processing of Program Budget Implications statements so that member states would receive timely notification of financial implications of resolutions. This initiative, originated by the United States, obtained 104 other sponsors in the First Committee.

5. Celebrating the Tenth Anniversary of the International Year of the Family

A/Res/59/111   December 6

Recalls Resolution 44/82 and welcomes the celebration of the 10th anniversary of the International Year of the Family on December 6, 2004, at UN Headquarters. Encourages governments to integrate a family perspective in the planning process.

Background: Resolution 44/82 of December 8, 1989, proclaimed 1994 the International Year of the Family as a measure to promote social progress and better standards of life through the stability and well-being of the family. The resolution encouraged UN agencies and intergovernmental and nongovernmental organizations to work closely with the Department of Economic and Social Affairs of the Secretariat on family-related issues.

U.S. Position: The United States joined consensus on this resolution as it believes that governments ought to honor and support the family as the most critical structure for ensuring the well-being of children. Primarily the United States believes that the governments should work to support and strengthen families by respecting the prerogatives of families, encouraging healthy marriages, and supporting all families that need assistance.

6. Providing Support to the Government of Afghanistan in Its Efforts to Eliminate Illicit Opium and Foster Stability and Security in the Region

A/Res/59/161   December 20

Recalls the UN Millennium Declaration and interrelated commitments to eliminate illicit opium, including Security Council Resolution 58/141 (2003) that recommended adequate help be provided to Afghanistan in support of the Transitional Administration of Afghanistan's commitment to eliminate illicit opium. Reaffirms commitments undertaken by member states that action against the world drug problem was a common and shared responsibility and that it must be addressed in a multilateral setting. Recalls the Joint Ministerial Statement from the 20th special session of the General Assembly that the United Nations and other multilateral forums should help in the provision of alternative livelihoods within Afghanistan and in the neighboring states and countries along trafficking routes, and that extensive efforts also needed to be made to reduce the global demand for illicit narcotics.

Calls upon the international community to enhance financial and technical support to Afghanistan to implement its national drug control strategy; urges stakeholders to accelerate efforts to implement a combined strategy of eradication, interdiction, demand reduction, awareness building, and provision of alternative, sustainable livelihoods; and encourages the Government of Afghanistan to accelerate implementation of the commitments it made in the five action plans adopted by the International Counter-narcotics Conference on Afghanistan of February 8 and 9, 2004. Reaffirms the need to strengthen global demand reduction, and requests the UN Office on Drugs and Crime (UNODC), subject to the availability of voluntary funds and with assistance from other international organizations and financial institutions, to assist the Government of Afghanistan so that sustainable alternative livelihoods are created in Afghanistan.

Background: In addition to the United States, other member states, principally European countries in the Group of Eight, have contributed substantial sums to fighting opium cultivation and trafficking in/from Afghanistan. In addition, a number of European countries contributed to the UNODC for ongoing counter-narcotics projects in Afghanistan. Projects funded include alternative development, monitoring of opium production, drug demand reduction, interdiction, border security, and counter-narcotics enforcement.

U.S. Position: Afghanistan remains the most serious, intractable problem facing the United States in counter-narcotics. The United States remains committed to working with the newly elected Government of Afghanistan and its neighbors to fight the trafficking in narcotics and to assist Afghan opium producers to find alternative livelihoods. The United States joined consensus in adopting this resolution.

7. Trafficking in Women and Girls

A/Res/59/166   December 20

Urges governments to take appropriate measures to address the root and external factors that encourage the trafficking of women and girls for prostitution and other forms of commercialized sex, forced marriage, and forced labor; and to devise, enforce, and strengthen effective measures to combat and eliminate all forms of trafficking in women and girls. Calls upon governments to criminalize all forms of trafficking in persons, to take appropriate measures to raise public awareness of the issue, particularly the trafficking of women and girls, including the demand side of the problem, and to provide or strengthen training for law enforcement, judicial, immigration, and other relevant officials in the prevention and combating of trafficking in persons. Further urges governments to strengthen national programs to combat trafficking through increased bilateral, regional, and international cooperation and to consider signing and ratifying relevant international instruments. Welcomes the appointment of the Special Rapporteur of the Commission on Human Rights on trafficking in Persons, especially women and children.

Background: The Philippines has introduced resolutions on trafficking for a number of years. The Philippines is also the main sponsor of a similar resolution adopted by the UN Commission on Human Rights.

U.S. Position: During negotiations, the United States supported the addition of references addressing sex tourism and sexual exploitation to the Philippines' draft resolution. The United States joined consensus on this resolution, but did not cosponsor because of a paragraph concerning the International Criminal Court.

8. Assistance to Refugees, Returnees, and Displaced Persons in Africa

A/Res/59/172   December 20

Notes the need for African states to address the root causes of forced displacement in Africa and to foster peace, stability, and prosperity so as to forestall refugee flows. Recognizes that women and children are the majority of the population affected by conflict and bear the brunt of atrocities and other consequences of conflict. Reiterates the importance of better addressing the specific protection needs of refugee children and adolescents, in particular, the need to ensure attention to unaccompanied children and former child soldiers in refugee settings as well as in voluntary repatriation and reintegration measures.

Notes with great concern that, despite all efforts made by the United Nations, the African Union, and others, the situation of refugees and other displaced persons in Africa remains precarious, and calls upon states and other parties to armed conflict to observe scrupulously international and humanitarian laws. Reaffirms that host states have the primary responsibility to ensure the civilian and humanitarian character of asylum, and calls upon states to take all necessary measures to ensure respect for the principles of refugee protection and, in particular, to ensure that refugee camps are not compromised by the presence or activities of armed elements or used for purposes incompatible with their civilian character. Recognizes the need to strengthen the capacity of states to provide assistance and protection to refugees, returnees, and displaced persons, and calls upon the international community to increase its assistance in this regard.

Condemns all acts that pose a threat to the security and well-being of refugees and asylum seekers. Deplores the deaths, injuries, and other violence sustained by staff members of the Office of the High Commissioner for Refugees and other humanitarian organizations, and urges states and other parties to conflict to take all measures to prevent attacks on and kidnapping of national and international humanitarian workers.

Reaffirms the right of return and the principle of voluntary repatriation. Notes with satisfaction the voluntary return of thousands of refugees to their countries of origin. Reaffirms that voluntary repatriation should not necessarily be conditioned on the accomplishment of political solutions in the country of origin in order not to impede refugees' right of return. Recognizes that repatriation and reintegration is normally guided by the conditions in the country of origin, in particular that voluntary repatriation can be accomplished with safety and dignity.

Appeals to the international community to respond positively to resettlement needs of African refugees and urges support for the refugee programs of the Office of the High Commissioner for Refugees. Calls upon international donors to provide financial and material assistance for community-based development programs intended for the rehabilitation of the environment and infrastructure affected by refugees in countries of asylum. Requests the Secretary-General to submit a comprehensive report on assistance to refugees, returnees, and displaced persons in Africa at its 60th session.

Background: This was a resolution led by South Africa and negotiated largely among African states themselves, though cosponsored by several Western countries as well. It drew primarily from the UN High Commission for Refugees (UNHCR) Executive Committee Conclusions made earlier in 2004.

U.S. Position: The United States joined consensus on this resolution, which called upon the international community to respond positively to appeals for assistance to UNHCR for its programs assisting African refugees, returnees, and displaced persons, and which reiterated that each host country is primarily responsible for the security and protection of refugees in their respective territories.

9. Torture and Other Cruel, Inhuman, or Degrading Treatment or Punishment

A/Res/59/182   December 20

Condemns all forms of torture and other cruel, inhuman, or degrading treatment or punishment, including through intimidation, which are and shall remain prohibited at any time and in any place whatsoever and can thus never be justified. Calls upon all governments to implement fully the prohibition on torture and other cruel, inhuman, or degrading treatment or punishment. Urges governments to take effective measures to prevent torture and other cruel, inhuman, or degrading treatment or punishment, including their gender-based manifestations.

Condemns any action or attempt by states or public officials to legalize or authorize torture and other cruel, inhuman, or degrading treatment or punishment under any circumstances, including on grounds of national security or through judicial decisions, and calls upon governments to eliminate any practices of torture and other cruel, inhuman, or degrading treatment or punishment. Stresses that all acts of torture must be made offences under domestic criminal law, and emphasizes that acts of torture are serious violations of international humanitarian law and can constitute crimes against humanity and war crimes, and that the perpetrators of all acts of torture must be prosecuted and punished.

Recalls that states shall not expel, return, or extradite a person to another state where there are substantial grounds for believing that the person would be in danger of being subjected to torture. Calls upon all governments to cooperate with and assist the Special Rapporteur on the torture and other cruel, inhuman, or degrading treatment or punishment in the performance of his task.

Background: The Convention against Torture established the Committee Against Torture, which, among other things, is charged with reviewing periodic reports submitted by the States Parties to the Convention. The UN Special Rapporteur on torture, who regularly undertakes fact-finding country visits, is strongly supported by the United States.

U.S. Position: The United States unequivocally condemns the practice of torture and is a party to the Convention against Torture. The United States cosponsored this resolution with many other countries.

10. Report of the Committee for Development Policy on Its Sixth Session (graduating countries from least developed country status)

A/Res/59/210   December 20

Recalling Economic and Social Council Resolution 2004/67, on the report of the Committee for Development Policy and taking into account its resolution 59/209 of December 20 on a smooth transition strategy for countries graduating from the group of least developed countries (LDCs), takes note of the recommendations of the Committee for Development Policy to graduate Cape Verde and Maldives from the group of least developed countries.

Background: The resolution on Smooth Transition Strategy for Countries Graduating From the List of Least Developed Countries outlines steps for the smooth transition of states graduating from least developed country status. It is a companion to this resolution which graduates the Maldives and Cape Verde from LDC status. The Secretary-General is requested to assist countries graduating from the list by providing a consultative mechanism to help forge a transition strategy. Development and trading partners are asked to consider extending to the graduating country trade preferences previously made available as a result of least developed country status. The UN's Committee for Development Policy is also asked to monitor the progress of the graduating country as a complement to its triennial review of the list of least developed countries and to report on that progress to the Economic and Social Council.

U.S. Position: The United States joined other council members in consensus to adopt and support this resolution.

11. Follow-Up to and Implementation of the Outcome of the International Conference on Financing for Development

A/Res/59/225   December 22

Notes international efforts, contributions, and discussions aimed at identifying possible innovative and additional sources of financing for development from all sources, public and private, domestic and external, within the follow-up to the International Conference on Financing for Development, recognizing that some of such sources and their use fall within the realm of sovereign action.

Underlines the importance of implementing sound policies, good governance, and the rule of law; mobilizing domestic resources; and coherent and consistent international monetary, financial, and trading systems. Recognizes the issues of concern to developing countries acknowledged in the Monterrey Consensus and the importance that a rule-based, open, and equitable multilateral trading system, as well as meaningful trade liberalization, can play in stimulating economic growth and development.

Acknowledges the role that the private sector can play in generating new financing for development and stresses the importance of pursuing policy and regulatory frameworks to foster a dynamic and well-functioning business sector to increase economic growth and reduce poverty.

Calls on developed countries to devise measures to encourage the flow of foreign direct investment and calls upon developing countries to create a conducive environment for attracting investments. Recalls the commitments made at the International Conference on Financing for Development to increase the levels and effectiveness of official development assistance and urges developed countries to make efforts towards the target of 0.7 percent of gross national product, and encourages developing countries to continue to work to ensure that assistance is used effectively. Stresses that debt relief can play a key role in liberating resources for activities consistent with poverty eradication, achieving economic growth and sustainable development, and internationally agreed development goals, and notes with concern that some countries have not achieved lasting debt sustainability. Stresses the importance of advancing in efforts to reform the international financial architecture as envisaged in the Monterrey Consensus. Emphasizes that corruption at all levels is a serious barrier to development.

Background: The International Conference on Financing for Development held in March 2002 broke new ground as a UN development conference. The final Consensus document stressed good governance and the need to mobilize private resources, both domestic and international, in order to achieve economic growth and development. Participants agreed that sustained follow-up within the UN system, including collaboration among the Bretton Woods institutions, World Trade Organization, and UN bodies, would underscore the importance of implementing proven success strategies as agreed to at the Conference.

U.S. Position: The United States joined consensus on this resolution. However, in its Explanation of Position, the U.S. delegate noted that the United States opposes global taxes as a means for financing development, that each country must decide how to raise funds for official development assistance (ODA), and that, although important, ODA only represents a small amount of the overall resources available for development. Finally, the United States reaffirmed that, while it had exceeded its pledge to increase ODA by 50 percent over 2000 levels by 2006, it does not accept international aid targets based on percentages of donor GNP. The United States believes that aid should be increased to those developing countries making a demonstrated commitment to govern justly, invest in their people, and promote enterprise and entrepreneurship.

12. Preventing and Combating Corrupt Practices and Transfer of Assets of Illicit Origin and Returning Such Assets to the Countries of Origin

A/Res/59/242   December 22

Condemns corruption in all its forms, including bribery, money-laundering, and transfer of assets of illicit origin. Welcomes the efforts of member states that have enacted laws in the fight against corruption in all its forms. Encourages all governments to prevent, combat, and penalize corruption. Further encourages regional cooperation in the efforts to prevent and combat corrupt practices and the transfer of assets of illicit origin. Calls for further international cooperation through the United Nations and reiterates its request to the international community to provide technical assistance to support national efforts aimed at preventing and combating corrupt practices,

Urges all member states to abide by the principles of proper management of public affairs and public property, fairness, responsibility, and equality. Calls upon the private sector to remain fully engaged in the fight against corruption. Emphasizes the need to continue to promote corporate responsibility and accountability. Encourages all member states to require financial institutions to properly implement comprehensive due diligence and vigilance programs.

Background: Members of the Group of 77 and China introduced this resolution into the Second Committee. The United States agrees that corruption at all levels is a serious barrier to development and is committed to the positive language of this resolution, which calls for further international cooperation and remaining fully engaged in the fight against corruption.

U.S. Position: The United States joined consensus on this resolution in agreement that good governance is essential to sustainable development. This resolution represents a very positive step forward in focusing attention on the importance of combating corruption.

13. Integration of the Economies in Transition into the World Economy

A/Res/59/243   December 22

Welcoming the progress made in countries with economies in transition towards market-oriented reforms and achieving macroeconomic and financial stability and economic growth, among other things, through sound macroeconomic policies, good governance, and rule of law, and noting the need to sustain these positive trends, welcomes the measures taken by the organizations of the UN system to implement General Assembly resolutions on the integration of the economies in transition into the world economy.

Calls upon the UN system, including the regional commissions, and invites the Bretton Woods institutions, in collaboration with relevant non-UN multilateral and regional institutions, to continue to conduct analytical activities and provide policy advice and targeted and substantial technical assistance to the governments of the countries with economies in transition aimed at strengthening the social, legal, and political framework for completing market-oriented reforms, supporting national development priorities with a view to sustaining the positive trends, and reversing any declines in the economic and social development of those countries.

Taking into account, among other things, the relevant provisions of the Monterrey Consensus of the International Conference of Financing for Development and the Plan of Implementation of the World Summit on Sustainable Development, stresses the need to focus international assistance to countries with economies in transition facing particular difficulties in socio-economic development; implementing market-oriented reforms; and meeting internationally agreed development goals, including those contained in the UN Millennium Declaration. Welcomes efforts made by countries with economies in transition to improve governance and institutional capabilities in order to use aid more effectively.

Welcomes the efforts made by countries with economies in transition implementing policies that promote sustained economic growth and sustainable development, including, among other things, by promoting competition, regulatory reform, respect for property rights, and expeditious contract enforcement; and calls on the UN system to highlight the success models as good practices.

Background: This resolution previously focused on actions the international community could take to help transition economies, such as ensuring favorable conditions for market access of exports, encouraging foreign direct investment, and recognizing the need for capacity building.

U.S. Position: In this resolution, the United States gained references to good governance and rule of law and a more detailed description of market oriented policies countries should pursue. This resolution also avoided calling for international assistance in general to help the slower transitioning economies. The United States succeeded in linking the effectiveness of aid to improved governance and accountability. Because of these positive changes, the United States was able to join consensus.

14. Situation of Human Rights in Myanmar (Burma)

A/Res/59/263   December 23

Expresses its grave concern at the ongoing systematic violation of human rights of the people of Burma; the events of May 30, 2003, and the continuing detention and house arrest of Aung San Suu Kyi and members of the National League for Democracy; and the Burmese authorities' failure to implement recommendations contained in previous General Assembly and Commission on Human Rights (CHR) resolutions or to permit the Special

Envoy of the Secretary-General for Burma to visit for over six months or the Special Rapporteur of the CHR on the situation of human rights in Burma to visit for almost 12 months, despite repeated requests.

Calls upon the Government of Burma to end the systematic violations of human rights in Burma to ensure full respect for all human rights and fundamental freedoms, and to end impunity; ensure that the National Convention is fully inclusive of all political parties and representatives and all major ethnic nationalities not represented by a political party; restore democracy and respect the results of the 1990 elections, including by releasing immediately and unconditionally the leadership of the National League for Democracy and all detained or imprisoned political prisoners; and initiate a full and independent inquiry into the Depayin incident of May 30, 2003. Requests the Secretary-General to continue to provide his good offices, assist his Special Envoy and the Special Rapporteur to discharge their mandate, and to report to the General Assembly and the CHR at their next session on progress made in implementation of the resolution.

Background: In 2003, the General Assembly adopted a resolution condemning Burma's human rights record. The resolution was adopted without a vote, although Burma disassociated from consensus. Burma's human rights record worsened during 2004. Burmese authorities have not allowed the Special Rapporteur to visit the country since November 2003, and the Envoy has not visited Burma since March 2004.

U.S. Position: The United States cosponsored this European Union resolution. The United States continues to call on the junta to release Aung San Suu Kyi, U Tin Oo, Hkun Htun Oo, and all political prisoners immediately and unconditionally; allow the National League for Democracy to re-open its offices nation-wide; engage the democratic opposition in a meaningful dialogue leading to genuine national reconciliation and the establishment of democracy; and to respect and ensure the free exercise of the fundamental human rights of the people of Burma. The National League for Democracy and ethnic political parties were not invited to participate in the National Convention, reconvened by the junta on February 17 for the purpose of drafting a new Constitution. Without their full participation, the Convention lacks the legitimacy to draw up a Constitution that is truly democratic and representative of the will of the Burmese people.

15. Review of the Implementation of Resolution 48/218B and 52/244

A/Res/59/272   December 23

Requests the Secretary-General to ensure that Office of Internal Oversight Services (OIOS) reports submitted to the General Assembly contain the titles and brief summaries of all OIOS reports issued during the year or reporting period, and that original versions of OIOS reports not submitted to the General Assembly are, upon request, made available to any member state.

Also decides that when access to a report would be inappropriate for reasons of confidentiality or the risk of violating the due process rights of individuals involved in OIOS investigations, the report may be modified, or withheld in extraordinary circumstances. Further decides that OIOS reports shall be submitted directly to the General Assembly as submitted by OIOS and that the Secretary-General may submit comments in a separate report. Regrets that despite previous information provided by the Secretary-General on the establishment of accountability mechanisms, including the accountability panel, such mechanisms are not in place. Concurs with the OIOS annual report that a high-level follow-up mechanism under the authority of the Secretary-General should be established to feed OIOS findings and recommendations, as well as relevant findings of the Joint Inspection Unit and the Board of Auditors, into the executive management processes, and requests the Secretary-General to establish this follow-up mechanism as soon as possible and to report to the General Assembly on the results achieved.

Background: The OIOS was established in 1994 to provide internal oversight to the United Nations and to promote stronger stewardship of resources, accountability, transparency, and performance.

U.S. Position: This resolution was a U.S. initiative. The United States was concerned that the United Nations had not made available to member states 55 OIOS audits on various aspects of the Oil-for-Food program conducted over the life of the program. During the 59th General Assembly, the United States made other proposals to strengthen OIOS, including giving OIOS budgetary independence from the offices that it audits and extending the nonrenewable term of the Under Secretary-General for Internal Oversight from the current five to seven years.

16. Program Budget for the Biennium 2004–2005

A/Res/59/277   December 23

Resolves that for the biennium 2004–2005, the amount of $3.18 billion appropriated in Resolutions 58/271 A and 58/295 shall be adjusted by an increase of $428 million. Resolves that for the biennium 2004–2005, the estimates of income of $415 million approved in Resolutions 58/271 B and 58/295 shall be increased by $28 million. Budget appropriations totaling $2.02 billion shall be financed in accordance with the UN Financial Regulations and Rules.

Background: This resolution brought the total biennial budget for 2004–2005, including inflation, currency fluctuations, additional mandates, and unforeseen expenses, to $3.608 billion. The resolution included an appropriation of $54 million to establish a new Department of Safety and Security in the United Nations, in keeping with the Secretary-General's November 1 recommendation to the Fifth Committee for an overhaul of the UN's security structure and a new directorate of security.

U.S. Position: This resolution was adopted unanimously. The United States supported the Secretary-General's recommendation for a new directorate of security.

COMPARISON WITH U.S. VOTES

The tables that follow summarize UN member state performance at the 59th UNGA in comparison with the United States on the 10 important votes. In these tables, "Identical Votes" is the total number of times the United States and the listed state both voted Yes or No on these issues. "Opposite Votes" is the total number of times the United States voted Yes and the listed state No, or the United States voted No and the listed state Yes. "Abstentions" and "Absences" are totals for the country being compared on these 10 votes. "Voting Coincidence (Votes Only)" is calculated by dividing the number of identical votes by the total of identical and opposite votes. The column headed "Voting Coincidence (Including Consensus)" presents the percentage of voting coincidence with the United States after including the 16 important consensus resolutions as identical votes. The extent of participation was also factored in. (See the second paragraph in this section.)

The first table lists all UN member states in alphabetical order. The second lists them by number of identical votes in descending order; those states with the same number of identical votes are further ranked by the number of opposite votes in ascending order. Countries with the same number of both identical votes and opposite votes are listed alphabetically. Subsequent tables are comparisons of UN members by regional and other groupings to which they belong, again ranked in descending order of identical votes.

All Countries (Alphabetical)

COUNTRY	IDENTICAL VOTES	OPPOSITE VOTES	ABSTEN-TIONS	ABSENCES	VOTING COINCIDENCE INCLUDING CONSENSUS	VOTES ONLY
Afghanistan	2	6	0	2	69.6%	25.0%
Albania	4	3	3	0	86.2%	57.1%
Algeria	2	8	0	0	69.0%	20.0%
Andorra	4	3	3	0	86.9%	57.1%
Angola	2	4	1	3	77.9%	33.3%
Antigua-Barbuda	2	3	2	3	84.2%	40.0%
Argentina	3	5	2	0	79.2%	37.5%
Armenia	3	6	1	0	75.8%	33.3%
Australia	7	2	1	0	91.9%	77.8%
Austria	4	3	3	0	87.0%	57.1%
Azerbaijan	2	8	0	0	67.7%	20.0%
Bahamas	2	5	2	1	77.2%	28.6%
Bahrain	2	8	0	0	68.6%	20.0%
Bangladesh	2	8	0	0	69.2%	20.0%
Barbados	2	6	1	1	74.0%	25.0%
Belarus	1	8	1	0	66.6%	11.1%
Belgium	4	3	3	0	86.8%	57.1%
Belize	3	7	0	0	72.5%	30.0%
Benin	2	7	1	0	70.8%	22.2%
Bhutan	1	5	2	2	72.1%	16.7%
Bolivia	4	6	0	0	76.9%	40.0%
Bosnia/Herzegovina	4	3	3	0	87.0%	57.1%
Botswana	2	7	1	0	69.1%	22.2%
Brazil	2	6	2	0	75.0%	25.0%
Brunei Darussalam	2	8	0	0	69.2%	20.0%
Bulgaria	4	3	3	0	87.0%	57.1%
Burkina Faso	2	7	1	0	71.4%	22.2%
Burundi	2	4	4	0	80.4%	33.3%
Cambodia	2	7	1	0	71.0%	22.2%
Cameroon	2	4	4	0	81.4%	33.3%
Canada	6	2	2	0	91.5%	75.0%
Cape Verde	2	6	1	1	72.3%	25.0%
Central African Rep.	2	6	1	1	71.6%	25.0%
Chad	2	1	0	7	86.2%	66.7%
Chile	4	6	0	0	76.6%	40.0%
China	1	8	1	0	67.5%	11.1%
Colombia	2	6	2	0	75.0%	25.0%
Comoros	2	6	0	2	72.3%	25.0%
Congo	0	6	0	4	62.4%	0.0%
Costa Rica	3	4	3	0	82.2%	42.9%
Cote d'Ivoire	2	6	2	0	73.4%	25.0%

All Countries (Alphabetical) (Cont'd)

COUNTRY	IDENTICAL VOTES	OPPOSITE VOTES	ABSTEN-TIONS	ABSENCES	VOTING COINCIDENCE INCLUDING CONSENSUS	VOTES ONLY
Croatia	4	3	3	0	87.0%	57.1%
Cuba	1	8	1	0	67.1%	11.1%
Cyprus	4	5	1	0	80.0%	44.4%
Czech Republic	4	3	3	0	86.8%	57.1%
DPR of Korea	1	7	1	1	67.7%	12.5%
Dem. Rep. Congo	2	3	0	5	74.9%	40.0%
Denmark	4	3	3	0	87.0%	57.1%
Djibouti	2	8	0	0	68.6%	20.0%
Dominica	2	5	1	2	77.0%	28.6%
Dominican Republic	2	3	5	0	85.5%	40.0%
Ecuador	2	6	2	0	74.8%	25.0%
Egypt	2	8	0	0	68.8%	20.0%
El Salvador	4	4	1	1	83.2%	50.0%
Equatorial Guinea	2	3	2	3	83.0%	40.0%
Eritrea	2	6	1	1	73.4%	25.0%
Estonia	4	3	3	0	86.8%	57.1%
Ethiopia	2	6	2	0	73.0%	25.0%
Fiji	2	4	3	1	80.7%	33.3%
Finland	4	3	3	0	87.0%	57.1%
France	4	3	3	0	86.9%	57.1%
Gabon	2	7	0	1	66.8%	22.2%
Gambia	2	6	0	2	66.9%	25.0%
Georgia	3	3	3	1	85.4%	50.0%
Germany	4	3	3	0	86.8%	57.1%
Ghana	2	7	1	0	71.4%	22.2%
Greece	4	3	3	0	86.9%	57.1%
Grenada	5	3	1	1	87.0%	62.5%
Guatemala	3	3	4	0	86.4%	50.0%
Guinea	2	6	0	2	65.6%	25.0%
Guinea-Bissau	2	6	1	1	72.3%	25.0%
Guyana	2	7	1	0	71.6%	22.2%
Haiti	3	3	3	1	84.6%	50.0%
Honduras	2	3	4	1	84.5%	40.0%
Hungary	4	3	3	0	86.9%	57.1%
Iceland	4	3	3	0	86.9%	57.1%
India	2	8	0	0	69.2%	20.0%
Indonesia	2	8	0	0	69.2%	20.0%
Iran	2	8	0	0	69.0%	20.0%
Iraq	2	6	1	1	68.5%	25.0%
Ireland	4	3	3	0	87.0%	57.1%
Israel	8	0	2	0	100.0%	100.0%

All Countries (Alphabetical) (Cont'd)

COUNTRY	IDENTICAL VOTES	OPPOSITE VOTES	ABSTEN-TIONS	ABSENCES	VOTING COINCIDENCE INCLUDING CONSENSUS	VOTES ONLY
Italy	4	3	3	0	86.9%	57.1%
Jamaica	2	6	2	0	73.8%	25.0%
Japan	4	2	4	0	90.9%	66.7%
Jordan	3	7	0	0	72.7%	30.0%
Kazakhstan	2	7	1	0	70.1%	22.2%
Kenya	2	4	4	0	81.8%	33.3%
Kiribati	1	1	0	8	57.5%	50.0%
Kuwait	2	8	0	0	68.6%	20.0%
Kyrgyzstan	2	5	1	2	75.8%	28.6%
Laos	1	7	2	0	68.0%	12.5%
Latvia	4	3	3	0	86.6%	57.1%
Lebanon	2	8	0	0	67.9%	20.0%
Lesotho	2	7	1	0	70.5%	22.2%
Liberia	2	5	2	1	75.8%	28.6%
Libya	1	8	1	0	67.5%	11.1%
Liechtenstein	4	3	3	0	87.0%	57.1%
Lithuania	4	3	3	0	87.0%	57.1%
Luxembourg	4	3	3	0	86.8%	57.1%
Madagascar	2	7	1	0	71.2%	22.2%
Malawi	3	3	0	4	81.0%	50.0%
Malaysia	2	8	0	0	69.2%	20.0%
Maldives	2	8	0	0	67.7%	20.0%
Mali	2	7	0	1	70.5%	22.2%
Malta	4	5	1	0	79.9%	44.4%
Marshall Islands	8	2	0	0	92.0%	80.0%
Mauritania	2	6	0	2	62.9%	25.0%
Mauritius	2	7	1	0	71.8%	22.2%
Mexico	4	5	1	0	80.0%	44.4%
Micronesia	7	2	1	0	90.9%	77.8%
Monaco	4	3	3	0	85.7%	57.1%
Mongolia	3	3	1	3	85.8%	50.0%
Morocco	2	6	0	2	74.2%	25.0%
Mozambique	2	7	1	0	68.1%	22.2%
Myanmar (Burma)	1	8	1	0	67.8%	11.1%
Namibia	2	7	1	0	71.8%	22.2%
Nauru	6	3	1	0	86.9%	66.7%
Nepal	2	7	1	0	71.6%	22.2%
Netherlands	4	3	3	0	87.0%	57.1%
New Zealand	4	2	4	0	90.9%	66.7%
Nicaragua	4	2	3	1	90.7%	66.7%
Niger	2	7	0	1	67.1%	22.2%

All Countries (Alphabetical) (Cont'd)

COUNTRY	IDENTICAL VOTES	OPPOSITE VOTES	ABSTEN-TIONS	ABSENCES	VOTING COINCIDENCE INCLUDING CONSENSUS	VOTES ONLY
Nigeria	2	8	0	0	69.0%	20.0%
Norway	4	3	3	0	86.9%	57.1%
Oman	2	8	0	0	68.8%	20.0%
Pakistan	2	8	0	0	68.8%	20.0%
Palau	10	0	0	0	100.0%	100.0%
Panama	4	5	1	0	79.9%	44.4%
Papua New Guinea	3	3	4	0	85.2%	50.0%
Paraguay	4	6	0	0	76.4%	40.0%
Peru	4	3	3	0	87.0%	57.1%
Philippines	2	6	2	0	74.8%	25.0%
Poland	4	3	3	0	87.0%	57.1%
Portugal	4	3	3	0	87.0%	57.1%
Qatar	2	8	0	0	68.6%	20.0%
Republic of Korea	3	2	5	0	90.4%	60.0%
Republic of Moldova	4	3	3	0	86.6%	57.1%
Romania	4	3	3	0	87.0%	57.1%
Russia	2	5	3	0	78.3%	28.6%
Rwanda	2	4	1	3	77.0%	33.3%
St. Kitts and Nevis	0	2	0	8	41.6%	0.0%
Saint Lucia	2	7	1	0	70.8%	22.2%
St.Vincent/Grenadines	3	6	1	0	75.3%	33.3%
Samoa	3	3	3	1	85.0%	50.0%
San Marino	4	3	3	0	87.0%	57.1%
Sao Tome/Principe	2	4	1	3	78.1%	33.3%
Saudi Arabia	1	8	1	0	67.3%	11.1%
Senegal	2	8	0	0	69.0%	20.0%
Serbia/Montenegro	4	3	3	0	87.0%	57.1%
Seychelles	2	4	0	4	74.4%	33.3%
Sierra Leone	2	7	1	0	71.4%	22.2%
Singapore	2	7	1	0	71.8%	22.2%
Slovak Republic	4	3	3	0	87.0%	57.1%
Slovenia	4	3	3	0	87.0%	57.1%
Solomon Islands	3	3	4	0	84.5%	50.0%
Somalia	3	7	0	0	72.1%	30.0%
South Africa	2	8	0	0	68.8%	20.0%
Spain	4	3	3	0	87.0%	57.1%
Sri Lanka	2	8	0	0	69.2%	20.0%
Sudan	2	8	0	0	69.0%	20.0%
Suriname	2	7	1	0	71.8%	22.2%
Swaziland	2	3	1	4	81.7%	40.0%
Sweden	4	3	3	0	87.0%	57.1%

All Countries (Alphabetical) (Cont'd)

COUNTRY	IDENTICAL VOTES	OPPOSITE VOTES	ABSTEN-TIONS	ABSENCES	VOTING COINCIDENCE INCLUDING CONSENSUS	VOTES ONLY
Switzerland	4	3	3	0	86.9%	57.1%
Syria	1	8	1	0	66.6%	11.1%
Tajikistan	2	7	0	1	66.8%	22.2%
Thailand	2	4	4	0	81.8%	33.3%
TFYR Macedonia	4	3	3	0	86.8%	57.1%
Timor-Leste	4	3	0	3	86.3%	57.1%
Togo	2	8	0	0	68.6%	20.0%
Tonga	0	3	3	4	78.6%	0.0%
Trinidad and Tobago	2	6	1	1	73.8%	25.0%
Tunisia	2	8	0	0	68.4%	20.0%
Turkey	2	6	0	2	74.0%	25.0%
Turkmenistan	1	7	1	1	65.2%	12.5%
Tuvalu	3	3	2	2	83.7%	50.0%
Uganda	2	4	4	0	81.1%	33.3%
Ukraine	2	4	3	1	81.5%	33.3%
United Arab Emirates	1	7	2	0	70.4%	12.5%
United Kingdom	4	2	4	0	90.9%	66.7%
UR Tanzania	2	6	1	1	74.4%	25.0%
Uruguay	3	4	3	0	82.3%	42.9%
Uzbekistan	2	4	1	3	77.2%	33.3%
Vanuatu	1	2	3	4	85.9%	33.3%
Venezuela	1	8	1	0	68.0%	11.1%
Vietnam	1	8	1	0	65.3%	11.1%
Yemen	2	8	0	0	69.2%	20.0%
Zambia	2	7	1	0	71.6%	22.2%
Zimbabwe	1	8	1	0	67.1%	11.1%
Average	2.7	5.1	1.6	0.6	77.5%	35.0%

All Countries (Ranked by Identical Votes)

COUNTRY	IDENTICAL VOTES	OPPOSITE VOTES	ABSTEN- TIONS	ABSENCES	VOTING COINCIDENCE INCLUDING CONSENSUS	VOTES ONLY
Palau	10	0	0	0	100.0%	100.0%
Israel	8	0	2	0	100.0%	100.0%
Marshall Islands	8	2	0	0	92.0%	80.0%
Australia	7	2	1	0	91.9%	77.8%
Micronesia	7	2	1	0	90.9%	77.8%
Canada	6	2	2	0	91.5%	75.0%
Nauru	6	3	1	0	86.9%	66.7%
Grenada	5	3	1	1	87.0%	62.5%
Japan	4	2	4	0	90.9%	66.7%
New Zealand	4	2	4	0	90.9%	66.7%
Nicaragua	4	2	3	1	90.7%	66.7%
United Kingdom	4	2	4	0	90.9%	66.7%
Albania	4	3	3	0	86.2%	57.1%
Andorra	4	3	3	0	86.9%	57.1%
Austria	4	3	3	0	87.0%	57.1%
Belgium	4	3	3	0	86.8%	57.1%
Bosnia/Herzegovina	4	3	3	0	87.0%	57.1%
Bulgaria	4	3	3	0	87.0%	57.1%
Croatia	4	3	3	0	87.0%	57.1%
Czech Republic	4	3	3	0	86.8%	57.1%
Denmark	4	3	3	0	87.0%	57.1%
Estonia	4	3	3	0	86.8%	57.1%
Finland	4	3	3	0	87.0%	57.1%
France	4	3	3	0	86.9%	57.1%
Germany	4	3	3	0	86.8%	57.1%
Greece	4	3	3	0	86.9%	57.1%
Hungary	4	3	3	0	86.9%	57.1%
Iceland	4	3	3	0	86.9%	57.1%
Ireland	4	3	3	0	87.0%	57.1%
Italy	4	3	3	0	86.9%	57.1%
Latvia	4	3	3	0	86.6%	57.1%
Liechtenstein	4	3	3	0	87.0%	57.1%
Lithuania	4	3	3	0	87.0%	57.1%
Luxembourg	4	3	3	0	86.8%	57.1%
Monaco	4	3	3	0	85.7%	57.1%
Netherlands	4	3	3	0	87.0%	57.1%
Norway	4	3	3	0	86.9%	57.1%
Peru	4	3	3	0	87.0%	57.1%
Poland	4	3	3	0	87.0%	57.1%
Portugal	4	3	3	0	87.0%	57.1%

All Countries (Ranked by Identical Votes) (Cont'd)

COUNTRY	IDENTICAL VOTES	OPPOSITE VOTES	ABSTEN-TIONS	ABSENCES	VOTING COINCIDENCE INCLUDING CONSENSUS	VOTES ONLY
Republic of Moldova	4	3	3	0	86.6%	57.1%
Romania	4	3	3	0	87.0%	57.1%
San Marino	4	3	3	0	87.0%	57.1%
Serbia/Montenegro	4	3	3	0	87.0%	57.1%
Slovak Republic	4	3	3	0	87.0%	57.1%
Slovenia	4	3	3	0	87.0%	57.1%
Spain	4	3	3	0	87.0%	57.1%
Sweden	4	3	3	0	87.0%	57.1%
Switzerland	4	3	3	0	86.9%	57.1%
TFYR Macedonia	4	3	3	0	86.8%	57.1%
Timor-Leste	4	3	0	3	86.3%	57.1%
El Salvador	4	4	1	1	83.2%	50.0%
Cyprus	4	5	1	0	80.0%	44.4%
Malta	4	5	1	0	79.9%	44.4%
Mexico	4	5	1	0	80.0%	44.4%
Panama	4	5	1	0	79.9%	44.4%
Bolivia	4	6	0	0	76.9%	40.0%
Chile	4	6	0	0	76.6%	40.0%
Paraguay	4	6	0	0	76.4%	40.0%
Republic of Korea	3	2	5	0	90.4%	60.0%
Georgia	3	3	3	1	85.4%	50.0%
Guatemala	3	3	4	0	86.4%	50.0%
Haiti	3	3	3	1	84.6%	50.0%
Malawi	3	3	0	4	81.0%	50.0%
Mongolia	3	3	1	3	85.8%	50.0%
Papua New Guinea	3	3	4	0	85.2%	50.0%
Samoa	3	3	3	1	85.0%	50.0%
Solomon Islands	3	3	4	0	84.5%	50.0%
Tuvalu	3	3	2	2	83.7%	50.0%
Costa Rica	3	4	3	0	82.2%	42.9%
Uruguay	3	4	3	0	82.3%	42.9%
Argentina	3	5	2	0	79.2%	37.5%
Armenia	3	6	1	0	75.8%	33.3%
St.Vincent/Grenadines	3	6	1	0	75.3%	33.3%
Belize	3	7	0	0	72.5%	30.0%
Jordan	3	7	0	0	72.7%	30.0%
Somalia	3	7	0	0	72.1%	30.0%
Chad	2	1	0	7	86.2%	66.7%
Antigua-Barbuda	2	3	2	3	84.2%	40.0%
Dem. Rep. Congo	2	3	0	5	74.9%	40.0%

All Countries (Ranked by Identical Votes) (Cont'd)

COUNTRY	IDENTICAL VOTES	OPPOSITE VOTES	ABSTEN- TIONS	ABSENCES	VOTING COINCIDENCE INCLUDING CONSENSUS	VOTES ONLY
Dominican Republic	2	3	5	0	85.5%	40.0%
Equatorial Guinea	2	3	2	3	83.0%	40.0%
Honduras	2	3	4	1	84.5%	40.0%
Swaziland	2	3	1	4	81.7%	40.0%
Angola	2	4	1	3	77.9%	33.3%
Burundi	2	4	4	0	80.4%	33.3%
Cameroon	2	4	4	0	81.4%	33.3%
Fiji	2	4	3	1	80.7%	33.3%
Kenya	2	4	4	0	81.8%	33.3%
Rwanda	2	4	1	3	77.0%	33.3%
Sao Tome/Principe	2	4	1	3	78.1%	33.3%
Seychelles	2	4	0	4	74.4%	33.3%
Thailand	2	4	4	0	81.8%	33.3%
Uganda	2	4	4	0	81.1%	33.3%
Ukraine	2	4	3	1	81.5%	33.3%
Uzbekistan	2	4	1	3	77.2%	33.3%
Bahamas	2	5	2	1	77.2%	28.6%
Dominica	2	5	1	2	77.0%	28.6%
Kyrgyzstan	2	5	1	2	75.8%	28.6%
Liberia	2	5	2	1	75.8%	28.6%
Russia	2	5	3	0	78.3%	28.6%
Afghanistan	2	6	0	2	69.6%	25.0%
Barbados	2	6	1	1	74.0%	25.0%
Brazil	2	6	2	0	75.0%	25.0%
Cape Verde	2	6	1	1	72.3%	25.0%
Central African. Rep.	2	6	1	1	71.6%	25.0%
Colombia	2	6	2	0	75.0%	25.0%
Comoros	2	6	0	2	72.3%	25.0%
Cote d'Ivoire	2	6	2	0	73.4%	25.0%
Ecuador	2	6	2	0	74.8%	25.0%
Eritrea	2	6	1	1	73.4%	25.0%
Ethiopia	2	6	2	0	73.0%	25.0%
Gambia	2	6	0	2	66.9%	25.0%
Guinea	2	6	0	2	65.6%	25.0%
Guinea-Bissau	2	6	1	1	72.3%	25.0%
Iraq	2	6	1	1	68.5%	25.0%
Jamaica	2	6	2	0	73.8%	25.0%
Mauritania	2	6	0	2	62.9%	25.0%
Morocco	2	6	0	2	74.2%	25.0%
Philippines	2	6	2	0	74.8%	25.0%
Trinidad and Tobago	2	6	1	1	73.8%	25.0%

All Countries (Ranked by Identical Votes) (Cont'd)

COUNTRY	IDENTICAL VOTES	OPPOSITE VOTES	ABSTEN-TIONS	ABSENCES	VOTING COINCIDENCE INCLUDING CONSENSUS	VOTES ONLY
Turkey	2	6	0	2	74.0%	25.0%
UR Tanzania	2	6	1	1	74.4%	25.0%
Benin	2	7	1	0	70.8%	22.2%
Botswana	2	7	1	0	69.1%	22.2%
Burkina Faso	2	7	1	0	71.4%	22.2%
Cambodia	2	7	1	0	71.0%	22.2%
Gabon	2	7	0	1	66.8%	22.2%
Ghana	2	7	1	0	71.4%	22.2%
Guyana	2	7	1	0	71.6%	22.2%
Kazakhstan	2	7	1	0	70.1%	22.2%
Lesotho	2	7	1	0	70.5%	22.2%
Madagascar	2	7	1	0	71.2%	22.2%
Mali	2	7	0	1	70.5%	22.2%
Mauritius	2	7	1	0	71.8%	22.2%
Mozambique	2	7	1	0	68.1%	22.2%
Namibia	2	7	1	0	71.8%	22.2%
Nepal	2	7	1	0	71.6%	22.2%
Niger	2	7	0	1	67.1%	22.2%
Saint Lucia	2	7	1	0	70.8%	22.2%
Sierra Leone	2	7	1	0	71.4%	22.2%
Singapore	2	7	1	0	71.8%	22.2%
Suriname	2	7	1	0	71.8%	22.2%
Tajikistan	2	7	0	1	66.8%	22.2%
Zambia	2	7	1	0	71.6%	22.2%
Algeria	2	8	0	0	69.0%	20.0%
Azerbaijan	2	8	0	0	67.7%	20.0%
Bahrain	2	8	0	0	68.6%	20.0%
Bangladesh	2	8	0	0	69.2%	20.0%
Brunei Darussalam	2	8	0	0	69.2%	20.0%
Djibouti	2	8	0	0	68.6%	20.0%
Egypt	2	8	0	0	68.8%	20.0%
India	2	8	0	0	69.2%	20.0%
Indonesia	2	8	0	0	69.2%	20.0%
Iran	2	8	0	0	69.0%	20.0%
Kuwait	2	8	0	0	68.6%	20.0%
Lebanon	2	8	0	0	67.9%	20.0%
Malaysia	2	8	0	0	69.2%	20.0%
Maldives	2	8	0	0	67.7%	20.0%
Nigeria	2	8	0	0	69.0%	20.0%
Oman	2	8	0	0	68.8%	20.0%

All Countries (Ranked by Identical Votes) (Cont'd)

COUNTRY	IDENTICAL VOTES	OPPOSITE VOTES	ABSTEN-TIONS	ABSENCES	VOTING COINCIDENCE INCLUDING CONSENSUS	VOTES ONLY
Pakistan	2	8	0	0	68.8%	20.0%
Qatar	2	8	0	0	68.6%	20.0%
Senegal	2	8	0	0	69.0%	20.0%
South Africa	2	8	0	0	68.8%	20.0%
Sri Lanka	2	8	0	0	69.2%	20.0%
Sudan	2	8	0	0	69.0%	20.0%
Togo	2	8	0	0	68.6%	20.0%
Tunisia	2	8	0	0	68.4%	20.0%
Yemen	2	8	0	0	69.2%	20.0%
Kiribati	1	1	0	8	57.5%	50.0%
Vanuatu	1	2	3	4	85.9%	33.3%
Bhutan	1	5	2	2	72.1%	16.7%
DPR of Korea	1	7	1	1	67.7%	12.5%
Laos	1	7	2	0	68.0%	12.5%
Turkmenistan	1	7	1	1	65.2%	12.5%
United Arab Emirates	1	7	2	0	70.4%	12.5%
Belarus	1	8	1	0	66.6%	11.1%
China	1	8	1	0	67.5%	11.1%
Cuba	1	8	1	0	67.1%	11.1%
Libya	1	8	1	0	67.5%	11.1%
Myanmar (Burma)	1	8	1	0	67.8%	11.1%
Saudi Arabia	1	8	1	0	67.3%	11.1%
Syria	1	8	1	0	66.6%	11.1%
Venezuela	1	8	1	0	68.0%	11.1%
Vietnam	1	8	1	0	65.3%	11.1%
Zimbabwe	1	8	1	0	67.1%	11.1%
St. Kitts and Nevis	0	2	0	8	41.6%	0.0%
Tonga	0	3	3	4	78.6%	0.0%
Congo	0	6	0	4	62.4%	0.0%
Average	2.7	5.1	1.6	0.6	77.5%	35.0%

UN REGIONAL GROUPS

The following tables show the voting coincidence percentage with U.S. votes on the 10 important votes.

African Group

COUNTRY	IDENTICAL VOTES	OPPOSITE VOTES	ABSTEN-TIONS	ABSENCES	VOTING COINCIDENCE INCLUDING CONSENSUS	VOTES ONLY
Malawi	3	3	0	4	81.0%	50.0%
Somalia	3	7	0	0	72.1%	30.0%
Chad	2	1	0	7	86.2%	66.7%
Dem. Rep. Congo	2	3	0	5	74.9%	40.0%
Equatorial Guinea	2	3	2	3	83.0%	40.0%
Swaziland	2	3	1	4	81.7%	40.0%
Angola	2	4	1	3	77.9%	33.3%
Burundi	2	4	4	0	80.4%	33.3%
Cameroon	2	4	4	0	81.4%	33.3%
Kenya	2	4	4	0	81.8%	33.3%
Rwanda	2	4	1	3	77.0%	33.3%
Sao Tome/Principe	2	4	1	3	78.1%	33.3%
Seychelles	2	4	0	4	74.4%	33.3%
Uganda	2	4	4	0	81.1%	33.3%
Liberia	2	5	2	1	75.8%	28.6%
Cape Verde	2	6	1	1	72.3%	25.0%
Central African Rep.	2	6	1	1	71.6%	25.0%
Comoros	2	6	0	2	72.3%	25.0%
Cote d'Ivoire	2	6	2	0	73.4%	25.0%
Eritrea	2	6	1	1	73.4%	25.0%
Ethiopia	2	6	2	0	73.0%	25.0%
Gambia	2	6	0	2	66.9%	25.0%
Guinea	2	6	0	2	65.6%	25.0%
Guinea-Bissau	2	6	1	1	72.3%	25.0%
Mauritania	2	6	0	2	62.9%	25.0%
Morocco	2	6	0	2	74.2%	25.0%
UR Tanzania	2	6	1	1	74.4%	25.0%
Benin	2	7	1	0	70.8%	22.2%
Botswana	2	7	1	0	69.1%	22.2%
Burkina Faso	2	7	1	0	71.4%	22.2%
Gabon	2	7	0	1	66.8%	22.2%
Ghana	2	7	1	0	71.4%	22.2%
Lesotho	2	7	1	0	70.5%	22.2%
Madagascar	2	7	1	0	71.2%	22.2%

African Group (Cont'd)

COUNTRY	IDENTICAL VOTES	OPPOSITE VOTES	ABSTEN- TIONS	ABSENCES	VOTING COINCIDENCE INCLUDING CONSENSUS	VOTES ONLY
Mali	2	7	0	1	70.5%	22.2%
Mauritius	2	7	1	0	71.8%	22.2%
Mozambique	2	7	1	0	68.1%	22.2%
Namibia	2	7	1	0	71.8%	22.2%
Niger	2	7	0	1	67.1%	22.2%
Sierra Leone	2	7	1	0	71.4%	22.2%
Zambia	2	7	1	0	71.6%	22.2%
Algeria	2	8	0	0	69.0%	20.0%
Djibouti	2	8	0	0	68.6%	20.0%
Egypt	2	8	0	0	68.8%	20.0%
Nigeria	2	8	0	0	69.0%	20.0%
Senegal	2	8	0	0	69.0%	20.0%
South Africa	2	8	0	0	68.8%	20.0%
Sudan	2	8	0	0	69.0%	20.0%
Togo	2	8	0	0	68.6%	20.0%
Tunisia	2	8	0	0	68.4%	20.0%
Libya	1	8	1	0	67.5%	11.1%
Zimbabwe	1	8	1	0	67.1%	11.1%
Congo	0	6	0	4	62.4%	0.0%
Average	2.0	6.1	0.9	1.1	72.0%	24.5%

Asian Group

COUNTRY	IDENTICAL VOTES	OPPOSITE VOTES	ABSTEN- TIONS	ABSENCES	VOTING COINCIDENCE INCLUDING CONSENSUS	VOTES ONLY
Marshall Islands	8	2	0	0	92.0%	80.0%
Micronesia	7	2	1	0	90.9%	77.8%
Nauru	6	3	1	0	86.9%	66.7%
Japan	4	2	4	0	90.9%	66.7%
Timor-Leste	4	3	0	3	86.3%	57.1%
Cyprus	4	5	1	0	80.0%	44.4%
Republic of Korea	3	2	5	0	90.4%	60.0%
Mongolia	3	3	1	3	85.8%	50.0%
Papua New Guinea	3	3	4	0	85.2%	50.0%
Samoa	3	3	3	1	85.0%	50.0%
Solomon Islands	3	3	4	0	84.5%	50.0%
Tuvalu	3	3	2	2	83.7%	50.0%
Jordan	3	7	0	0	72.7%	30.0%
Fiji	2	4	3	1	80.7%	33.3%

Asian Group (Cont'd)

COUNTRY	IDENTICAL VOTES	OPPOSITE VOTES	ABSTEN-TIONS	ABSENCES	VOTING COINCIDENCE INCLUDING CONSENSUS	VOTES ONLY
Thailand	2	4	4	0	81.8%	33.3%
Uzbekistan	2	4	1	3	77.2%	33.3%
Kyrgyzstan	2	5	1	2	75.8%	28.6%
Afghanistan	2	6	0	2	69.6%	25.0%
Iraq	2	6	1	1	68.5%	25.0%
Philippines	2	6	2	0	74.8%	25.0%
Cambodia	2	7	1	0	71.0%	22.2%
Kazakhstan	2	7	1	0	70.1%	22.2%
Nepal	2	7	1	0	71.6%	22.2%
Singapore	2	7	1	0	71.8%	22.2%
Tajikistan	2	7	0	1	66.8%	22.2%
Bahrain	2	8	0	0	68.6%	20.0%
Bangladesh	2	8	0	0	69.2%	20.0%
Brunei Darussalam	2	8	0	0	69.2%	20.0%
India	2	8	0	0	69.2%	20.0%
Indonesia	2	8	0	0	69.2%	20.0%
Iran	2	8	0	0	69.0%	20.0%
Kuwait	2	8	0	0	68.6%	20.0%
Lebanon	2	8	0	0	67.9%	20.0%
Malaysia	2	8	0	0	69.2%	20.0%
Maldives	2	8	0	0	67.7%	20.0%
Oman	2	8	0	0	68.8%	20.0%
Pakistan	2	8	0	0	68.8%	20.0%
Qatar	2	8	0	0	68.6%	20.0%
Sri Lanka	2	8	0	0	69.2%	20.0%
Yemen	2	8	0	0	69.2%	20.0%
Vanuatu	1	2	3	4	85.9%	33.3%
Bhutan	1	5	2	2	72.1%	16.7%
DPR of Korea	1	7	1	1	67.7%	12.5%
Laos	1	7	2	0	68.0%	12.5%
Turkmenistan	1	7	1	1	65.2%	12.5%
United Arab Emirates	1	7	2	0	70.4%	12.5%
China	1	8	1	0	67.5%	11.1%
Myanmar (Burma)	1	8	1	0	67.8%	11.1%
Saudi Arabia	1	8	1	0	67.3%	11.1%
Syria	1	8	1	0	66.6%	11.1%
Vietnam	1	8	1	0	65.3%	11.1%
Tonga	0	3	3	4	78.6%	0.0%
Average	2.3	5.9	1.2	0.6	73.9%	27.8%

Latin American and Caribbean Group (LAC)

COUNTRY	IDENTICAL VOTES	OPPOSITE VOTES	ABSTEN-TIONS	ABSENCES	VOTING COINCIDENCE INCLUDING CONSENSUS	VOTES ONLY
Grenada	5	3	1	1	87.0%	62.5%
Nicaragua	4	2	3	1	90.7%	66.7%
Peru	4	3	3	0	87.0%	57.1%
El Salvador	4	4	1	1	83.2%	50.0%
Mexico	4	5	1	0	80.0%	44.4%
Panama	4	5	1	0	79.9%	44.4%
Bolivia	4	6	0	0	76.9%	40.0%
Chile	4	6	0	0	76.6%	40.0%
Paraguay	4·	6	0	0	76.4%	40.0%
Guatemala	3	3	4	0	86.4%	50.0%
Haiti	3	3	3	1	84.6%	50.0%
Costa Rica	3	4	3	0	82.2%	42.9%
Uruguay	3	4	3	0	82.3%	42.9%
Argentina	3	5	2	0	79.2%	37.5%
St.Vincent/Grenadines	3	6	1	0	75.3%	33.3%
Belize	3	7	0	0	72.5%	30.0%
Antigua-Barbuda	2	3	2	3	84.2%	40.0%
Dominican Republic	2	3	5	0	85.5%	40.0%
Honduras	2	3	4	1	84.5%	40.0%
Bahamas	2	5	2	1	77.2%	28.6%
Dominica	2	5	1	2	77.0%	28.6%
Barbados	2	6	1	1	74.0%	25.0%
Brazil	2	6	2	0	75.0%	25.0%
Colombia	2	6	2	0	75.0%	25.0%
Ecuador	2	6	2	0	74.8%	25.0%
Jamaica	2	6	2	0	73.8%	25.0%
Trinidad and Tobago	2	6	1	1	73.8%	25.0%
Guyana	2	7	1	0	71.6%	22.2%
Saint Lucia	2	7	1	0	70.8%	22.2%
Suriname	2	7	1	0	71.8%	22.2%
Cuba	1	8	1	0	67.1%	11.1%
Venezuela	1	8	1	0	68.0%	11.1%
St. Kitts and Nevis	0	2	0	8	41.6%	0.0%
Average	2.7	5.0	1.7	0.6	77.8%	34.6%

Western European and Others Group (WEOG)

COUNTRY	IDENTICAL VOTES	OPPOSITE VOTES	ABSTEN- TIONS	ABSENCES	VOTING COINCIDENCE INCLUDING CONSENSUS	VOTES ONLY
Israel	8	0	2	0	100.0%	100.0%
Australia	7	2	1	0	91.9%	77.8%
Canada	6	2	2	0	91.5%	75.0%
New Zealand	4	2	4	0	90.9%	66.7%
United Kingdom	4	2	4	0	90.9%	66.7%
Andorra	4	3	3	0	86.9%	57.1%
Austria	4	3	3	0	87.0%	57.1%
Belgium	4	3	3	0	86.8%	57.1%
Denmark	4	3	3	0	87.0%	57.1%
Finland	4	3	3	0	87.0%	57.1%
France	4	3	3	0	86.9%	57.1%
Germany	4	3	3	0	86.8%	57.1%
Greece	4	3	3	0	86.9%	57.1%
Iceland	4	3	3	0	86.9%	57.1%
Ireland	4	3	3	0	87.0%	57.1%
Italy	4	3	3	0	86.9%	57.1%
Liechtenstein	4	3	3	0	87.0%	57.1%
Luxembourg	4	3	3	0	86.8%	57.1%
Monaco	4	3	3	0	85.7%	57.1%
Netherlands	4	3	3	0	87.0%	57.1%
Norway	4	3	3	0	86.9%	57.1%
Portugal	4	3	3	0	87.0%	57.1%
San Marino	4	3	3	0	87.0%	57.1%
Spain	4	3	3	0	87.0%	57.1%
Sweden	4	3	3	0	87.0%	57.1%
Switzerland	4	3	3	0	86.9%	57.1%
Malta	4	5	1	0	79.9%	44.4%
Turkey	2	6	0	2	74.0%	25.0%
Average	4.3	2.9	2.8	0.1	87.2%	59.2%

Eastern European Group (EE)

COUNTRY	IDENTICAL VOTES	OPPOSITE VOTES	ABSTEN- TIONS	ABSENCES	VOTING COINCIDENCE INCLUDING CONSENSUS	VOTES ONLY
Albania	4	3	3	0	86.2%	57.1%
Bosnia/Herzegovina	4	3	3	0	87.0%	57.1%
Bulgaria	4	3	3	0	87.0%	57.1%
Croatia	4	3	3	0	87.0%	57.1%
Czech Republic	4	3	3	0	86.8%	57.1%
Estonia	4	3	3	0	86.8%	57.1%

Eastern European Group (EE) (Cont'd)

COUNTRY	IDENTICAL VOTES	OPPOSITE VOTES	ABSTEN- TIONS	ABSENCES	VOTING COINCIDENCE INCLUDING CONSENSUS	VOTES ONLY
Hungary	4	3	3	0	86.9%	57.1%
Latvia	4	3	3	0	86.6%	57.1%
Lithuania	4	3	3	0	87.0%	57.1%
Poland	4	3	3	0	87.0%	57.1%
Republic of Moldova	4	3	3	0	86.6%	57.1%
Romania	4	3	3	0	87.0%	57.1%
Serbia/Montenegro	4	3	3	0	87.0%	57.1%
Slovak Republic	4	3	3	0	87.0%	57.1%
Slovenia	4	3	3	0	87.0%	57.1%
TFYR Macedonia	4	3	3	0	86.8%	57.1%
Georgia	3	3	3	1	85.4%	50.0%
Armenia	3	6	1	0	75.8%	33.3%
Ukraine	2	4	3	1	81.5%	33.3%
Russia	2	5	3	0	78.3%	28.6%
Azerbaijan	2	8	0	0	67.7%	20.0%
Belarus	1	8	1	0	66.6%	11.1%
Average	3.5	3.7	2.7	0.1	83.7%	48.4%

OTHER GROUPINGS

The following tables show percentage of voting coincidence with U.S. votes for major groups, in rank order by identical votes.

Arab Group

COUNTRY	IDENTICAL VOTES	OPPOSITE VOTES	ABSTEN- TIONS	ABSENCES	VOTING COINCIDENCE INCLUDING CONSENSUS	VOTES ONLY
Jordan	3	7	0	0	72.7%	30.0%
Somalia	3	7	0	0	72.1%	30.0%
Iraq	2	6	1	1	68.5%	25.0%
Mauritania	2	6	0	2	62.9%	25.0%
Morocco	2	6	0	2	74.2%	25.0%
Algeria	2	8	0	0	69.0%	20.0%
Bahrain	2	8	0	0	68.6%	20.0%
Djibouti	2	8	0	0	68.6%	20.0%
Egypt	2	8	0	0	68.8%	20.0%
Kuwait	2	8	0	0	68.6%	20.0%
Lebanon	2	8	0	0	67.9%	20.0%
Oman	2	8	0	0	68.8%	20.0%
Qatar	2	8	0	0	68.6%	20.0%
Sudan	2	8	0	0	69.0%	20.0%
Tunisia	2	8	0	0	68.4%	20.0%
Yemen	2	8	0	0	69.2%	20.0%
United Arab Emirates	1	7	2	0	70.4%	12.5%
Libya	1	8	1	0	67.5%	11.1%
Saudi Arabia	1	8	1	0	67.3%	11.1%
Syria	1	8	1	0	66.6%	11.1%
Average	1.9	7.6	0.3	0.3	69.0%	20.1%

Association of Southeast Asian Nations (ASEAN)

COUNTRY	IDENTICAL VOTES	OPPOSITE VOTES	ABSTEN- TIONS	ABSENCES	VOTING COINCIDENCE INCLUDING CONSENSUS	VOTES ONLY
Thailand	2	4	4	0	81.8%	33.3%
Philippines	2	6	2	0	74.8%	25.0%
Cambodia	2	7	1	0	71.0%	22.2%
Singapore	2	7	1	0	71.8%	22.2%
Brunei Darussalam	2	8	0	0	69.2%	20.0%
Indonesia	2	8	0	0	69.2%	20.0%
Malaysia	2	8	0	0	69.2%	20.0%
Laos	1	7	2	0	68.0%	12.5%
Myanmar (Burma)	1	8	1	0	67.8%	11.1%

Association of Southeast Asian Nations (ASEAN) (Cont'd)

COUNTRY	IDENTICAL VOTES	OPPOSITE VOTES	ABSTEN-TIONS	ABSENCES	VOTING COINCIDENCE INCLUDING CONSENSUS	VOTES ONLY
Vietnam	1	8	1	0	65.3%	11.1%
Average	1.7	7.1	1.2	0.0	70.7%	19.3%

European Union (EU)

COUNTRY	IDENTICAL VOTES	OPPOSITE VOTES	ABSTEN-IONS	ABSENCES	VOTING COINCIDENCE INCLUDING CONSENSUS	VOTES ONLY
United Kingdom	4	2	4	0	90.9%	66.7%
Austria	4	3	3	0	87.0%	57.1%
Belgium	4	3	3	0	86.8%	57.1%
Czech Republic	4	3	3	0	86.8%	57.1%
Denmark	4	3	3	0	87.0%	57.1%
Estonia	4	3	3	0	86.8%	57.1%
Finland	4	3	3	0	87.0%	57.1%
France	4	3	3	0	86.9%	57.1%
Germany	4	3	3	0	86.8%	57.1%
Greece	4	3	3	0	86.9%	57.1%
Hungary	4	3	3	0	86.9%	57.1%
Ireland	4	3	3	0	87.0%	57.1%
Italy	4	3	3	0	86.9%	57.1%
Latvia	4	3	3	0	86.6%	57.1%
Lithuania	4	3	3	0	87.0%	57.1%
Luxembourg	4	3	3	0	86.8%	57.1%
Netherlands	4	3	3	0	87.0%	57.1%
Poland	4	3	3	0	87.0%	57.1%
Portugal	4	3	3	0	87.0%	57.1%
Slovak Republic	4	3	3	0	87.0%	57.1%
Slovenia	4	3	3	0	87.0%	57.1%
Spain	4	3	3	0	87.0%	57.1%
Sweden	4	3	3	0	87.0%	57.1%
Cyprus	4	5	1	0	80.0%	44.4%
Malta	4	5	1	0	79.9%	44.4%
Average	4.0	3.1	2.9	0.0	86.4%	56.2%

Islamic Conference (OIC)

COUNTRY	IDENTICAL VOTES	OPPOSITE VOTES	ABSTEN-TIONS	ABSENCES	VOTING COINCIDENCE INCLUDING CONSENSUS	VOTES ONLY
Albania	4	3	3	0	86.2%	57.1%

Islamic Conference (OIC) (Cont'd)

COUNTRY	IDENTICAL VOTES	OPPOSITE VOTES	ABSTEN-TIONS	ABSENCES	VOTING COINCIDENCE INCLUDING CONSENSUS	VOTES ONLY
Jordan	3	7	0	0	72.7%	30.0%
Somalia	3	7	0	0	72.1%	30.0%
Chad	2	1	0	7	86.2%	66.7%
Cameroon	2	4	4	0	81.4%	33.3%
Uganda	2	4	4	0	81.1%	33.3%
Uzbekistan	2	4	1	3	77.2%	33.3%
Kyrgyzstan	2	5	1	2	75.8%	28.6%
Afghanistan	2	6	0	2	69.6%	25.0%
Comoros	2	6	0	2	72.3%	25.0%
Cote d'Ivoire	2	6	2	0	73.4%	25.0%
Gambia	2	6	0	2	66.9%	25.0%
Guinea	2	6	0	2	65.6%	25.0%
Guinea-Bissau	2	6	1	1	72.3%	25.0%
Iraq	2	6	1	1	68.5%	25.0%
Mauritania	2	6	0	2	62.9%	25.0%
Morocco	2	6	0	2	74.2%	25.0%
Turkey	2	6	0	2	74.0%	25.0%
Benin	2	7	1	0	70.8%	22.2%
Burkina Faso	2	7	1	0	71.4%	22.2%
Gabon	2	7	0	1	66.8%	22.2%
Guyana	2	7	1	0	71.6%	22.2%
Kazakhstan	2	7	1	0	70.1%	22.2%
Mali	2	7	0	1	70.5%	22.2%
Mozambique	2	7	1	0	68.1%	22.2%
Niger	2	7	0	1	67.1%	22.2%
Sierra Leone	2	7	1	0	71.4%	22.2%
Suriname	2	7	1	0	71.8%	22.2%
Tajikistan	2	7	0	1	66.8%	22.2%
Algeria	2	8	0	0	69.0%	20.0%
Azerbaijan	2	8	0	0	67.7%	20.0%
Bahrain	2	8	0	0	68.6%	20.0%
Bangladesh	2	8	0	0	69.2%	20.0%
Brunei Darussalam	2	8	0	0	69.2%	20.0%
Djibouti	2	8	0	0	68.6%	20.0%
Egypt	2	8	0	0	68.8%	20.0%
Indonesia	2	8	0	0	69.2%	20.0%
Iran	2	8	0	0	69.0%	20.0%
Kuwait	2	8	0	0	68.6%	20.0%
Lebanon	2	8	0	0	67.9%	20.0%
Malaysia	2	8	0	0	69.2%	20.0%

Islamic Conference (OIC) (Cont'd)

COUNTRY	IDENTICAL VOTES	OPPOSITE VOTES	ABSTEN-TIONS	ABSENCES	VOTING COINCIDENCE INCLUDING CONSENSUS	VOTES ONLY
Maldives	2	8	0	0	67.7%	20.0%
Nigeria	2	8	0	0	69.0%	20.0%
Oman	2	8	0	0	68.8%	20.0%
Pakistan	2	8	0	0	68.8%	20.0%
Qatar	2	8	0	0	68.6%	20.0%
Senegal	2	8	0	0	69.0%	20.0%
Sudan	2	8	0	0	69.0%	20.0%
Togo	2	8	0	0	68.6%	20.0%
Tunisia	2	8	0	0	68.4%	20.0%
Yemen	2	8	0	0	69.2%	20.0%
Turkmenistan	1	7	1	1	65.2%	12.5%
United Arab Emirates	1	7	2	0	70.4%	12.5%
Libya	1	8	1	0	67.5%	11.1%
Saudi Arabia	1	8	1	0	67.3%	11.1%
Syria	1	8	1	0	66.6%	11.1%
Average	2.0	6.9	0.5	0.6	70.3%	22.3%

Non-Aligned Movement (NAM)

COUNTRY	IDENTICAL VOTES	OPPOSITE VOTES	ABSTEN-TIONS	ABSENCES	VOTING COINCIDENCE INCLUDING CONSENSUS	VOTES ONLY
Grenada	5	3	1	1	87.0%	62.5%
Nicaragua	4	2	3	1	90.7%	66.7%
Peru	4	3	3	0	87.0%	57.1%
Cyprus	4	5	1	0	80.0%	44.4%
Malta	4	5	1	0	79.9%	44.4%
Panama	4	5	1	0	79.9%	44.4%
Bolivia	4	6	0	0	76.9%	40.0%
Chile	4	6	0	0	76.6%	40.0%
Guatemala	3	3	4	0	86.4%	50.0%
Malawi	3	3	0	4	81.0%	50.0%
Mongolia	3	3	1	3	85.8%	50.0%
Papua New Guinea	3	3	4	0	85.2%	50.0%
Belize	3	7	0	0	72.5%	30.0%
Jordan	3	7	0	0	72.7%	30.0%
Somalia	3	7	0	0	72.1%	30.0%
Chad	2	1	0	7	86.2%	66.7%
Dem. Rep. Congo	2	3	0	5	74.9%	40.0%
Dominican Republic	2	3	5	0	85.5%	40.0%
Equatorial Guinea	2	3	2	3	83.0%	40.0%

Non-Aligned Movement (NAM) (Cont'd)

COUNTRY	IDENTICAL VOTES	OPPOSITE VOTES	ABSTEN-TIONS	ABSENCES	VOTING COINCIDENCE INCLUDING CONSENSUS	VOTES ONLY
Honduras	2	3	4	1	84.5%	40.0%
Swaziland	2	3	1	4	81.7%	40.0%
Angola	2	4	1	3	77.9%	33.3%
Burundi	2	4	4	0	80.4%	33.3%
Cameroon	2	4	4	0	81.4%	33.3%
Kenya	2	4	4	0	81.8%	33.3%
Rwanda	2	4	1	3	77.0%	33.3%
Sao Tome/Principe	2	4	1	3	78.1%	33.3%
Seychelles	2	4	0	4	74.4%	33.3%
Thailand	2	4	4	0	81.8%	33.3%
Uganda	2	4	4	0	81.1%	33.3%
Uzbekistan	2	4	1	3	77.2%	33.3%
Bahamas	2	5	2	1	77.2%	28.6%
Liberia	2	5	2	1	75.8%	28.6%
Afghanistan	2	6	0	2	69.6%	25.0%
Barbados	2	6	1	1	74.0%	25.0%
Cape Verde	2	6	1	1	72.3%	25.0%
Central African Rep.	2	6	1	1	71.6%	25.0%
Colombia	2	6	2	0	75.0%	25.0%
Comoros	2	6	0	2	72.3%	25.0%
Cote d'Ivoire	2	6	2	0	73.4%	25.0%
Ecuador	2	6	2	0	74.8%	25.0%
Eritrea	2	6	1	1	73.4%	25.0%
Ethiopia	2	6	2	0	73.0%	25.0%
Gambia	2	6	0	2	66.9%	25.0%
Guinea	2	6	0	2	65.6%	25.0%
Guinea-Bissau	2	6	1	1	72.3%	25.0%
Iraq	2	6	1	1	68.5%	25.0%
Jamaica	2	6	2	0	73.8%	25.0%
Mauritania	2	6	0	2	62.9%	25.0%
Morocco	2	6	0	2	74.2%	25.0%
Philippines	2	6	2	0	74.8%	25.0%
Trinidad and Tobago	2	6	1	1	73.8%	25.0%
UR Tanzania	2	6	1	1	74.4%	25.0%
Benin	2	7	1	0	70.8%	22.2%
Botswana	2	7	1	0	69.1%	22.2%
Burkina Faso	2	7	1	0	71.4%	22.2%
Cambodia	2	7	1	0	71.0%	22.2%
Gabon	2	7	0	1	66.8%	22.2%
Ghana	2	7	1	0	71.4%	22.2%

Non-Aligned Movement (NAM) (Cont'd)

COUNTRY	IDENTICAL VOTES	OPPOSITE VOTES	ABSTEN-TIONS	ABSENCES	VOTING COINCIDENCE INCLUDING CONSENSUS	VOTES ONLY
Guyana	2	7	1	0	71.6%	22.2%
Lesotho	2	7	1	0	70.5%	22.2%
Madagascar	2	7	1	0	71.2%	22.2%
Mali	2	7	0	1	70.5%	22.2%
Mauritius	2	7	1	0	71.8%	22.2%
Mozambique	2	7	1	0	68.1%	22.2%
Namibia	2	7	1	0	71.8%	22.2%
Nepal	2	7	1	0	71.6%	22.2%
Niger	2	7	0	1	67.1%	22.2%
Saint Lucia	2	7	1	0	70.8%	22.2%
Sierra Leone	2	7	1	0	71.4%	22.2%
Singapore	2	7	1	0	71.8%	22.2%
Suriname	2	7	1	0	71.8%	22.2%
Zambia	2	7	1	0	71.6%	22.2%
Algeria	2	8	0	0	69.0%	20.0%
Bahrain	2	8	0	0	68.6%	20.0%
Bangladesh	2	8	0	0	69.2%	20.0%
Brunei Darussalam	2	8	0	0	69.2%	20.0%
Djibouti	2	8	0	0	68.6%	20.0%
Egypt	2	8	0	0	68.8%	20.0%
India	2	8	0	0	69.2%	20.0%
Indonesia	2	8	0	0	69.2%	20.0%
Iran	2	8	0	0	69.0%	20.0%
Kuwait	2	8	0	0	68.6%	20.0%
Lebanon	2	8	0	0	67.9%	20.0%
Malaysia	2	8	0	0	69.2%	20.0%
Maldives	2	8	0	0	67.7%	20.0%
Nigeria	2	8	0	0	69.0%	20.0%
Oman	2	8	0	0	68.8%	20.0%
Pakistan	2	8	0	0	68.8%	20.0%
Qatar	2	8	0	0	68.6%	20.0%
Senegal	2	8	0	0	69.0%	20.0%
South Africa	2	8	0	0	68.8%	20.0%
Sri Lanka	2	8	0	0	69.2%	20.0%
Sudan	2	8	0	0	69.0%	20.0%
Togo	2	8	0	0	68.6%	20.0%
Tunisia	2	8	0	0	68.4%	20.0%
Yemen	2	8	0	0	69.2%	20.0%
Vanuatu	1	2	3	4	85.9%	33.3%

Non-Aligned Movement (NAM) (Cont'd)

COUNTRY	IDENTICAL VOTES	OPPOSITE VOTES	ABSTEN-TIONS	ABSENCES	VOTING COINCIDENCE INCLUDING CONSENSUS	VOTES ONLY
Bhutan	1	5	2	2	72.1%	16.7%
DPR of Korea	1	7	1	1	67.7%	12.5%
Laos	1	7	2	0	68.0%	12.5%
Turkmenistan	1	7	1	1	65.2%	12.5%
United Arab Emirates	1	7	2	0	70.4%	12.5%
Belarus	1	8	1	0	66.6%	11.1%
Cuba	1	8	1	0	67.1%	11.1%
Libya	1	8	1	0	67.5%	11.1%
Myanmar (Burma)	1	8	1	0	67.8%	11.1%
Saudi Arabia	1	8	1	0	67.3%	11.1%
Syria	1	8	1	0	66.6%	11.1%
Venezuela	1	8	1	0	68.0%	11.1%
Vietnam	1	8	1	0	65.3%	11.1%
Zimbabwe	1	8	1	0	67.1%	11.1%
Congo	0	6	0	4	62.4%	0.0%
Average	2.1	6.2	1.0	0.7	72.7%	25.0%

Nordic Group

COUNTRY	IDENTICAL VOTES	OPPOSITE VOTES	ABSTEN-TIONS	ABSENCES	VOTING COINCIDENCE INCLUDING CONSENSUS	VOTES ONLY
Denmark	4	3	3	0	87.0%	57.1%
Finland	4	3	3	0	87.0%	57.1%
Iceland	4	3	3	0	86.9%	57.1%
Norway	4	3	3	0	86.9%	57.1%
Sweden	4	3	3	0	87.0%	57.1%
Average	4.0	3.0	3.0	0.0	86.9%	57.1%

North Atlantic Treaty Organization (NATO)

COUNTRY	IDENTICAL VOTES	OPPOSITE VOTES	ABSTEN-TIONS	ABSENCES	VOTING COINCIDENCE INCLUDING CONSENSUS	VOTES ONLY
Canada	6	2	2	0	91.5%	75.0%
United Kingdom	4	2	4	0	90.9%	66.7%
Belgium	4	3	3	0	86.8%	57.1%
Bulgaria	4	3	3	0	87.0%	57.1%
Czech Republic	4	3	3	0	86.8%	57.1%
Denmark	4	3	3	0	87.0%	57.1%
Estonia	4	3	3	0	86.8%	57.1%

North Atlantic Treaty Organization (NATO) (Cont'd)

COUNTRY	IDENTICAL VOTES	OPPOSITE VOTES	ABSTEN-TIONS	ABSENCES	VOTING COINCIDENCE INCLUDING CONSENSUS	VOTES ONLY
France	4	3	3	0	86.9%	57.1%
Germany	4	3	3	0	86.8%	57.1%
Greece	4	3	3	0	86.9%	57.1%
Hungary	4	3	3	0	86.9%	57.1%
Iceland	4	3	3	0	86.9%	57.1%
Italy	4	3	3	0	86.9%	57.1%
Latvia	4	3	3	0	86.6%	57.1%
Lithuania	4	3	3	0	87.0%	57.1%
Luxembourg	4	3	3	0	86.8%	57.1%
Netherlands	4	3	3	0	87.0%	57.1%
Norway	4	3	3	0	86.9%	57.1%
Poland	4	3	3	0	87.0%	57.1%
Portugal	4	3	3	0	87.0%	57.1%
Romania	4	3	3	0	87.0%	57.1%
Slovak Republic	4	3	3	0	87.0%	57.1%
Slovenia	4	3	3	0	87.0%	57.1%
Spain	4	3	3	0	87.0%	57.1%
Turkey	2	6	0	2	74.0%	25.0%
Average	4.0	3.0	2.9	0.1	86.7%	56.8%

COMPARISON OF IMPORTANT AND OVERALL VOTES

The following table shows the percentage of voting coincidence with the United States in 2004 for both important votes and all Plenary votes, in a side-by-side comparison.

Comparison of Important and Overall Votes

COUNTRY	IMPORTANT VOTES IDENTICAL VOTES	OPPOSITE VOTES	PERCENT	OVERALL VOTES IDENTICAL VOTES	OPPOSITE VOTES	PERCENT
Afghanistan	2	6	25.0%	5	52	8.8%
Albania	4	3	57.1%	29	29	50.0%
Algeria	2	8	20.0%	7	63	10.0%
Andorra	4	3	57.1%	29	40	42.0%
Angola	2	4	33.3%	9	43	17.3%
Antigua-Barbuda	2	3	40.0%	6	50	10.7%
Argentina	3	5	37.5%	17	51	25.0%
Armenia	3	6	33.3%	18	49	26.9%
Australia	7	2	77.8%	34	26	56.7%
Austria	4	3	57.1%	29	39	42.6%
Azerbaijan	2	8	20.0%	8	56	12.5%
Bahamas	2	5	28.6%	7	57	10.9%
Bahrain	2	8	20.0%	6	62	8.8%
Bangladesh	2	8	20.0%	6	64	8.6%
Barbados	2	6	25.0%	6	57	9.5%
Belarus	1	8	11.1%	5	57	8.1%
Belgium	4	3	57.1%	29	37	43.9%
Belize	3	7	30.0%	8	61	11.6%
Benin	2	7	22.2%	10	57	14.9%
Bhutan	1	5	16.7%	3	39	7.1%
Bolivia	4	6	40.0%	18	60	23.1%
Bosnia/Herzegovina	4	3	57.1%	29	39	42.6%
Botswana	2	7	22.2%	8	56	12.5%
Brazil	2	6	25.0%	10	57	14.9%
Brunei Darussalam	2	8	20.0%	6	63	8.7%
Bulgaria	4	3	57.1%	30	38	44.1%
Burkina Faso	2	7	22.2%	10	60	14.3%
Burundi	2	4	33.3%	6	55	9.8%
Cambodia	2	7	22.2%	8	60	11.8%
Cameroon	2	4	33.3%	12	44	21.4%
Canada	6	2	75.0%	32	32	50.0%
Cape Verde	2	6	25.0%	5	57	8.1%
Central African Rep	2	6	25.0%	10	52	16.1%
Chad	2	1	66.7%	5	17	22.7%
Chile	4	6	40.0%	20	54	27.0%
China	1	8	11.1%	6	62	8.8%

Comparison of Important and Overall Votes (Cont'd)

COUNTRY	IMPORTANT VOTES			OVERALL VOTES		
	IDENTICAL VOTES	OPPOSITE VOTES	PERCENT	IDENTICAL VOTES	OPPOSITE VOTES	PERCENT
Colombia	2	6	25.0%	7	59	10.6%
Comoros	2	6	25.0%	5	57	8.1%
Congo	0	6	0.0%	3	43	6.5%
Costa Rica	3	4	42.9%	15	56	21.1%
Cote d'Ivoire	2	6	25.0%	11	50	18.0%
Croatia	4	3	57.1%	29	39	42.6%
Cuba	1	8	11.1%	5	63	7.4%
Cyprus	4	5	44.4%	29	43	40.3%
Czech Republic	4	3	57.1%	30	37	44.8%
Dem. Rep. of the Congo	2	3	40.0%	9	24	27.3%
DPR of Korea	1	7	12.5%	2	59	3.3%
Denmark	4	3	57.1%	31	38	44.9%
Djibouti	2	8	20.0%	9	62	12.7%
Dominica	2	5	28.6%	6	57	9.5%
Dominican Republic	2	3	40.0%	16	52	23.5%
Ecuador	2	6	25.0%	11	59	15.7%
Egypt	2	8	20.0%	6	65	8.5%
El Salvador	4	4	50.0%	18	56	24.3%
Equatorial Guinea	2	3	40.0%	11	43	20.4%
Eritrea	2	6	25.0%	7	59	10.6%
Estonia	4	3	57.1%	27	38	41.5%
Ethiopia	2	6	25.0%	8	50	13.8%
Fiji	2	4	33.3%	12	53	18.5%
Finland	4	3	57.1%	30	39	43.5%
France	4	3	57.1%	33	28	54.1%
Gabon	2	7	22.2%	7	51	12.1%
Gambia	2	6	25.0%	6	44	12.0%
Georgia	3	3	50.0%	22	38	36.7%
Germany	4	3	57.1%	30	37	44.8%
Ghana	2	7	22.2%	10	59	14.5%
Greece	4	3	57.1%	30	39	43.5%
Grenada	5	3	62.5%	19	46	29.2%
Guatemala	3	3	50.0%	17	54	23.9%
Guinea	2	6	25.0%	8	38	17.4%
Guinea-Bissau	2	6	25.0%	14	52	21.2%
Guyana	2	7	22.2%	9	60	13.0%
Haiti	3	3	50.0%	8	36	18.2%
Honduras	2	3	40.0%	14	45	23.7%
Hungary	4	3	57.1%	29	38	43.3%
Iceland	4	3	57.1%	30	36	45.5%
India	2	8	20.0%	13	52	20.0%
Indonesia	2	8	20.0%	6	66	8.3%
Iran	2	8	20.0%	6	65	8.5%

Comparison of Important and Overall Votes (Cont'd)

COUNTRY	IMPORTANT VOTES IDENTICAL VOTES	IMPORTANT VOTES OPPOSITE VOTES	PERCENT	OVERALL VOTES IDENTICAL VOTES	OVERALL VOTES OPPOSITE VOTES	PERCENT
Iraq	2	6	25.0%	3	51	5.6%
Ireland	4	3	57.1%	28	40	41.2%
Israel	8	0	100.0%	55	4	93.2%
Italy	4	3	57.1%	30	39	43.5%
Jamaica	2	6	25.0%	8	56	12.5%
Japan	4	2	66.7%	27	36	42.9%
Jordan	3	7	30.0%	12	63	16.0%
Kazakhstan	2	7	22.2%	7	57	10.9%
Kenya	2	4	33.3%	8	56	12.5%
Kiribati	1	1	50.0%	1	1	50.0%
Kuwait	2	8	20.0%	7	63	10.0%
Kyrgyzstan	2	5	28.6%	8	52	13.3%
Laos	1	7	12.5%	3	57	5.0%
Latvia	4	3	57.1%	32	36	47.1%
Lebanon	2	8	20.0%	6	63	8.7%
Lesotho	2	7	22.2%	6	61	9.0%
Liberia	2	5	28.6%	8	51	13.6%
Libya	1	8	11.1%	7	65	9.7%
Liechtenstein	4	3	57.1%	28	39	41.8%
Lithuania	4	3	57.1%	30	39	43.5%
Luxembourg	4	3	57.1%	29	38	43.3%
Madagascar	2	7	22.2%	9	62	12.7%
Malawi	3	3	50.0%	9	31	22.5%
Malaysia	2	8	20.0%	6	64	8.6%
Maldives	2	8	20.0%	7	62	10.1%
Mali	2	7	22.2%	10	61	14.1%
Malta	4	5	44.4%	28	42	40.0%
Marshall Islands	8	2	80.0%	44	28	61.1%
Mauritania	2	6	25.0%	3	32	8.6%
Mauritius	2	7	22.2%	8	59	11.9%
Mexico	4	5	44.4%	17	57	23.0%
Micronesia	7	2	77.8%	46	13	78.0%
Monaco	4	3	57.1%	29	33	46.8%
Mongolia	3	3	50.0%	10	58	14.7%
Morocco	2	6	25.0%	8	62	11.4%
Mozambique	2	7	22.2%	6	54	10.0%
Myanmar (Burma)	1	8	11.1%	8	60	11.8%
Namibia	2	7	22.2%	11	62	15.1%
Nauru	6	3	66.7%	21	32	39.6%
Nepal	2	7	22.2%	9	62	12.7%
Netherlands	4	3	57.1%	30	40	42.9%
New Zealand	4	2	66.7%	28	41	40.6%
Nicaragua	4	2	66.7%	18	51	26.1%

Comparison of Important and Overall Votes (Cont'd)

COUNTRY	IMPORTANT VOTES IDENTICAL VOTES	OPPOSITE VOTES	PERCENT	OVERALL VOTES IDENTICAL VOTES	OPPOSITE VOTES	PERCENT
Niger	2	7	22.2%	9	52	14.8%
Nigeria	2	8	20.0%	11	63	14.9%
Norway	4	3	57.1%	29	39	42.6%
Oman	2	8	20.0%	7	64	9.9%
Pakistan	2	8	20.0%	6	56	9.7%
Palau	10	0	100.0%	67	1	98.5%
Panama	4	5	44.4%	18	59	23.4%
Papua New Guinea	3	3	50.0%	11	40	21.6%
Paraguay	4	6	40.0%	18	55	24.7%
Peru	4	3	57.1%	18	54	25.0%
Philippines	2	6	25.0%	9	60	13.0%
Poland	4	3	57.1%	32	38	45.7%
Portugal	4	3	57.1%	30	39	43.5%
Qatar	2	8	20.0%	7	63	10.0%
Republic of Korea	3	2	60.0%	24	37	39.3%
Republic of Moldova	4	3	57.1%	22	38	36.7%
Romania	4	3	57.1%	30	38	44.1%
Russia	2	5	28.6%	11	48	18.6%
Rwanda	2	4	33.3%	6	47	11.3%
St. Kitts and Nevis	0	2	0.0%	1	5	16.7%
Saint Lucia	2	7	22.2%	9	58	13.4%
St. Vincent/Grenadines	3	6	33.3%	9	58	13.4%
Samoa	3	3	50.0%	17	40	29.8%
San Marino	4	3	57.1%	28	40	41.2%
Sao Tome and Principe	2	4	33.3%	5	49	9.3%
Saudi Arabia	1	8	11.1%	5	64	7.2%
Senegal	2	8	20.0%	10	65	13.3%
Serbia/Montenegro	4	3	57.1%	29	39	42.6%
Seychelles	2	4	33.3%	7	40	14.9%
Sierra Leone	2	7	22.2%	8	58	12.1%
Singapore	2	7	22.2%	9	57	13.6%
Slovak Republic	4	3	57.1%	30	39	43.5%
Slovenia	4	3	57.1%	30	38	44.1%
Solomon Islands	3	3	50.0%	12	41	22.6%
Somalia	3	7	30.0%	6	62	8.8%
South Africa	2	8	20.0%	8	62	11.4%
Spain	4	3	57.1%	30	36	45.5%
Sri Lanka	2	8	20.0%	9	61	12.9%
Sudan	2	8	20.0%	10	65	13.3%
Suriname	2	7	22.2%	6	63	8.7%
Swaziland	2	3	40.0%	7	43	14.0%
Sweden	4	3	57.1%	29	39	42.6%
Switzerland	4	3	57.1%	28	38	42.4%

161

Comparison of Important and Overall Votes (Cont'd)

COUNTRY	IMPORTANT VOTES			OVERALL VOTES		
	IDENTICAL VOTES	OPPOSITE VOTES	PERCENT	IDENTICAL VOTES	OPPOSITE VOTES	PERCENT
Syria 1	8	11.1%	7	62	10.1%
Tajikistan 2	7	22.2%	6	49	10.9%
Thailand 2	4	33.3%	10	57	14.9%
TFYR Macedonia. 4	3	57.1%	28	38	42.4%
Timor-Leste 4	3	57.1%	18	55	24.7%
Togo 2	8	20.0%	8	64	11.1%
Tonga 0	3	0.0%	3	35	7.9%
Trinidad and Tobago 2	6	25.0%	11	57	16.2%
Tunisia 2	8	20.0%	7	63	10.0%
Turkey 2	6	25.0%	24	45	34.8%
Turkmenistan 1	7	12.5%	3	49	5.8%
Tuvalu 3	3	50.0%	7	39	15.2%
Uganda 2	4	33.3%	5	55	8.3%
Ukraine 2	4	33.3%	18	45	28.6%
United Arab Emirates 1	7	12.5%	5	62	7.5%
United Kingdom 4	2	66.7%	38	29	56.7%
UR Tanzania 2	6	25.0%	8	59	11.9%
Uruguay 3	4	42.9%	14	54	20.6%
Uzbekistan 2	4	33.3%	5	35	12.5%
Vanuatu 1	2	33.3%	4	29	12.1%
Venezuela 1	8	11.1%	8	65	11.0%
Vietnam 1	8	11.1%	4	63	6.0%
Yemen 2	8	20.0%	6	64	8.6%
Zambia 2	7	22.2%	9	62	12.7%
Zimbabwe 1	8	11.1%	5	64	7.2%
Average 2.7	5.1	35.0%	14.8	48.8	23.3%

V—COUNTRY VOTING PRACTICES

This section consolidates previous information, and presents it by country for 190 UN members (all except the United States). The countries appear in the alphabetical order by which they are seated at the UN General Assembly. Thus, the Democratic People's Republic of Korea is listed under "D," Republic of Korea and Republic of Moldova under "R," The Former Yugoslav Republic of Macedonia under "T," and United Republic of Tanzania under "U." The Democratic Republic of the Congo, formerly Zaire, is listed under "D." Congo (Brazzaville) remains under "C." Burma, which changed its name to Myanmar and is so designated at the United Nations, is listed under "M." Ivory Coast, which changed its name to Cote d'Ivoire, appears under "C." Each country listing contains the following:

—Summary coincidence percentages drawn from Sections III and IV, and, for Security Council members, Section II. Coincidence percentages for selected issue categories are included. These percentages are derived by the same methodology used for overall Plenary votes, i.e., identical votes divided by the sum of identical and opposite votes; abstentions and absences are not included, nor are consensus resolutions.

—Vote totals in the Plenary and on the 10 important Plenary votes.

—Every vote on the 16 important issues, with the U.S. vote in parentheses for comparison. Symbols used are Y=Yes, N=No, A=Abstain, and X=Absent.

Countries two years in arrears in payment of UN dues are not permitted to vote in the Plenary. For 2004, all countries voted. The Palestinian Authority is not a UN member, and therefore has no voting privileges.

AFGHANISTAN

Voting Coincidence Percentages

Overall Votes (79): Agree 5, Disagree 52, Abstain 0, Absent 22: 8.8%
—Including All 213 Consensus Resolutions: 75.6%
—Arms Control: 8.3%; Human Rights: 33.3%; Middle East: 0.0%
Important Votes (10): Agree 2, Disagree 6, Abstain 0, Absent 2: 25.0%
—Including the 16 Important Consensus Resolutions: 69.6%

Important Issues   **VOTES**
1. U.S. Embargo of Cuba..(N) Y
2. Human Rights in Sudan ....(N) X
3. Committee on the Inalienable Rights of the Palestinian People.......(N) Y
4. Division for Palestinian Rights of the Secretariat ....(N) Y
5. Fissile Material Cutoff Treaty...(N) Y
6. Work of the Special Committee to Investigate Israeli Practices ......(N) Y
7. Elimination of all Forms of Religious Intolerance ....(Y) Y
8. Enhancing the Role of Organizations to Promote Democracy.........(Y) Y
9. Human Rights in Iran..(Y) X
10. International Trade and Development...(N) Y

ALBANIA

Voting Coincidence Percentages

Overall Votes (79): Agree 29, Disagree 29, Abstain 15, Absent 6: 50.0%
—Including All 213 Consensus Resolutions: 88.6%
—Arms Control: 38.1%; Human Rights: 76.0%; Middle East: 25.0%
Important Votes (10): Agree 4, Disagree 3, Abstain 3, Absent 0: 57.1%
—Including the 16 Important Consensus Resolutions: 86.2%

Important Issues   **VOTES**
1. U.S. Embargo of Cuba..(N) Y
2. Human Rights in Sudan ....(N) N
3. Committee on the Inalienable Rights of the Palestinian People.......(N) A
4. Division for Palestinian Rights of the Secretariat ....(N) A
5. Fissile Material Cutoff Treaty...(N) Y
6. Work of the Special Committee to Investigate Israeli Practices ......(N) A
7. Elimination of all Forms of Religious Intolerance ....(Y) Y
8. Enhancing the Role of Organizations to Promote Democracy.........(Y) Y
9. Human Rights in Iran..(Y) Y
10. International Trade and Development...(N) Y

Votes: Y=Yes, N=No, A=Abstain, X=Absent, ( )=U.S. Vote

ALGERIA

Voting Coincidence Percentages

Overall Votes (79): Agree 7, Disagree 63, Abstain 8, Absent 1: 10.0%
—Including All 213 Consensus Resolutions: 77.6%
—Arms Control: 9.1%; Human Rights: 18.2%; Middle East: 5.9%
Important Votes (10): Agree 2, Disagree 8, Abstain 0, Absent 0: 20.0%
—Including the 16 Important Consensus Resolutions: 69.0%
Security Council votes: 96.6%

Important Issues	**VOTES**
1. U.S. Embargo of Cuba	(N) Y
2. Human Rights in Sudan	(N) Y
3. Committee on the Inalienable Rights of the Palestinian People	(N) Y
4. Division for Palestinian Rights of the Secretariat	(N) Y
5. Fissile Material Cutoff Treaty	(N) Y
6. Work of the Special Committee to Investigate Israeli Practices	(N) Y
7. Elimination of all Forms of Religious Intolerance	(Y) Y
8. Enhancing the Role of Organizations to Promote Democracy	(Y) Y
9. Human Rights in Iran	(Y) N
10. International Trade and Development	(N) Y

ANDORRA

Voting Coincidence Percentages

Overall Votes (79): Agree 29, Disagree 40, Abstain 9, Absent 1: 42.0%
—Including All 213 Consensus Resolutions: 85.7%
—Arms Control: 33.3%; Human Rights: 76.0%; Middle East: 14.3%
Important Votes (10): Agree 4, Disagree 3, Abstain 3, Absent 0: 57.1%
—Including the 16 Important Consensus Resolutions: 86.9%

Important Issues	**VOTES**
1. U.S. Embargo of Cuba	(N) Y
2. Human Rights in Sudan	(N) N
3. Committee on the Inalienable Rights of the Palestinian People	(N) A
4. Division for Palestinian Rights of the Secretariat	(N) A
5. Fissile Material Cutoff Treaty	(N) Y
6. Work of the Special Committee to Investigate Israeli Practices	(N) A
7. Elimination of all Forms of Religious Intolerance	(Y) Y
8. Enhancing the Role of Organizations to Promote Democracy	(Y) Y
9. Human Rights in Iran	(Y) Y
10. International Trade and Development	(N) Y

Votes: Y=Yes, N=No, A=Abstain, X=Absent, ( )=U.S. Vote

ANGOLA

Voting Coincidence Percentages

Overall Votes (79): Agree 9, Disagree 43, Abstain 7, Absent 20: 17.3%
—Including All 213 Consensus Resolutions: 79.8%
—Arms Control: 13.0%; Human Rights: 35.3%; Middle East: 16.7%
Important Votes (10): Agree 2, Disagree 4, Abstain 1, Absent 3: 33.3%
—Including the 16 Important Consensus Resolutions: 77.9%
Security Council votes: 96.7%

Important Issues	**VOTES**
1. U.S. Embargo of Cuba	(N) Y
2. Human Rights in Sudan	(N) Y
3. Committee on the Inalienable Rights of the Palestinian People	(N) X
4. Division for Palestinian Rights of the Secretariat	(N) X
5. Fissile Material Cutoff Treaty	(N) Y
6. Work of the Special Committee to Investigate Israeli Practices	(N) X
7. Elimination of all Forms of Religious Intolerance	(Y) Y
8. Enhancing the Role of Organizations to Promote Democracy	(Y) Y
9. Human Rights in Iran	(Y) A
10. International Trade and Development	(N) Y

ANTIGUA AND BARBUDA

Voting Coincidence Percentages

Overall Votes (79): Agree 6, Disagree 50, Abstain 12, Absent 11: 10.7%
—Including All 213 Consensus Resolutions: 79.4%
—Arms Control: 8.7%; Human Rights: 21.4%; Middle East: 0.0%
Important Votes (10): Agree 2, Disagree 3, Abstain 2, Absent 3: 40.0%
—Including the 16 Important Consensus Resolutions: 84.2%

Important Issues	**VOTES**
1. U.S. Embargo of Cuba	(N) Y
2. Human Rights in Sudan	(N) X
3. Committee on the Inalienable Rights of the Palestinian People	(N) X
4. Division for Palestinian Rights of the Secretariat	(N) X
5. Fissile Material Cutoff Treaty	(N) Y
6. Work of the Special Committee to Investigate Israeli Practices	(N) A
7. Elimination of all Forms of Religious Intolerance	(Y) Y
8. Enhancing the Role of Organizations to Promote Democracy	(Y) Y
9. Human Rights in Iran	(Y) A
10. International Trade and Development	(N) Y

Votes: Y=Yes, N=No, A=Abstain, X=Absent, ( )=U.S. Vote

ARGENTINA

Voting Coincidence Percentages

<u>Overall Votes (79):</u> Agree 17, Disagree 51, Abstain 11, Absent 0: 25.0%
—Including All 213 Consensus Resolutions: 81.9%
—Arms Control: 15.8%; Human Rights: 56.5%; Middle East: 5.9%
<u>Important Votes (10):</u> Agree 3, Disagree 5, Abstain 2, Absent 0: 37.5%
—Including the 16 Important Consensus Resolutions: 79.2%

Important Issues	**VOTES**
1. U.S. Embargo of Cuba	(N) Y
2. Human Rights in Sudan	(N) N
3. Committee on the Inalienable Rights of the Palestinian People	(N) Y
4. Division for Palestinian Rights of the Secretariat	(N) Y
5. Fissile Material Cutoff Treaty	(N) Y
6. Work of the Special Committee to Investigate Israeli Practices	(N) A
7. Elimination of all Forms of Religious Intolerance	(Y) Y
8. Enhancing the Role of Organizations to Promote Democracy	(Y) Y
9. Human Rights in Iran	(Y) A
10. International Trade and Development	(N) Y

ARMENIA

Voting Coincidence Percentages

<u>Overall Votes (79):</u> Agree 18, Disagree 49, Abstain 11, Absent 1: 26.9%
—Including All 213 Consensus Resolutions: 82.4%
—Arms Control: 16.7%; Human Rights: 54.2%; Middle East: 6.3%
<u>Important Votes (10):</u> Agree 3, Disagree 6, Abstain 1, Absent 0: 33.3%
—Including the 16 Important Consensus Resolutions: 75.8%

Important Issues	**VOTES**
1. U.S. Embargo of Cuba	(N) Y
2. Human Rights in Sudan	(N) N
3. Committee on the Inalienable Rights of the Palestinian People	(N) Y
4. Division for Palestinian Rights of the Secretariat	(N) A
5. Fissile Material Cutoff Treaty	(N) Y
6. Work of the Special Committee to Investigate Israeli Practices	(N) Y
7. Elimination of all Forms of Religious Intolerance	(Y) Y
8. Enhancing the Role of Organizations to Promote Democracy	(Y) Y
9. Human Rights in Iran	(Y) N
10. International Trade and Development	(N) Y

Votes: Y=Yes, N=No, A=Abstain, X=Absent, ( )=U.S. Vote

AUSTRALIA

Voting Coincidence Percentages

Overall Votes (79): Agree 34, Disagree 26, Abstain 17, Absent 2: 56.7%
—Including All 213 Consensus Resolutions: 90.3%
—Arms Control: 35.3%; Human Rights: 82.6%; Middle East: 58.3%
Important Votes (10): Agree 7, Disagree 2, Abstain 1, Absent 0: 77.8%
—Including the 16 Important Consensus Resolutions: 91.9%

Important Issues	**VOTES**
1. U.S. Embargo of Cuba	(N) Y
2. Human Rights in Sudan	(N) N
3. Committee on the Inalienable Rights of the Palestinian People	(N) N
4. Division for Palestinian Rights of the Secretariat	(N) N
5. Fissile Material Cutoff Treaty	(N) Y
6. Work of the Special Committee to Investigate Israeli Practices	(N) N
7. Elimination of all Forms of Religious Intolerance	(Y) Y
8. Enhancing the Role of Organizations to Promote Democracy	(Y) Y
9. Human Rights in Iran	(Y) Y
10. International Trade and Development	(N) A

AUSTRIA

Voting Coincidence Percentages

Overall Votes (79): Agree 29, Disagree 39, Abstain 11, Absent 0: 42.6%
—Including All 213 Consensus Resolutions: 86.1%
—Arms Control: 33.3%; Human Rights: 76.0%; Middle East: 14.3%
Important Votes (10): Agree 4, Disagree 3, Abstain 3, Absent 0: 57.1%
—Including the 16 Important Consensus Resolutions: 87.0%

Important Issues	**VOTES**
1. U.S. Embargo of Cuba	(N) Y
2. Human Rights in Sudan	(N) N
3. Committee on the Inalienable Rights of the Palestinian People	(N) A
4. Division for Palestinian Rights of the Secretariat	(N) A
5. Fissile Material Cutoff Treaty	(N) Y
6. Work of the Special Committee to Investigate Israeli Practices	(N) A
7. Elimination of all Forms of Religious Intolerance	(Y) Y
8. Enhancing the Role of Organizations to Promote Democracy	(Y) Y
9. Human Rights in Iran	(Y) Y
10. International Trade and Development	(N) Y

Votes: Y=Yes, N=No, A=Abstain, X=Absent, ( )=U.S. Vote

AZERBAIJAN

Voting Coincidence Percentages

Overall Votes (79): Agree 8, Disagree 56, Abstain 8, Absent 7: 12.5%
—Including All 213 Consensus Resolutions: 78.5%
—Arms Control: 16.7%; Human Rights: 23.8%; Middle East: 5.9%
Important Votes (10): Agree 2, Disagree 8, Abstain 0, Absent 0: 20.0%
—Including the 16 Important Consensus Resolutions: 67.7%

Important Issues	**VOTES**
1. U.S. Embargo of Cuba	(N) Y
2. Human Rights in Sudan	(N) Y
3. Committee on the Inalienable Rights of the Palestinian People	(N) Y
4. Division for Palestinian Rights of the Secretariat	(N) Y
5. Fissile Material Cutoff Treaty	(N) Y
6. Work of the Special Committee to Investigate Israeli Practices	(N) Y
7. Elimination of all Forms of Religious Intolerance	(Y) Y
8. Enhancing the Role of Organizations to Promote Democracy	(Y) Y
9. Human Rights in Iran	(Y) N
10. International Trade and Development	(N) Y

BAHAMAS

Voting Coincidence Percentages

Overall Votes (79): Agree 7, Disagree 57, Abstain 10, Absent 5: 10.9%
—Including All 213 Consensus Resolutions: 78.3%
—Arms Control: 8.7%; Human Rights: 25.0%; Middle East: 0.0%
Important Votes (10): Agree 2, Disagree 5, Abstain 2, Absent 1: 28.6%
—Including the 16 Important Consensus Resolutions: 77.2%

Important Issues	**VOTES**
1. U.S. Embargo of Cuba	(N) Y
2. Human Rights in Sudan	(N) X
3. Committee on the Inalienable Rights of the Palestinian People	(N) Y
4. Division for Palestinian Rights of the Secretariat	(N) Y
5. Fissile Material Cutoff Treaty	(N) Y
6. Work of the Special Committee to Investigate Israeli Practices	(N) A
7. Elimination of all Forms of Religious Intolerance	(Y) Y
8. Enhancing the Role of Organizations to Promote Democracy	(Y) Y
9. Human Rights in Iran	(Y) A
10. International Trade and Development	(N) Y

Votes: Y=Yes, N=No, A=Abstain, X=Absent, ( )=U.S. Vote

BAHRAIN

Voting Coincidence Percentages

Overall Votes (79): Agree 6, Disagree 62, Abstain 8, Absent 3: 8.8%
—Including All 213 Consensus Resolutions: 77.4%
—Arms Control: 8.7%; Human Rights: 15.0%; Middle East: 5.9%
Important Votes (10): Agree 2, Disagree 8, Abstain 0, Absent 0: 20.0%
—Including the 16 Important Consensus Resolutions: 68.6%

Important Issues	**VOTES**
1. U.S. Embargo of Cuba	(N) Y
2. Human Rights in Sudan	(N) Y
3. Committee on the Inalienable Rights of the Palestinian People	(N) Y
4. Division for Palestinian Rights of the Secretariat	(N) Y
5. Fissile Material Cutoff Treaty	(N) Y
6. Work of the Special Committee to Investigate Israeli Practices	(N) Y
7. Elimination of all Forms of Religious Intolerance	(Y) Y
8. Enhancing the Role of Organizations to Promote Democracy	(Y) Y
9. Human Rights in Iran	(Y) N
10. International Trade and Development	(N) Y

BANGLADESH

Voting Coincidence Percentages

Overall Votes (79): Agree 6, Disagree 64, Abstain 9, Absent 0: 8.6%
—Including All 213 Consensus Resolutions: 77.4%
—Arms Control: 8.3%; Human Rights: 15.0%; Middle East: 5.9%
Important Votes (10): Agree 2, Disagree 8, Abstain 0, Absent 0: 20.0%
—Including the 16 Important Consensus Resolutions: 69.2%

Important Issues	**VOTES**
1. U.S. Embargo of Cuba	(N) Y
2. Human Rights in Sudan	(N) Y
3. Committee on the Inalienable Rights of the Palestinian People	(N) Y
4. Division for Palestinian Rights of the Secretariat	(N) Y
5. Fissile Material Cutoff Treaty	(N) Y
6. Work of the Special Committee to Investigate Israeli Practices	(N) Y
7. Elimination of all Forms of Religious Intolerance	(Y) Y
8. Enhancing the Role of Organizations to Promote Democracy	(Y) Y
9. Human Rights in Iran	(Y) N
10. International Trade and Development	(N) Y

Votes: Y=Yes, N=No, A=Abstain, X=Absent, ( )=U.S. Vote

BARBADOS

Voting Coincidence Percentages

Overall Votes (79): Agree 6, Disagree 57, Abstain 11, Absent 5: 9.5%
—Including All 213 Consensus Resolutions: 78.4%
—Arms Control: 8.7%; Human Rights: 25.0%; Middle East: 0.0%
Important Votes (10): Agree 2, Disagree 6, Abstain 1, Absent 1: 25.0%
—Including the 16 Important Consensus Resolutions: 74.0%

Important Issues	**VOTES**
1. U.S. Embargo of Cuba	(N) Y
2. Human Rights in Sudan	(N) Y
3. Committee on the Inalienable Rights of the Palestinian People	(N) X
4. Division for Palestinian Rights of the Secretariat	(N) Y
5. Fissile Material Cutoff Treaty	(N) Y
6. Work of the Special Committee to Investigate Israeli Practices	(N) Y
7. Elimination of all Forms of Religious Intolerance	(Y) Y
8. Enhancing the Role of Organizations to Promote Democracy	(Y) Y
9. Human Rights in Iran	(Y) A
10. International Trade and Development	(N) Y

BELARUS

Voting Coincidence Percentages

Overall Votes (79): Agree 5, Disagree 57, Abstain 12, Absent 5: 8.1%
—Including All 213 Consensus Resolutions: 78.1%
—Arms Control: 16.7%; Human Rights: 11.1%; Middle East: 5.6%
Important Votes (10): Agree 1, Disagree 8, Abstain 1, Absent 0: 11.1%
—Including the 16 Important Consensus Resolutions: 66.6%

Important Issues	**VOTES**
1. U.S. Embargo of Cuba	(N) Y
2. Human Rights in Sudan	(N) Y
3. Committee on the Inalienable Rights of the Palestinian People	(N) Y
4. Division for Palestinian Rights of the Secretariat	(N) Y
5. Fissile Material Cutoff Treaty	(N) Y
6. Work of the Special Committee to Investigate Israeli Practices	(N) Y
7. Elimination of all Forms of Religious Intolerance	(Y) Y
8. Enhancing the Role of Organizations to Promote Democracy	(Y) A
9. Human Rights in Iran	(Y) N
10. International Trade and Development	(N) Y

Votes: Y=Yes, N=No, A=Abstain, X=Absent, ( )=U.S. Vote

BELGIUM

Voting Coincidence Percentages

Overall Votes (79): Agree 29, Disagree 37, Abstain 11, Absent 2: 43.9%
—Including All 213 Consensus Resolutions: 86.5%
—Arms Control: 35.0%; Human Rights: 76.0%; Middle East: 7.7%
Important Votes (10): Agree 4, Disagree 3, Abstain 3, Absent 0: 57.1%
—Including the 16 Important Consensus Resolutions: 86.8%

Important Issues	**VOTES**
1. U.S. Embargo of Cuba	(N) Y
2. Human Rights in Sudan	(N) N
3. Committee on the Inalienable Rights of the Palestinian People	(N) A
4. Division for Palestinian Rights of the Secretariat	(N) A
5. Fissile Material Cutoff Treaty	(N) Y
6. Work of the Special Committee to Investigate Israeli Practices	(N) A
7. Elimination of all Forms of Religious Intolerance	(Y) Y
8. Enhancing the Role of Organizations to Promote Democracy	(Y) Y
9. Human Rights in Iran	(Y) Y
10. International Trade and Development	(N) Y

BELIZE

Voting Coincidence Percentages

Overall Votes (79): Agree 8, Disagree 61, Abstain 8, Absent 2: 11.6%
—Including All 213 Consensus Resolutions: 77.8%
—Arms Control: 8.7%; Human Rights: 26.3%; Middle East: 0.0%
Important Votes (10): Agree 3, Disagree 7, Abstain 0, Absent 0: 30.0%
—Including the 16 Important Consensus Resolutions: 72.5%

Important Issues	**VOTES**
1. U.S. Embargo of Cuba	(N) Y
2. Human Rights in Sudan	(N) Y
3. Committee on the Inalienable Rights of the Palestinian People	(N) Y
4. Division for Palestinian Rights of the Secretariat	(N) Y
5. Fissile Material Cutoff Treaty	(N) Y
6. Work of the Special Committee to Investigate Israeli Practices	(N) Y
7. Elimination of all Forms of Religious Intolerance	(Y) Y
8. Enhancing the Role of Organizations to Promote Democracy	(Y) Y
9. Human Rights in Iran	(Y) Y
10. International Trade and Development	(N) Y

Votes: Y=Yes, N=No, A=Abstain, X=Absent, ( )=U.S. Vote

BENIN

Voting Coincidence Percentages

<u>Overall Votes (79):</u> Agree 10, Disagree 57, Abstain 6, Absent 6: 14.9%
—Including All 213 Consensus Resolutions: 78.6%
—Arms Control: 12.5%; Human Rights: 38.9%; Middle East: 5.9%
<u>Important Votes (10):</u> Agree 2, Disagree 7, Abstain 1, Absent 0: 22.2%
—Including the 16 Important Consensus Resolutions: 70.8%
Security Council votes: 96.7%

Important Issues	**VOTES**
1. U.S. Embargo of Cuba	(N) Y
2. Human Rights in Sudan	(N) Y
3. Committee on the Inalienable Rights of the Palestinian People	(N) Y
4. Division for Palestinian Rights of the Secretariat	(N) Y
5. Fissile Material Cutoff Treaty	(N) Y
6. Work of the Special Committee to Investigate Israeli Practices	(N) Y
7. Elimination of all Forms of Religious Intolerance	(Y) Y
8. Enhancing the Role of Organizations to Promote Democracy	(Y) Y
9. Human Rights in Iran	(Y) A
10. International Trade and Development	(N) Y

BHUTAN

Voting Coincidence Percentages

<u>Overall Votes (79):</u> Agree 3, Disagree 39, Abstain 19, Absent 18: 7.1%
—Including All 213 Consensus Resolutions: 80.6%
—Arms Control: 6.3%; Human Rights: 13.3%; Middle East: 0.0%
<u>Important Votes (10):</u> Agree 1, Disagree 5, Abstain 2, Absent 2: 16.7%
—Including the 16 Important Consensus Resolutions: 72.1%

Important Issues	**VOTES**
1. U.S. Embargo of Cuba	(N) Y
2. Human Rights in Sudan	(N) Y
3. Committee on the Inalienable Rights of the Palestinian People	(N) Y
4. Division for Palestinian Rights of the Secretariat	(N) Y
5. Fissile Material Cutoff Treaty	(N) Y
6. Work of the Special Committee to Investigate Israeli Practices	(N) X
7. Elimination of all Forms of Religious Intolerance	(Y) Y
8. Enhancing the Role of Organizations to Promote Democracy	(Y) A
9. Human Rights in Iran	(Y) A
10. International Trade and Development	(N) X

Votes: Y=Yes, N=No, A=Abstain, X=Absent, ( )=U.S. Vote

BOLIVIA

Voting Coincidence Percentages

Overall Votes (79): Agree 18, Disagree 60, Abstain 1, Absent 0: 23.1%
—Including All 213 Consensus Resolutions: 79.4%
—Arms Control: 12.5%; Human Rights: 51.9%; Middle East: 5.6%
Important Votes (10): Agree 4, Disagree 6, Abstain 0, Absent 0: 40.0%
—Including the 16 Important Consensus Resolutions: 76.9%

Important Issues	**VOTES**
1. U.S. Embargo of Cuba	(N) Y
2. Human Rights in Sudan	(N) N
3. Committee on the Inalienable Rights of the Palestinian People	(N) Y
4. Division for Palestinian Rights of the Secretariat	(N) Y
5. Fissile Material Cutoff Treaty	(N) Y
6. Work of the Special Committee to Investigate Israeli Practices	(N) Y
7. Elimination of all Forms of Religious Intolerance	(Y) Y
8. Enhancing the Role of Organizations to Promote Democracy	(Y) Y
9. Human Rights in Iran	(Y) Y
10. International Trade and Development	(N) Y

BOSNIA AND HERZEGOVINA

Voting Coincidence Percentages

Overall Votes (79): Agree 29, Disagree 39, Abstain 11, Absent 0: 42.6%
—Including All 213 Consensus Resolutions: 86.1%
—Arms Control: 35.0%; Human Rights: 76.0%; Middle East: 14.3%
Important Votes (10): Agree 4, Disagree 3, Abstain 3, Absent 0: 57.1%
—Including the 16 Important Consensus Resolutions: 87.0%

Important Issues	**VOTES**
1. U.S. Embargo of Cuba	(N) Y
2. Human Rights in Sudan	(N) N
3. Committee on the Inalienable Rights of the Palestinian People	(N) A
4. Division for Palestinian Rights of the Secretariat	(N) A
5. Fissile Material Cutoff Treaty	(N) Y
6. Work of the Special Committee to Investigate Israeli Practices	(N) A
7. Elimination of all Forms of Religious Intolerance	(Y) Y
8. Enhancing the Role of Organizations to Promote Democracy	(Y) Y
9. Human Rights in Iran	(Y) Y
10. International Trade and Development	(N) Y

Votes: Y=Yes, N=No, A=Abstain, X=Absent, ( )=U.S. Vote

BOTSWANA

Voting Coincidence Percentages

Overall Votes (79): Agree 8, Disagree 56, Abstain 5, Absent 10: 12.5%
—Including All 213 Consensus Resolutions: 77.3%
—Arms Control: 8.7%; Human Rights: 31.3%; Middle East: 0.0%
Important Votes (10): Agree 2, Disagree 7, Abstain 1, Absent 0: 22.2%
—Including the 16 Important Consensus Resolutions: 69.1%

Important Issues	**VOTES**
1. U.S. Embargo of Cuba	(N) Y
2. Human Rights in Sudan	(N) Y
3. Committee on the Inalienable Rights of the Palestinian People	(N) Y
4. Division for Palestinian Rights of the Secretariat	(N) Y
5. Fissile Material Cutoff Treaty	(N) Y
6. Work of the Special Committee to Investigate Israeli Practices	(N) Y
7. Elimination of all Forms of Religious Intolerance	(Y) Y
8. Enhancing the Role of Organizations to Promote Democracy	(Y) Y
9. Human Rights in Iran	(Y) A
10. International Trade and Development	(N) Y

BRAZIL

Voting Coincidence Percentages

Overall Votes (79): Agree 10, Disagree 57, Abstain 12, Absent 0: 14.9%
—Including All 213 Consensus Resolutions: 79.6%
—Arms Control: 8.7%; Human Rights: 38.9%; Middle East: 5.6%
Important Votes (10): Agree 2, Disagree 6, Abstain 2, Absent 0: 25.0%
—Including the 16 Important Consensus Resolutions: 75.0%
Security Council votes: 96.7%

Important Issues	**VOTES**
1. U.S. Embargo of Cuba	(N) Y
2. Human Rights in Sudan	(N) A
3. Committee on the Inalienable Rights of the Palestinian People	(N) Y
4. Division for Palestinian Rights of the Secretariat	(N) Y
5. Fissile Material Cutoff Treaty	(N) Y
6. Work of the Special Committee to Investigate Israeli Practices	(N) Y
7. Elimination of all Forms of Religious Intolerance	(Y) Y
8. Enhancing the Role of Organizations to Promote Democracy	(Y) Y
9. Human Rights in Iran	(Y) A
10. International Trade and Development	(N) Y

Votes: Y=Yes, N=No, A=Abstain, X=Absent, ( )=U.S. Vote

BRUNEI DARUSSALAM

Voting Coincidence Percentages

Overall Votes (79): Agree 6, Disagree 63, Abstain 10, Absent 0: 8.7%
—Including All 213 Consensus Resolutions: 77.7%
—Arms Control: 12.0%; Human Rights: 11.1%; Middle East: 5.9%
Important Votes (10): Agree 2, Disagree 8, Abstain 0, Absent 0: 20.0%
—Including the 16 Important Consensus Resolutions: 69.2%

Important Issues	**VOTES**
1. U.S. Embargo of Cuba	(N) Y
2. Human Rights in Sudan	(N) Y
3. Committee on the Inalienable Rights of the Palestinian People	(N) Y
4. Division for Palestinian Rights of the Secretariat	(N) Y
5. Fissile Material Cutoff Treaty	(N) Y
6. Work of the Special Committee to Investigate Israeli Practices	(N) Y
7. Elimination of all Forms of Religious Intolerance	(Y) Y
8. Enhancing the Role of Organizations to Promote Democracy	(Y) Y
9. Human Rights in Iran	(Y) N
10. International Trade and Development	(N) Y

BULGARIA

Voting Coincidence Percentages

Overall Votes (79): Agree 30, Disagree 38, Abstain 11, Absent 0: 44.1%
—Including All 213 Consensus Resolutions: 86.5%
—Arms Control: 38.1%; Human Rights: 76.0%; Middle East: 14.3%
Important Votes (10): Agree 4, Disagree 3, Abstain 3, Absent 0: 57.1%
—Including the 16 Important Consensus Resolutions: 87.0%

Important Issues	**VOTES**
1. U.S. Embargo of Cuba	(N) Y
2. Human Rights in Sudan	(N) N
3. Committee on the Inalienable Rights of the Palestinian People	(N) A
4. Division for Palestinian Rights of the Secretariat	(N) A
5. Fissile Material Cutoff Treaty	(N) Y
6. Work of the Special Committee to Investigate Israeli Practices	(N) A
7. Elimination of all Forms of Religious Intolerance	(Y) Y
8. Enhancing the Role of Organizations to Promote Democracy	(Y) Y
9. Human Rights in Iran	(Y) Y
10. International Trade and Development	(N) Y

Votes: Y=Yes, N=No, A=Abstain, X=Absent, ( )=U.S. Vote

BURKINA FASO

Voting Coincidence Percentages

<u>Overall Votes (79):</u> Agree 10, Disagree 60, Abstain 6, Absent 3: 14.3%
—Including All 213 Consensus Resolutions: 78.3%
—Arms Control: 12.5%; Human Rights: 33.3%; Middle East: 5.9%
<u>Important Votes (10):</u> Agree 2, Disagree 7, Abstain 1, Absent 0: 22.2%
—Including the 16 Important Consensus Resolutions: 71.4%

Important Issues	**VOTES**
1. U.S. Embargo of Cuba	(N) Y
2. Human Rights in Sudan	(N) Y
3. Committee on the Inalienable Rights of the Palestinian People	(N) Y
4. Division for Palestinian Rights of the Secretariat	(N) Y
5. Fissile Material Cutoff Treaty	(N) Y
6. Work of the Special Committee to Investigate Israeli Practices	(N) Y
7. Elimination of all Forms of Religious Intolerance	(Y) Y
8. Enhancing the Role of Organizations to Promote Democracy	(Y) Y
9. Human Rights in Iran	(Y) A
10. International Trade and Development	(N) Y

BURUNDI

Voting Coincidence Percentages

<u>Overall Votes (79):</u> Agree 6, Disagree 55, Abstain 9, Absent 9: 9.8%
—Including All 213 Consensus Resolutions: 78.2%
—Arms Control: 8.7%; Human Rights: 22.2%; Middle East: 0.0%
<u>Important Votes (10):</u> Agree 2, Disagree 4, Abstain 4, Absent 0: 33.3%
—Including the 16 Important Consensus Resolutions: 80.4%

Important Issues	**VOTES**
1. U.S. Embargo of Cuba	(N) Y
2. Human Rights in Sudan	(N) Y
3. Committee on the Inalienable Rights of the Palestinian People	(N) A
4. Division for Palestinian Rights of the Secretariat	(N) A
5. Fissile Material Cutoff Treaty	(N) Y
6. Work of the Special Committee to Investigate Israeli Practices	(N) A
7. Elimination of all Forms of Religious Intolerance	(Y) Y
8. Enhancing the Role of Organizations to Promote Democracy	(Y) Y
9. Human Rights in Iran	(Y) A
10. International Trade and Development	(N) Y

Votes: Y=Yes, N=No, A=Abstain, X=Absent, ( )=U.S. Vote

CAMBODIA

Voting Coincidence Percentages

Overall Votes (79): Agree 8, Disagree 60, Abstain 7, Absent 4: 11.8%
—Including All 213 Consensus Resolutions: 77.7%
—Arms Control: 8.7%; Human Rights: 30.0%; Middle East: 0.0%
Important Votes (10): Agree 2, Disagree 7, Abstain 1, Absent 0: 22.2%
—Including the 16 Important Consensus Resolutions: 71.0%

Important Issues   **VOTES**
1. U.S. Embargo of Cuba ....(N) Y
2. Human Rights in Sudan ....(N) Y
3. Committee on the Inalienable Rights of the Palestinian People ....(N) Y
4. Division for Palestinian Rights of the Secretariat ....(N) Y
5. Fissile Material Cutoff Treaty ....(N) Y
6. Work of the Special Committee to Investigate Israeli Practices ......(N) Y
7. Elimination of all Forms of Religious Intolerance ....(Y) Y
8. Enhancing the Role of Organizations to Promote Democracy ....(Y) Y
9. Human Rights in Iran ....(Y) A
10. International Trade and Development ....(N) Y

CAMEROON

Voting Coincidence Percentages

Overall Votes (79): Agree 12, Disagree 44, Abstain 20, Absent 3: 21.4%
—Including All 213 Consensus Resolutions: 83.2%
—Arms Control: 13.6%; Human Rights: 36.4%; Middle East: 33.3%
Important Votes (10): Agree 2, Disagree 4, Abstain 4, Absent 0: 33.3%
—Including the 16 Important Consensus Resolutions: 81.4%

Important Issues   **VOTES**
1. U.S. Embargo of Cuba ....(N) Y
2. Human Rights in Sudan ....(N) Y
3. Committee on the Inalienable Rights of the Palestinian People ....(N) A
4. Division for Palestinian Rights of the Secretariat ....(N) Y
5. Fissile Material Cutoff Treaty ....(N) Y
6. Work of the Special Committee to Investigate Israeli Practices ......(N) A
7. Elimination of all Forms of Religious Intolerance ....(Y) Y
8. Enhancing the Role of Organizations to Promote Democracy ....(Y) Y
9. Human Rights in Iran ....(Y) A
10. International Trade and Development ....(N) Y

Votes: Y=Yes, N=No, A=Abstain, X=Absent, ( )=U.S. Vote

CANADA

Voting Coincidence Percentages

Overall Votes (79): Agree 32, Disagree 32, Abstain 13, Absent 2: 50.0%
—Including All 213 Consensus Resolutions: 88.2%
—Arms Control: 36.8%; Human Rights: 82.6%; Middle East: 26.7%
Important Votes (10): Agree 6, Disagree 2, Abstain 2, Absent 0: 75.0%
—Including the 16 Important Consensus Resolutions: 91.5%

Important Issues	**VOTES**
1. U.S. Embargo of Cuba	(N) Y
2. Human Rights in Sudan	(N) N
3. Committee on the Inalienable Rights of the Palestinian People	(N) N
4. Division for Palestinian Rights of the Secretariat	(N) A
5. Fissile Material Cutoff Treaty	(N) Y
6. Work of the Special Committee to Investigate Israeli Practices	(N) N
7. Elimination of all Forms of Religious Intolerance	(Y) Y
8. Enhancing the Role of Organizations to Promote Democracy	(Y) Y
9. Human Rights in Iran	(Y) Y
10. International Trade and Development	(N) A

CAPE VERDE

Voting Coincidence Percentages

Overall Votes (79): Agree 5, Disagree 57, Abstain 5, Absent 12: 8.1%
—Including All 213 Consensus Resolutions: 76.7%
—Arms Control: 8.7%; Human Rights: 20.0%; Middle East: 0.0%
Important Votes (10): Agree 2, Disagree 6, Abstain 1, Absent 1: 25.0%
—Including the 16 Important Consensus Resolutions: 72.3%

Important Issues	**VOTES**
1. U.S. Embargo of Cuba	(N) Y
2. Human Rights in Sudan	(N) Y
3. Committee on the Inalienable Rights of the Palestinian People	(N) Y
4. Division for Palestinian Rights of the Secretariat	(N) Y
5. Fissile Material Cutoff Treaty	(N) Y
6. Work of the Special Committee to Investigate Israeli Practices	(N) Y
7. Elimination of all Forms of Religious Intolerance	(Y) Y
8. Enhancing the Role of Organizations to Promote Democracy	(Y) Y
9. Human Rights in Iran	(Y) A
10. International Trade and Development	(N) X

Votes: Y=Yes, N=No, A=Abstain, X=Absent, ( )=U.S. Vote

CENTRAL AFRICAN REPUBLIC

Voting Coincidence Percentages

Overall Votes (79): Agree 10, Disagree 52, Abstain 4, Absent 13: 16.1%
—Including All 213 Consensus Resolutions: 78.1%
—Arms Control: 12.0%; Human Rights: 35.0%; Middle East: 11.1%
Important Votes (10): Agree 2, Disagree 6, Abstain 1, Absent 1: 25.0%
—Including the 16 Important Consensus Resolutions: 71.6%

Important Issues	**VOTES**
1. U.S. Embargo of Cuba	(N) Y
2. Human Rights in Sudan	(N) Y
3. Committee on the Inalienable Rights of the Palestinian People	(N) Y
4. Division for Palestinian Rights of the Secretariat	(N) Y
5. Fissile Material Cutoff Treaty	(N) Y
6. Work of the Special Committee to Investigate Israeli Practices	(N) X
7. Elimination of all Forms of Religious Intolerance	(Y) Y
8. Enhancing the Role of Organizations to Promote Democracy	(Y) Y
9. Human Rights in Iran	(Y) A
10. International Trade and Development	(N) Y

CHAD

Voting Coincidence Percentages

Overall Votes (79): Agree 5, Disagree 17, Abstain 1, Absent 56: 22.7%
—Including All 213 Consensus Resolutions: 78.4%
—Arms Control: 0.0%; Human Rights: 26.3%; Middle East: 0.0%
Important Votes (10): Agree 2, Disagree 1, Abstain 0, Absent 7: 66.7%
—Including the 16 Important Consensus Resolutions: 86.2%

Important Issues	**VOTES**
1. U.S. Embargo of Cuba	(N) X
2. Human Rights in Sudan	(N) X
3. Committee on the Inalienable Rights of the Palestinian People	(N) X
4. Division for Palestinian Rights of the Secretariat	(N) X
5. Fissile Material Cutoff Treaty	(N) X
6. Work of the Special Committee to Investigate Israeli Practices	(N) X
7. Elimination of all Forms of Religious Intolerance	(Y) Y
8. Enhancing the Role of Organizations to Promote Democracy	(Y) Y
9. Human Rights in Iran	(Y) N
10. International Trade and Development	(N) X

Votes: Y=Yes, N=No, A=Abstain, X=Absent, ( )=U.S. Vote

CHILE

Voting Coincidence Percentages

Overall Votes (79): Agree 20, Disagree 54, Abstain 4, Absent 1: 27.0%
—Including All 213 Consensus Resolutions: 80.9%
—Arms Control: 12.5%; Human Rights: 62.5%; Middle East: 5.6%
Important Votes (10): Agree 4, Disagree 6, Abstain 0, Absent 0: 40.0%
—Including the 16 Important Consensus Resolutions: 76.6%
Security Council votes: 96.7%

Important Issues	**VOTES**
1. U.S. Embargo of Cuba	(N) Y
2. Human Rights in Sudan	(N) N
3. Committee on the Inalienable Rights of the Palestinian People	(N) Y
4. Division for Palestinian Rights of the Secretariat	(N) Y
5. Fissile Material Cutoff Treaty	(N) Y
6. Work of the Special Committee to Investigate Israeli Practices	(N) Y
7. Elimination of all Forms of Religious Intolerance	(Y) Y
8. Enhancing the Role of Organizations to Promote Democracy	(Y) Y
9. Human Rights in Iran	(Y) Y
10. International Trade and Development	(N) Y

CHINA

Voting Coincidence Percentages

Overall Votes (79): Agree 6, Disagree 62, Abstain 10, Absent 1: 8.8%
—Including All 213 Consensus Resolutions: 77.6%
—Arms Control: 13.0%; Human Rights: 10.5%; Middle East: 5.9%
Important Votes (10): Agree 1, Disagree 8, Abstain 1, Absent 0: 11.1%
—Including the 16 Important Consensus Resolutions: 67.5%
Security Council votes: 96.6%

Important Issues	**VOTES**
1. U.S. Embargo of Cuba	(N) Y
2. Human Rights in Sudan	(N) Y
3. Committee on the Inalienable Rights of the Palestinian People	(N) Y
4. Division for Palestinian Rights of the Secretariat	(N) Y
5. Fissile Material Cutoff Treaty	(N) Y
6. Work of the Special Committee to Investigate Israeli Practices	(N) Y
7. Elimination of all Forms of Religious Intolerance	(Y) Y
8. Enhancing the Role of Organizations to Promote Democracy	(Y) A
9. Human Rights in Iran	(Y) N
10. International Trade and Development	(N) Y

Votes: Y=Yes, N=No, A=Abstain, X=Absent, ( )=U.S. Vote

COLOMBIA

Voting Coincidence Percentages

Overall Votes (79): Agree 7, Disagree 59, Abstain 13, Absent 0: 10.6%
—Including All 213 Consensus Resolutions: 78.9%
—Arms Control: 12.5%; Human Rights: 25.0%; Middle East: 5.6%
Important Votes (10): Agree 2, Disagree 6, Abstain 2, Absent 0: 25.0%
—Including the 16 Important Consensus Resolutions: 75.0%

Important Issues	**VOTES**
1. U.S. Embargo of Cuba	(N) Y
2. Human Rights in Sudan	(N) A
3. Committee on the Inalienable Rights of the Palestinian People	(N) Y
4. Division for Palestinian Rights of the Secretariat	(N) Y
5. Fissile Material Cutoff Treaty	(N) Y
6. Work of the Special Committee to Investigate Israeli Practices	(N) Y
7. Elimination of all Forms of Religious Intolerance	(Y) Y
8. Enhancing the Role of Organizations to Promote Democracy	(Y) Y
9. Human Rights in Iran	(Y) A
10. International Trade and Development	(N) Y

COMOROS

Voting Coincidence Percentages

Overall Votes (79): Agree 5, Disagree 57, Abstain 4, Absent 13: 8.1%
—Including All 213 Consensus Resolutions: 76.7%
—Arms Control: 8.7%; Human Rights: 15.0%; Middle East: 0.0%
Important Votes (10): Agree 2, Disagree 6, Abstain 0, Absent 2: 25.0%
—Including the 16 Important Consensus Resolutions: 72.3%

Important Issues	**VOTES**
1. U.S. Embargo of Cuba	(N) Y
2. Human Rights in Sudan	(N) Y
3. Committee on the Inalienable Rights of the Palestinian People	(N) X
4. Division for Palestinian Rights of the Secretariat	(N) X
5. Fissile Material Cutoff Treaty	(N) Y
6. Work of the Special Committee to Investigate Israeli Practices	(N) Y
7. Elimination of all Forms of Religious Intolerance	(Y) Y
8. Enhancing the Role of Organizations to Promote Democracy	(Y) Y
9. Human Rights in Iran	(Y) N
10. International Trade and Development	(N) Y

Votes: Y=Yes, N=No, A=Abstain, X=Absent, ( )=U.S. Vote

CONGO

Voting Coincidence Percentages

Overall Votes (79): Agree 3, Disagree 43, Abstain 1, Absent 32: 6.5%
—Including All 213 Consensus Resolutions: 75.9%
—Arms Control: 8.3%; Human Rights: 0.0%; Middle East: 0.0%
Important Votes (10): Agree 0, Disagree 6, Abstain 0, Absent 4: 0.0%
—Including the 16 Important Consensus Resolutions: 62.4%

Important Issues	**VOTES**
1. U.S. Embargo of Cuba	(N) Y
2. Human Rights in Sudan	(N) Y
3. Committee on the Inalienable Rights of the Palestinian People	(N) Y
4. Division for Palestinian Rights of the Secretariat	(N) Y
5. Fissile Material Cutoff Treaty	(N) Y
6. Work of the Special Committee to Investigate Israeli Practices	(N) X
7. Elimination of all Forms of Religious Intolerance	(Y) X
8. Enhancing the Role of Organizations to Promote Democracy	(Y) X
9. Human Rights in Iran	(Y) X
10. International Trade and Development	(N) Y

COSTA RICA

Voting Coincidence Percentages

Overall Votes (79): Agree 15, Disagree 56, Abstain 5, Absent 3: 21.1%
—Including All 213 Consensus Resolutions: 79.8%
—Arms Control: 8.7%; Human Rights: 40.7%; Middle East: 9.1%
Important Votes (10): Agree 3, Disagree 4, Abstain 3, Absent 0: 42.9%
—Including the 16 Important Consensus Resolutions: 82.2%

Important Issues	**VOTES**
1. U.S. Embargo of Cuba	(N) Y
2. Human Rights in Sudan	(N) Y
3. Committee on the Inalienable Rights of the Palestinian People	(N) A
4. Division for Palestinian Rights of the Secretariat	(N) A
5. Fissile Material Cutoff Treaty	(N) Y
6. Work of the Special Committee to Investigate Israeli Practices	(N) A
7. Elimination of all Forms of Religious Intolerance	(Y) Y
8. Enhancing the Role of Organizations to Promote Democracy	(Y) Y
9. Human Rights in Iran	(Y) Y
10. International Trade and Development	(N) Y

Votes: Y=Yes, N=No, A=Abstain, X=Absent, ( )=U.S. Vote

COTE D'IVOIRE

Voting Coincidence Percentages

Overall Votes (79): Agree 11, Disagree 50, Abstain 11, Absent 7: 18.0%
—Including All 213 Consensus Resolutions: 80.4%
—Arms Control: 12.5%; Human Rights: 35.0%; Middle East: 11.1%
Important Votes (10): Agree 2, Disagree 6, Abstain 2, Absent 0: 25.0%
—Including the 16 Important Consensus Resolutions: 73.4%

Important Issues	**VOTES**
1. U.S. Embargo of Cuba	(N) Y
2. Human Rights in Sudan	(N) Y
3. Committee on the Inalienable Rights of the Palestinian People	(N) Y
4. Division for Palestinian Rights of the Secretariat	(N) Y
5. Fissile Material Cutoff Treaty	(N) Y
6. Work of the Special Committee to Investigate Israeli Practices	(N) A
7. Elimination of all Forms of Religious Intolerance	(Y) Y
8. Enhancing the Role of Organizations to Promote Democracy	(Y) Y
9. Human Rights in Iran	(Y) A
10. International Trade and Development	(N) Y

CROATIA

Voting Coincidence Percentages

Overall Votes (79): Agree 29, Disagree 39, Abstain 11, Absent 0: 42.6%
—Including All 213 Consensus Resolutions: 86.1%
—Arms Control: 33.3%; Human Rights: 76.0%; Middle East: 14.3%
Important Votes (10): Agree 4, Disagree 3, Abstain 3, Absent 0: 57.1%
—Including the 16 Important Consensus Resolutions: 87.0%

Important Issues	**VOTES**
1. U.S. Embargo of Cuba	(N) Y
2. Human Rights in Sudan	(N) N
3. Committee on the Inalienable Rights of the Palestinian People	(N) A
4. Division for Palestinian Rights of the Secretariat	(N) A
5. Fissile Material Cutoff Treaty	(N) Y
6. Work of the Special Committee to Investigate Israeli Practices	(N) A
7. Elimination of all Forms of Religious Intolerance	(Y) Y
8. Enhancing the Role of Organizations to Promote Democracy	(Y) Y
9. Human Rights in Iran	(Y) Y
10. International Trade and Development	(N) Y

Votes: Y=Yes, N=No, A=Abstain, X=Absent, ( )=U.S. Vote

CUBA

Voting Coincidence Percentages

Overall Votes (79): Agree 5, Disagree 63, Abstain 8, Absent 3: 7.4%
—Including All 213 Consensus Resolutions: 76.8%
—Arms Control: 4.5%; Human Rights: 15.0%; Middle East: 5.9%
Important Votes (10): Agree 1, Disagree 8, Abstain 1, Absent 0: 11.1%
—Including the 16 Important Consensus Resolutions: 67.1%

Important Issues	**VOTES**
1. U.S. Embargo of Cuba	(N) Y
2. Human Rights in Sudan	(N) Y
3. Committee on the Inalienable Rights of the Palestinian People	(N) Y
4. Division for Palestinian Rights of the Secretariat	(N) Y
5. Fissile Material Cutoff Treaty	(N) Y
6. Work of the Special Committee to Investigate Israeli Practices	(N) Y
7. Elimination of all Forms of Religious Intolerance	(Y) Y
8. Enhancing the Role of Organizations to Promote Democracy	(Y) A
9. Human Rights in Iran	(Y) N
10. International Trade and Development	(N) Y

CYPRUS

Voting Coincidence Percentages

Overall Votes (79): Agree 29, Disagree 43, Abstain 7, Absent 0: 40.3%
—Including All 213 Consensus Resolutions: 84.9%
—Arms Control: 31.8%; Human Rights: 76.0%; Middle East: 12.5%
Important Votes (10): Agree 4, Disagree 5, Abstain 1, Absent 0: 44.4%
—Including the 16 Important Consensus Resolutions: 80.0%

Important Issues	**VOTES**
1. U.S. Embargo of Cuba	(N) Y
2. Human Rights in Sudan	(N) N
3. Committee on the Inalienable Rights of the Palestinian People	(N) Y
4. Division for Palestinian Rights of the Secretariat	(N) Y
5. Fissile Material Cutoff Treaty	(N) Y
6. Work of the Special Committee to Investigate Israeli Practices	(N) A
7. Elimination of all Forms of Religious Intolerance	(Y) Y
8. Enhancing the Role of Organizations to Promote Democracy	(Y) Y
9. Human Rights in Iran	(Y) Y
10. International Trade and Development	(N) Y

Votes: Y=Yes, N=No, A=Abstain, X=Absent, ( )=U.S. Vote

CZECH REPUBLIC

Voting Coincidence Percentages

Overall Votes (79): Agree 30, Disagree 37, Abstain 10, Absent 2: 44.8%
—Including All 213 Consensus Resolutions: 86.6%
—Arms Control: 40.0%; Human Rights: 76.0%; Middle East: 14.3%
Important Votes (10): Agree 4, Disagree 3, Abstain 3, Absent 0: 57.1%
—Including the 16 Important Consensus Resolutions: 86.8%

Important Issues	VOTES
1. U.S. Embargo of Cuba	(N) Y
2. Human Rights in Sudan	(N) N
3. Committee on the Inalienable Rights of the Palestinian People	(N) A
4. Division for Palestinian Rights of the Secretariat	(N) A
5. Fissile Material Cutoff Treaty	(N) Y
6. Work of the Special Committee to Investigate Israeli Practices	(N) A
7. Elimination of all Forms of Religious Intolerance	(Y) Y
8. Enhancing the Role of Organizations to Promote Democracy	(Y) Y
9. Human Rights in Iran	(Y) Y
10. International Trade and Development	(N) Y

DEMOCRATIC PEOPLE'S REPUBLIC OF KOREA

Voting Coincidence Percentages

Overall Votes (79): Agree 2, Disagree 59, Abstain 8, Absent 10: 3.3%
—Including All 213 Consensus Resolutions: 75.7%
—Arms Control: 0.0%; Human Rights: 11.1%; Middle East: 0.0%
Important Votes (10): Agree 1, Disagree 7, Abstain 1, Absent 1: 12.5%
—Including the 16 Important Consensus Resolutions: 67.7%

Important Issues	VOTES
1. U.S. Embargo of Cuba	(N) Y
2. Human Rights in Sudan	(N) Y
3. Committee on the Inalienable Rights of the Palestinian People	(N) Y
4. Division for Palestinian Rights of the Secretariat	(N) Y
5. Fissile Material Cutoff Treaty	(N) X
6. Work of the Special Committee to Investigate Israeli Practices	(N) Y
7. Elimination of all Forms of Religious Intolerance	(Y) Y
8. Enhancing the Role of Organizations to Promote Democracy	(Y) A
9. Human Rights in Iran	(Y) N
10. International Trade and Development	(N) Y

Votes: Y=Yes, N=No, A=Abstain, X=Absent, ( )=U.S. Vote

DEMOCRATIC REPUBLIC OF THE CONGO

Voting Coincidence Percentages

Overall Votes (79): Agree 9, Disagree 24, Abstain 2, Absent 44: 27.3%
—Including All 213 Consensus Resolutions: 80.6%
—Arms Control: 100.0%; Human Rights: 30.4%; Middle East: 33.3%
Important Votes (10): Agree 2, Disagree 3, Abstain 0, Absent 5: 40.0%
—Including the 16 Important Consensus Resolutions: 74.9%

Important Issues	**VOTES**
1. U.S. Embargo of Cuba	(N) Y
2. Human Rights in Sudan	(N) Y
3. Committee on the Inalienable Rights of the Palestinian People	(N) X
4. Division for Palestinian Rights of the Secretariat	(N) X
5. Fissile Material Cutoff Treaty	(N) X
6. Work of the Special Committee to Investigate Israeli Practices	(N) X
7. Elimination of all Forms of Religious Intolerance	(Y) Y
8. Enhancing the Role of Organizations to Promote Democracy	(Y) Y
9. Human Rights in Iran	(Y) N
10. International Trade and Development	(N) X

DENMARK

Voting Coincidence Percentages

Overall Votes (79): Agree 31, Disagree 38, Abstain 10, Absent 0: 44.9%
—Including All 213 Consensus Resolutions: 86.5%
—Arms Control: 38.1%; Human Rights: 76.0%; Middle East: 14.3%
Important Votes (10): Agree 4, Disagree 3, Abstain 3, Absent 0: 57.1%
—Including the 16 Important Consensus Resolutions: 87.0%

Important Issues	**VOTES**
1. U.S. Embargo of Cuba	(N) Y
2. Human Rights in Sudan	(N) N
3. Committee on the Inalienable Rights of the Palestinian People	(N) A
4. Division for Palestinian Rights of the Secretariat	(N) A
5. Fissile Material Cutoff Treaty	(N) Y
6. Work of the Special Committee to Investigate Israeli Practices	(N) A
7. Elimination of all Forms of Religious Intolerance	(Y) Y
8. Enhancing the Role of Organizations to Promote Democracy	(Y) Y
9. Human Rights in Iran	(Y) Y
10. International Trade and Development	(N) Y

Votes: Y=Yes, N=No, A=Abstain, X=Absent, ( )=U.S. Vote

DJIBOUTI

Voting Coincidence Percentages

Overall Votes (79): Agree 9, Disagree 62, Abstain 6, Absent 2: 12.7%
—Including All 213 Consensus Resolutions: 77.6%
—Arms Control: 8.7%; Human Rights: 28.6%; Middle East: 5.6%
Important Votes (10): Agree 2, Disagree 8, Abstain 0, Absent 0: 20.0%
—Including the 16 Important Consensus Resolutions: 68.6%

Important Issues	**VOTES**
1. U.S. Embargo of Cuba	(N) Y
2. Human Rights in Sudan	(N) Y
3. Committee on the Inalienable Rights of the Palestinian People	(N) Y
4. Division for Palestinian Rights of the Secretariat	(N) Y
5. Fissile Material Cutoff Treaty	(N) Y
6. Work of the Special Committee to Investigate Israeli Practices	(N) Y
7. Elimination of all Forms of Religious Intolerance	(Y) Y
8. Enhancing the Role of Organizations to Promote Democracy	(Y) Y
9. Human Rights in Iran	(Y) N
10. International Trade and Development	(N) Y

DOMINICA

Voting Coincidence Percentages

Overall Votes (79): Agree 6, Disagree 57, Abstain 10, Absent 6: 9.5%
—Including All 213 Consensus Resolutions: 78.0%
—Arms Control: 9.1%; Human Rights: 25.0%; Middle East: 0.0%
Important Votes (10): Agree 2, Disagree 5, Abstain 1, Absent 2: 28.6%
—Including the 16 Important Consensus Resolutions: 77.0%

Important Issues	**VOTES**
1. U.S. Embargo of Cuba	(N) Y
2. Human Rights in Sudan	(N) X
3. Committee on the Inalienable Rights of the Palestinian People	(N) Y
4. Division for Palestinian Rights of the Secretariat	(N) X
5. Fissile Material Cutoff Treaty	(N) Y
6. Work of the Special Committee to Investigate Israeli Practices	(N) Y
7. Elimination of all Forms of Religious Intolerance	(Y) Y
8. Enhancing the Role of Organizations to Promote Democracy	(Y) Y
9. Human Rights in Iran	(Y) A
10. International Trade and Development	(N) Y

Votes: Y=Yes, N=No, A=Abstain, X=Absent, ( )=U.S. Vote

DOMINICAN REPUBLIC

Voting Coincidence Percentages

Overall Votes (79): Agree 16, Disagree 52, Abstain 10, Absent 1: 23.5%
—Including All 213 Consensus Resolutions: 81.2%
—Arms Control: 12.5%; Human Rights: 48.0%; Middle East: 10.0%
Important Votes (10): Agree 2, Disagree 3, Abstain 5, Absent 0: 40.0%
—Including the 16 Important Consensus Resolutions: 85.5%

Important Issues	**VOTES**
1. U.S. Embargo of Cuba	(N) Y
2. Human Rights in Sudan	(N) A
3. Committee on the Inalienable Rights of the Palestinian People	(N) A
4. Division for Palestinian Rights of the Secretariat	(N) A
5. Fissile Material Cutoff Treaty	(N) Y
6. Work of the Special Committee to Investigate Israeli Practices	(N) A
7. Elimination of all Forms of Religious Intolerance	(Y) Y
8. Enhancing the Role of Organizations to Promote Democracy	(Y) Y
9. Human Rights in Iran	(Y) A
10. International Trade and Development	(N) Y

ECUADOR

Voting Coincidence Percentages

Overall Votes (79): Agree 11, Disagree 59, Abstain 8, Absent 1: 15.7%
—Including All 213 Consensus Resolutions: 79.0%
—Arms Control: 13.0%; Human Rights: 35.0%; Middle East: 5.6%
Important Votes (10): Agree 2, Disagree 6, Abstain 2, Absent 0: 25.0%
—Including the 16 Important Consensus Resolutions: 74.8%

Important Issues	**VOTES**
1. U.S. Embargo of Cuba	(N) Y
2. Human Rights in Sudan	(N) A
3. Committee on the Inalienable Rights of the Palestinian People	(N) Y
4. Division for Palestinian Rights of the Secretariat	(N) Y
5. Fissile Material Cutoff Treaty	(N) Y
6. Work of the Special Committee to Investigate Israeli Practices	(N) Y
7. Elimination of all Forms of Religious Intolerance	(Y) Y
8. Enhancing the Role of Organizations to Promote Democracy	(Y) Y
9. Human Rights in Iran	(Y) A
10. International Trade and Development	(N) Y

Votes: Y=Yes, N=No, A=Abstain, X=Absent, ( )=U.S. Vote

EGYPT

Voting Coincidence Percentages

Overall Votes (79): Agree 6, Disagree 65, Abstain 6, Absent 2: 8.5%
—Including All 213 Consensus Resolutions: 76.7%
—Arms Control: 4.5%; Human Rights: 18.2%; Middle East: 0.0%
Important Votes (10): Agree 2, Disagree 8, Abstain 0, Absent 0: 20.0%
—Including the 16 Important Consensus Resolutions: 68.8%

Important Issues	VOTES
1. U.S. Embargo of Cuba	(N) Y
2. Human Rights in Sudan	(N) Y
3. Committee on the Inalienable Rights of the Palestinian People	(N) Y
4. Division for Palestinian Rights of the Secretariat	(N) Y
5. Fissile Material Cutoff Treaty	(N) Y
6. Work of the Special Committee to Investigate Israeli Practices	(N) Y
7. Elimination of all Forms of Religious Intolerance	(Y) Y
8. Enhancing the Role of Organizations to Promote Democracy	(Y) Y
9. Human Rights in Iran	(Y) N
10. International Trade and Development	(N) Y

EL SALVADOR

Voting Coincidence Percentages

Overall Votes (79): Agree 18, Disagree 56, Abstain 4, Absent 1: 24.3%
—Including All 213 Consensus Resolutions: 80.3%
—Arms Control: 12.0%; Human Rights: 53.8%; Middle East: 6.7%
Important Votes (10): Agree 4, Disagree 4, Abstain 1, Absent 1: 50.0%
—Including the 16 Important Consensus Resolutions: 83.2%

Important Issues	VOTES
1. U.S. Embargo of Cuba	(N) X
2. Human Rights in Sudan	(N) N
3. Committee on the Inalienable Rights of the Palestinian People	(N) Y
4. Division for Palestinian Rights of the Secretariat	(N) Y
5. Fissile Material Cutoff Treaty	(N) Y
6. Work of the Special Committee to Investigate Israeli Practices	(N) A
7. Elimination of all Forms of Religious Intolerance	(Y) Y
8. Enhancing the Role of Organizations to Promote Democracy	(Y) Y
9. Human Rights in Iran	(Y) Y
10. International Trade and Development	(N) Y

Votes: Y=Yes, N=No, A=Abstain, X=Absent, ( )=U.S. Vote

EQUATORIAL GUINEA

Voting Coincidence Percentages

Overall Votes (79): Agree 11, Disagree 43, Abstain 7, Absent 18: 20.4%
—Including All 213 Consensus Resolutions: 80.6%
—Arms Control: 8.7%; Human Rights: 42.9%; Middle East: 0.0%
Important Votes (10): Agree 2, Disagree 3, Abstain 2, Absent 3: 40.0%
—Including the 16 Important Consensus Resolutions: 83.0%

Important Issues	**VOTES**
1. U.S. Embargo of Cuba	(N) Y
2. Human Rights in Sudan	(N) Y
3. Committee on the Inalienable Rights of the Palestinian People	(N) X
4. Division for Palestinian Rights of the Secretariat	(N) X
5. Fissile Material Cutoff Treaty	(N) Y
6. Work of the Special Committee to Investigate Israeli Practices	(N) A
7. Elimination of all Forms of Religious Intolerance	(Y) Y
8. Enhancing the Role of Organizations to Promote Democracy	(Y) Y
9. Human Rights in Iran	(Y) A
10. International Trade and Development	(N) X

ERITREA

Voting Coincidence Percentages

Overall Votes (79): Agree 7, Disagree 59, Abstain 7, Absent 6: 10.6%
—Including All 213 Consensus Resolutions: 77.3%
—Arms Control: 8.7%; Human Rights: 26.3%; Middle East: 0.0%
Important Votes (10): Agree 2, Disagree 6, Abstain 1, Absent 1: 25.0%
—Including the 16 Important Consensus Resolutions: 73.4%

Important Issues	**VOTES**
1. U.S. Embargo of Cuba	(N) Y
2. Human Rights in Sudan	(N) Y
3. Committee on the Inalienable Rights of the Palestinian People	(N) Y
4. Division for Palestinian Rights of the Secretariat	(N) Y
5. Fissile Material Cutoff Treaty	(N) Y
6. Work of the Special Committee to Investigate Israeli Practices	(N) X
7. Elimination of all Forms of Religious Intolerance	(Y) Y
8. Enhancing the Role of Organizations to Promote Democracy	(Y) Y
9. Human Rights in Iran	(Y) A
10. International Trade and Development	(N) Y

Votes: Y=Yes, N=No, A=Abstain, X=Absent, ( )=U.S. Vote

ESTONIA

Voting Coincidence Percentages

Overall Votes (79): Agree 27, Disagree 38, Abstain 12, Absent 2: 41.5%
—Including All 213 Consensus Resolutions: 86.1%
—Arms Control: 31.6%; Human Rights: 76.0%; Middle East: 7.7%
Important Votes (10): Agree 4, Disagree 3, Abstain 3, Absent 0: 57.1%
—Including the 16 Important Consensus Resolutions: 86.8%

Important Issues	VOTES
1. U.S. Embargo of Cuba	(N) Y
2. Human Rights in Sudan	(N) N
3. Committee on the Inalienable Rights of the Palestinian People	(N) A
4. Division for Palestinian Rights of the Secretariat	(N) A
5. Fissile Material Cutoff Treaty	(N) Y
6. Work of the Special Committee to Investigate Israeli Practices	(N) A
7. Elimination of all Forms of Religious Intolerance	(Y) Y
8. Enhancing the Role of Organizations to Promote Democracy	(Y) Y
9. Human Rights in Iran	(Y) Y
10. International Trade and Development	(N) Y

ETHIOPIA

Voting Coincidence Percentages

Overall Votes (79): Agree 8, Disagree 50, Abstain 11, Absent 10: 13.8%
—Including All 213 Consensus Resolutions: 79.8%
—Arms Control: 15.0%; Human Rights: 26.7%; Middle East: 6.7%
Important Votes (10): Agree 2, Disagree 6, Abstain 2, Absent 0: 25.0%
—Including the 16 Important Consensus Resolutions: 73.0%

Important Issues	VOTES
1. U.S. Embargo of Cuba	(N) Y
2. Human Rights in Sudan	(N) Y
3. Committee on the Inalienable Rights of the Palestinian People	(N) Y
4. Division for Palestinian Rights of the Secretariat	(N) Y
5. Fissile Material Cutoff Treaty	(N) Y
6. Work of the Special Committee to Investigate Israeli Practices	(N) A
7. Elimination of all Forms of Religious Intolerance	(Y) Y
8. Enhancing the Role of Organizations to Promote Democracy	(Y) Y
9. Human Rights in Iran	(Y) A
10. International Trade and Development	(N) Y

Votes: Y=Yes, N=No, A=Abstain, X=Absent, ( )=U.S. Vote

FIJI

Voting Coincidence Percentages

Overall Votes (79): Agree 12, Disagree 53, Abstain 9, Absent 5: 18.5%
—Including All 213 Consensus Resolutions: 79.7%
—Arms Control: 9.1%; Human Rights: 45.0%; Middle East: 0.0%
Important Votes (10): Agree 2, Disagree 4, Abstain 3, Absent 1: 33.3%
—Including the 16 Important Consensus Resolutions: 80.7%

Important Issues	**VOTES**
1. U.S. Embargo of Cuba	(N) Y
2. Human Rights in Sudan	(N) X
3. Committee on the Inalienable Rights of the Palestinian People	(N) Y
4. Division for Palestinian Rights of the Secretariat	(N) A
5. Fissile Material Cutoff Treaty	(N) Y
6. Work of the Special Committee to Investigate Israeli Practices	(N) A
7. Elimination of all Forms of Religious Intolerance	(Y) Y
8. Enhancing the Role of Organizations to Promote Democracy	(Y) Y
9. Human Rights in Iran	(Y) A
10. International Trade and Development	(N) Y

FINLAND

Voting Coincidence Percentages

Overall Votes (79): Agree 30, Disagree 39, Abstain 10, Absent 0: 43.5%
—Including All 213 Consensus Resolutions: 86.2%
—Arms Control: 33.3%; Human Rights: 76.0%; Middle East: 14.3%
Important Votes (10): Agree 4, Disagree 3, Abstain 3, Absent 0: 57.1%
—Including the 16 Important Consensus Resolutions: 87.0%

Important Issues	**VOTES**
1. U.S. Embargo of Cuba	(N) Y
2. Human Rights in Sudan	(N) N
3. Committee on the Inalienable Rights of the Palestinian People	(N) A
4. Division for Palestinian Rights of the Secretariat	(N) A
5. Fissile Material Cutoff Treaty	(N) Y
6. Work of the Special Committee to Investigate Israeli Practices	(N) A
7. Elimination of all Forms of Religious Intolerance	(Y) Y
8. Enhancing the Role of Organizations to Promote Democracy	(Y) Y
9. Human Rights in Iran	(Y) Y
10. International Trade and Development	(N) Y

Votes: Y=Yes, N=No, A=Abstain, X=Absent, ( )=U.S. Vote

FRANCE

Voting Coincidence Percentages

Overall Votes (79): Agree 33, Disagree 28, Abstain 17, Absent 1: 54.1%
—Including All 213 Consensus Resolutions: 89.7%
—Arms Control: 64.7%; Human Rights: 76.0%; Middle East: 14.3%
Important Votes (10): Agree 4, Disagree 3, Abstain 3, Absent 0: 57.1%
—Including the 16 Important Consensus Resolutions: 86.9%
Security Council votes: 96.7%

Important Issues	**VOTES**
1. U.S. Embargo of Cuba	(N) Y
2. Human Rights in Sudan	(N) N
3. Committee on the Inalienable Rights of the Palestinian People	(N) A
4. Division for Palestinian Rights of the Secretariat	(N) A
5. Fissile Material Cutoff Treaty	(N) Y
6. Work of the Special Committee to Investigate Israeli Practices	(N) A
7. Elimination of all Forms of Religious Intolerance	(Y) Y
8. Enhancing the Role of Organizations to Promote Democracy	(Y) Y
9. Human Rights in Iran	(Y) Y
10. International Trade and Development	(N) Y

GABON

Voting Coincidence Percentages

Overall Votes (79): Agree 7, Disagree 51, Abstain 1, Absent 20: 12.1%
—Including All 213 Consensus Resolutions: 76.7%
—Arms Control: 10.5%; Human Rights: 25.0%; Middle East: 0.0%
Important Votes (10): Agree 2, Disagree 7, Abstain 0, Absent 1: 22.2%
—Including the 16 Important Consensus Resolutions: 66.8%

Important Issues	**VOTES**
1. U.S. Embargo of Cuba	(N) Y
2. Human Rights in Sudan	(N) Y
3. Committee on the Inalienable Rights of the Palestinian People	(N) Y
4. Division for Palestinian Rights of the Secretariat	(N) Y
5. Fissile Material Cutoff Treaty	(N) Y
6. Work of the Special Committee to Investigate Israeli Practices	(N) Y
7. Elimination of all Forms of Religious Intolerance	(Y) Y
8. Enhancing the Role of Organizations to Promote Democracy	(Y) Y
9. Human Rights in Iran	(Y) X
10. International Trade and Development	(N) Y

Votes: Y=Yes, N=No, A=Abstain, X=Absent, ( )=U.S. Vote

GAMBIA

Voting Coincidence Percentages

Overall Votes (79): Agree 6, Disagree 44, Abstain 1, Absent 28: 12.0%
—Including All 213 Consensus Resolutions: 76.2%
—Arms Control: 9.5%; Human Rights: 17.6%; Middle East: 0.0%
Important Votes (10): Agree 2, Disagree 6, Abstain 0, Absent 2: 25.0%
—Including the 16 Important Consensus Resolutions: 66.9%

Important Issues	**VOTES**
1. U.S. Embargo of Cuba	(N) Y
2. Human Rights in Sudan	(N) Y
3. Committee on the Inalienable Rights of the Palestinian People	(N) Y
4. Division for Palestinian Rights of the Secretariat	(N) Y
5. Fissile Material Cutoff Treaty	(N) Y
6. Work of the Special Committee to Investigate Israeli Practices	(N) X
7. Elimination of all Forms of Religious Intolerance	(Y) Y
8. Enhancing the Role of Organizations to Promote Democracy	(Y) Y
9. Human Rights in Iran	(Y) N
10. International Trade and Development	(N) X

GEORGIA

Voting Coincidence Percentages

Overall Votes (79): Agree 22, Disagree 38, Abstain 15, Absent 4: 36.7%
—Including All 213 Consensus Resolutions: 85.0%
—Arms Control: 18.8%; Human Rights: 72.7%; Middle East: 7.7%
Important Votes (10): Agree 3, Disagree 3, Abstain 3, Absent 1: 50.0%
—Including the 16 Important Consensus Resolutions: 85.4%

Important Issues	**VOTES**
1. U.S. Embargo of Cuba	(N) Y
2. Human Rights in Sudan	(N) N
3. Committee on the Inalienable Rights of the Palestinian People	(N) A
4. Division for Palestinian Rights of the Secretariat	(N) A
5. Fissile Material Cutoff Treaty	(N) Y
6. Work of the Special Committee to Investigate Israeli Practices	(N) A
7. Elimination of all Forms of Religious Intolerance	(Y) Y
8. Enhancing the Role of Organizations to Promote Democracy	(Y) Y
9. Human Rights in Iran	(Y) X
10. International Trade and Development	(N) Y

Votes: Y=Yes, N=No, A=Abstain, X=Absent, ( )=U.S. Vote

GERMANY

Voting Coincidence Percentages

Overall Votes (79): Agree 30, Disagree 37, Abstain 11, Absent 1: 44.8%
—Including All 213 Consensus Resolutions: 86.6%
—Arms Control: 38.1%; Human Rights: 76.0%; Middle East: 14.3%
Important Votes (10): Agree 4, Disagree 3, Abstain 3, Absent 0: 57.1%
—Including the 16 Important Consensus Resolutions: 86.8%
Security Council votes: 100.0%

Important Issues	**VOTES**
1. U.S. Embargo of Cuba	(N) Y
2. Human Rights in Sudan	(N) N
3. Committee on the Inalienable Rights of the Palestinian People	(N) A
4. Division for Palestinian Rights of the Secretariat	(N) A
5. Fissile Material Cutoff Treaty	(N) Y
6. Work of the Special Committee to Investigate Israeli Practices	(N) A
7. Elimination of all Forms of Religious Intolerance	(Y) Y
8. Enhancing the Role of Organizations to Promote Democracy	(Y) Y
9. Human Rights in Iran	(Y) Y
10. International Trade and Development	(N) Y

GHANA

Voting Coincidence Percentages

Overall Votes (79): Agree 10, Disagree 59, Abstain 8, Absent 2: 14.5%
—Including All 213 Consensus Resolutions: 78.5%
—Arms Control: 12.5%; Human Rights: 31.6%; Middle East: 5.9%
Important Votes (10): Agree 2, Disagree 7, Abstain 1, Absent 0: 22.2%
—Including the 16 Important Consensus Resolutions: 71.4%

Important Issues	**VOTES**
1. U.S. Embargo of Cuba	(N) Y
2. Human Rights in Sudan	(N) Y
3. Committee on the Inalienable Rights of the Palestinian People	(N) Y
4. Division for Palestinian Rights of the Secretariat	(N) Y
5. Fissile Material Cutoff Treaty	(N) Y
6. Work of the Special Committee to Investigate Israeli Practices	(N) Y
7. Elimination of all Forms of Religious Intolerance	(Y) Y
8. Enhancing the Role of Organizations to Promote Democracy	(Y) Y
9. Human Rights in Iran	(Y) A
10. International Trade and Development	(N) Y

Votes: Y=Yes, N=No, A=Abstain, X=Absent, ( )=U.S. Vote

GREECE

Voting Coincidence Percentages

Overall Votes (79): Agree 30, Disagree 39, Abstain 9, Absent 1: 43.5%
—Including All 213 Consensus Resolutions: 86.1%
—Arms Control: 36.4%; Human Rights: 76.0%; Middle East: 14.3%
Important Votes (10): Agree 4, Disagree 3, Abstain 3, Absent 0: 57.1%
—Including the 16 Important Consensus Resolutions: 86.9%

Important Issues	**VOTES**
1. U.S. Embargo of Cuba	(N) Y
2. Human Rights in Sudan	(N) N
3. Committee on the Inalienable Rights of the Palestinian People	(N) A
4. Division for Palestinian Rights of the Secretariat	(N) A
5. Fissile Material Cutoff Treaty	(N) Y
6. Work of the Special Committee to Investigate Israeli Practices	(N) A
7. Elimination of all Forms of Religious Intolerance	(Y) Y
8. Enhancing the Role of Organizations to Promote Democracy	(Y) Y
9. Human Rights in Iran	(Y) Y
10. International Trade and Development	(N) Y

GRENADA

Voting Coincidence Percentages

Overall Votes (79): Agree 19, Disagree 46, Abstain 10, Absent 4: 29.2%
—Including All 213 Consensus Resolutions: 82.7%
—Arms Control: 8.7%; Human Rights: 31.6%; Middle East: 78.6%
Important Votes (10): Agree 5, Disagree 3, Abstain 1, Absent 1: 62.5%
—Including the 16 Important Consensus Resolutions: 87.0%

Important Issues	**VOTES**
1. U.S. Embargo of Cuba	(N) Y
2. Human Rights in Sudan	(N) A
3. Committee on the Inalienable Rights of the Palestinian People	(N) X
4. Division for Palestinian Rights of the Secretariat	(N) N
5. Fissile Material Cutoff Treaty	(N) Y
6. Work of the Special Committee to Investigate Israeli Practices	(N) N
7. Elimination of all Forms of Religious Intolerance	(Y) Y
8. Enhancing the Role of Organizations to Promote Democracy	(Y) Y
9. Human Rights in Iran	(Y) Y
10. International Trade and Development	(N) Y

Votes: Y=Yes, N=No, A=Abstain, X=Absent, ( )=U.S. Vote

GUATEMALA

Voting Coincidence Percentages

Overall Votes (79): Agree 17, Disagree 54, Abstain 8, Absent 0: 23.9%
—Including All 213 Consensus Resolutions: 81.0%
—Arms Control: 12.0%; Human Rights: 52.0%; Middle East: 8.3%
Important Votes (10): Agree 3, Disagree 3, Abstain 4, Absent 0: 50.0%
—Including the 16 Important Consensus Resolutions: 86.4%

Important Issues	**VOTES**
1. U.S. Embargo of Cuba	(N) Y
2. Human Rights in Sudan	(N) N
3. Committee on the Inalienable Rights of the Palestinian People	(N) A
4. Division for Palestinian Rights of the Secretariat	(N) A
5. Fissile Material Cutoff Treaty	(N) Y
6. Work of the Special Committee to Investigate Israeli Practices	(N) A
7. Elimination of all Forms of Religious Intolerance	(Y) Y
8. Enhancing the Role of Organizations to Promote Democracy	(Y) Y
9. Human Rights in Iran	(Y) A
10. International Trade and Development	(N) Y

GUINEA

Voting Coincidence Percentages

Overall Votes (79): Agree 8, Disagree 38, Abstain 2, Absent 31: 17.4%
—Including All 213 Consensus Resolutions: 77.8%
—Arms Control: 0.0%; Human Rights: 30.4%; Middle East: 0.0%
Important Votes (10): Agree 2, Disagree 6, Abstain 0, Absent 2: 25.0%
—Including the 16 Important Consensus Resolutions: 65.6%

Important Issues	**VOTES**
1. U.S. Embargo of Cuba	(N) Y
2. Human Rights in Sudan	(N) Y
3. Committee on the Inalienable Rights of the Palestinian People	(N) Y
4. Division for Palestinian Rights of the Secretariat	(N) Y
5. Fissile Material Cutoff Treaty	(N) X
6. Work of the Special Committee to Investigate Israeli Practices	(N) Y
7. Elimination of all Forms of Religious Intolerance	(Y) Y
8. Enhancing the Role of Organizations to Promote Democracy	(Y) Y
9. Human Rights in Iran	(Y) N
10. International Trade and Development	(N) X

Votes: Y=Yes, N=No, A=Abstain, X=Absent, ( )=U.S. Vote

GUINEA-BISSAU

Voting Coincidence Percentages

Overall Votes (79): Agree 14, Disagree 52, Abstain 1, Absent 12: 21.2%
—Including All 213 Consensus Resolutions: 79.1%
—Arms Control: 8.7%; Human Rights: 50.0%; Middle East: 0.0%
Important Votes (10): Agree 2, Disagree 6, Abstain 1, Absent 1: 25.0%
—Including the 16 Important Consensus Resolutions: 72.3%

Important Issues	VOTES
1. U.S. Embargo of Cuba	(N) Y
2. Human Rights in Sudan	(N) Y
3. Committee on the Inalienable Rights of the Palestinian People	(N) Y
4. Division for Palestinian Rights of the Secretariat	(N) Y
5. Fissile Material Cutoff Treaty	(N) Y
6. Work of the Special Committee to Investigate Israeli Practices	(N) Y
7. Elimination of all Forms of Religious Intolerance	(Y) Y
8. Enhancing the Role of Organizations to Promote Democracy	(Y) Y
9. Human Rights in Iran	(Y) A
10. International Trade and Development	(N) X

GUYANA

Voting Coincidence Percentages

Overall Votes (79): Agree 9, Disagree 60, Abstain 8, Absent 2: 13.0%
—Including All 213 Consensus Resolutions: 78.4%
—Arms Control: 12.0%; Human Rights: 27.8%; Middle East: 5.9%
Important Votes (10): Agree 2, Disagree 7, Abstain 1, Absent 0: 22.2%
—Including the 16 Important Consensus Resolutions: 71.6%

Important Issues	VOTES
1. U.S. Embargo of Cuba	(N) Y
2. Human Rights in Sudan	(N) Y
3. Committee on the Inalienable Rights of the Palestinian People	(N) Y
4. Division for Palestinian Rights of the Secretariat	(N) Y
5. Fissile Material Cutoff Treaty	(N) Y
6. Work of the Special Committee to Investigate Israeli Practices	(N) Y
7. Elimination of all Forms of Religious Intolerance	(Y) Y
8. Enhancing the Role of Organizations to Promote Democracy	(Y) Y
9. Human Rights in Iran	(Y) A
10. International Trade and Development	(N) Y

Votes: Y=Yes, N=No, A=Abstain, X=Absent, ( )=U.S. Vote

HAITI

Voting Coincidence Percentages

Overall Votes (79): Agree 8, Disagree 36, Abstain 23, Absent 12: 18.2%
—Including All 213 Consensus Resolutions: 83.9%
—Arms Control: 10.5%; Human Rights: 37.5%; Middle East: 0.0%
Important Votes (10): Agree 3, Disagree 3, Abstain 3, Absent 1: 50.0%
—Including the 16 Important Consensus Resolutions: 84.6%

Important Issues	VOTES
1. U.S. Embargo of Cuba	(N) Y
2. Human Rights in Sudan	(N) X
3. Committee on the Inalienable Rights of the Palestinian People	(N) A
4. Division for Palestinian Rights of the Secretariat	(N) A
5. Fissile Material Cutoff Treaty	(N) Y
6. Work of the Special Committee to Investigate Israeli Practices	(N) A
7. Elimination of all Forms of Religious Intolerance	(Y) Y
8. Enhancing the Role of Organizations to Promote Democracy	(Y) Y
9. Human Rights in Iran	(Y) Y
10. International Trade and Development	(N) Y

HONDURAS

Voting Coincidence Percentages

Overall Votes (79): Agree 14, Disagree 45, Abstain 11, Absent 9: 23.7%
—Including All 213 Consensus Resolutions: 82.1%
—Arms Control: 13.0%; Human Rights: 43.5%; Middle East: 14.3%
Important Votes (10): Agree 2, Disagree 3, Abstain 4, Absent 1: 40.0%
—Including the 16 Important Consensus Resolutions: 84.5%

Important Issues	VOTES
1. U.S. Embargo of Cuba	(N) Y
2. Human Rights in Sudan	(N) Y
3. Committee on the Inalienable Rights of the Palestinian People	(N) A
4. Division for Palestinian Rights of the Secretariat	(N) A
5. Fissile Material Cutoff Treaty	(N) Y
6. Work of the Special Committee to Investigate Israeli Practices	(N) A
7. Elimination of all Forms of Religious Intolerance	(Y) Y
8. Enhancing the Role of Organizations to Promote Democracy	(Y) Y
9. Human Rights in Iran	(Y) A
10. International Trade and Development	(N) X

Votes: Y=Yes, N=No, A=Abstain, X=Absent, ( )=U.S. Vote

HUNGARY

Voting Coincidence Percentages

Overall Votes (79): Agree 29, Disagree 38, Abstain 11, Absent 1: 43.3%
—Including All 213 Consensus Resolutions: 86.3%
—Arms Control: 38.1%; Human Rights: 76.0%; Middle East: 14.3%
Important Votes (10): Agree 4, Disagree 3, Abstain 3, Absent 0: 57.1%
—Including the 16 Important Consensus Resolutions: 86.9%

Important Issues	**VOTES**
1. U.S. Embargo of Cuba	(N) Y
2. Human Rights in Sudan	(N) N
3. Committee on the Inalienable Rights of the Palestinian People	(N) A
4. Division for Palestinian Rights of the Secretariat	(N) A
5. Fissile Material Cutoff Treaty	(N) Y
6. Work of the Special Committee to Investigate Israeli Practices	(N) A
7. Elimination of all Forms of Religious Intolerance	(Y) Y
8. Enhancing the Role of Organizations to Promote Democracy	(Y) Y
9. Human Rights in Iran	(Y) Y
10. International Trade and Development	(N) Y

ICELAND

Voting Coincidence Percentages

Overall Votes (79): Agree 30, Disagree 36, Abstain 12, Absent 1: 45.5%
—Including All 213 Consensus Resolutions: 87.0%
—Arms Control: 38.1%; Human Rights: 76.0%; Middle East: 16.7%
Important Votes (10): Agree 4, Disagree 3, Abstain 3, Absent 0: 57.1%
—Including the 16 Important Consensus Resolutions: 86.9%

Important Issues	**VOTES**
1. U.S. Embargo of Cuba	(N) Y
2. Human Rights in Sudan	(N) N
3. Committee on the Inalienable Rights of the Palestinian People	(N) A
4. Division for Palestinian Rights of the Secretariat	(N) A
5. Fissile Material Cutoff Treaty	(N) Y
6. Work of the Special Committee to Investigate Israeli Practices	(N) A
7. Elimination of all Forms of Religious Intolerance	(Y) Y
8. Enhancing the Role of Organizations to Promote Democracy	(Y) Y
9. Human Rights in Iran	(Y) Y
10. International Trade and Development	(N) Y

Votes: Y=Yes, N=No, A=Abstain, X=Absent, ( )=U.S. Vote

INDIA

Voting Coincidence Percentages

Overall Votes (79): Agree 13, Disagree 52, Abstain 14, Absent 0: 20.0%
—Including All 213 Consensus Resolutions: 81.3%
—Arms Control: 31.6%; Human Rights: 30.0%; Middle East: 5.9%
Important Votes (10): Agree 2, Disagree 8, Abstain 0, Absent 0: 20.0%
—Including the 16 Important Consensus Resolutions: 69.2%

Important Issues	**VOTES**
1. U.S. Embargo of Cuba	(N) Y
2. Human Rights in Sudan	(N) Y
3. Committee on the Inalienable Rights of the Palestinian People	(N) Y
4. Division for Palestinian Rights of the Secretariat	(N) Y
5. Fissile Material Cutoff Treaty	(N) Y
6. Work of the Special Committee to Investigate Israeli Practices	(N) Y
7. Elimination of all Forms of Religious Intolerance	(Y) Y
8. Enhancing the Role of Organizations to Promote Democracy	(Y) Y
9. Human Rights in Iran	(Y) N
10. International Trade and Development	(N) Y

INDONESIA

Voting Coincidence Percentages

Overall Votes (79): Agree 6, Disagree 66, Abstain 7, Absent 0: 8.3%
—Including All 213 Consensus Resolutions: 76.8%
—Arms Control: 8.3%; Human Rights: 13.6%; Middle East: 5.9%
Important Votes (10): Agree 2, Disagree 8, Abstain 0, Absent 0: 20.0%
—Including the 16 Important Consensus Resolutions: 69.2%

Important Issues	**VOTES**
1. U.S. Embargo of Cuba	(N) Y
2. Human Rights in Sudan	(N) Y
3. Committee on the Inalienable Rights of the Palestinian People	(N) Y
4. Division for Palestinian Rights of the Secretariat	(N) Y
5. Fissile Material Cutoff Treaty	(N) Y
6. Work of the Special Committee to Investigate Israeli Practices	(N) Y
7. Elimination of all Forms of Religious Intolerance	(Y) Y
8. Enhancing the Role of Organizations to Promote Democracy	(Y) Y
9. Human Rights in Iran	(Y) N
10. International Trade and Development	(N) Y

Votes: Y=Yes, N=No, A=Abstain, X=Absent, ( )=U.S. Vote

IRAN

Voting Coincidence Percentages

Overall Votes (79): Agree 6, Disagree 65, Abstain 8, Absent 0: 8.5%
—Including All 213 Consensus Resolutions: 76.9%
—Arms Control: 8.3%; Human Rights: 15.0%; Middle East: 5.6%
Important Votes (10): Agree 2, Disagree 8, Abstain 0, Absent 0: 20.0%
—Including the 16 Important Consensus Resolutions: 69.0%

Important Issues	**VOTES**
1. U.S. Embargo of Cuba	(N) Y
2. Human Rights in Sudan	(N) Y
3. Committee on the Inalienable Rights of the Palestinian People	(N) Y
4. Division for Palestinian Rights of the Secretariat	(N) Y
5. Fissile Material Cutoff Treaty	(N) Y
6. Work of the Special Committee to Investigate Israeli Practices	(N) Y
7. Elimination of all Forms of Religious Intolerance	(Y) Y
8. Enhancing the Role of Organizations to Promote Democracy	(Y) Y
9. Human Rights in Iran	(Y) N
10. International Trade and Development	(N) Y

IRAQ

Voting Coincidence Percentages

Overall Votes (79): Agree 3, Disagree 51, Abstain 3, Absent 22: 5.6%
—Including All 213 Consensus Resolutions: 74.6%
—Arms Control: 0.0%; Human Rights: 14.3%; Middle East: 0.0%
Important Votes (10): Agree 2, Disagree 6, Abstain 1, Absent 1: 25.0%
—Including the 16 Important Consensus Resolutions: 68.5%

Important Issues	**VOTES**
1. U.S. Embargo of Cuba	(N) X
2. Human Rights in Sudan	(N) A
3. Committee on the Inalienable Rights of the Palestinian People	(N) Y
4. Division for Palestinian Rights of the Secretariat	(N) Y
5. Fissile Material Cutoff Treaty	(N) Y
6. Work of the Special Committee to Investigate Israeli Practices	(N) Y
7. Elimination of all Forms of Religious Intolerance	(Y) Y
8. Enhancing the Role of Organizations to Promote Democracy	(Y) Y
9. Human Rights in Iran	(Y) N
10. International Trade and Development	(N) Y

Votes: Y=Yes, N=No, A=Abstain, X=Absent, ( )=U.S. Vote

IRELAND

Voting Coincidence Percentages

Overall Votes (79): Agree 28, Disagree 40, Abstain 11, Absent 0: 41.2%
—Including All 213 Consensus Resolutions: 85.8%
—Arms Control: 28.6%; Human Rights: 76.0%; Middle East: 14.3%
Important Votes (10): Agree 4, Disagree 3, Abstain 3, Absent 0: 57.1%
—Including the 16 Important Consensus Resolutions: 87.0%

Important Issues	**VOTES**
1. U.S. Embargo of Cuba	(N) Y
2. Human Rights in Sudan	(N) N
3. Committee on the Inalienable Rights of the Palestinian People	(N) A
4. Division for Palestinian Rights of the Secretariat	(N) A
5. Fissile Material Cutoff Treaty	(N) Y
6. Work of the Special Committee to Investigate Israeli Practices	(N) A
7. Elimination of all Forms of Religious Intolerance	(Y) Y
8. Enhancing the Role of Organizations to Promote Democracy	(Y) Y
9. Human Rights in Iran	(Y) Y
10. International Trade and Development	(N) Y

ISRAEL

Voting Coincidence Percentages

Overall Votes (79): Agree 55, Disagree 4, Abstain 14, Absent 6: 93.2%
—Including All 213 Consensus Resolutions: 98.4%
—Arms Control: 87.5%; Human Rights: 90.9%; Middle East: 100.0%
Important Votes (10): Agree 8, Disagree 0, Abstain 2, Absent 0: 100.0%
—Including the 16 Important Consensus Resolutions: 100.0%

Important Issues	**VOTES**
1. U.S. Embargo of Cuba	(N) N
2. Human Rights in Sudan	(N) N
3. Committee on the Inalienable Rights of the Palestinian People	(N) N
4. Division for Palestinian Rights of the Secretariat	(N) N
5. Fissile Material Cutoff Treaty	(N) A
6. Work of the Special Committee to Investigate Israeli Practices	(N) N
7. Elimination of all Forms of Religious Intolerance	(Y) Y
8. Enhancing the Role of Organizations to Promote Democracy	(Y) Y
9. Human Rights in Iran	(Y) Y
10. International Trade and Development	(N) A

Votes: Y=Yes, N=No, A=Abstain, X=Absent, ( )=U.S. Vote

ITALY

Voting Coincidence Percentages

Overall Votes (79): Agree 30, Disagree 39, Abstain 10, Absent 0: 43.5%
—Including All 213 Consensus Resolutions: 86.1%
—Arms Control: 38.1%; Human Rights: 76.0%; Middle East: 14.3%
Important Votes (10): Agree 4, Disagree 3, Abstain 3, Absent 0: 57.1%
—Including the 16 Important Consensus Resolutions: 86.9%

Important Issues	VOTES
1. U.S. Embargo of Cuba	(N) Y
2. Human Rights in Sudan	(N) N
3. Committee on the Inalienable Rights of the Palestinian People	(N) A
4. Division for Palestinian Rights of the Secretariat	(N) A
5. Fissile Material Cutoff Treaty	(N) Y
6. Work of the Special Committee to Investigate Israeli Practices	(N) A
7. Elimination of all Forms of Religious Intolerance	(Y) Y
8. Enhancing the Role of Organizations to Promote Democracy	(Y) Y
9. Human Rights in Iran	(Y) Y
10. International Trade and Development	(N) Y

JAMAICA

Voting Coincidence Percentages

Overall Votes (79): Agree 8, Disagree 56, Abstain 9, Absent 6: 12.5%
—Including All 213 Consensus Resolutions: 78.7%
—Arms Control: 12.5%; Human Rights: 28.6%; Middle East: 5.6%
Important Votes (10): Agree 2, Disagree 6, Abstain 2, Absent 0: 25.0%
—Including the 16 Important Consensus Resolutions: 73.8%

Important Issues	VOTES
1. U.S. Embargo of Cuba	(N) Y
2. Human Rights in Sudan	(N) A
3. Committee on the Inalienable Rights of the Palestinian People	(N) Y
4. Division for Palestinian Rights of the Secretariat	(N) Y
5. Fissile Material Cutoff Treaty	(N) Y
6. Work of the Special Committee to Investigate Israeli Practices	(N) Y
7. Elimination of all Forms of Religious Intolerance	(Y) Y
8. Enhancing the Role of Organizations to Promote Democracy	(Y) Y
9. Human Rights in Iran	(Y) A
10. International Trade and Development	(N) Y

Votes: Y=Yes, N=No, A=Abstain, X=Absent, ( )=U.S. Vote

JAPAN

Voting Coincidence Percentages

Overall Votes (79): Agree 27, Disagree 36, Abstain 16, Absent 0: 42.9%
—Including All 213 Consensus Resolutions: 87.0%
—Arms Control: 16.7%; Human Rights: 83.3%; Middle East: 14.3%
Important Votes (10): Agree 4, Disagree 2, Abstain 4, Absent 0: 66.7%
—Including the 16 Important Consensus Resolutions: 90.9%

Important Issues	**VOTES**
1. U.S. Embargo of Cuba	(N) Y
2. Human Rights in Sudan	(N) N
3. Committee on the Inalienable Rights of the Palestinian People	(N) A
4. Division for Palestinian Rights of the Secretariat	(N) A
5. Fissile Material Cutoff Treaty	(N) Y
6. Work of the Special Committee to Investigate Israeli Practices	(N) A
7. Elimination of all Forms of Religious Intolerance	(Y) Y
8. Enhancing the Role of Organizations to Promote Democracy	(Y) Y
9. Human Rights in Iran	(Y) Y
10. International Trade and Development	(N) A

JORDAN

Voting Coincidence Percentages

Overall Votes (79): Agree 12, Disagree 63, Abstain 2, Absent 2: 16.0%
—Including All 213 Consensus Resolutions: 77.8%
—Arms Control: 12.5%; Human Rights: 33.3%; Middle East: 5.6%
Important Votes (10): Agree 3, Disagree 7, Abstain 0, Absent 0: 30.0%
—Including the 16 Important Consensus Resolutions: 72.7%

Important Issues	**VOTES**
1. U.S. Embargo of Cuba	(N) Y
2. Human Rights in Sudan	(N) Y
3. Committee on the Inalienable Rights of the Palestinian People	(N) Y
4. Division for Palestinian Rights of the Secretariat	(N) Y
5. Fissile Material Cutoff Treaty	(N) Y
6. Work of the Special Committee to Investigate Israeli Practices	(N) Y
7. Elimination of all Forms of Religious Intolerance	(Y) Y
8. Enhancing the Role of Organizations to Promote Democracy	(Y) Y
9. Human Rights in Iran	(Y) Y
10. International Trade and Development	(N) Y

Votes: Y=Yes, N=No, A=Abstain, X=Absent, ( )=U.S. Vote

KAZAKHSTAN

Voting Coincidence Percentages

Overall Votes (79): Agree 7, Disagree 57, Abstain 8, Absent 7: 10.9%
—Including All 213 Consensus Resolutions: 77.7%
—Arms Control: 15.0%; Human Rights: 15.0%; Middle East: 6.3%
Important Votes (10): Agree 2, Disagree 7, Abstain 1, Absent 0: 22.2%
—Including the 16 Important Consensus Resolutions: 70.1%

Important Issues	**VOTES**
1. U.S. Embargo of Cuba	(N) Y
2. Human Rights in Sudan	(N) Y
3. Committee on the Inalienable Rights of the Palestinian People	(N) Y
4. Division for Palestinian Rights of the Secretariat	(N) Y
5. Fissile Material Cutoff Treaty	(N) Y
6. Work of the Special Committee to Investigate Israeli Practices	(N) A
7. Elimination of all Forms of Religious Intolerance	(Y) Y
8. Enhancing the Role of Organizations to Promote Democracy	(Y) Y
9. Human Rights in Iran	(Y) N
10. International Trade and Development	(N) Y

KENYA

Voting Coincidence Percentages

Overall Votes (79): Agree 8, Disagree 56, Abstain 15, Absent 0: 12.5%
—Including All 213 Consensus Resolutions: 79.8%
—Arms Control: 12.0%; Human Rights: 21.1%; Middle East: 9.1%
Important Votes (10): Agree 2, Disagree 4, Abstain 4, Absent 0: 33.3%
—Including the 16 Important Consensus Resolutions: 81.8%

Important Issues	**VOTES**
1. U.S. Embargo of Cuba	(N) Y
2. Human Rights in Sudan	(N) Y
3. Committee on the Inalienable Rights of the Palestinian People	(N) A
4. Division for Palestinian Rights of the Secretariat	(N) A
5. Fissile Material Cutoff Treaty	(N) Y
6. Work of the Special Committee to Investigate Israeli Practices	(N) A
7. Elimination of all Forms of Religious Intolerance	(Y) Y
8. Enhancing the Role of Organizations to Promote Democracy	(Y) Y
9. Human Rights in Iran	(Y) A
10. International Trade and Development	(N) Y

Votes: Y=Yes, N=No, A=Abstain, X=Absent, ( )=U.S. Vote

KIRIBATI

Voting Coincidence Percentages

Overall Votes (79): Agree 1, Disagree 1, Abstain 0, Absent 77: 50.0%
—Including All 213 Consensus Resolutions: 85.1%
—Arms Control: 0.0%; Human Rights: 100.0%; Middle East: 0.0%
Important Votes (10): Agree 1, Disagree 1, Abstain 0, Absent 8: 50.0%
—Including the 16 Important Consensus Resolutions: 57.5%

Important Issues	**VOTES**
1. U.S. Embargo of Cuba	(N) Y
2. Human Rights in Sudan	(N) X
3. Committee on the Inalienable Rights of the Palestinian People	(N) X
4. Division for Palestinian Rights of the Secretariat	(N) X
5. Fissile Material Cutoff Treaty	(N) X
6. Work of the Special Committee to Investigate Israeli Practices	(N) X
7. Elimination of all Forms of Religious Intolerance	(Y) X
8. Enhancing the Role of Organizations to Promote Democracy	(Y) X
9. Human Rights in Iran	(Y) Y
10. International Trade and Development	(N) X

KUWAIT

Voting Coincidence Percentages

Overall Votes (79): Agree 7, Disagree 63, Abstain 7, Absent 2: 10.0%
—Including All 213 Consensus Resolutions: 77.2%
—Arms Control: 12.0%; Human Rights: 15.0%; Middle East: 5.9%
Important Votes (10): Agree 2, Disagree 8, Abstain 0, Absent 0: 20.0%
—Including the 16 Important Consensus Resolutions: 68.6%

Important Issues	**VOTES**
1. U.S. Embargo of Cuba	(N) Y
2. Human Rights in Sudan	(N) Y
3. Committee on the Inalienable Rights of the Palestinian People	(N) Y
4. Division for Palestinian Rights of the Secretariat	(N) Y
5. Fissile Material Cutoff Treaty	(N) Y
6. Work of the Special Committee to Investigate Israeli Practices	(N) Y
7. Elimination of all Forms of Religious Intolerance	(Y) Y
8. Enhancing the Role of Organizations to Promote Democracy	(Y) Y
9. Human Rights in Iran	(Y) N
10. International Trade and Development	(N) Y

Votes: Y=Yes, N=No, A=Abstain, X=Absent, ( )=U.S. Vote

KYRGYZSTAN

Voting Coincidence Percentages

Overall Votes (79): Agree 8, Disagree 52, Abstain 6, Absent 13: 13.3%
—Including All 213 Consensus Resolutions: 78.5%
—Arms Control: 10.5%; Human Rights: 30.0%; Middle East: 0.0%
Important Votes (10): Agree 2, Disagree 5, Abstain 1, Absent 2: 28.6%
—Including the 16 Important Consensus Resolutions: 75.8%

Important Issues	**VOTES**
1. U.S. Embargo of Cuba	(N) Y
2. Human Rights in Sudan	(N) A
3. Committee on the Inalienable Rights of the Palestinian People	(N) Y
4. Division for Palestinian Rights of the Secretariat	(N) Y
5. Fissile Material Cutoff Treaty	(N) Y
6. Work of the Special Committee to Investigate Israeli Practices	(N) X
7. Elimination of all Forms of Religious Intolerance	(Y) Y
8. Enhancing the Role of Organizations to Promote Democracy	(Y) Y
9. Human Rights in Iran	(Y) N
10. International Trade and Development	(N) X

LAOS

Voting Coincidence Percentages

Overall Votes (79): Agree 3, Disagree 57, Abstain 9, Absent 10: 5.0%
—Including All 213 Consensus Resolutions: 76.7%
—Arms Control: 4.8%; Human Rights: 7.1%; Middle East: 5.9%
Important Votes (10): Agree 1, Disagree 7, Abstain 2, Absent 0: 12.5%
—Including the 16 Important Consensus Resolutions: 68.0%

Important Issues	**VOTES**
1. U.S. Embargo of Cuba	(N) Y
2. Human Rights in Sudan	(N) Y
3. Committee on the Inalienable Rights of the Palestinian People	(N) Y
4. Division for Palestinian Rights of the Secretariat	(N) Y
5. Fissile Material Cutoff Treaty	(N) Y
6. Work of the Special Committee to Investigate Israeli Practices	(N) Y
7. Elimination of all Forms of Religious Intolerance	(Y) Y
8. Enhancing the Role of Organizations to Promote Democracy	(Y) A
9. Human Rights in Iran	(Y) A
10. International Trade and Development	(N) Y

Votes: Y=Yes, N=No, A=Abstain, X=Absent, ( )=U.S. Vote

LATVIA

Voting Coincidence Percentages

Overall Votes (79): Agree 32, Disagree 36, Abstain 9, Absent 2: 47.1%
—Including All 213 Consensus Resolutions: 86.9%
—Arms Control: 45.0%; Human Rights: 76.0%; Middle East: 14.3%
Important Votes (10): Agree 4, Disagree 3, Abstain 3, Absent 0: 57.1%
—Including the 16 Important Consensus Resolutions: 86.6%

Important Issues	**VOTES**
1. U.S. Embargo of Cuba	(N) Y
2. Human Rights in Sudan	(N) N
3. Committee on the Inalienable Rights of the Palestinian People	(N) A
4. Division for Palestinian Rights of the Secretariat	(N) A
5. Fissile Material Cutoff Treaty	(N) Y
6. Work of the Special Committee to Investigate Israeli Practices	(N) A
7. Elimination of all Forms of Religious Intolerance	(Y) Y
8. Enhancing the Role of Organizations to Promote Democracy	(Y) Y
9. Human Rights in Iran	(Y) Y
10. International Trade and Development	(N) Y

LEBANON

Voting Coincidence Percentages

Overall Votes (79): Agree 6, Disagree 63, Abstain 5, Absent 5: 8.7%
—Including All 213 Consensus Resolutions: 76.5%
—Arms Control: 8.7%; Human Rights: 19.0%; Middle East: 5.6%
Important Votes (10): Agree 2, Disagree 8, Abstain 0, Absent 0: 20.0%
—Including the 16 Important Consensus Resolutions: 67.9%

Important Issues	**VOTES**
1. U.S. Embargo of Cuba	(N) Y
2. Human Rights in Sudan	(N) Y
3. Committee on the Inalienable Rights of the Palestinian People	(N) Y
4. Division for Palestinian Rights of the Secretariat	(N) Y
5. Fissile Material Cutoff Treaty	(N) Y
6. Work of the Special Committee to Investigate Israeli Practices	(N) Y
7. Elimination of all Forms of Religious Intolerance	(Y) Y
8. Enhancing the Role of Organizations to Promote Democracy	(Y) Y
9. Human Rights in Iran	(Y) N
10. International Trade and Development	(N) Y

Votes: Y=Yes, N=No, A=Abstain, X=Absent, ( )=U.S. Vote

LESOTHO

Voting Coincidence Percentages

Overall Votes (79): Agree 6, Disagree 61, Abstain 6, Absent 6: 9.0%
—Including All 213 Consensus Resolutions: 76.8%
—Arms Control: 8.7%; Human Rights: 22.2%; Middle East: 0.0%
Important Votes (10): Agree 2, Disagree 7, Abstain 1, Absent 0: 22.2%
—Including the 16 Important Consensus Resolutions: 70.5%

Important Issues	**VOTES**
1. U.S. Embargo of Cuba	(N) Y
2. Human Rights in Sudan	(N) Y
3. Committee on the Inalienable Rights of the Palestinian People	(N) Y
4. Division for Palestinian Rights of the Secretariat	(N) Y
5. Fissile Material Cutoff Treaty	(N) Y
6. Work of the Special Committee to Investigate Israeli Practices	(N) Y
7. Elimination of all Forms of Religious Intolerance	(Y) Y
8. Enhancing the Role of Organizations to Promote Democracy	(Y) Y
9. Human Rights in Iran	(Y) A
10. International Trade and Development	(N) Y

LIBERIA

Voting Coincidence Percentages

Overall Votes (79): Agree 8, Disagree 51, Abstain 9, Absent 11: 13.6%
—Including All 213 Consensus Resolutions: 78.9%
—Arms Control: 9.1%; Human Rights: 31.6%; Middle East: 0.0%
Important Votes (10): Agree 2, Disagree 5, Abstain 2, Absent 1: 28.6%
—Including the 16 Important Consensus Resolutions: 75.8%

Important Issues	**VOTES**
1. U.S. Embargo of Cuba	(N) Y
2. Human Rights in Sudan	(N) A
3. Committee on the Inalienable Rights of the Palestinian People	(N) Y
4. Division for Palestinian Rights of the Secretariat	(N) Y
5. Fissile Material Cutoff Treaty	(N) Y
6. Work of the Special Committee to Investigate Israeli Practices	(N) X
7. Elimination of all Forms of Religious Intolerance	(Y) Y
8. Enhancing the Role of Organizations to Promote Democracy	(Y) Y
9. Human Rights in Iran	(Y) A
10. International Trade and Development	(N) Y

Votes: Y=Yes, N=No, A=Abstain, X=Absent, ( )=U.S. Vote

LIBYA

Voting Coincidence Percentages

Overall Votes (79): Agree 7, Disagree 65, Abstain 6, Absent 1: 9.7%
—Including All 213 Consensus Resolutions: 76.8%
—Arms Control: 12.0%; Human Rights: 14.3%; Middle East: 5.9%
Important Votes (10): Agree 1, Disagree 8, Abstain 1, Absent 0: 11.1%
—Including the 16 Important Consensus Resolutions: 67.5%

Important Issues	**VOTES**
1. U.S. Embargo of Cuba	(N) Y
2. Human Rights in Sudan	(N) Y
3. Committee on the Inalienable Rights of the Palestinian People	(N) Y
4. Division for Palestinian Rights of the Secretariat	(N) Y
5. Fissile Material Cutoff Treaty	(N) Y
6. Work of the Special Committee to Investigate Israeli Practices	(N) Y
7. Elimination of all Forms of Religious Intolerance	(Y) Y
8. Enhancing the Role of Organizations to Promote Democracy	(Y) A
9. Human Rights in Iran	(Y) N
10. International Trade and Development	(N) Y

LIECHTENSTEIN

Voting Coincidence Percentages

Overall Votes (79): Agree 28, Disagree 39, Abstain 12, Absent 0: 41.8%
—Including All 213 Consensus Resolutions: 86.1%
—Arms Control: 33.3%; Human Rights: 76.0%; Middle East: 14.3%
Important Votes (10): Agree 4, Disagree 3, Abstain 3, Absent 0: 57.1%
—Including the 16 Important Consensus Resolutions: 87.0%

Important Issues	**VOTES**
1. U.S. Embargo of Cuba	(N) Y
2. Human Rights in Sudan	(N) N
3. Committee on the Inalienable Rights of the Palestinian People	(N) A
4. Division for Palestinian Rights of the Secretariat	(N) A
5. Fissile Material Cutoff Treaty	(N) Y
6. Work of the Special Committee to Investigate Israeli Practices	(N) A
7. Elimination of all Forms of Religious Intolerance	(Y) Y
8. Enhancing the Role of Organizations to Promote Democracy	(Y) Y
9. Human Rights in Iran	(Y) Y
10. International Trade and Development	(N) Y

Votes: Y=Yes, N=No, A=Abstain, X=Absent, ( )=U.S. Vote

LITHUANIA

Voting Coincidence Percentages

Overall Votes (79): Agree 30, Disagree 39, Abstain 10, Absent 0: 43.5%
—Including All 213 Consensus Resolutions: 86.2%
—Arms Control: 36.4%; Human Rights: 76.0%; Middle East: 14.3%
Important Votes (10): Agree 4, Disagree 3, Abstain 3, Absent 0: 57.1%
—Including the 16 Important Consensus Resolutions: 87.0%

Important Issues	VOTES
1. U.S. Embargo of Cuba	(N) Y
2. Human Rights in Sudan	(N) N
3. Committee on the Inalienable Rights of the Palestinian People	(N) A
4. Division for Palestinian Rights of the Secretariat	(N) A
5. Fissile Material Cutoff Treaty	(N) Y
6. Work of the Special Committee to Investigate Israeli Practices	(N) A
7. Elimination of all Forms of Religious Intolerance	(Y) Y
8. Enhancing the Role of Organizations to Promote Democracy	(Y) Y
9. Human Rights in Iran	(Y) Y
10. International Trade and Development	(N) Y

LUXEMBOURG

Voting Coincidence Percentages

Overall Votes (79): Agree 29, Disagree 38, Abstain 10, Absent 2: 43.3%
—Including All 213 Consensus Resolutions: 86.2%
—Arms Control: 38.1%; Human Rights: 76.0%; Middle East: 14.3%
Important Votes (10): Agree 4, Disagree 3, Abstain 3, Absent 0: 57.1%
—Including the 16 Important Consensus Resolutions: 86.8%

Important Issues	VOTES
1. U.S. Embargo of Cuba	(N) Y
2. Human Rights in Sudan	(N) N
3. Committee on the Inalienable Rights of the Palestinian People	(N) A
4. Division for Palestinian Rights of the Secretariat	(N) A
5. Fissile Material Cutoff Treaty	(N) Y
6. Work of the Special Committee to Investigate Israeli Practices	(N) A
7. Elimination of all Forms of Religious Intolerance	(Y) Y
8. Enhancing the Role of Organizations to Promote Democracy	(Y) Y
9. Human Rights in Iran	(Y) Y
10. International Trade and Development	(N) Y

Votes: Y=Yes, N=No, A=Abstain, X=Absent, ( )=U.S. Vote

MADAGASCAR

Voting Coincidence Percentages

Overall Votes (79): Agree 9, Disagree 62, Abstain 5, Absent 3: 12.7%
—Including All 213 Consensus Resolutions: 77.4%
—Arms Control: 8.3%; Human Rights: 30.0%; Middle East: 0.0%
Important Votes (10): Agree 2, Disagree 7, Abstain 1, Absent 0: 22.2%
—Including the 16 Important Consensus Resolutions: 71.2%

Important Issues	VOTES
1. U.S. Embargo of Cuba	(N) Y
2. Human Rights in Sudan	(N) Y
3. Committee on the Inalienable Rights of the Palestinian People	(N) Y
4. Division for Palestinian Rights of the Secretariat	(N) Y
5. Fissile Material Cutoff Treaty	(N) Y
6. Work of the Special Committee to Investigate Israeli Practices	(N) Y
7. Elimination of all Forms of Religious Intolerance	(Y) Y
8. Enhancing the Role of Organizations to Promote Democracy	(Y) Y
9. Human Rights in Iran	(Y) A
10. International Trade and Development	(N) Y

MALAWI

Voting Coincidence Percentages

Overall Votes (79): Agree 9, Disagree 31, Abstain 10, Absent 29: 22.5%
—Including All 213 Consensus Resolutions: 81.8%
—Arms Control: 9.1%; Human Rights: 46.7%; Middle East: 0.0%
Important Votes (10): Agree 3, Disagree 3, Abstain 0, Absent 4: 50.0%
—Including the 16 Important Consensus Resolutions: 81.0%

Important Issues	VOTES
1. U.S. Embargo of Cuba	(N) Y
2. Human Rights in Sudan	(N) Y
3. Committee on the Inalienable Rights of the Palestinian People	(N) X
4. Division for Palestinian Rights of the Secretariat	(N) X
5. Fissile Material Cutoff Treaty	(N) Y
6. Work of the Special Committee to Investigate Israeli Practices	(N) X
7. Elimination of all Forms of Religious Intolerance	(Y) Y
8. Enhancing the Role of Organizations to Promote Democracy	(Y) Y
9. Human Rights in Iran	(Y) Y
10. International Trade and Development	(N) X

Votes: Y=Yes, N=No, A=Abstain, X=Absent, ( )=U.S. Vote

MALAYSIA

Voting Coincidence Percentages

Overall Votes (79): Agree 6, Disagree 64, Abstain 9, Absent 0: 8.6%
—Including All 213 Consensus Resolutions: 77.4%
—Arms Control: 8.3%; Human Rights: 15.0%; Middle East: 5.9%
Important Votes (10): Agree 2, Disagree 8, Abstain 0, Absent 0: 20.0%
—Including the 16 Important Consensus Resolutions: 69.2%

Important Issues	**VOTES**
1. U.S. Embargo of Cuba	(N) Y
2. Human Rights in Sudan	(N) Y
3. Committee on the Inalienable Rights of the Palestinian People	(N) Y
4. Division for Palestinian Rights of the Secretariat	(N) Y
5. Fissile Material Cutoff Treaty	(N) Y
6. Work of the Special Committee to Investigate Israeli Practices	(N) Y
7. Elimination of all Forms of Religious Intolerance	(Y) Y
8. Enhancing the Role of Organizations to Promote Democracy	(Y) Y
9. Human Rights in Iran	(Y) N
10. International Trade and Development	(N) Y

MALDIVES

Voting Coincidence Percentages

Overall Votes (79): Agree 7, Disagree 62, Abstain 3, Absent 7: 10.1%
—Including All 213 Consensus Resolutions: 76.6%
—Arms Control: 12.5%; Human Rights: 15.8%; Middle East: 6.3%
Important Votes (10): Agree 2, Disagree 8, Abstain 0, Absent 0: 20.0%
—Including the 16 Important Consensus Resolutions: 67.7%

Important Issues	**VOTES**
1. U.S. Embargo of Cuba	(N) Y
2. Human Rights in Sudan	(N) Y
3. Committee on the Inalienable Rights of the Palestinian People	(N) Y
4. Division for Palestinian Rights of the Secretariat	(N) Y
5. Fissile Material Cutoff Treaty	(N) Y
6. Work of the Special Committee to Investigate Israeli Practices	(N) Y
7. Elimination of all Forms of Religious Intolerance	(Y) Y
8. Enhancing the Role of Organizations to Promote Democracy	(Y) Y
9. Human Rights in Iran	(Y) N
10. International Trade and Development	(N) Y

Votes: Y=Yes, N=No, A=Abstain, X=Absent, ( )=U.S. Vote

MALI

Voting Coincidence Percentages

Overall Votes (79): Agree 10, Disagree 61, Abstain 3, Absent 5: 14.1%
—Including All 213 Consensus Resolutions: 77.2%
—Arms Control: 8.7%; Human Rights: 30.4%; Middle East: 0.0%
Important Votes (10): Agree 2, Disagree 7, Abstain 0, Absent 1: 22.2%
—Including the 16 Important Consensus Resolutions: 70.5%

Important Issues	**VOTES**
1. U.S. Embargo of Cuba	(N) Y
2. Human Rights in Sudan	(N) Y
3. Committee on the Inalienable Rights of the Palestinian People	(N) Y
4. Division for Palestinian Rights of the Secretariat	(N) Y
5. Fissile Material Cutoff Treaty	(N) Y
6. Work of the Special Committee to Investigate Israeli Practices	(N) Y
7. Elimination of all Forms of Religious Intolerance	(Y) Y
8. Enhancing the Role of Organizations to Promote Democracy	(Y) Y
9. Human Rights in Iran	(Y) X
10. International Trade and Development	(N) Y

MALTA

Voting Coincidence Percentages

Overall Votes (79): Agree 28, Disagree 42, Abstain 8, Absent 1: 40.0%
—Including All 213 Consensus Resolutions: 85.0%
—Arms Control: 30.0%; Human Rights: 76.0%; Middle East: 12.5%
Important Votes (10): Agree 4, Disagree 5, Abstain 1, Absent 0: 44.4%
—Including the 16 Important Consensus Resolutions: 79.9%

Important Issues	**VOTES**
1. U.S. Embargo of Cuba	(N) Y
2. Human Rights in Sudan	(N) N
3. Committee on the Inalienable Rights of the Palestinian People	(N) Y
4. Division for Palestinian Rights of the Secretariat	(N) Y
5. Fissile Material Cutoff Treaty	(N) Y
6. Work of the Special Committee to Investigate Israeli Practices	(N) A
7. Elimination of all Forms of Religious Intolerance	(Y) Y
8. Enhancing the Role of Organizations to Promote Democracy	(Y) Y
9. Human Rights in Iran	(Y) Y
10. International Trade and Development	(N) Y

Votes: Y=Yes, N=No, A=Abstain, X=Absent, ( )=U.S. Vote

MARSHALL ISLANDS

Voting Coincidence Percentages

Overall Votes (79): Agree 44, Disagree 28, Abstain 3, Absent 4: 61.1%
—Including All 213 Consensus Resolutions: 89.7%
—Arms Control: 28.6%; Human Rights: 83.3%; Middle East: 94.4%
Important Votes (10): Agree 8, Disagree 2, Abstain 0, Absent 0: 80.0%
—Including the 16 Important Consensus Resolutions: 92.0%

Important Issues	**VOTES**
1. U.S. Embargo of Cuba	(N) N
2. Human Rights in Sudan	(N) N
3. Committee on the Inalienable Rights of the Palestinian People	(N) N
4. Division for Palestinian Rights of the Secretariat	(N) N
5. Fissile Material Cutoff Treaty	(N) Y
6. Work of the Special Committee to Investigate Israeli Practices	(N) N
7. Elimination of all Forms of Religious Intolerance	(Y) Y
8. Enhancing the Role of Organizations to Promote Democracy	(Y) Y
9. Human Rights in Iran	(Y) Y
10. International Trade and Development	(N) Y

MAURITANIA

Voting Coincidence Percentages

Overall Votes (79): Agree 3, Disagree 32, Abstain 5, Absent 39: 8.6%
—Including All 213 Consensus Resolutions: 77.8%
—Arms Control: 0.0%; Human Rights: 11.8%; Middle East: 6.7%
Important Votes (10): Agree 2, Disagree 6, Abstain 0, Absent 2: 25.0%
—Including the 16 Important Consensus Resolutions: 62.9%

Important Issues	**VOTES**
1. U.S. Embargo of Cuba	(N) Y
2. Human Rights in Sudan	(N) Y
3. Committee on the Inalienable Rights of the Palestinian People	(N) Y
4. Division for Palestinian Rights of the Secretariat	(N) Y
5. Fissile Material Cutoff Treaty	(N) X
6. Work of the Special Committee to Investigate Israeli Practices	(N) Y
7. Elimination of all Forms of Religious Intolerance	(Y) Y
8. Enhancing the Role of Organizations to Promote Democracy	(Y) Y
9. Human Rights in Iran	(Y) N
10. International Trade and Development	(N) X

Votes: Y=Yes, N=No, A=Abstain, X=Absent, ( )=U.S. Vote

MAURITIUS

Voting Coincidence Percentages

Overall Votes (79): Agree 8, Disagree 59, Abstain 11, Absent 1: 11.9%
—Including All 213 Consensus Resolutions: 78.7%
—Arms Control: 5.3%; Human Rights: 28.6%; Middle East: 0.0%
Important Votes (10): Agree 2, Disagree 7, Abstain 1, Absent 0: 22.2%
—Including the 16 Important Consensus Resolutions: 71.8%

Important Issues	**VOTES**
1. U.S. Embargo of Cuba	(N) Y
2. Human Rights in Sudan	(N) Y
3. Committee on the Inalienable Rights of the Palestinian People	(N) Y
4. Division for Palestinian Rights of the Secretariat	(N) Y
5. Fissile Material Cutoff Treaty	(N) Y
6. Work of the Special Committee to Investigate Israeli Practices	(N) Y
7. Elimination of all Forms of Religious Intolerance	(Y) Y
8. Enhancing the Role of Organizations to Promote Democracy	(Y) Y
9. Human Rights in Iran	(Y) A
10. International Trade and Development	(N) Y

MEXICO

Voting Coincidence Percentages

Overall Votes (79): Agree 17, Disagree 57, Abstain 5, Absent 0: 23.0%
—Including All 213 Consensus Resolutions: 80.1%
—Arms Control: 8.7%; Human Rights: 56.0%; Middle East: 5.9%
Important Votes (10): Agree 4, Disagree 5, Abstain 1, Absent 0: 44.4%
—Including the 16 Important Consensus Resolutions: 80.0%

Important Issues	**VOTES**
1. U.S. Embargo of Cuba	(N) Y
2. Human Rights in Sudan	(N) N
3. Committee on the Inalienable Rights of the Palestinian People	(N) Y
4. Division for Palestinian Rights of the Secretariat	(N) Y
5. Fissile Material Cutoff Treaty	(N) Y
6. Work of the Special Committee to Investigate Israeli Practices	(N) A
7. Elimination of all Forms of Religious Intolerance	(Y) Y
8. Enhancing the Role of Organizations to Promote Democracy	(Y) Y
9. Human Rights in Iran	(Y) Y
10. International Trade and Development	(N) Y

Votes: Y=Yes, N=No, A=Abstain, X=Absent, ( )=U.S. Vote

MICRONESIA

Voting Coincidence Percentages

Overall Votes (79): Agree 46, Disagree 13, Abstain 4, Absent 16: 78.0%
—Including All 213 Consensus Resolutions: 94.4%
—Arms Control: 62.5%; Human Rights: 86.4%; Middle East: 100.0%
Important Votes (10): Agree 7, Disagree 2, Abstain 1, Absent 0: 77.8%
—Including the 16 Important Consensus Resolutions: 90.9%

Important Issues	VOTES
1. U.S. Embargo of Cuba	(N) A
2. Human Rights in Sudan	(N) N
3. Committee on the Inalienable Rights of the Palestinian People	(N) N
4. Division for Palestinian Rights of the Secretariat	(N) N
5. Fissile Material Cutoff Treaty	(N) Y
6. Work of the Special Committee to Investigate Israeli Practices	(N) N
7. Elimination of all Forms of Religious Intolerance	(Y) Y
8. Enhancing the Role of Organizations to Promote Democracy	(Y) Y
9. Human Rights in Iran	(Y) Y
10. International Trade and Development	(N) Y

MONACO

Voting Coincidence Percentages

Overall Votes (79): Agree 29, Disagree 33, Abstain 8, Absent 9: 46.8%
—Including All 213 Consensus Resolutions: 86.7%
—Arms Control: 50.0%; Human Rights: 75.0%; Middle East: 14.3%
Important Votes (10): Agree 4, Disagree 3, Abstain 3, Absent 0: 57.1%
—Including the 16 Important Consensus Resolutions: 85.7%

Important Issues	VOTES
1. U.S. Embargo of Cuba	(N) Y
2. Human Rights in Sudan	(N) N
3. Committee on the Inalienable Rights of the Palestinian People	(N) A
4. Division for Palestinian Rights of the Secretariat	(N) A
5. Fissile Material Cutoff Treaty	(N) Y
6. Work of the Special Committee to Investigate Israeli Practices	(N) A
7. Elimination of all Forms of Religious Intolerance	(Y) Y
8. Enhancing the Role of Organizations to Promote Democracy	(Y) Y
9. Human Rights in Iran	(Y) Y
10. International Trade and Development	(N) Y

Votes: Y=Yes, N=No, A=Abstain, X=Absent, ( )=U.S. Vote

MONGOLIA

Voting Coincidence Percentages

Overall Votes (79): Agree 10, Disagree 58, Abstain 7, Absent 4: 14.7%
—Including All 213 Consensus Resolutions: 78.5%
—Arms Control: 12.0%; Human Rights: 31.6%; Middle East: 6.7%
Important Votes (10): Agree 3, Disagree 3, Abstain 1, Absent 3: 50.0%
—Including the 16 Important Consensus Resolutions: 85.8%

Important Issues	**VOTES**
1. U.S. Embargo of Cuba	(N) Y
2. Human Rights in Sudan	(N) N
3. Committee on the Inalienable Rights of the Palestinian People	(N) X
4. Division for Palestinian Rights of the Secretariat	(N) X
5. Fissile Material Cutoff Treaty	(N) Y
6. Work of the Special Committee to Investigate Israeli Practices	(N) A
7. Elimination of all Forms of Religious Intolerance	(Y) Y
8. Enhancing the Role of Organizations to Promote Democracy	(Y) Y
9. Human Rights in Iran	(Y) X
10. International Trade and Development	(N) Y

MOROCCO

Voting Coincidence Percentages

Overall Votes (79): Agree 8, Disagree 62, Abstain 5, Absent 4: 11.4%
—Including All 213 Consensus Resolutions: 77.3%
—Arms Control: 12.0%; Human Rights: 20.0%; Middle East: 5.9%
Important Votes (10): Agree 2, Disagree 6, Abstain 0, Absent 2: 25.0%
—Including the 16 Important Consensus Resolutions: 74.2%

Important Issues	**VOTES**
1. U.S. Embargo of Cuba	(N) X
2. Human Rights in Sudan	(N) X
3. Committee on the Inalienable Rights of the Palestinian People	(N) Y
4. Division for Palestinian Rights of the Secretariat	(N) Y
5. Fissile Material Cutoff Treaty	(N) Y
6. Work of the Special Committee to Investigate Israeli Practices	(N) Y
7. Elimination of all Forms of Religious Intolerance	(Y) Y
8. Enhancing the Role of Organizations to Promote Democracy	(Y) Y
9. Human Rights in Iran	(Y) N
10. International Trade and Development	(N) Y

Votes: Y=Yes, N=No, A=Abstain, X=Absent, ( )=U.S. Vote

MOZAMBIQUE

Voting Coincidence Percentages

Overall Votes (79): Agree 6, Disagree 54, Abstain 3, Absent 16: 10.0%
—Including All 213 Consensus Resolutions: 76.8%
—Arms Control: 15.0%; Human Rights: 20.0%; Middle East: 5.9%
Important Votes (10): Agree 2, Disagree 7, Abstain 1, Absent 0: 22.2%
—Including the 16 Important Consensus Resolutions: 68.1%

Important Issues	**VOTES**
1. U.S. Embargo of Cuba	(N) Y
2. Human Rights in Sudan	(N) Y
3. Committee on the Inalienable Rights of the Palestinian People	(N) Y
4. Division for Palestinian Rights of the Secretariat	(N) Y
5. Fissile Material Cutoff Treaty	(N) Y
6. Work of the Special Committee to Investigate Israeli Practices	(N) Y
7. Elimination of all Forms of Religious Intolerance	(Y) Y
8. Enhancing the Role of Organizations to Promote Democracy	(Y) Y
9. Human Rights in Iran	(Y) A
10. International Trade and Development	(N) Y

MYANMAR (BURMA)

Voting Coincidence Percentages

Overall Votes (79): Agree 8, Disagree 60, Abstain 10, Absent 1: 11.8%
—Including All 213 Consensus Resolutions: 78.5%
—Arms Control: 13.0%; Human Rights: 21.1%; Middle East: 5.9%
Important Votes (10): Agree 1, Disagree 8, Abstain 1, Absent 0: 11.1%
—Including the 16 Important Consensus Resolutions: 67.8%

Important Issues	**VOTES**
1. U.S. Embargo of Cuba	(N) Y
2. Human Rights in Sudan	(N) Y
3. Committee on the Inalienable Rights of the Palestinian People	(N) Y
4. Division for Palestinian Rights of the Secretariat	(N) Y
5. Fissile Material Cutoff Treaty	(N) Y
6. Work of the Special Committee to Investigate Israeli Practices	(N) Y
7. Elimination of all Forms of Religious Intolerance	(Y) Y
8. Enhancing the Role of Organizations to Promote Democracy	(Y) A
9. Human Rights in Iran	(Y) N
10. International Trade and Development	(N) Y

Votes: Y=Yes, N=No, A=Abstain, X=Absent, ( )=U.S. Vote

NAMIBIA

Voting Coincidence Percentages

Overall Votes (79): Agree 11, Disagree 62, Abstain 5, Absent 1: 15.1%
—Including All 213 Consensus Resolutions: 78.1%
—Arms Control: 8.3%; Human Rights: 36.4%; Middle East: 0.0%
Important Votes (10): Agree 2, Disagree 7, Abstain 1, Absent 0: 22.2%
—Including the 16 Important Consensus Resolutions: 71.8%

Important Issues	**VOTES**
1. U.S. Embargo of Cuba	(N) Y
2. Human Rights in Sudan	(N) Y
3. Committee on the Inalienable Rights of the Palestinian People	(N) Y
4. Division for Palestinian Rights of the Secretariat	(N) Y
5. Fissile Material Cutoff Treaty	(N) Y
6. Work of the Special Committee to Investigate Israeli Practices	(N) Y
7. Elimination of all Forms of Religious Intolerance	(Y) Y
8. Enhancing the Role of Organizations to Promote Democracy	(Y) Y
9. Human Rights in Iran	(Y) A
10. International Trade and Development	(N) Y

NAURU

Voting Coincidence Percentages

Overall Votes (79): Agree 21, Disagree 32, Abstain 16, Absent 10: 39.6%
—Including All 213 Consensus Resolutions: 86.5%
—Arms Control: 11.1%; Human Rights: 68.4%; Middle East: 62.5%
Important Votes (10): Agree 6, Disagree 3, Abstain 1, Absent 0: 66.7%
—Including the 16 Important Consensus Resolutions: 86.9%

Important Issues	**VOTES**
1. U.S. Embargo of Cuba	(N) Y
2. Human Rights in Sudan	(N) N
3. Committee on the Inalienable Rights of the Palestinian People	(N) A
4. Division for Palestinian Rights of the Secretariat	(N) N
5. Fissile Material Cutoff Treaty	(N) Y
6. Work of the Special Committee to Investigate Israeli Practices	(N) N
7. Elimination of all Forms of Religious Intolerance	(Y) Y
8. Enhancing the Role of Organizations to Promote Democracy	(Y) Y
9. Human Rights in Iran	(Y) Y
10. International Trade and Development	(N) Y

Votes: Y=Yes, N=No, A=Abstain, X=Absent, ( )=U.S. Vote

NEPAL

Voting Coincidence Percentages

Overall Votes (79): Agree 9, Disagree 62, Abstain 7, Absent 1: 12.7%
—Including All 213 Consensus Resolutions: 77.8%
—Arms Control: 12.5%; Human Rights: 23.8%; Middle East: 5.9%
Important Votes (10): Agree 2, Disagree 7, Abstain 1, Absent 0: 22.2%
—Including the 16 Important Consensus Resolutions: 71.6%

Important Issues	**VOTES**
1. U.S. Embargo of Cuba	(N) Y
2. Human Rights in Sudan	(N) Y
3. Committee on the Inalienable Rights of the Palestinian People	(N) Y
4. Division for Palestinian Rights of the Secretariat	(N) Y
5. Fissile Material Cutoff Treaty	(N) Y
6. Work of the Special Committee to Investigate Israeli Practices	(N) Y
7. Elimination of all Forms of Religious Intolerance	(Y) Y
8. Enhancing the Role of Organizations to Promote Democracy	(Y) Y
9. Human Rights in Iran	(Y) A
10. International Trade and Development	(N) Y

NETHERLANDS

Voting Coincidence Percentages

Overall Votes (79): Agree 30, Disagree 40, Abstain 9, Absent 0: 42.9%
—Including All 213 Consensus Resolutions: 85.9%
—Arms Control: 34.8%; Human Rights: 76.0%; Middle East: 14.3%
Important Votes (10): Agree 4, Disagree 3, Abstain 3, Absent 0: 57.1%
—Including the 16 Important Consensus Resolutions: 87.0%

Important Issues	**VOTES**
1. U.S. Embargo of Cuba	(N) Y
2. Human Rights in Sudan	(N) N
3. Committee on the Inalienable Rights of the Palestinian People	(N) A
4. Division for Palestinian Rights of the Secretariat	(N) A
5. Fissile Material Cutoff Treaty	(N) Y
6. Work of the Special Committee to Investigate Israeli Practices	(N) A
7. Elimination of all Forms of Religious Intolerance	(Y) Y
8. Enhancing the Role of Organizations to Promote Democracy	(Y) Y
9. Human Rights in Iran	(Y) Y
10. International Trade and Development	(N) Y

Votes: Y=Yes, N=No, A=Abstain, X=Absent, ( )=U.S. Vote

NEW ZEALAND

Voting Coincidence Percentages

Overall Votes (79): Agree 28, Disagree 41, Abstain 10, Absent 0: 40.6%
—Including All 213 Consensus Resolutions: 85.5%
—Arms Control: 26.1%; Human Rights: 76.0%; Middle East: 14.3%
Important Votes (10): Agree 4, Disagree 2, Abstain 4, Absent 0: 66.7%
—Including the 16 Important Consensus Resolutions: 90.9%

Important Issues	**VOTES**
1. U.S. Embargo of Cuba	(N) Y
2. Human Rights in Sudan	(N) N
3. Committee on the Inalienable Rights of the Palestinian People	(N) A
4. Division for Palestinian Rights of the Secretariat	(N) A
5. Fissile Material Cutoff Treaty	(N) Y
6. Work of the Special Committee to Investigate Israeli Practices	(N) A
7. Elimination of all Forms of Religious Intolerance	(Y) Y
8. Enhancing the Role of Organizations to Promote Democracy	(Y) Y
9. Human Rights in Iran	(Y) Y
10. International Trade and Development	(N) A

NICARAGUA

Voting Coincidence Percentages

Overall Votes (79): Agree 18, Disagree 51, Abstain 7, Absent 3: 26.1%
—Including All 213 Consensus Resolutions: 81.4%
—Arms Control: 12.0%; Human Rights: 53.8%; Middle East: 10.0%
Important Votes (10): Agree 4, Disagree 2, Abstain 3, Absent 1: 66.7%
—Including the 16 Important Consensus Resolutions: 90.7%

Important Issues	**VOTES**
1. U.S. Embargo of Cuba	(N) X
2. Human Rights in Sudan	(N) N
3. Committee on the Inalienable Rights of the Palestinian People	(N) A
4. Division for Palestinian Rights of the Secretariat	(N) A
5. Fissile Material Cutoff Treaty	(N) Y
6. Work of the Special Committee to Investigate Israeli Practices	(N) A
7. Elimination of all Forms of Religious Intolerance	(Y) Y
8. Enhancing the Role of Organizations to Promote Democracy	(Y) Y
9. Human Rights in Iran	(Y) Y
10. International Trade and Development	(N) Y

Votes: Y=Yes, N=No, A=Abstain, X=Absent, ( )=U.S. Vote

NIGER

Voting Coincidence Percentages

Overall Votes (79): Agree 9, Disagree 52, Abstain 2, Absent 16: 14.8%
—Including All 213 Consensus Resolutions: 76.8%
—Arms Control: 9.1%; Human Rights: 29.2%; Middle East: 0.0%
Important Votes (10): Agree 2, Disagree 7, Abstain 0, Absent 1: 22.2%
—Including the 16 Important Consensus Resolutions: 67.1%

Important Issues	**VOTES**
1. U.S. Embargo of Cuba	(N) Y
2. Human Rights in Sudan	(N) Y
3. Committee on the Inalienable Rights of the Palestinian People	(N) Y
4. Division for Palestinian Rights of the Secretariat	(N) Y
5. Fissile Material Cutoff Treaty	(N) Y
6. Work of the Special Committee to Investigate Israeli Practices	(N) X
7. Elimination of all Forms of Religious Intolerance	(Y) Y
8. Enhancing the Role of Organizations to Promote Democracy	(Y) Y
9. Human Rights in Iran	(Y) N
10. International Trade and Development	(N) Y

NIGERIA

Voting Coincidence Percentages

Overall Votes (79): Agree 11, Disagree 63, Abstain 5, Absent 0: 14.9%
—Including All 213 Consensus Resolutions: 77.9%
—Arms Control: 12.0%; Human Rights: 31.8%; Middle East: 5.6%
Important Votes (10): Agree 2, Disagree 8, Abstain 0, Absent 0: 20.0%
—Including the 16 Important Consensus Resolutions: 69.0%

Important Issues	**VOTES**
1. U.S. Embargo of Cuba	(N) Y
2. Human Rights in Sudan	(N) Y
3. Committee on the Inalienable Rights of the Palestinian People	(N) Y
4. Division for Palestinian Rights of the Secretariat	(N) Y
5. Fissile Material Cutoff Treaty	(N) Y
6. Work of the Special Committee to Investigate Israeli Practices	(N) Y
7. Elimination of all Forms of Religious Intolerance	(Y) Y
8. Enhancing the Role of Organizations to Promote Democracy	(Y) Y
9. Human Rights in Iran	(Y) N
10. International Trade and Development	(N) Y

Votes: Y=Yes, N=No, A=Abstain, X=Absent, ( )=U.S. Vote

NORWAY

Voting Coincidence Percentages

Overall Votes (79): Agree 29, Disagree 39, Abstain 10, Absent 1: 42.6%
—Including All 213 Consensus Resolutions: 86.0%
—Arms Control: 36.4%; Human Rights: 76.0%; Middle East: 14.3%
Important Votes (10): Agree 4, Disagree 3, Abstain 3, Absent 0: 57.1%
—Including the 16 Important Consensus Resolutions: 86.9%

Important Issues	**VOTES**
1. U.S. Embargo of Cuba	(N) Y
2. Human Rights in Sudan	(N) N
3. Committee on the Inalienable Rights of the Palestinian People	(N) A
4. Division for Palestinian Rights of the Secretariat	(N) A
5. Fissile Material Cutoff Treaty	(N) Y
6. Work of the Special Committee to Investigate Israeli Practices	(N) A
7. Elimination of all Forms of Religious Intolerance	(Y) Y
8. Enhancing the Role of Organizations to Promote Democracy	(Y) Y
9. Human Rights in Iran	(Y) Y
10. International Trade and Development	(N) Y

OMAN

Voting Coincidence Percentages

Overall Votes (79): Agree 7, Disagree 64, Abstain 7, Absent 1: 9.9%
—Including All 213 Consensus Resolutions: 77.1%
—Arms Control: 12.0%; Human Rights: 15.0%; Middle East: 5.9%
Important Votes (10): Agree 2, Disagree 8, Abstain 0, Absent 0: 20.0%
—Including the 16 Important Consensus Resolutions: 68.8%

Important Issues	**VOTES**
1. U.S. Embargo of Cuba	(N) Y
2. Human Rights in Sudan	(N) Y
3. Committee on the Inalienable Rights of the Palestinian People	(N) Y
4. Division for Palestinian Rights of the Secretariat	(N) Y
5. Fissile Material Cutoff Treaty	(N) Y
6. Work of the Special Committee to Investigate Israeli Practices	(N) Y
7. Elimination of all Forms of Religious Intolerance	(Y) Y
8. Enhancing the Role of Organizations to Promote Democracy	(Y) Y
9. Human Rights in Iran	(Y) N
10. International Trade and Development	(N) Y

Votes: Y=Yes, N=No, A=Abstain, X=Absent, ( )=U.S. Vote

PAKISTAN

Voting Coincidence Percentages

Overall Votes (79): Agree 6, Disagree 56, Abstain 15, Absent 2: 9.7%
—Including All 213 Consensus Resolutions: 79.3%
—Arms Control: 17.6%; Human Rights: 10.5%; Middle East: 5.9%
Important Votes (10): Agree 2, Disagree 8, Abstain 0, Absent 0: 20.0%
—Including the 16 Important Consensus Resolutions: 68.8%
Security Council votes: 96.6%

Important Issues	VOTES
1. U.S. Embargo of Cuba	(N) Y
2. Human Rights in Sudan	(N) Y
3. Committee on the Inalienable Rights of the Palestinian People	(N) Y
4. Division for Palestinian Rights of the Secretariat	(N) Y
5. Fissile Material Cutoff Treaty	(N) Y
6. Work of the Special Committee to Investigate Israeli Practices	(N) Y
7. Elimination of all Forms of Religious Intolerance	(Y) Y
8. Enhancing the Role of Organizations to Promote Democracy	(Y) Y
9. Human Rights in Iran	(Y) N
10. International Trade and Development	(N) Y

PALAU

Voting Coincidence Percentages

Overall Votes (79): Agree 67, Disagree 1, Abstain 0, Absent 11: 98.5%
—Including All 213 Consensus Resolutions: 99.6%
—Arms Control: 100.0%; Human Rights: 100.0%; Middle East: 100.0%
Important Votes (10): Agree 10, Disagree 0, Abstain 0, Absent 0: 100.0%
—Including the 16 Important Consensus Resolutions: 100.0%

Important Issues	VOTES
1. U.S. Embargo of Cuba	(N) N
2. Human Rights in Sudan	(N) N
3. Committee on the Inalienable Rights of the Palestinian People	(N) N
4. Division for Palestinian Rights of the Secretariat	(N) N
5. Fissile Material Cutoff Treaty	(N) N
6. Work of the Special Committee to Investigate Israeli Practices	(N) N
7. Elimination of all Forms of Religious Intolerance	(Y) Y
8. Enhancing the Role of Organizations to Promote Democracy	(Y) Y
9. Human Rights in Iran	(Y) Y
10. International Trade and Development	(N) N

Votes: Y=Yes, N=No, A=Abstain, X=Absent, ( )=U.S. Vote

PANAMA

Voting Coincidence Percentages

Overall Votes (79): Agree 18, Disagree 59, Abstain 1, Absent 1: 23.4%
—Including All 213 Consensus Resolutions: 79.5%
—Arms Control: 12.5%; Human Rights: 51.9%; Middle East: 5.9%
Important Votes (10): Agree 4, Disagree 5, Abstain 1, Absent 0: 44.4%
—Including the 16 Important Consensus Resolutions: 79.9%

Important Issues	VOTES
1. U.S. Embargo of Cuba	(N) Y
2. Human Rights in Sudan	(N) N
3. Committee on the Inalienable Rights of the Palestinian People	(N) Y
4. Division for Palestinian Rights of the Secretariat	(N) Y
5. Fissile Material Cutoff Treaty	(N) Y
6. Work of the Special Committee to Investigate Israeli Practices	(N) A
7. Elimination of all Forms of Religious Intolerance	(Y) Y
8. Enhancing the Role of Organizations to Promote Democracy	(Y) Y
9. Human Rights in Iran	(Y) Y
10. International Trade and Development	(N) Y

PAPUA NEW GUINEA

Voting Coincidence Percentages

Overall Votes (79): Agree 11, Disagree 40, Abstain 21, Absent 7: 21.6%
—Including All 213 Consensus Resolutions: 83.4%
—Arms Control: 10.5%; Human Rights: 42.9%; Middle East: 0.0%
Important Votes (10): Agree 3, Disagree 3, Abstain 4, Absent 0: 50.0%
—Including the 16 Important Consensus Resolutions: 85.2%

Important Issues	VOTES
1. U.S. Embargo of Cuba	(N) Y
2. Human Rights in Sudan	(N) A
3. Committee on the Inalienable Rights of the Palestinian People	(N) A
4. Division for Palestinian Rights of the Secretariat	(N) A
5. Fissile Material Cutoff Treaty	(N) Y
6. Work of the Special Committee to Investigate Israeli Practices	(N) A
7. Elimination of all Forms of Religious Intolerance	(Y) Y
8. Enhancing the Role of Organizations to Promote Democracy	(Y) Y
9. Human Rights in Iran	(Y) Y
10. International Trade and Development	(N) Y

Votes: Y=Yes, N=No, A=Abstain, X=Absent, ( )=U.S. Vote

PARAGUAY

Voting Coincidence Percentages

Overall Votes (79): Agree 18, Disagree 55, Abstain 5, Absent 1: 24.7%
—Including All 213 Consensus Resolutions: 80.3%
—Arms Control: 13.6%; Human Rights: 56.0%; Middle East: 5.6%
Important Votes (10): Agree 4, Disagree 6, Abstain 0, Absent 0: 40.0%
—Including the 16 Important Consensus Resolutions: 76.4%

Important Issues	**VOTES**
1. U.S. Embargo of Cuba	(N) Y
2. Human Rights in Sudan	(N) N
3. Committee on the Inalienable Rights of the Palestinian People	(N) Y
4. Division for Palestinian Rights of the Secretariat	(N) Y
5. Fissile Material Cutoff Treaty	(N) Y
6. Work of the Special Committee to Investigate Israeli Practices	(N) Y
7. Elimination of all Forms of Religious Intolerance	(Y) Y
8. Enhancing the Role of Organizations to Promote Democracy	(Y) Y
9. Human Rights in Iran	(Y) Y
10. International Trade and Development	(N) Y

PERU

Voting Coincidence Percentages

Overall Votes (79): Agree 18, Disagree 54, Abstain 7, Absent 0: 25.0%
—Including All 213 Consensus Resolutions: 81.1%
—Arms Control: 12.0%; Human Rights: 58.3%; Middle East: 7.1%
Important Votes (10): Agree 4, Disagree 3, Abstain 3, Absent 0: 57.1%
—Including the 16 Important Consensus Resolutions: 87.0%

Important Issues	**VOTES**
1. U.S. Embargo of Cuba	(N) Y
2. Human Rights in Sudan	(N) N
3. Committee on the Inalienable Rights of the Palestinian People	(N) A
4. Division for Palestinian Rights of the Secretariat	(N) A
5. Fissile Material Cutoff Treaty	(N) Y
6. Work of the Special Committee to Investigate Israeli Practices	(N) A
7. Elimination of all Forms of Religious Intolerance	(Y) Y
8. Enhancing the Role of Organizations to Promote Democracy	(Y) Y
9. Human Rights in Iran	(Y) Y
10. International Trade and Development	(N) Y

Votes: Y=Yes, N=No, A=Abstain, X=Absent, ( )=U.S. Vote

PHILIPPINES

Voting Coincidence Percentages

Overall Votes (79): Agree 9, Disagree 60, Abstain 9, Absent 1: 13.0%
—Including All 213 Consensus Resolutions: 78.5%
—Arms Control: 12.0%; Human Rights: 26.3%; Middle East: 6.3%
Important Votes (10): Agree 2, Disagree 6, Abstain 2, Absent 0: 25.0%
—Including the 16 Important Consensus Resolutions: 74.8%
Security Council votes: 96.7%

Important Issues	**VOTES**
1. U.S. Embargo of Cuba	(N) Y
2. Human Rights in Sudan	(N) Y
3. Committee on the Inalienable Rights of the Palestinian People	(N) Y
4. Division for Palestinian Rights of the Secretariat	(N) Y
5. Fissile Material Cutoff Treaty	(N) Y
6. Work of the Special Committee to Investigate Israeli Practices	(N) A
7. Elimination of all Forms of Religious Intolerance	(Y) Y
8. Enhancing the Role of Organizations to Promote Democracy	(Y) Y
9. Human Rights in Iran	(Y) A
10. International Trade and Development	(N) Y

POLAND

Voting Coincidence Percentages

Overall Votes (79): Agree 32, Disagree 38, Abstain 9, Absent 0: 45.7%
—Including All 213 Consensus Resolutions: 86.6%
—Arms Control: 43.5%; Human Rights: 76.0%; Middle East: 14.3%
Important Votes (10): Agree 4, Disagree 3, Abstain 3, Absent 0: 57.1%
—Including the 16 Important Consensus Resolutions: 87.0%

Important Issues	**VOTES**
1. U.S. Embargo of Cuba	(N) Y
2. Human Rights in Sudan	(N) N
3. Committee on the Inalienable Rights of the Palestinian People	(N) A
4. Division for Palestinian Rights of the Secretariat	(N) A
5. Fissile Material Cutoff Treaty	(N) Y
6. Work of the Special Committee to Investigate Israeli Practices	(N) A
7. Elimination of all Forms of Religious Intolerance	(Y) Y
8. Enhancing the Role of Organizations to Promote Democracy	(Y) Y
9. Human Rights in Iran	(Y) Y
10. International Trade and Development	(N) Y

Votes: Y=Yes, N=No, A=Abstain, X=Absent, ( )=U.S. Vote

PORTUGAL

Voting Coincidence Percentages

Overall Votes (79): Agree 30, Disagree 39, Abstain 10, Absent 0: 43.5%
—Including All 213 Consensus Resolutions: 86.2%
—Arms Control: 38.1%; Human Rights: 76.0%; Middle East: 14.3%
Important Votes (10): Agree 4, Disagree 3, Abstain 3, Absent 0: 57.1%
—Including the 16 Important Consensus Resolutions: 87.0%

Important Issues	**VOTES**
1. U.S. Embargo of Cuba	(N) Y
2. Human Rights in Sudan	(N) N
3. Committee on the Inalienable Rights of the Palestinian People	(N) A
4. Division for Palestinian Rights of the Secretariat	(N) A
5. Fissile Material Cutoff Treaty	(N) Y
6. Work of the Special Committee to Investigate Israeli Practices	(N) A
7. Elimination of all Forms of Religious Intolerance	(Y) Y
8. Enhancing the Role of Organizations to Promote Democracy	(Y) Y
9. Human Rights in Iran	(Y) Y
10. International Trade and Development	(N) Y

QATAR

Voting Coincidence Percentages

Overall Votes (79): Agree 7, Disagree 63, Abstain 7, Absent 2: 10.0%
—Including All 213 Consensus Resolutions: 77.2%
—Arms Control: 12.5%; Human Rights: 15.0%; Middle East: 5.9%
Important Votes (10): Agree 2, Disagree 8, Abstain 0, Absent 0: 20.0%
—Including the 16 Important Consensus Resolutions: 68.6%

Important Issues	**VOTES**
1. U.S. Embargo of Cuba	(N) Y
2. Human Rights in Sudan	(N) Y
3. Committee on the Inalienable Rights of the Palestinian People	(N) Y
4. Division for Palestinian Rights of the Secretariat	(N) Y
5. Fissile Material Cutoff Treaty	(N) Y
6. Work of the Special Committee to Investigate Israeli Practices	(N) Y
7. Elimination of all Forms of Religious Intolerance	(Y) Y
8. Enhancing the Role of Organizations to Promote Democracy	(Y) Y
9. Human Rights in Iran	(Y) N
10. International Trade and Development	(N) Y

Votes: Y=Yes, N=No, A=Abstain, X=Absent, ( )=U.S. Vote

231

REPUBLIC OF KOREA

Voting Coincidence Percentages

Overall Votes (79): Agree 24, Disagree 37, Abstain 18, Absent 0: 39.3%
—Including All 213 Consensus Resolutions: 86.4%
—Arms Control: 22.2%; Human Rights: 78.3%; Middle East: 14.3%
Important Votes (10): Agree 3, Disagree 2, Abstain 5, Absent 0: 60.0%
—Including the 16 Important Consensus Resolutions: 90.4%

Important Issues	**VOTES**
1. U.S. Embargo of Cuba	(N) Y
2. Human Rights in Sudan	(N) N
3. Committee on the Inalienable Rights of the Palestinian People	(N) A
4. Division for Palestinian Rights of the Secretariat	(N) A
5. Fissile Material Cutoff Treaty	(N) Y
6. Work of the Special Committee to Investigate Israeli Practices	(N) A
7. Elimination of all Forms of Religious Intolerance	(Y) Y
8. Enhancing the Role of Organizations to Promote Democracy	(Y) Y
9. Human Rights in Iran	(Y) A
10. International Trade and Development	(N) A

REPUBLIC OF MOLDOVA

Voting Coincidence Percentages

Overall Votes (79): Agree 22, Disagree 38, Abstain 16, Absent 3: 36.7%
—Including All 213 Consensus Resolutions: 85.7%
—Arms Control: 17.6%; Human Rights: 72.7%; Middle East: 8.3%
Important Votes (10): Agree 4, Disagree 3, Abstain 3, Absent 0: 57.1%
—Including the 16 Important Consensus Resolutions: 86.6%

Important Issues	**VOTES**
1. U.S. Embargo of Cuba	(N) Y
2. Human Rights in Sudan	(N) N
3. Committee on the Inalienable Rights of the Palestinian People	(N) A
4. Division for Palestinian Rights of the Secretariat	(N) A
5. Fissile Material Cutoff Treaty	(N) Y
6. Work of the Special Committee to Investigate Israeli Practices	(N) A
7. Elimination of all Forms of Religious Intolerance	(Y) Y
8. Enhancing the Role of Organizations to Promote Democracy	(Y) Y
9. Human Rights in Iran	(Y) Y
10. International Trade and Development	(N) Y

Votes: Y=Yes, N=No, A=Abstain, X=Absent, ( )=U.S. Vote

ROMANIA

Voting Coincidence Percentages

Overall Votes (79): Agree 30, Disagree 38, Abstain 11, Absent 0: 44.1%
—Including All 213 Consensus Resolutions: 86.5%
—Arms Control: 38.1%; Human Rights: 76.0%; Middle East: 14.3%
Important Votes (10): Agree 4, Disagree 3, Abstain 3, Absent 0: 57.1%
—Including the 16 Important Consensus Resolutions: 87.0%
Security Council votes: 100.0%

Important Issues	**VOTES**
1. U.S. Embargo of Cuba	(N) Y
2. Human Rights in Sudan	(N) N
3. Committee on the Inalienable Rights of the Palestinian People	(N) A
4. Division for Palestinian Rights of the Secretariat	(N) A
5. Fissile Material Cutoff Treaty	(N) Y
6. Work of the Special Committee to Investigate Israeli Practices	(N) A
7. Elimination of all Forms of Religious Intolerance	(Y) Y
8. Enhancing the Role of Organizations to Promote Democracy	(Y) Y
9. Human Rights in Iran	(Y) Y
10. International Trade and Development	(N) Y

RUSSIA

Voting Coincidence Percentages

Overall Votes (79): Agree 11, Disagree 48, Abstain 20, Absent 0: 18.6%
—Including All 213 Consensus Resolutions: 82.4%
—Arms Control: 33.3%; Human Rights: 23.8%; Middle East: 6.7%
Important Votes (10): Agree 2, Disagree 5, Abstain 3, Absent 0: 28.6%
—Including the 16 Important Consensus Resolutions: 78.3%
Security Council votes: 94.9%

Important Issues	**VOTES**
1. U.S. Embargo of Cuba	(N) Y
2. Human Rights in Sudan	(N) Y
3. Committee on the Inalienable Rights of the Palestinian People	(N) A
4. Division for Palestinian Rights of the Secretariat	(N) A
5. Fissile Material Cutoff Treaty	(N) Y
6. Work of the Special Committee to Investigate Israeli Practices	(N) A
7. Elimination of all Forms of Religious Intolerance	(Y) Y
8. Enhancing the Role of Organizations to Promote Democracy	(Y) Y
9. Human Rights in Iran	(Y) N
10. International Trade and Development	(N) Y

Votes: Y=Yes, N=No, A=Abstain, X=Absent, ( )=U.S. Vote

RWANDA

Voting Coincidence Percentages

Overall Votes (79): Agree 6, Disagree 47, Abstain 3, Absent 23: 11.3%
—Including All 213 Consensus Resolutions: 77.0%
—Arms Control: 9.5%; Human Rights: 19.0%; Middle East: 0.0%
Important Votes (10): Agree 2, Disagree 4, Abstain 1, Absent 3: 33.3%
—Including the 16 Important Consensus Resolutions: 77.0%

Important Issues	**VOTES**
1. U.S. Embargo of Cuba	(N) Y
2. Human Rights in Sudan	(N) Y
3. Committee on the Inalienable Rights of the Palestinian People	(N) X
4. Division for Palestinian Rights of the Secretariat	(N) X
5. Fissile Material Cutoff Treaty	(N) Y
6. Work of the Special Committee to Investigate Israeli Practices	(N) X
7. Elimination of all Forms of Religious Intolerance	(Y) Y
8. Enhancing the Role of Organizations to Promote Democracy	(Y) Y
9. Human Rights in Iran	(Y) A
10. International Trade and Development	(N) Y

ST. KITTS AND NEVIS

Voting Coincidence Percentages

Overall Votes (79): Agree 1, Disagree 5, Abstain 0, Absent 73: 16.7%
—Including All 213 Consensus Resolutions: 79.9%
—Arms Control: 50.0%; Human Rights: 0.0%; Middle East: 0.0%
Important Votes (10): Agree 0, Disagree 2, Abstain 0, Absent 8: 0.0%
—Including the 16 Important Consensus Resolutions: 41.6%

Important Issues	**VOTES**
1. U.S. Embargo of Cuba	(N) Y
2. Human Rights in Sudan	(N) X
3. Committee on the Inalienable Rights of the Palestinian People	(N) X
4. Division for Palestinian Rights of the Secretariat	(N) X
5. Fissile Material Cutoff Treaty	(N) X
6. Work of the Special Committee to Investigate Israeli Practices	(N) X
7. Elimination of all Forms of Religious Intolerance	(Y) X
8. Enhancing the Role of Organizations to Promote Democracy	(Y) X
9. Human Rights in Iran	(Y) X
10. International Trade and Development	(N) Y

Votes: Y=Yes, N=No, A=Abstain, X=Absent, ( )=U.S. Vote

SAINT LUCIA

Voting Coincidence Percentages

Overall Votes (79): Agree 9, Disagree 58, Abstain 7, Absent 5: 13.4%
—Including All 213 Consensus Resolutions: 78.2%
—Arms Control: 8.7%; Human Rights: 36.8%; Middle East: 0.0%
Important Votes (10): Agree 2, Disagree 7, Abstain 1, Absent 0: 22.2%
—Including the 16 Important Consensus Resolutions: 70.8%

Important Issues	**VOTES**
1. U.S. Embargo of Cuba	(N) Y
2. Human Rights in Sudan	(N) Y
3. Committee on the Inalienable Rights of the Palestinian People	(N) Y
4. Division for Palestinian Rights of the Secretariat	(N) Y
5. Fissile Material Cutoff Treaty	(N) Y
6. Work of the Special Committee to Investigate Israeli Practices	(N) Y
7. Elimination of all Forms of Religious Intolerance	(Y) Y
8. Enhancing the Role of Organizations to Promote Democracy	(Y) Y
9. Human Rights in Iran	(Y) A
10. International Trade and Development	(N) Y

ST. VINCENT AND THE GRENADINES

Voting Coincidence Percentages

Overall Votes (79): Agree 9, Disagree 58, Abstain 8, Absent 4: 13.4%
—Including All 213 Consensus Resolutions: 78.6%
—Arms Control: 9.1%; Human Rights: 33.3%; Middle East: 0.0%
Important Votes (10): Agree 3, Disagree 6, Abstain 1, Absent 0: 33.3%
—Including the 16 Important Consensus Resolutions: 75.3%

Important Issues	**VOTES**
1. U.S. Embargo of Cuba	(N) Y
2. Human Rights in Sudan	(N) Y
3. Committee on the Inalienable Rights of the Palestinian People	(N) Y
4. Division for Palestinian Rights of the Secretariat	(N) Y
5. Fissile Material Cutoff Treaty	(N) Y
6. Work of the Special Committee to Investigate Israeli Practices	(N) A
7. Elimination of all Forms of Religious Intolerance	(Y) Y
8. Enhancing the Role of Organizations to Promote Democracy	(Y) Y
9. Human Rights in Iran	(Y) Y
10. International Trade and Development	(N) Y

Votes: Y=Yes, N=No, A=Abstain, X=Absent, ( )=U.S. Vote

SAMOA

Voting Coincidence Percentages

Overall Votes (79): Agree 17, Disagree 40, Abstain 12, Absent 10: 29.8%
—Including All 213 Consensus Resolutions: 83.6%
—Arms Control: 10.0%; Human Rights: 70.0%; Middle East: 0.0%
Important Votes (10): Agree 3, Disagree 3, Abstain 3, Absent 1: 50.0%
—Including the 16 Important Consensus Resolutions: 85.0%

Important Issues	**VOTES**
1. U.S. Embargo of Cuba	(N) Y
2. Human Rights in Sudan	(N) X
3. Committee on the Inalienable Rights of the Palestinian People	(N) A
4. Division for Palestinian Rights of the Secretariat	(N) A
5. Fissile Material Cutoff Treaty	(N) Y
6. Work of the Special Committee to Investigate Israeli Practices	(N) A
7. Elimination of all Forms of Religious Intolerance	(Y) Y
8. Enhancing the Role of Organizations to Promote Democracy	(Y) Y
9. Human Rights in Iran	(Y) Y
10. International Trade and Development	(N) Y

SAN MARINO

Voting Coincidence Percentages

Overall Votes (79): Agree 28, Disagree 40, Abstain 11, Absent 0: 41.2%
—Including All 213 Consensus Resolutions: 85.8%
—Arms Control: 31.8%; Human Rights: 76.0%; Middle East: 14.3%
Important Votes (10): Agree 4, Disagree 3, Abstain 3, Absent 0: 57.1%
—Including the 16 Important Consensus Resolutions: 87.0%

Important Issues	**VOTES**
1. U.S. Embargo of Cuba	(N) Y
2. Human Rights in Sudan	(N) N
3. Committee on the Inalienable Rights of the Palestinian People	(N) A
4. Division for Palestinian Rights of the Secretariat	(N) A
5. Fissile Material Cutoff Treaty	(N) Y
6. Work of the Special Committee to Investigate Israeli Practices	(N) A
7. Elimination of all Forms of Religious Intolerance	(Y) Y
8. Enhancing the Role of Organizations to Promote Democracy	(Y) Y
9. Human Rights in Iran	(Y) Y
10. International Trade and Development	(N) Y

Votes: Y=Yes, N=No, A=Abstain, X=Absent, ( )=U.S. Vote

SAO TOME AND PRINCIPE

Voting Coincidence Percentages

Overall Votes (79): Agree 5, Disagree 49, Abstain 4, Absent 21: 9.3%
—Including All 213 Consensus Resolutions: 77.5%
—Arms Control: 8.7%; Human Rights: 23.1%; Middle East: 0.0%
Important Votes (10): Agree 2, Disagree 4, Abstain 1, Absent 3: 33.3%
—Including the 16 Important Consensus Resolutions: 78.1%

Important Issues	**VOTES**
1. U.S. Embargo of Cuba	(N) Y
2. Human Rights in Sudan	(N) X
3. Committee on the Inalienable Rights of the Palestinian People	(N) X
4. Division for Palestinian Rights of the Secretariat	(N) X
5. Fissile Material Cutoff Treaty	(N) Y
6. Work of the Special Committee to Investigate Israeli Practices	(N) Y
7. Elimination of all Forms of Religious Intolerance	(Y) Y
8. Enhancing the Role of Organizations to Promote Democracy	(Y) Y
9. Human Rights in Iran	(Y) A
10. International Trade and Development	(N) Y

SAUDI ARABIA

Voting Coincidence Percentages

Overall Votes (79): Agree 5, Disagree 64, Abstain 8, Absent 2: 7.2%
—Including All 213 Consensus Resolutions: 76.7%
—Arms Control: 8.3%; Human Rights: 10.5%; Middle East: 5.9%
Important Votes (10): Agree 1, Disagree 8, Abstain 1, Absent 0: 11.1%
—Including the 16 Important Consensus Resolutions: 67.3%

Important Issues	**VOTES**
1. U.S. Embargo of Cuba	(N) Y
2. Human Rights in Sudan	(N) Y
3. Committee on the Inalienable Rights of the Palestinian People	(N) Y
4. Division for Palestinian Rights of the Secretariat	(N) Y
5. Fissile Material Cutoff Treaty	(N) Y
6. Work of the Special Committee to Investigate Israeli Practices	(N) Y
7. Elimination of all Forms of Religious Intolerance	(Y) Y
8. Enhancing the Role of Organizations to Promote Democracy	(Y) A
9. Human Rights in Iran	(Y) N
10. International Trade and Development	(N) Y

Votes: Y=Yes, N=No, A=Abstain, X=Absent, ( )=U.S. Vote

SENEGAL

Voting Coincidence Percentages

Overall Votes (79): Agree 10, Disagree 65, Abstain 4, Absent 0: 13.3%
—Including All 213 Consensus Resolutions: 77.2%
—Arms Control: 12.0%; Human Rights: 25.0%; Middle East: 5.9%
Important Votes (10): Agree 2, Disagree 8, Abstain 0, Absent 0: 20.0%
—Including the 16 Important Consensus Resolutions: 69.0%

Important Issues	VOTES
1. U.S. Embargo of Cuba	(N) Y
2. Human Rights in Sudan	(N) Y
3. Committee on the Inalienable Rights of the Palestinian People	(N) Y
4. Division for Palestinian Rights of the Secretariat	(N) Y
5. Fissile Material Cutoff Treaty	(N) Y
6. Work of the Special Committee to Investigate Israeli Practices	(N) Y
7. Elimination of all Forms of Religious Intolerance	(Y) Y
8. Enhancing the Role of Organizations to Promote Democracy	(Y) Y
9. Human Rights in Iran	(Y) N
10. International Trade and Development	(N) Y

SERBIA/MONTENEGRO

Voting Coincidence Percentages

Overall Votes (79): Agree 29, Disagree 39, Abstain 11, Absent 0: 42.6%
—Including All 213 Consensus Resolutions: 86.1%
—Arms Control: 35.0%; Human Rights: 76.0%; Middle East: 14.3%
Important Votes (10): Agree 4, Disagree 3, Abstain 3, Absent 0: 57.1%
—Including the 16 Important Consensus Resolutions: 87.0%

Important Issues	VOTES
1. U.S. Embargo of Cuba	(N) Y
2. Human Rights in Sudan	(N) N
3. Committee on the Inalienable Rights of the Palestinian People	(N) A
4. Division for Palestinian Rights of the Secretariat	(N) A
5. Fissile Material Cutoff Treaty	(N) Y
6. Work of the Special Committee to Investigate Israeli Practices	(N) A
7. Elimination of all Forms of Religious Intolerance	(Y) Y
8. Enhancing the Role of Organizations to Promote Democracy	(Y) Y
9. Human Rights in Iran	(Y) Y
10. International Trade and Development	(N) Y

Votes: Y=Yes, N=No, A=Abstain, X=Absent, ( )=U.S. Vote

SEYCHELLES

Voting Coincidence Percentages

Overall Votes (79): Agree 7, Disagree 40, Abstain 0, Absent 32: 14.9%
—Including All 213 Consensus Resolutions: 77.1%
—Arms Control: 18.8%; Human Rights: 30.0%; Middle East: 6.7%
Important Votes (10): Agree 2, Disagree 4, Abstain 0, Absent 4: 33.3%
—Including the 16 Important Consensus Resolutions: 74.4%

Important Issues	**VOTES**
1. U.S. Embargo of Cuba	(N) Y
2. Human Rights in Sudan	(N) X
3. Committee on the Inalienable Rights of the Palestinian People	(N) Y
4. Division for Palestinian Rights of the Secretariat	(N) Y
5. Fissile Material Cutoff Treaty	(N) Y
6. Work of the Special Committee to Investigate Israeli Practices	(N) X
7. Elimination of all Forms of Religious Intolerance	(Y) Y
8. Enhancing the Role of Organizations to Promote Democracy	(Y) Y
9. Human Rights in Iran	(Y) X
10. International Trade and Development	(N) X

SIERRA LEONE

Voting Coincidence Percentages

Overall Votes (79): Agree 8, Disagree 58, Abstain 10, Absent 3: 12.1%
—Including All 213 Consensus Resolutions: 78.7%
—Arms Control: 8.7%; Human Rights: 29.4%; Middle East: 0.0%
Important Votes (10): Agree 2, Disagree 7, Abstain 1, Absent 0: 22.2%
—Including the 16 Important Consensus Resolutions: 71.4%

Important Issues	**VOTES**
1. U.S. Embargo of Cuba	(N) Y
2. Human Rights in Sudan	(N) Y
3. Committee on the Inalienable Rights of the Palestinian People	(N) Y
4. Division for Palestinian Rights of the Secretariat	(N) Y
5. Fissile Material Cutoff Treaty	(N) Y
6. Work of the Special Committee to Investigate Israeli Practices	(N) Y
7. Elimination of all Forms of Religious Intolerance	(Y) Y
8. Enhancing the Role of Organizations to Promote Democracy	(Y) Y
9. Human Rights in Iran	(Y) A
10. International Trade and Development	(N) Y

Votes: Y=Yes, N=No, A=Abstain, X=Absent, ( )=U.S. Vote

SINGAPORE

Voting Coincidence Percentages

Overall Votes (79): Agree 9, Disagree 57, Abstain 12, Absent 1: 13.6%
—Including All 213 Consensus Resolutions: 79.4%
—Arms Control: 13.0%; Human Rights: 29.4%; Middle East: 5.9%
Important Votes (10): Agree 2, Disagree 7, Abstain 1, Absent 0: 22.2%
—Including the 16 Important Consensus Resolutions: 71.8%

Important Issues	**VOTES**
1. U.S. Embargo of Cuba	(N) Y
2. Human Rights in Sudan	(N) Y
3. Committee on the Inalienable Rights of the Palestinian People	(N) Y
4. Division for Palestinian Rights of the Secretariat	(N) Y
5. Fissile Material Cutoff Treaty	(N) Y
6. Work of the Special Committee to Investigate Israeli Practices	(N) Y
7. Elimination of all Forms of Religious Intolerance	(Y) Y
8. Enhancing the Role of Organizations to Promote Democracy	(Y) Y
9. Human Rights in Iran	(Y) A
10. International Trade and Development	(N) Y

SLOVAK REPUBLIC

Voting Coincidence Percentages

Overall Votes (79): Agree 30, Disagree 39, Abstain 10, Absent 0: 43.5%
—Including All 213 Consensus Resolutions: 86.2%
—Arms Control: 38.1%; Human Rights: 76.0%; Middle East: 14.3%
Important Votes (10): Agree 4, Disagree 3, Abstain 3, Absent 0: 57.1%
—Including the 16 Important Consensus Resolutions: 87.0%

Important Issues	**VOTES**
1. U.S. Embargo of Cuba	(N) Y
2. Human Rights in Sudan	(N) N
3. Committee on the Inalienable Rights of the Palestinian People	(N) A
4. Division for Palestinian Rights of the Secretariat	(N) A
5. Fissile Material Cutoff Treaty	(N) Y
6. Work of the Special Committee to Investigate Israeli Practices	(N) A
7. Elimination of all Forms of Religious Intolerance	(Y) Y
8. Enhancing the Role of Organizations to Promote Democracy	(Y) Y
9. Human Rights in Iran	(Y) Y
10. International Trade and Development	(N) Y

Votes: Y=Yes, N=No, A=Abstain, X=Absent, ( )=U.S. Vote

SLOVENIA

Voting Coincidence Percentages

<u>Overall Votes (79):</u> Agree 30, Disagree 38, Abstain 11, Absent 0: 44.1%
—Including All 213 Consensus Resolutions: 86.5%
—Arms Control: 38.1%; Human Rights: 76.0%; Middle East: 14.3%
<u>Important Votes (10):</u> Agree 4, Disagree 3, Abstain 3, Absent 0: 57.1%
—Including the 16 Important Consensus Resolutions: 87.0%

Important Issues	<u>**VOTES**</u>
1. U.S. Embargo of Cuba	(N) Y
2. Human Rights in Sudan	(N) N
3. Committee on the Inalienable Rights of the Palestinian People	(N) A
4. Division for Palestinian Rights of the Secretariat	(N) A
5. Fissile Material Cutoff Treaty	(N) Y
6. Work of the Special Committee to Investigate Israeli Practices	(N) A
7. Elimination of all Forms of Religious Intolerance	(Y) Y
8. Enhancing the Role of Organizations to Promote Democracy	(Y) Y
9. Human Rights in Iran	(Y) Y
10. International Trade and Development	(N) Y

SOLOMON ISLANDS

Voting Coincidence Percentages

<u>Overall Votes (79):</u> Agree 12, Disagree 41, Abstain 13, Absent 13: 22.6%
—Including All 213 Consensus Resolutions: 82.2%
—Arms Control: 9.5%; Human Rights: 56.3%; Middle East: 0.0%
<u>Important Votes (10):</u> Agree 3, Disagree 3, Abstain 4, Absent 0: 50.0%
—Including the 16 Important Consensus Resolutions: 84.5%

Important Issues	<u>**VOTES**</u>
1. U.S. Embargo of Cuba	(N) Y
2. Human Rights in Sudan	(N) A
3. Committee on the Inalienable Rights of the Palestinian People	(N) A
4. Division for Palestinian Rights of the Secretariat	(N) A
5. Fissile Material Cutoff Treaty	(N) Y
6. Work of the Special Committee to Investigate Israeli Practices	(N) A
7. Elimination of all Forms of Religious Intolerance	(Y) Y
8. Enhancing the Role of Organizations to Promote Democracy	(Y) Y
9. Human Rights in Iran	(Y) Y
10. International Trade and Development	(N) Y

Votes: Y=Yes, N=No, A=Abstain, X=Absent, ( )=U.S. Vote

241

SOMALIA

Voting Coincidence Percentages

Overall Votes (79): Agree 6, Disagree 62, Abstain 6, Absent 5: 8.8%
—Including All 213 Consensus Resolutions: 77.0%
—Arms Control: 8.7%; Human Rights: 20.0%; Middle East: 0.0%
Important Votes (10): Agree 3, Disagree 7, Abstain 0, Absent 0: 30.0%
—Including the 16 Important Consensus Resolutions: 72.1%

Important Issues	**VOTES**
1. U.S. Embargo of Cuba	(N) Y
2. Human Rights in Sudan	(N) N
3. Committee on the Inalienable Rights of the Palestinian People	(N) Y
4. Division for Palestinian Rights of the Secretariat	(N) Y
5. Fissile Material Cutoff Treaty	(N) Y
6. Work of the Special Committee to Investigate Israeli Practices	(N) Y
7. Elimination of all Forms of Religious Intolerance	(Y) Y
8. Enhancing the Role of Organizations to Promote Democracy	(Y) Y
9. Human Rights in Iran	(Y) N
10. International Trade and Development	(N) Y

SOUTH AFRICA

Voting Coincidence Percentages

Overall Votes (79): Agree 8, Disagree 62, Abstain 8, Absent 1: 11.4%
—Including All 213 Consensus Resolutions: 77.7%
—Arms Control: 13.6%; Human Rights: 19.0%; Middle East: 5.6%
Important Votes (10): Agree 2, Disagree 8, Abstain 0, Absent 0: 20.0%
—Including the 16 Important Consensus Resolutions: 68.8%

Important Issues	**VOTES**
1. U.S. Embargo of Cuba	(N) Y
2. Human Rights in Sudan	(N) Y
3. Committee on the Inalienable Rights of the Palestinian People	(N) Y
4. Division for Palestinian Rights of the Secretariat	(N) Y
5. Fissile Material Cutoff Treaty	(N) Y
6. Work of the Special Committee to Investigate Israeli Practices	(N) Y
7. Elimination of all Forms of Religious Intolerance	(Y) Y
8. Enhancing the Role of Organizations to Promote Democracy	(Y) Y
9. Human Rights in Iran	(Y) N
10. International Trade and Development	(N) Y

Votes: Y=Yes, N=No, A=Abstain, X=Absent, ( )=U.S. Vote

SPAIN

Voting Coincidence Percentages

Overall Votes (79): Agree 30, Disagree 36, Abstain 13, Absent 0: 45.5%
—Including All 213 Consensus Resolutions: 87.1%
—Arms Control: 44.4%; Human Rights: 76.0%; Middle East: 14.3%
Important Votes (10): Agree 4, Disagree 3, Abstain 3, Absent 0: 57.1%
—Including the 16 Important Consensus Resolutions: 87.0%
Security Council votes: 96.7%

Important Issues	**VOTES**
1. U.S. Embargo of Cuba	(N) Y
2. Human Rights in Sudan	(N) N
3. Committee on the Inalienable Rights of the Palestinian People	(N) A
4. Division for Palestinian Rights of the Secretariat	(N) A
5. Fissile Material Cutoff Treaty	(N) A
6. Work of the Special Committee to Investigate Israeli Practices	(N) A
7. Elimination of all Forms of Religious Intolerance	(Y) Y
8. Enhancing the Role of Organizations to Promote Democracy	(Y) Y
9. Human Rights in Iran	(Y) Y
10. International Trade and Development	(N) Y

SRI LANKA

Voting Coincidence Percentages

Overall Votes (79): Agree 9, Disagree 61, Abstain 9, Absent 0: 12.9%
—Including All 213 Consensus Resolutions: 78.4%
—Arms Control: 12.0%; Human Rights: 26.3%; Middle East: 5.9%
Important Votes (10): Agree 2, Disagree 8, Abstain 0, Absent 0: 20.0%
—Including the 16 Important Consensus Resolutions: 69.2%

Important Issues	**VOTES**
1. U.S. Embargo of Cuba	(N) Y
2. Human Rights in Sudan	(N) Y
3. Committee on the Inalienable Rights of the Palestinian People	(N) Y
4. Division for Palestinian Rights of the Secretariat	(N) Y
5. Fissile Material Cutoff Treaty	(N) Y
6. Work of the Special Committee to Investigate Israeli Practices	(N) Y
7. Elimination of all Forms of Religious Intolerance	(Y) Y
8. Enhancing the Role of Organizations to Promote Democracy	(Y) Y
9. Human Rights in Iran	(Y) N
10. International Trade and Development	(N) Y

Votes: Y=Yes, N=No, A=Abstain, X=Absent, ( )=U.S. Vote

SUDAN

Voting Coincidence Percentages

Overall Votes (79): Agree 10, Disagree 65, Abstain 4, Absent 0: 13.3%
—Including All 213 Consensus Resolutions: 77.2%
—Arms Control: 12.0%; Human Rights: 26.1%; Middle East: 5.6%
Important Votes (10): Agree 2, Disagree 8, Abstain 0, Absent 0: 20.0%
—Including the 16 Important Consensus Resolutions: 69.0%

Important Issues	**VOTES**
1. U.S. Embargo of Cuba	(N) Y
2. Human Rights in Sudan	(N) Y
3. Committee on the Inalienable Rights of the Palestinian People	(N) Y
4. Division for Palestinian Rights of the Secretariat	(N) Y
5. Fissile Material Cutoff Treaty	(N) Y
6. Work of the Special Committee to Investigate Israeli Practices	(N) Y
7. Elimination of all Forms of Religious Intolerance	(Y) Y
8. Enhancing the Role of Organizations to Promote Democracy	(Y) Y
9. Human Rights in Iran	(Y) N
10. International Trade and Development	(N) Y

SURINAME

Voting Coincidence Percentages

Overall Votes (79): Agree 6, Disagree 63, Abstain 9, Absent 1: 8.7%
—Including All 213 Consensus Resolutions: 77.5%
—Arms Control: 8.3%; Human Rights: 16.7%; Middle East: 0.0%
Important Votes (10): Agree 2, Disagree 7, Abstain 1, Absent 0: 22.2%
—Including the 16 Important Consensus Resolutions: 71.8%

Important Issues	**VOTES**
1. U.S. Embargo of Cuba	(N) Y
2. Human Rights in Sudan	(N) Y
3. Committee on the Inalienable Rights of the Palestinian People	(N) Y
4. Division for Palestinian Rights of the Secretariat	(N) Y
5. Fissile Material Cutoff Treaty	(N) Y
6. Work of the Special Committee to Investigate Israeli Practices	(N) Y
7. Elimination of all Forms of Religious Intolerance	(Y) Y
8. Enhancing the Role of Organizations to Promote Democracy	(Y) Y
9. Human Rights in Iran	(Y) A
10. International Trade and Development	(N) Y

Votes: Y=Yes, N=No, A=Abstain, X=Absent, ( )=U.S. Vote

SWAZILAND

Voting Coincidence Percentages

Overall Votes (79): Agree 7, Disagree 43, Abstain 7, Absent 22: 14.0%
—Including All 213 Consensus Resolutions: 78.7%
—Arms Control: 12.5%; Human Rights: 28.6%; Middle East: 11.1%
Important Votes (10): Agree 2, Disagree 3, Abstain 1, Absent 4: 40.0%
—Including the 16 Important Consensus Resolutions: 81.7%

Important Issues	VOTES
1. U.S. Embargo of Cuba	(N) Y
2. Human Rights in Sudan	(N) Y
3. Committee on the Inalienable Rights of the Palestinian People	(N) X
4. Division for Palestinian Rights of the Secretariat	(N) X
5. Fissile Material Cutoff Treaty	(N) Y
6. Work of the Special Committee to Investigate Israeli Practices	(N) X
7. Elimination of all Forms of Religious Intolerance	(Y) Y
8. Enhancing the Role of Organizations to Promote Democracy	(Y) Y
9. Human Rights in Iran	(Y) A
10. International Trade and Development	(N) X

SWEDEN

Voting Coincidence Percentages

Overall Votes (79): Agree 29, Disagree 39, Abstain 11, Absent 0: 42.6%
—Including All 213 Consensus Resolutions: 86.1%
—Arms Control: 28.6%; Human Rights: 79.2%; Middle East: 14.3%
Important Votes (10): Agree 4, Disagree 3, Abstain 3, Absent 0: 57.1%
—Including the 16 Important Consensus Resolutions: 87.0%

Important Issues	VOTES
1. U.S. Embargo of Cuba	(N) Y
2. Human Rights in Sudan	(N) N
3. Committee on the Inalienable Rights of the Palestinian People	(N) A
4. Division for Palestinian Rights of the Secretariat	(N) A
5. Fissile Material Cutoff Treaty	(N) Y
6. Work of the Special Committee to Investigate Israeli Practices	(N) A
7. Elimination of all Forms of Religious Intolerance	(Y) Y
8. Enhancing the Role of Organizations to Promote Democracy	(Y) Y
9. Human Rights in Iran	(Y) Y
10. International Trade and Development	(N) Y

Votes: Y=Yes, N=No, A=Abstain, X=Absent, ( )=U.S. Vote

SWITZERLAND

Voting Coincidence Percentages

Overall Votes (79): Agree 28, Disagree 38, Abstain 12, Absent 1: 42.4%
—Including All 213 Consensus Resolutions: 86.3%
—Arms Control: 35.0%; Human Rights: 76.0%; Middle East: 14.3%
Important Votes (10): Agree 4, Disagree 3, Abstain 3, Absent 0: 57.1%
—Including the 16 Important Consensus Resolutions: 86.9%

Important Issues	**VOTES**
1. U.S. Embargo of Cuba	(N) Y
2. Human Rights in Sudan	(N) N
3. Committee on the Inalienable Rights of the Palestinian People	(N) A
4. Division for Palestinian Rights of the Secretariat	(N) A
5. Fissile Material Cutoff Treaty	(N) Y
6. Work of the Special Committee to Investigate Israeli Practices	(N) A
7. Elimination of all Forms of Religious Intolerance	(Y) Y
8. Enhancing the Role of Organizations to Promote Democracy	(Y) Y
9. Human Rights in Iran	(Y) Y
10. International Trade and Development	(N) Y

SYRIA

Voting Coincidence Percentages

Overall Votes (79): Agree 7, Disagree 62, Abstain 6, Absent 4: 10.1%
—Including All 213 Consensus Resolutions: 76.8%
—Arms Control: 9.1%; Human Rights: 23.8%; Middle East: 5.6%
Important Votes (10): Agree 1, Disagree 8, Abstain 1, Absent 0: 11.1%
—Including the 16 Important Consensus Resolutions: 66.6%

Important Issues	**VOTES**
1. U.S. Embargo of Cuba	(N) Y
2. Human Rights in Sudan	(N) Y
3. Committee on the Inalienable Rights of the Palestinian People	(N) Y
4. Division for Palestinian Rights of the Secretariat	(N) Y
5. Fissile Material Cutoff Treaty	(N) Y
6. Work of the Special Committee to Investigate Israeli Practices	(N) Y
7. Elimination of all Forms of Religious Intolerance	(Y) Y
8. Enhancing the Role of Organizations to Promote Democracy	(Y) A
9. Human Rights in Iran	(Y) N
10. International Trade and Development	(N) Y

Votes: Y=Yes, N=No, A=Abstain, X=Absent, ( )=U.S. Vote

TAJIKISTAN

Voting Coincidence Percentages

Overall Votes (79): Agree 6, Disagree 49, Abstain 5, Absent 19: 10.9%
—Including All 213 Consensus Resolutions: 77.3%
—Arms Control: 11.8%; Human Rights: 22.2%; Middle East: 0.0%
Important Votes (10): Agree 2, Disagree 7, Abstain 0, Absent 1: 22.2%
—Including the 16 Important Consensus Resolutions: 66.8%

Important Issues	**VOTES**
1. U.S. Embargo of Cuba	(N) Y
2. Human Rights in Sudan	(N) Y
3. Committee on the Inalienable Rights of the Palestinian People	(N) Y
4. Division for Palestinian Rights of the Secretariat	(N) Y
5. Fissile Material Cutoff Treaty	(N) Y
6. Work of the Special Committee to Investigate Israeli Practices	(N) Y
7. Elimination of all Forms of Religious Intolerance	(Y) Y
8. Enhancing the Role of Organizations to Promote Democracy	(Y) Y
9. Human Rights in Iran	(Y) N
10. International Trade and Development	(N) X

THAILAND

Voting Coincidence Percentages

Overall Votes (79): Agree 10, Disagree 57, Abstain 12, Absent 0: 14.9%
—Including All 213 Consensus Resolutions: 79.6%
—Arms Control: 12.0%; Human Rights: 31.6%; Middle East: 7.1%
Important Votes (10): Agree 2, Disagree 4, Abstain 4, Absent 0: 33.3%
—Including the 16 Important Consensus Resolutions: 81.8%

Important Issues	**VOTES**
1. U.S. Embargo of Cuba	(N) Y
2. Human Rights in Sudan	(N) Y
3. Committee on the Inalienable Rights of the Palestinian People	(N) A
4. Division for Palestinian Rights of the Secretariat	(N) A
5. Fissile Material Cutoff Treaty	(N) Y
6. Work of the Special Committee to Investigate Israeli Practices	(N) A
7. Elimination of all Forms of Religious Intolerance	(Y) Y
8. Enhancing the Role of Organizations to Promote Democracy	(Y) Y
9. Human Rights in Iran	(Y) A
10. International Trade and Development	(N) Y

Votes: Y=Yes, N=No, A=Abstain, X=Absent, ( )=U.S. Vote

TFYR MACEDONIA

Voting Coincidence Percentages

Overall Votes (79): Agree 28, Disagree 38, Abstain 11, Absent 2: 42.4%
—Including All 213 Consensus Resolutions: 86.1%
—Arms Control: 33.3%; Human Rights: 76.0%; Middle East: 7.7%
Important Votes (10): Agree 4, Disagree 3, Abstain 3, Absent 0: 57.1%
—Including the 16 Important Consensus Resolutions: 86.8%

Important Issues	VOTES
1. U.S. Embargo of Cuba	(N) Y
2. Human Rights in Sudan	(N) N
3. Committee on the Inalienable Rights of the Palestinian People	(N) A
4. Division for Palestinian Rights of the Secretariat	(N) A
5. Fissile Material Cutoff Treaty	(N) Y
6. Work of the Special Committee to Investigate Israeli Practices	(N) A
7. Elimination of all Forms of Religious Intolerance	(Y) Y
8. Enhancing the Role of Organizations to Promote Democracy	(Y) Y
9. Human Rights in Iran	(Y) Y
10. International Trade and Development	(N) Y

TIMOR-LESTE

Voting Coincidence Percentages

Overall Votes (79): Agree 18, Disagree 55, Abstain 0, Absent 6: 24.7%
—Including All 213 Consensus Resolutions: 79.8%
—Arms Control: 12.5%; Human Rights: 53.8%; Middle East: 7.1%
Important Votes (10): Agree 4, Disagree 3, Abstain 0, Absent 3: 57.1%
—Including the 16 Important Consensus Resolutions: 86.3%

Important Issues	VOTES
1. U.S. Embargo of Cuba	(N) Y
2. Human Rights in Sudan	(N) N
3. Committee on the Inalienable Rights of the Palestinian People	(N) X
4. Division for Palestinian Rights of the Secretariat	(N) X
5. Fissile Material Cutoff Treaty	(N) Y
6. Work of the Special Committee to Investigate Israeli Practices	(N) X
7. Elimination of all Forms of Religious Intolerance	(Y) Y
8. Enhancing the Role of Organizations to Promote Democracy	(Y) Y
9. Human Rights in Iran	(Y) Y
10. International Trade and Development	(N) Y

Votes: Y=Yes, N=No, A=Abstain, X=Absent, ( )=U.S. Vote

TOGO

Voting Coincidence Percentages

Overall Votes (79): Agree 8, Disagree 64, Abstain 5, Absent 2: 11.1%
—Including All 213 Consensus Resolutions: 77.0%
—Arms Control: 12.5%; Human Rights: 19.0%; Middle East: 5.6%
Important Votes (10): Agree 2, Disagree 8, Abstain 0, Absent 0: 20.0%
—Including the 16 Important Consensus Resolutions: 68.6%

Important Issues	**VOTES**
1. U.S. Embargo of Cuba	(N) Y
2. Human Rights in Sudan	(N) Y
3. Committee on the Inalienable Rights of the Palestinian People	(N) Y
4. Division for Palestinian Rights of the Secretariat	(N) Y
5. Fissile Material Cutoff Treaty	(N) Y
6. Work of the Special Committee to Investigate Israeli Practices	(N) Y
7. Elimination of all Forms of Religious Intolerance	(Y) Y
8. Enhancing the Role of Organizations to Promote Democracy	(Y) Y
9. Human Rights in Iran	(Y) N
10. International Trade and Development	(N) Y

TONGA

Voting Coincidence Percentages

Overall Votes (79): Agree 3, Disagree 35, Abstain 15, Absent 26: 7.9%
—Including All 213 Consensus Resolutions: 81.1%
—Arms Control: 11.1%; Human Rights: 0.0%; Middle East: 16.7%
Important Votes (10): Agree 0, Disagree 3, Abstain 3, Absent 4: 0.0%
—Including the 16 Important Consensus Resolutions: 78.6%

Important Issues	**VOTES**
1. U.S. Embargo of Cuba	(N) Y
2. Human Rights in Sudan	(N) X
3. Committee on the Inalienable Rights of the Palestinian People	(N) A
4. Division for Palestinian Rights of the Secretariat	(N) A
5. Fissile Material Cutoff Treaty	(N) Y
6. Work of the Special Committee to Investigate Israeli Practices	(N) A
7. Elimination of all Forms of Religious Intolerance	(Y) X
8. Enhancing the Role of Organizations to Promote Democracy	(Y) X
9. Human Rights in Iran	(Y) X
10. International Trade and Development	(N) Y

Votes: Y=Yes, N=No, A=Abstain, X=Absent, ( )=U.S. Vote

TRINIDAD AND TOBAGO

Voting Coincidence Percentages

Overall Votes (79): Agree 11, Disagree 57, Abstain 6, Absent 5: 16.2%
—Including All 213 Consensus Resolutions: 78.6%
—Arms Control: 9.1%; Human Rights: 40.0%; Middle East: 0.0%
Important Votes (10): Agree 2, Disagree 6, Abstain 1, Absent 1: 25.0%
—Including the 16 Important Consensus Resolutions: 73.8%

Important Issues	**VOTES**
1. U.S. Embargo of Cuba	(N) Y
2. Human Rights in Sudan	(N) X
3. Committee on the Inalienable Rights of the Palestinian People	(N) Y
4. Division for Palestinian Rights of the Secretariat	(N) Y
5. Fissile Material Cutoff Treaty	(N) Y
6. Work of the Special Committee to Investigate Israeli Practices	(N) Y
7. Elimination of all Forms of Religious Intolerance	(Y) Y
8. Enhancing the Role of Organizations to Promote Democracy	(Y) Y
9. Human Rights in Iran	(Y) A
10. International Trade and Development	(N) Y

TUNISIA

Voting Coincidence Percentages

Overall Votes (79): Agree 7, Disagree 63, Abstain 7, Absent 2: 10.0%
—Including All 213 Consensus Resolutions: 77.0%
—Arms Control: 12.0%; Human Rights: 15.8%; Middle East: 5.9%
Important Votes (10): Agree 2, Disagree 8, Abstain 0, Absent 0: 20.0%
—Including the 16 Important Consensus Resolutions: 68.4%

Important Issues	**VOTES**
1. U.S. Embargo of Cuba	(N) Y
2. Human Rights in Sudan	(N) Y
3. Committee on the Inalienable Rights of the Palestinian People	(N) Y
4. Division for Palestinian Rights of the Secretariat	(N) Y
5. Fissile Material Cutoff Treaty	(N) Y
6. Work of the Special Committee to Investigate Israeli Practices	(N) Y
7. Elimination of all Forms of Religious Intolerance	(Y) Y
8. Enhancing the Role of Organizations to Promote Democracy	(Y) Y
9. Human Rights in Iran	(Y) N
10. International Trade and Development	(N) Y

Votes: Y=Yes, N=No, A=Abstain, X=Absent, ( )=U.S. Vote

TURKEY

Voting Coincidence Percentages

Overall Votes (79): Agree 24, Disagree 45, Abstain 5, Absent 5: 34.8%
—Including All 213 Consensus Resolutions: 83.3%
—Arms Control: 36.4%; Human Rights: 66.7%; Middle East: 11.1%
Important Votes (10): Agree 2, Disagree 6, Abstain 0, Absent 2: 25.0%
—Including the 16 Important Consensus Resolutions: 74.0%

Important Issues	VOTES
1. U.S. Embargo of Cuba	(N) Y
2. Human Rights in Sudan	(N) X
3. Committee on the Inalienable Rights of the Palestinian People	(N) Y
4. Division for Palestinian Rights of the Secretariat	(N) Y
5. Fissile Material Cutoff Treaty	(N) Y
6. Work of the Special Committee to Investigate Israeli Practices	(N) Y
7. Elimination of all Forms of Religious Intolerance	(Y) Y
8. Enhancing the Role of Organizations to Promote Democracy	(Y) Y
9. Human Rights in Iran	(Y) X
10. International Trade and Development	(N) Y

TURKMENISTAN

Voting Coincidence Percentages

Overall Votes (79): Agree 3, Disagree 49, Abstain 7, Absent 20: 5.8%
—Including All 213 Consensus Resolutions: 77.0%
—Arms Control: 8.3%; Human Rights: 11.1%; Middle East: 0.0%
Important Votes (10): Agree 1, Disagree 7, Abstain 1, Absent 1: 12.5%
—Including the 16 Important Consensus Resolutions: 65.2%

Important Issues	VOTES
1. U.S. Embargo of Cuba	(N) Y
2. Human Rights in Sudan	(N) Y
3. Committee on the Inalienable Rights of the Palestinian People	(N) Y
4. Division for Palestinian Rights of the Secretariat	(N) Y
5. Fissile Material Cutoff Treaty	(N) X
6. Work of the Special Committee to Investigate Israeli Practices	(N) Y
7. Elimination of all Forms of Religious Intolerance	(Y) Y
8. Enhancing the Role of Organizations to Promote Democracy	(Y) A
9. Human Rights in Iran	(Y) N
10. International Trade and Development	(N) Y

Votes: Y=Yes, N=No, A=Abstain, X=Absent, ( )=U.S. Vote

TUVALU

Voting Coincidence Percentages

Overall Votes (79): Agree 7, Disagree 39, Abstain 15, Absent 18: 15.2%
—Including All 213 Consensus Resolutions: 81.6%
—Arms Control: 9.5%; Human Rights: 28.6%; Middle East: 0.0%
Important Votes (10): Agree 3, Disagree 3, Abstain 2, Absent 2: 50.0%
—Including the 16 Important Consensus Resolutions: 83.7%

Important Issues	VOTES
1. U.S. Embargo of Cuba	(N) Y
2. Human Rights in Sudan	(N) A
3. Committee on the Inalienable Rights of the Palestinian People	(N) X
4. Division for Palestinian Rights of the Secretariat	(N) X
5. Fissile Material Cutoff Treaty	(N) Y
6. Work of the Special Committee to Investigate Israeli Practices	(N) A
7. Elimination of all Forms of Religious Intolerance	(Y) Y
8. Enhancing the Role of Organizations to Promote Democracy	(Y) Y
9. Human Rights in Iran	(Y) Y
10. International Trade and Development	(N) Y

UGANDA

Voting Coincidence Percentages

Overall Votes (79): Agree 5, Disagree 55, Abstain 16, Absent 3: 8.3%
—Including All 213 Consensus Resolutions: 78.9%
—Arms Control: 8.7%; Human Rights: 10.0%; Middle East: 0.0%
Important Votes (10): Agree 2, Disagree 4, Abstain 4, Absent 0: 33.3%
—Including the 16 Important Consensus Resolutions: 81.1%

Important Issues	VOTES
1. U.S. Embargo of Cuba	(N) Y
2. Human Rights in Sudan	(N) Y
3. Committee on the Inalienable Rights of the Palestinian People	(N) A
4. Division for Palestinian Rights of the Secretariat	(N) Y
5. Fissile Material Cutoff Treaty	(N) Y
6. Work of the Special Committee to Investigate Israeli Practices	(N) A
7. Elimination of all Forms of Religious Intolerance	(Y) Y
8. Enhancing the Role of Organizations to Promote Democracy	(Y) Y
9. Human Rights in Iran	(Y) A
10. International Trade and Development	(N) Y

Votes: Y=Yes, N=No, A=Abstain, X=Absent, ( )=U.S. Vote

UKRAINE

Voting Coincidence Percentages

<u>Overall Votes (79):</u> Agree 18, Disagree 45, Abstain 14, Absent 2: 28.6%
—Including All 213 Consensus Resolutions: 83.4%
—Arms Control: 15.0%; Human Rights: 60.9%; Middle East: 14.3%
<u>Important Votes (10):</u> Agree 2, Disagree 4, Abstain 3, Absent 1: 33.3%
—Including the 16 Important Consensus Resolutions: 81.5%

Important Issues	<u>**VOTES**</u>
1. U.S. Embargo of Cuba	(N) Y
2. Human Rights in Sudan	(N) X
3. Committee on the Inalienable Rights of the Palestinian People	(N) A
4. Division for Palestinian Rights of the Secretariat	(N) A
5. Fissile Material Cutoff Treaty	(N) Y
6. Work of the Special Committee to Investigate Israeli Practices	(N) A
7. Elimination of all Forms of Religious Intolerance	(Y) Y
8. Enhancing the Role of Organizations to Promote Democracy	(Y) Y
9. Human Rights in Iran	(Y) N
10. International Trade and Development	(N) Y

UNITED ARAB EMIRATES

Voting Coincidence Percentages

<u>Overall Votes (79):</u> Agree 5, Disagree 62, Abstain 10, Absent 2: 7.5%
—Including All 213 Consensus Resolutions: 77.5%
—Arms Control: 8.3%; Human Rights: 11.1%; Middle East: 5.9%
<u>Important Votes (10):</u> Agree 1, Disagree 7, Abstain 2, Absent 0: 12.5%
—Including the 16 Important Consensus Resolutions: 70.4%

Important Issues	<u>**VOTES**</u>
1. U.S. Embargo of Cuba	(N) Y
2. Human Rights in Sudan	(N) Y
3. Committee on the Inalienable Rights of the Palestinian People	(N) Y
4. Division for Palestinian Rights of the Secretariat	(N) Y
5. Fissile Material Cutoff Treaty	(N) Y
6. Work of the Special Committee to Investigate Israeli Practices	(N) Y
7. Elimination of all Forms of Religious Intolerance	(Y) Y
8. Enhancing the Role of Organizations to Promote Democracy	(Y) A
9. Human Rights in Iran	(Y) A
10. International Trade and Development	(N) Y

Votes: Y=Yes, N=No, A=Abstain, X=Absent, ( )=U.S. Vote

UNITED KINGDOM

Voting Coincidence Percentages

Overall Votes (79): Agree 38, Disagree 29, Abstain 12, Absent 0: 56.7%
—Including All 213 Consensus Resolutions: 89.6%
—Arms Control: 65.0%; Human Rights: 76.0%; Middle East: 14.3%
Important Votes (10): Agree 4, Disagree 2, Abstain 4, Absent 0: 66.7%
—Including the 16 Important Consensus Resolutions: 90.9%
Security Council votes: 100.0%

Important Issues	**VOTES**
1. U.S. Embargo of Cuba	(N) Y
2. Human Rights in Sudan	(N) N
3. Committee on the Inalienable Rights of the Palestinian People	(N) A
4. Division for Palestinian Rights of the Secretariat	(N) A
5. Fissile Material Cutoff Treaty	(N) A
6. Work of the Special Committee to Investigate Israeli Practices	(N) A
7. Elimination of all Forms of Religious Intolerance	(Y) Y
8. Enhancing the Role of Organizations to Promote Democracy	(Y) Y
9. Human Rights in Iran	(Y) Y
10. International Trade and Development	(N) Y

UNITED REPUBLIC OF TANZANIA

Voting Coincidence Percentages

Overall Votes (79): Agree 8, Disagree 59, Abstain 9, Absent 3: 11.9%
—Including All 213 Consensus Resolutions: 78.4%
—Arms Control: 12.5%; Human Rights: 23.5%; Middle East: 5.9%
Important Votes (10): Agree 2, Disagree 6, Abstain 1, Absent 1: 25.0%
—Including the 16 Important Consensus Resolutions: 74.4%

Important Issues	**VOTES**
1. U.S. Embargo of Cuba	(N) Y
2. Human Rights in Sudan	(N) X
3. Committee on the Inalienable Rights of the Palestinian People	(N) Y
4. Division for Palestinian Rights of the Secretariat	(N) Y
5. Fissile Material Cutoff Treaty	(N) Y
6. Work of the Special Committee to Investigate Israeli Practices	(N) Y
7. Elimination of all Forms of Religious Intolerance	(Y) Y
8. Enhancing the Role of Organizations to Promote Democracy	(Y) Y
9. Human Rights in Iran	(Y) A
10. International Trade and Development	(N) Y

Votes: Y=Yes, N=No, A=Abstain, X=Absent, ( )=U.S. Vote

URUGUAY

Voting Coincidence Percentages

Overall Votes (79): Agree 14, Disagree 54, Abstain 10, Absent 1: 20.6%
—Including All 213 Consensus Resolutions: 80.5%
—Arms Control: 9.1%; Human Rights: 50.0%; Middle East: 0.0%
Important Votes (10): Agree 3, Disagree 4, Abstain 3, Absent 0: 42.9%
—Including the 16 Important Consensus Resolutions: 82.3%

Important Issues	**VOTES**
1. U.S. Embargo of Cuba	(N) Y
2. Human Rights in Sudan	(N) N
3. Committee on the Inalienable Rights of the Palestinian People	(N) A
4. Division for Palestinian Rights of the Secretariat	(N) Y
5. Fissile Material Cutoff Treaty	(N) Y
6. Work of the Special Committee to Investigate Israeli Practices	(N) A
7. Elimination of all Forms of Religious Intolerance	(Y) Y
8. Enhancing the Role of Organizations to Promote Democracy	(Y) Y
9. Human Rights in Iran	(Y) A
10. International Trade and Development	(N) Y

UZBEKISTAN

Voting Coincidence Percentages

Overall Votes (79): Agree 5, Disagree 35, Abstain 18, Absent 21: 12.5%
—Including All 213 Consensus Resolutions: 81.9%
—Arms Control: 14.3%; Human Rights: 18.8%; Middle East: 0.0%
Important Votes (10): Agree 2, Disagree 4, Abstain 1, Absent 3: 33.3%
—Including the 16 Important Consensus Resolutions: 77.2%

Important Issues	**VOTES**
1. U.S. Embargo of Cuba	(N) X
2. Human Rights in Sudan	(N) X
3. Committee on the Inalienable Rights of the Palestinian People	(N) Y
4. Division for Palestinian Rights of the Secretariat	(N) Y
5. Fissile Material Cutoff Treaty	(N) Y
6. Work of the Special Committee to Investigate Israeli Practices	(N) A
7. Elimination of all Forms of Religious Intolerance	(Y) Y
8. Enhancing the Role of Organizations to Promote Democracy	(Y) Y
9. Human Rights in Iran	(Y) N
10. International Trade and Development	(N) X

Votes: Y=Yes, N=No, A=Abstain, X=Absent, ( )=U.S. Vote

VANUATU

Voting Coincidence Percentages

Overall Votes (79): Agree 4, Disagree 29, Abstain 21, Absent 25: 12.1%
—Including All 213 Consensus Resolutions: 84.1%
—Arms Control: 15.0%; Human Rights: 12.5%; Middle East: 50.0%
Important Votes (10): Agree 1, Disagree 2, Abstain 3, Absent 4: 33.3%
—Including the 16 Important Consensus Resolutions: 85.9%

Important Issues	**VOTES**
1. U.S. Embargo of Cuba	(N) X
2. Human Rights in Sudan	(N) X
3. Committee on the Inalienable Rights of the Palestinian People	(N) A
4. Division for Palestinian Rights of the Secretariat	(N) A
5. Fissile Material Cutoff Treaty	(N) Y
6. Work of the Special Committee to Investigate Israeli Practices	(N) A
7. Elimination of all Forms of Religious Intolerance	(Y) X
8. Enhancing the Role of Organizations to Promote Democracy	(Y) Y
9. Human Rights in Iran	(Y) X
10. International Trade and Development	(N) Y

VENEZUELA

Voting Coincidence Percentages

Overall Votes (79): Agree 8, Disagree 65, Abstain 6, Absent 0: 11.0%
—Including All 213 Consensus Resolutions: 77.3%
—Arms Control: 12.0%; Human Rights: 22.7%; Middle East: 5.6%
Important Votes (10): Agree 1, Disagree 8, Abstain 1, Absent 0: 11.1%
—Including the 16 Important Consensus Resolutions: 68.0%

Important Issues	**VOTES**
1. U.S. Embargo of Cuba	(N) Y
2. Human Rights in Sudan	(N) Y
3. Committee on the Inalienable Rights of the Palestinian People	(N) Y
4. Division for Palestinian Rights of the Secretariat	(N) Y
5. Fissile Material Cutoff Treaty	(N) Y
6. Work of the Special Committee to Investigate Israeli Practices	(N) Y
7. Elimination of all Forms of Religious Intolerance	(Y) Y
8. Enhancing the Role of Organizations to Promote Democracy	(Y) A
9. Human Rights in Iran	(Y) N
10. International Trade and Development	(N) Y

Votes: Y=Yes, N=No, A=Abstain, X=Absent, ( )=U.S. Vote

VIETNAM

Voting Coincidence Percentages

Overall Votes (79): Agree 4, Disagree 63, Abstain 2, Absent 10: 6.0%
—Including All 213 Consensus Resolutions: 75.2%
—Arms Control: 0.0%; Human Rights: 15.0%; Middle East: 0.0%
Important Votes (10): Agree 1, Disagree 8, Abstain 1, Absent 0: 11.1%
—Including the 16 Important Consensus Resolutions: 65.3%

Important Issues	**VOTES**
1. U.S. Embargo of Cuba	(N) Y
2. Human Rights in Sudan	(N) Y
3. Committee on the Inalienable Rights of the Palestinian People	(N) Y
4. Division for Palestinian Rights of the Secretariat	(N) Y
5. Fissile Material Cutoff Treaty	(N) Y
6. Work of the Special Committee to Investigate Israeli Practices	(N) Y
7. Elimination of all Forms of Religious Intolerance	(Y) Y
8. Enhancing the Role of Organizations to Promote Democracy	(Y) A
9. Human Rights in Iran	(Y) N
10. International Trade and Development	(N) Y

YEMEN

Voting Coincidence Percentages

Overall Votes (79): Agree 6, Disagree 64, Abstain 9, Absent 0: 8.6%
—Including All 213 Consensus Resolutions: 77.4%
—Arms Control: 8.3%; Human Rights: 15.0%; Middle East: 5.9%
Important Votes (10): Agree 2, Disagree 8, Abstain 0, Absent 0: 20.0%
—Including the 16 Important Consensus Resolutions: 69.2%

Important Issues	**VOTES**
1. U.S. Embargo of Cuba	(N) Y
2. Human Rights in Sudan	(N) Y
3. Committee on the Inalienable Rights of the Palestinian People	(N) Y
4. Division for Palestinian Rights of the Secretariat	(N) Y
5. Fissile Material Cutoff Treaty	(N) Y
6. Work of the Special Committee to Investigate Israeli Practices	(N) Y
7. Elimination of all Forms of Religious Intolerance	(Y) Y
8. Enhancing the Role of Organizations to Promote Democracy	(Y) Y
9. Human Rights in Iran	(Y) N
10. International Trade and Development	(N) Y

Votes: Y=Yes, N=No, A=Abstain, X=Absent, ( )=U.S. Vote

ZAMBIA

Voting Coincidence Percentages

Overall Votes (79): Agree 9, Disagree 62, Abstain 7, Absent 1: 12.7%
—Including All 213 Consensus Resolutions: 77.8%
—Arms Control: 12.5%; Human Rights: 23.8%; Middle East: 5.9%
Important Votes (10): Agree 2, Disagree 7, Abstain 1, Absent 0: 22.2%
—Including the 16 Important Consensus Resolutions: 71.6%

Important Issues	**VOTES**
1. U.S. Embargo of Cuba	(N) Y
2. Human Rights in Sudan	(N) Y
3. Committee on the Inalienable Rights of the Palestinian People	(N) Y
4. Division for Palestinian Rights of the Secretariat	(N) Y
5. Fissile Material Cutoff Treaty	(N) Y
6. Work of the Special Committee to Investigate Israeli Practices	(N) Y
7. Elimination of all Forms of Religious Intolerance	(Y) Y
8. Enhancing the Role of Organizations to Promote Democracy	(Y) Y
9. Human Rights in Iran	(Y) A
10. International Trade and Development	(N) Y

ZIMBABWE

Voting Coincidence Percentages

Overall Votes (79): Agree 5, Disagree 64, Abstain 7, Absent 3: 7.2%
—Including All 213 Consensus Resolutions: 76.5%
—Arms Control: 9.1%; Human Rights: 9.5%; Middle East: 0.0%
Important Votes (10): Agree 1, Disagree 8, Abstain 1, Absent 0: 11.1%
—Including the 16 Important Consensus Resolutions: 67.1%

Important Issues	**VOTES**
1. U.S. Embargo of Cuba	(N) Y
2. Human Rights in Sudan	(N) Y
3. Committee on the Inalienable Rights of the Palestinian People	(N) Y
4. Division for Palestinian Rights of the Secretariat	(N) Y
5. Fissile Material Cutoff Treaty	(N) Y
6. Work of the Special Committee to Investigate Israeli Practices	(N) Y
7. Elimination of all Forms of Religious Intolerance	(Y) Y
8. Enhancing the Role of Organizations to Promote Democracy	(Y) A
9. Human Rights in Iran	(Y) N
10. International Trade and Development	(N) Y

Votes: Y=Yes, N=No, A=Abstain, X=Absent, ( )=U.S. Vote

ANNEX—RESOLUTIONS RELATED TO ISRAEL OPPOSED BY THE UNITED STATES

Public Law 101-246 as amended by Public Law 108-447 calls for a separate listing of all Plenary votes cast by UN member countries in the General Assembly on resolutions specifically related to Israel that are opposed by the United States. For the 59th UN General Assembly (UNGA), 17 resolutions meet this criteria. Six of these resolutions relate to special bodies in the UN system that the United States believes perpetuate an anti-Israel bias in the United Nations.

The Annex contains two parts: (1) a listing and description of the 14 votes related to Israel at the 59th UNGA not covered in Section IV, and (2) voting coincidence percentages with the United States, arranged both alphabetically by country and in rank order by voting coincidence percentage. An additional column in the tables presents the voting coincidence percentage with the the the one resolution adopted by consensus factored in. Since not all states are equally active at the United Nations, these coincidence percentages were refined to reflect a country's rate of participation in all UN voting overall. The participation rate was calculated by dividing the number of Yes-No-Abstain votes cast by a UN member in Plenary (i.e., the number of times it was not absent) by the total number of Plenary votes related to Israel. Also, the United States abstained on two Israel-related resolutions. These two votes are included in the calculations to maintain consistency with the calculations in Section III of this report.

RESOLUTIONS RELATED TO ISRAEL OPPOSED BY THE UNITED STATES

The following 14 resolutions are identified by a short title, document number, date of vote, and results (Yes-No-Abstain), with the U.S. vote noted. The first paragraph gives a summary description of the resolution using language from the document ("General Assembly" is the subject of the verbs in the first paragraph) and the subsequent paragraph provides background, if pertinent. The resolutions are listed in order by the date adopted, and then in numerical order. Resolutions 59/28 (Committee on the Inalienable Rights of Palestinians), 59/29 (Division for Palestinian Rights of the Secretariat), and 59/121 (Work of the Special Committee to Investigate Israeli Practices) are previously discussed in Section IV – General Assembly Important Votes.

1. Special Information Program on the Question of Palestine of the Department of Public Information of the Secretariat

A/Res/59/30   December 1   162-7(US)-9

Considers that the special information program on the question of Palestine of the Department is very useful in raising the awareness of the international community concerning the question of Palestine and the situation

259

in the Middle East and that the program is contributing effectively to an atmosphere conducive to dialogue and supportive of the peace process. Requests the Department to continue its information program.

Background: The General Assembly established the Special Information Program by Resolution 32/40 B (1977).

U.S. Position: The United States believes that the continuation of this Program that embodies institutional discrimination against Israel is inconsistent with UN support for the efforts of the Quartet to achieve a just and durable solution. (The Quartet is a group comprised of the United States, the United Nations, the European Union, and Russia.)

2. Peaceful Settlement of the Question of Palestine

A/Res/59/31   December 1   161-7(US)-10

Expressing its grave concern over the tragic events in the Occupied Palestinian Territory since September 28, 2000, and the rising number of deaths and injuries, mostly among Palestinian civilians, the deepening humanitarian crisis facing the Palestinian people, and the widespread destruction of Palestinian property and infrastructure; and also expressing its grave concern over the repeated military actions in the Occupied Palestinian Territory and the reoccupation of Palestinian population centers by the Israeli occupying forces, stresses the need for a speedy end to the reoccupation of Palestinian population centers and for the complete cessation of all acts of violence, including military attacks, destruction, and acts of terror.

Demands that Israel, the occupying power, and all UN member states comply with their legal obligations. Reaffirms its commitment to the two-state solution of Israel and Palestine, living side-by-side in peace and security within recognized borders, based on the pre-1967 borders. Reiterates its demand for complete cessation of all Israeli settlement activities in the Occupied Palestinian Territory and in the occupied Syrian Golan.

Also stresses the need for resolving the problem of the Palestine refugees in conformity with its Resolution 194 (1948). Reaffirms the necessity of achieving a peaceful settlement of the question of Palestine, the core of the Arab-Israeli conflict and calls upon both parties to fulfill their obligations in implementation of the Roadmap by taking parallel and reciprocal steps in this direction. Stresses the importance and urgency of establishing a credible and effective third-party monitoring mechanism including all members of the Quartet.

Background: Since 1967, the General Assembly has consistently adopted a resolution concerning the Israeli-Palestinian conflict.

U.S. Position: While the United States agrees with the necessity of achieving a peaceful settlement to the conflict and that both parties need to fulfill their obligations implementing the Roadmap, the United States feels that the resolution is one-sided in its criticism of Israel. The resolution also states how issues should be resolved; the United States believes these issues should be resolved between the parties through negotiations.

3. Jerusalem

A/Res/59/32   December 1   155-7(US)-15

Reiterates its determination that any actions taken by Israel to impose its laws, jurisdiction, and administration on the Holy City of Jerusalem are illegal and therefore null and void, and have no validity whatsoever. Stresses that a comprehensive, just, and lasting solution to the question of the City of Jerusalem should take into account the legitimate concerns of both the Palestinian and Israeli sides and should include internationally guaranteed provisions to ensure the freedom of religion and of conscience of its inhabitants, as well as permanent, free, and unhindered access to the holy places by all people.

Background: Since the June 1967 hostilities, the General Assembly has consistently adopted a resolution concerning Jerusalem.

U.S. Position: The United States believes that the final status of Jerusalem should be resolved by the parties to the conflict as part of a final, permanent status resolution that also includes the status of borders, refugees and settlements as called for in Phase III of the Roadmap. Parties to the conflict should resolve the final status issue of Jerusalem through the Roadmap and direct negotiations.

4. The Syrian Golan

A/Res/59/33   December 1   111-6(US)-60

Declares that the Israeli decision of December 14, 1981, to impose its laws, jurisdiction, and administration on the occupied Syrian Golan is null and void and has no validity whatsoever and calls upon Israel to rescind it. Determines that the continued occupation of the Syrian Golan and its de facto annexation constitute a stumbling block in the way of achieving a just, comprehensive, and lasting peace in the region. Demands that Israel withdraw from all the occupied Syrian Golan to the line of June 4, 1967, in implementation of the relevant Security Council resolutions.

Background: Since the June 1967 hostilities, the General Assembly has consistently adopted a resolution concerning the Syrian Golan.

U.S. Position: The United States believes that Israel and Syria should resolve the issue of the Syrian Golan through negotiations.

5. The Risk of Nuclear Proliferation in the Middle East

A/Res/59/106   December 3   170-5(US)-9

Welcomes the conclusions on the Middle East of the 2000 Review Conference of the Parties to the Treaty on the Non-Proliferation of Nuclear

Weapons; reaffirms the importance of Israel's accession to the Treaty on the Non-Proliferation of Nuclear Weapons (NPT) and placement of all its nuclear facilities under comprehensive International Atomic Energy Agency (IAEA) safeguards, in realizing the goal of universal adherence to the Treaty in the Middle East; and calls upon that state to accede to the NPT without further delay and not to develop, produce, test, or otherwise acquire nuclear weapons, and to renounce possession of nuclear weapons, and to place all its unsafeguarded nuclear facilities under full-scope IAEA safeguards as an important confidence-building measure among all states for the region and as a step towards enhancing peace and security.

Background: A resolution on this issue was first adopted by the General Assembly in 1979.

U.S. Position: The United States voted against this resolution. This resolution confines itself to expressions of concern about the activities of Israel without reference to other questions regarding the problem of nuclear proliferation in the region.

6. Persons Displaced as a Result of the June 1967 and Subsequent Hostilities

A/Res/59/118   December 10   162-6(US)-9

Reaffirms the right of all persons displaced as a result of the June 1967 and subsequent hostilities to return to their homes or former places of residence in the territories occupied by Israel since 1967. Expresses deep concern that the mechanism agreed upon by the parties in the Declaration of Principles on Interim Self-Government Arrangements of 1993 on the return of displaced persons has not been complied with, and stresses the necessity for an accelerated return of displaced persons. Endorses the efforts of the Commissioner-General of the UN Relief and Works Agency for Palestine Refugees in the Near East to continue to provide humanitarian assistance, as far as practicable, on an emergency basis, and as a temporary measure, to persons in the area who are currently displaced and in serious need of continued assistance as a result of the June 1967 and subsequent hostilities.

Background: Since the June 1967 hostilities, the General Assembly has consistently adopted a resolution concerning displaced persons.

U.S. Position: The United States believes that the parties to the conflict should resolve the issue of displaced persons through final-status negotiations between themselves.

7. Operations of the UN Relief and Works Agency for Palestine Refugees in the Near East (UNRWA)

A/Res/59/119   December 10   163-6(US)-7

Expresses its appreciation to the Commissioner-General of the UN Relief and Works Agency, as well as to all of the staff of the Agency, for their tireless efforts and valuable work. Calls upon Israel, the occupying power, to comply fully with the provisions of the Geneva Convention relative to the Protection of Civilian Persons in Time of War. Also calls upon Israel to abide by Articles 100, 104, and 105 of the UN Charter and the Convention on the Privileges and Immunities of the United Nations in order to ensure the safety of the personnel of the Agency, the protection of its institutions, and the safeguarding of the security of its facilities in the Occupied Palestinian Territory. Urges the Government of Israel to speedily compensate the Agency for damage to its property and facilities resulting from actions by the Israeli side.

Background: The General Assembly established UNRWA by Resolution 302 in 1949.

U.S. Position: The United States believes that singling out Israel, without taking into account the context of Israel's actions, is not useful in settling the Israeli-Palestinian conflict. The United States also believes that these issues are extraneous issues and are not appropriate in a resolution that renews UNRWA's mandate.

8. Palestine Refugees' Properties and Their Revenues

A/Res/59/120   December 10   161-6(US)-9

Reaffirms that the Palestine refugees are entitled to their property and to the income derived therefrom, in conformity with the principles of equity and justice. Requests the Secretary-General to take all appropriate steps, in consultation with the UN Conciliation Commission for Palestine, for the protection of Arab property, assets, and property rights in Israel.

Background: The General Assembly established the UN Conciliation Commission for Palestine in 1948. Among other tasks, the Commission is mandated to facilitate the repatriation, resettlement, and economic and social rehabilitation of the Palestinian refugees and their compensation.

U.S. Position: The United States believes that the parties to the conflict should resolve the issue of properties and their revenues through final-status negotiations.

9. Applicability of the Geneva Convention relative to the Protection of Civilian Persons in Time of War, of August 12, 1949, to the Occupied Palestinian Territory, including East Jerusalem, and the other occupied Arab territories

A/Res/59/122   December 10   160-7(US)-11

Reaffirms that this Geneva Convention is applicable to the Occupied Palestinian Territory occupied by Israel since 1967 and demands that Israel accept the legal applicability of the Convention and that it scrupulously comply with its provisions.

Background: The General Assembly first adopted this resolution in 1973.

U.S. Position: The United States believes that this resolution singles out Israel, isolates it for criticism, and implicitly prejudges the outcome of final-status negotiations.

10. Israeli Settlements in the Occupied Palestinian Territory, including East Jerusalem, and the Occupied Syrian Golan

A/Res/59/123   December 10   155-8(US)-15

Reaffirms that Israeli settlements in the Palestinian territory, including East Jerusalem, and in the occupied Syrian Golan are illegal and an obstacle to peace and economic and social development. Demands that Israel, the occupying Power, comply with its legal obligations, as mentioned in the advisory opinion rendered on July 9, 2004, by the International Court of Justice. Stresses the need for full implementation of Security Council Resolution 904 (1994), in which, among other things, the Council called upon Israel to continue to take and implement measures with the aim of preventing illegal acts of violence by Israeli settlers, and called for measures to be taken to guarantee the safety and protection of the Palestinian civilians in the occupied territory. Reiterates its calls for the prevention of all acts of violence by Israeli settlers, especially against Palestinian civilians and properties.

Background: Since 1967, the General Assembly has consistently adopted a resolution on the Israeli-Palestinian conflict.

U.S. Position: The United States believes that mention of the advisory opinion of the International Court of Justice regarding the separation barrier is inappropriate and could undercut efforts by the Quartet to reinvigorate the Roadmap. The United States also objects to singling out Israeli practices for criticism in the absence of corresponding criticism of Palestinian policies.

11. Israeli Practices Affecting the Human Rights of the Palestinian People in the Occupied Palestinian Territory, including East Jerusalem

A/Res/59/124   December 10   149-7(US)-22

Condemns all acts of violence, including all acts of terror, provocation, incitement, and destruction, especially the excessive use of force by the Israeli occupying forces against Palestinian civilians, and expresses grave concern at the use of suicide bombing attacks against Israeli civilians. Demands that Israel, the occupying power, cease all practices and actions which violate the human rights of the Palestinian people, respect human rights law, and comply with its obligations.

Stresses the need to preserve the territorial integrity of all the Occupied Palestinian Territory and to guarantee the freedom of movement of persons and goods within the Palestinian territory, including the removal of restrictions on movement into and from East Jerusalem, and the freedom of movement to and from the outside world.

Background: Since 1967, the General Assembly has consistenly adopted a resolution on the Israeli-Palestinian conflict.

U.S. Position: The United States believes that the provision concerning the preservation of territorial integrity should be decided between the parties, not in a resolution. The United States also objects to singling out Israeli practices for criticism in the absence of corresponding criticism of Palestinian policies.

12. The Situation of and Assistance to Palestinian Children

A/Res/59/173   December 20   117-5(US)-62

Stresses the urgent need for Palestinian children to live a normal life free from foreign occupation, destruction, and fear in their own state. Demands that Israel respect relevant provisions of the Convention on the Rights of the Child, and comply fully with the provisions of the Geneva Convention relative to the Protection of Civilian Persons in Time of War (1949) in order to ensure the well-being and protection of Palestinian children and their families.

Calls upon the international community to provide urgently needed assistance and services in an effort to alleviate the dire humanitarian crisis being faced by Palestinian children and their families.

Background: The General Assembly first adopted this resolution in 2003.

U.S. Position: While deeply concerned over the effect the Israeli-Palestinian conflict has had on Palestinian children, the United States feels that this resolution politicizes their plight. The resolution inappropriately singles out one group of children while children in Israel and other regions in conflict are also suffering.

13. The Right of the Palestinian People to Self-Determination

A/Res/59/179   December 20   179-5(US)-3

Reaffirms the right of the Palestinian people to self-determination, including the right to their independent state of Palestine. Urges all states and the specialized agencies and organizations of the UN system to continue to support and assist the Palestinian people in the early realization of their right to self-determination.

Background: The General Assembly first adopted this resolution in 1994.

U.S. Position: The United States believes that renewing this resolution is unhelpful to resolving the Israeli-Palestinian conflict. President Bush has reiterated his vision of a two-state solution. This vision can only be achieved through direct negotiations between the parties, not UN resolutions. The United States also objects to preambular language regarding the construction of a separation barrier that attempts to raise to the level of a requirement an advisory opinion of the International Court of Justice.

14. Permanent Sovereignty of the Palestinian People in the Occupied Palestinian Territory, Including East Jerusalem, and of the Arab Population in the Occupied Syrian Golan Over Their Natural Resources

A/Res/59/251   December 22   156-5(US)-11

Reaffirms the inalienable rights of the Palestinian people and the population of the occupied Syrian Golan over their natural resources, including land and water. Calls upon Israel not to exploit, damage, cause loss or depletion of, or endanger the natural resources in the Occupied Palestinian Territory. Recognizes the right of the Palestinian people to claim restitution as a result of any exploitation, damage, loss or depletion, or endangerment of their natural resources, and expresses the hope that this issue will be dealt with in the framework of the final status negotiations between the Palestinian and Israeli sides.

Background: The General Assembly first adopted a resolution on this issue in 1997.

U.S. Position: The United States believes that this resolution prejudges the final status outcome. The parties to the conflict should resolve the issues concerning natural resources between themselves through negotiations.

COMPARISON WITH U.S. VOTES

The tables that follow summarize UN member state performance at the 59th UNGA in comparison with the United States on the 18 votes related to Israel (this number includes one paragraph vote on Resolution 59/106), plus two Israel-related resolutions on which the United States abstained. In these tables, "Identical Votes" is the total number of times the United States and the listed state both voted Yes or No on these issues. "Opposite Votes" is the total number of times the United States voted Yes and the listed state No, or the United States voted No and the listed state Yes. "Abstentions" and "Absences" are totals for the country being compared on these 18 votes. "Voting Coincidence (Votes Only)" is calculated by dividing the number of identical votes by the total of identical and opposite votes. The column headed "Voting Coincidence (Including Consensus)" presents the percentage of voting coincidence with the United States after including the one consensus resolution as identical votes. The extent of participation was also factored in. (See the second paragraph in this Annex.)

The first table lists all UN member states in alphabetical order. The second lists them in rank order by voting coincidence percentage. Countries with the same voting coincidence are listed alphabetically.

All Countries (Alphabetical)

COUNTRY	IDENTICAL VOTES	OPPOSITE VOTES	ABSTEN-TIONS	ABSENCES	VOTING COINCIDENCE INCLUDING CONSENSUS	VOTES ONLY
Afghanistan	0	18	0	0	5.3%	0.0%
Albania	0	5	10	3	13.8%	0.0%
Algeria	0	18	0	0	5.3%	0.0%
Andorra	0	13	5	0	7.1%	0.0%
Angola	0	7	0	11	5.4%	0.0%
Antigua-Barbuda	0	11	1	6	6.0%	0.0%
Argentina	0	17	1	0	5.6%	0.0%
Armenia	0	17	1	0	5.6%	0.0%
Australia	6	5	7	0	58.3%	54.5%
Austria	0	13	5	0	7.1%	0.0%
Azerbaijan	0	18	0	0	5.3%	0.0%
Bahamas	0	17	1	0	5.6%	0.0%
Bahrain	0	18	0	0	5.3%	0.0%
Bangladesh	0	18	0	0	5.3%	0.0%
Barbados	0	17	0	1	5.3%	0.0%
Belarus	0	18	0	0	5.3%	0.0%
Belgium	0	13	5	0	7.1%	0.0%
Belize	0	18	0	0	5.3%	0.0%
Benin	0	17	1	0	5.6%	0.0%
Bhutan	0	9	1	8	5.3%	0.0%
Bolivia	0	18	0	0	5.3%	0.0%
Bosnia/Herzegovina	0	13	5	0	7.1%	0.0%
Botswana	0	18	0	0	5.3%	0.0%
Brazil	0	18	0	0	5.3%	0.0%
Brunei Darussalam	0	18	0	0	5.3%	0.0%
Bulgaria	0	13	5	0	7.1%	0.0%
Burkina Faso	0	18	0	0	5.3%	0.0%
Burundi	0	13	5	0	7.1%	0.0%
Cambodia	0	18	0	0	5.3%	0.0%
Cameroon	0	1	16	1	48.7%	0.0%
Canada	2	12	4	0	20.0%	14.3%
Cape Verde	0	18	0	0	5.3%	0.0%
Central African Rep.	0	9	1	8	5.8%	0.0%
Chad	0	2	0	16	4.8%	0.0%
Chile	0	18	0	0	5.3%	0.0%
China	0	18	0	0	5.3%	0.0%
Colombia	0	17	1	0	5.6%	0.0%
Comoros	0	12	0	6	5.5%	0.0%
Congo	0	13	0	5	5.5%	0.0%
Costa Rica	1	12	5	0	14.3%	7.7%
Cote d'Ivoire	0	10	8	0	9.1%	0.0%

All Countries (Alphabetical) (Cont'd)

COUNTRY	IDENTICAL VOTES	OPPOSITE VOTES	ABSTEN- TIONS	ABSENCES	VOTING COINCIDENCE INCLUDING CONSENSUS	VOTES ONLY
Croatia	0	13	5	0	7.1%	0.0%
Cuba	0	18	0	0	5.3%	0.0%
Cyprus	0	15	3	0	6.3%	0.0%
Czech Republic	0	13	5	0	7.1%	0.0%
DPR of Korea	0	18	0	0	5.3%	0.0%
Dem. Rep. Congo	0	2	0	16	4.8%	0.0%
Denmark	0	13	5	0	7.1%	0.0%
Djibouti	0	18	0	0	5.3%	0.0%
Dominica	0	17	0	1	5.3%	0.0%
Dominican Republic	0	10	8	0	9.1%	0.0%
Ecuador	0	18	0	0	5.3%	0.0%
Egypt	0	18	0	0	5.3%	0.0%
El Salvador	0	14	4	0	6.7%	0.0%
Equatorial Guinea	0	7	3	8	7.9%	0.0%
Eritrea	0	17	0	1	5.3%	0.0%
Estonia	0	13	5	0	7.1%	0.0%
Ethiopia	0	14	2	2	6.0%	0.0%
Fiji	0	15	3	0	6.3%	0.0%
Finland	0	13	5	0	7.1%	0.0%
France	0	13	5	0	7.1%	0.0%
Gabon	0	18	0	0	5.3%	0.0%
Gambia	0	10	0	8	4.8%	0.0%
Georgia	0	13	5	0	7.1%	0.0%
Germany	0	13	5	0	7.1%	0.0%
Ghana	0	18	0	0	5.3%	0.0%
Greece	0	13	5	0	7.1%	0.0%
Grenada	11	5	1	1	70.5%	68.8%
Guatemala	0	11	7	0	8.3%	0.0%
Guinea	0	15	0	3	5.4%	0.0%
Guinea-Bissau	0	17	0	1	5.3%	0.0%
Guyana	0	18	0	0	5.3%	0.0%
Haiti	0	3	15	0	25.0%	0.0%
Honduras	0	8	9	1	10.6%	0.0%
Hungary	0	13	5	0	7.1%	0.0%
Iceland	0	12	6	0	7.7%	0.0%
India	1	16	1	0	11.1%	5.9%
Indonesia	0	18	0	0	5.3%	0.0%
Iran	0	18	0	0	5.3%	0.0%
Iraq	0	17	0	1	5.0%	0.0%
Ireland	0	13	5	0	7.1%	0.0%
Israel	18	0	0	0	100.0%	100.0%

All Countries (Alphabetical) (Cont'd)

COUNTRY	IDENTICAL VOTES	OPPOSITE VOTES	ABSTEN- TIONS	ABSENCES	VOTING COINCIDENCE INCLUDING CONSENSUS	VOTES ONLY
Italy	0	13	5	0	7.1%	0.0%
Jamaica	0	18	0	0	5.3%	0.0%
Japan	0	13	5	0	7.1%	0.0%
Jordan	0	18	0	0	5.3%	0.0%
Kazakhstan	0	17	1	0	5.6%	0.0%
Kenya	0	11	7	0	8.3%	0.0%
Kiribati	0	0	0	18	**	**
Kuwait	0	18	0	0	5.3%	0.0%
Kyrgyzstan	0	16	0	2	5.3%	0.0%
Laos	0	18	0	0	5.3%	0.0%
Latvia	0	13	5	0	7.1%	0.0%
Lebanon	0	18	0	0	5.3%	0.0%
Lesotho	0	18	0	0	5.3%	0.0%
Liberia	0	11	0	7	4.8%	0.0%
Libya	0	18	0	0	5.3%	0.0%
Liechtenstein	0	13	5	0	7.1%	0.0%
Lithuania	0	13	5	0	7.1%	0.0%
Luxembourg	0	13	5	0	7.1%	0.0%
Madagascar	0	18	0	0	5.3%	0.0%
Malawi	0	4	0	14	4.8%	0.0%
Malaysia	0	18	0	0	5.3%	0.0%
Maldives	0	18	0	0	5.3%	0.0%
Mali	0	18	0	0	5.3%	0.0%
Malta	0	15	3	0	6.3%	0.0%
Marshall Islands	18	0	0	0	100.0%	100.0%
Mauritania	1	14	0	3	11.7%	6.7%
Mauritius	0	17	1	0	5.6%	0.0%
Mexico	0	16	2	0	5.9%	0.0%
Micronesia	18	0	0	0	100.0%	100.0%
Monaco	0	13	5	0	7.1%	0.0%
Mongolia	0	15	1	2	5.7%	0.0%
Morocco	0	18	0	0	5.3%	0.0%
Mozambique	0	17	0	1	5.3%	0.0%
Myanmar (Burma)	0	18	0	0	5.3%	0.0%
Namibia	0	18	0	0	5.3%	0.0%
Nauru	5	4	9	0	60.0%	55.6%
Nepal	0	18	0	0	5.3%	0.0%
Netherlands	0	13	5	0	7.1%	0.0%
New Zealand	0	13	5	0	7.1%	0.0%
Nicaragua	0	10	7	1	8.7%	0.0%
Niger	0	11	0	7	4.8%	0.0%

All Countries (Alphabetical) (Cont'd)

COUNTRY	IDENTICAL VOTES	OPPOSITE VOTES	ABSTEN-TIONS	ABSENCES	VOTING COINCIDENCE INCLUDING CONSENSUS	VOTES ONLY
Nigeria	0	18	0	0	5.3%	0.0%
Norway	0	13	5	0	7.1%	0.0%
Oman	0	18	0	0	5.3%	0.0%
Pakistan	0	17	1	0	5.6%	0.0%
Palau	18	0	0	0	100.0%	100.0%
Panama	0	17	1	0	5.6%	0.0%
Papua New Guinea	0	1	16	1	48.7%	0.0%
Paraguay	0	18	0	0	5.3%	0.0%
Peru	0	13	5	0	7.1%	0.0%
Philippines	0	17	1	0	5.6%	0.0%
Poland	0	13	5	0	7.1%	0.0%
Portugal	0	13	5	0	7.1%	0.0%
Qatar	0	18	0	0	5.3%	0.0%
Republic of Korea	0	13	5	0	7.1%	0.0%
Republic of Moldova	0	13	5	0	7.1%	0.0%
Romania	0	13	5	0	7.1%	0.0%
Russia	0	15	3	0	6.3%	0.0%
Rwanda	0	1	0	17	4.8%	0.0%
St. Kitts and Nevis	0	0	0	18	**	**
Saint Lucia	0	18	0	0	5.3%	0.0%
St.Vincent/Grenadines	0	17	1	0	5.6%	0.0%
Samoa	0	9	8	1	9.5%	0.0%
San Marino	0	13	5	0	7.1%	0.0%
Sao Tome/Principe	0	12	0	6	5.5%	0.0%
Saudi Arabia	0	18	0	0	5.3%	0.0%
Senegal	0	18	0	0	5.3%	0.0%
Serbia/Montenegro	0	13	5	0	7.1%	0.0%
Seychelles	0	16	0	2	5.3%	0.0%
Sierra Leone	0	18	0	0	5.3%	0.0%
Singapore	0	18	0	0	5.3%	0.0%
Slovak Republic	0	13	5	0	7.1%	0.0%
Slovenia	0	13	5	0	7.1%	0.0%
Solomon Islands	0	7	9	2	10.8%	0.0%
Somalia	0	18	0	0	5.3%	0.0%
South Africa	0	18	0	0	5.3%	0.0%
Spain	0	13	5	0	7.1%	0.0%
Sri Lanka	0	18	0	0	5.3%	0.0%
Sudan	0	18	0	0	5.3%	0.0%
Suriname	0	18	0	0	5.3%	0.0%
Swaziland	0	9	0	9	5.3%	0.0%
Sweden	0	13	5	0	7.1%	0.0%

All Countries (Alphabetical) (Cont'd)

COUNTRY	IDENTICAL VOTES	OPPOSITE VOTES	ABSTEN-TIONS	ABSENCES	VOTING COINCIDENCE INCLUDING CONSENSUS	VOTES ONLY
Switzerland	0	13	5	0	7.1%	0.0%
Syria	0	18	0	0	5.3%	0.0%
Tajikistan	0	17	0	1	5.3%	0.0%
Thailand	0	15	3	0	6.3%	0.0%
TFYR Macedonia	0	13	5	0	7.1%	0.0%
Timor-Leste	0	13	0	5	5.5%	0.0%
Togo	0	18	0	0	5.3%	0.0%
Tonga	0	5	12	1	16.0%	0.0%
Trinidad and Tobago	0	16	1	1	5.6%	0.0%
Tunisia	0	18	0	0	5.3%	0.0%
Turkey	0	18	0	0	5.3%	0.0%
Turkmenistan	0	18	0	0	5.3%	0.0%
Tuvalu	0	3	8	7	17.8%	0.0%
Uganda	0	9	8	1	9.5%	0.0%
Ukraine	0	13	5	0	7.1%	0.0%
United Arab Emirates	0	18	0	0	5.3%	0.0%
United Kingdom	0	13	5	0	7.1%	0.0%
UR Tanzania	0	18	0	0	5.3%	0.0%
Uruguay	0	14	4	0	6.7%	0.0%
Uzbekistan	0	12	5	1	7.3%	0.0%
Vanuatu	0	1	16	1	48.7%	0.0%
Venezuela	0	18	0	0	5.3%	0.0%
Vietnam	0	18	0	0	5.3%	0.0%
Yemen	0	18	0	0	5.3%	0.0%
Zambia	0	18	0	0	5.3%	0.0%
Zimbabwe	0	18	0	0	5.3%	0.0%
Average	0.5	13.8	2.4	1.2	9.6%	3.6%

All Countries (By Voting Coincidence Percentage)

COUNTRY	IDENTICAL VOTES	OPPOSITE VOTES	ABSTEN-TIONS	ABSENCES	VOTING COINCIDENCE INCLUDING CONSENSUS	VOTES ONLY
Israel	18	0	0	0	100.0%	100.0%
Marshall Islands	18	0	0	0	100.0%	100.0%
Micronesia	18	0	0	0	100.0%	100.0%
Palau	18	0	0	0	100.0%	100.0%
Grenada	11	5	1	1	70.5%	68.8%
Nauru	5	4	9	0	60.0%	55.6%
Australia	6	5	7	0	58.3%	54.5%
Cameroon	0	1	16	1	48.7%	0.0%
Papua New Guinea	0	1	16	1	48.7%	0.0%
Vanuatu	0	1	16	1	48.7%	0.0%
Haiti	0	3	15	0	25.0%	0.0%
Canada	2	12	4	0	20.0%	14.3%
Tuvalu	0	3	8	7	17.8%	0.0%
Tonga	0	5	12	1	16.0%	0.0%
Costa Rica	1	12	5	0	14.3%	7.7%
Albania	0	5	10	3	13.8%	0.0%
Mauritania	1	14	0	3	11.7%	6.7%
India	1	16	1	0	11.1%	5.9%
Solomon Islands	0	7	9	2	10.8%	0.0%
Honduras	0	8	9	1	10.6%	0.0%
Samoa	0	9	8	1	9.5%	0.0%
Uganda	0	9	8	1	9.5%	0.0%
Cote d'Ivoire	0	10	8	0	9.1%	0.0%
Dominican Republic	0	10	8	0	9.1%	0.0%
Nicaragua	0	10	7	1	8.7%	0.0%
Guatemala	0	11	7	0	8.3%	0.0%
Kenya	0	11	7	0	8.3%	0.0%
Equatorial Guinea	0	7	3	8	7.9%	0.0%
Iceland	0	12	6	0	7.7%	0.0%
Uzbekistan	0	12	5	1	7.3%	0.0%
Andorra	0	13	5	0	7.1%	0.0%
Austria	0	13	5	0	7.1%	0.0%
Belgium	0	13	5	0	7.1%	0.0%
Bosnia-Herzegovina	0	13	5	0	7.1%	0.0%
Bulgaria	0	13	5	0	7.1%	0.0%
Burundi	0	13	5	0	7.1%	0.0%
Croatia	0	13	5	0	7.1%	0.0%
Czech Republic	0	13	5	0	7.1%	0.0%
Denmark	0	13	5	0	7.1%	0.0%
Estonia	0	13	5	0	7.1%	0.0%
Finland	0	13	5	0	7.1%	0.0%

273

All Countries (By Voting Coincidence Percentage) (Cont'd)

COUNTRY	IDENTICAL VOTES	OPPOSITE VOTES	ABSTEN-TIONS	ABSENCES	VOTING COINCIDENCE INCLUDING CONSENSUS	VOTES ONLY
France	0	13	5	0	7.1%	0.0%
Georgia	0	13	5	0	7.1%	0.0%
Germany	0	13	5	0	7.1%	0.0%
Greece	0	13	5	0	7.1%	0.0%
Hungary	0	13	5	0	7.1%	0.0%
Ireland	0	13	5	0	7.1%	0.0%
Italy	0	13	5	0	7.1%	0.0%
Japan	0	13	5	0	7.1%	0.0%
Latvia	0	13	5	0	7.1%	0.0%
Liechtenstein	0	13	5	0	7.1%	0.0%
Lithuania	0	13	5	0	7.1%	0.0%
Luxembourg	0	13	5	0	7.1%	0.0%
Monaco	0	13	5	0	7.1%	0.0%
Netherlands	0	13	5	0	7.1%	0.0%
New Zealand	0	13	5	0	7.1%	0.0%
Norway	0	13	5	0	7.1%	0.0%
Peru	0	13	5	0	7.1%	0.0%
Poland	0	13	5	0	7.1%	0.0%
Portugal	0	13	5	0	7.1%	0.0%
Republic of Korea	0	13	5	0	7.1%	0.0%
Republic of Moldova	0	13	5	0	7.1%	0.0%
Romania	0	13	5	0	7.1%	0.0%
San Marino	0	13	5	0	7.1%	0.0%
Serbia/Montenegro	0	13	5	0	7.1%	0.0%
Slovak Republic	0	13	5	0	7.1%	0.0%
Slovenia	0	13	5	0	7.1%	0.0%
Spain	0	13	5	0	7.1%	0.0%
Sweden	0	13	5	0	7.1%	0.0%
Switzerland	0	13	5	0	7.1%	0.0%
TFYR Macedonia	0	13	5	0	7.1%	0.0%
Ukraine	0	13	5	0	7.1%	0.0%
United Kingdom	0	13	5	0	7.1%	0.0%
El Salvador	0	14	4	0	6.7%	0.0%
Uruguay	0	14	4	0	6.7%	0.0%
Cyprus	0	15	3	0	6.3%	0.0%
Fiji	0	15	3	0	6.3%	0.0%
Malta	0	15	3	0	6.3%	0.0%
Russia	0	15	3	0	6.3%	0.0%
Thailand	0	15	3	0	6.3%	0.0%
Antigua-Barbuda	0	11	1	6	6.0%	0.0%
Ethiopia	0	14	2	2	6.0%	0.0%

All Countries (By Voting Coincidence Percentage) (Cont'd)

COUNTRY	IDENTICAL VOTES	OPPOSITE VOTES	ABSTEN- TIONS	ABSENCES	VOTING COINCIDENCE INCLUDING CONSENSUS	VOTES ONLY
Mexico	0	16	2	0	5.9%	0.0%
Central African Rep.	0	9	1	8	5.8%	0.0%
Mongolia	0	15	1	2	5.7%	0.0%
Argentina	0	17	1	0	5.6%	0.0%
Armenia	0	17	1	0	5.6%	0.0%
Bahamas	0	17	1	0	5.6%	0.0%
Benin	0	17	1	0	5.6%	0.0%
Colombia	0	17	1	0	5.6%	0.0%
Kazakhstan	0	17	1	0	5.6%	0.0%
Mauritius	0	17	1	0	5.6%	0.0%
Pakistan	0	17	1	0	5.6%	0.0%
Panama	0	17	1	0	5.6%	0.0%
Philippines	0	17	1	0	5.6%	0.0%
St.Vincent/Grenadines	0	17	1	0	5.6%	0.0%
Trinidad/Tobago	0	16	1	1	5.6%	0.0%
Comoros	0	12	0	6	5.5%	0.0%
Congo	0	13	0	5	5.5%	0.0%
Sao Tome/Principe	0	12	0	6	5.5%	0.0%
Timor-Leste	0	13	0	5	5.5%	0.0%
Angola	0	7	0	11	5.4%	0.0%
Guinea	0	15	0	3	5.4%	0.0%
Afghanistan	0	18	0	0	5.3%	0.0%
Algeria	0	18	0	0	5.3%	0.0%
Azerbaijan	0	18	0	0	5.3%	0.0%
Bahrain	0	18	0	0	5.3%	0.0%
Bangladesh	0	18	0	0	5.3%	0.0%
Barbados	0	17	0	1	5.3%	0.0%
Belarus	0	18	0	0	5.3%	0.0%
Belize	0	18	0	0	5.3%	0.0%
Bhutan	0	9	1	8	5.3%	0.0%
Bolivia	0	18	0	0	5.3%	0.0%
Botswana	0	18	0	0	5.3%	0.0%
Brazil	0	18	0	0	5.3%	0.0%
Brunei Darussalam	0	18	0	0	5.3%	0.0%
Burkina Faso	0	18	0	0	5.3%	0.0%
Cambodia	0	18	0	0	5.3%	0.0%
Cape Verde	0	18	0	0	5.3%	0.0%
Chile	0	18	0	0	5.3%	0.0%
China	0	18	0	0	5.3%	0.0%
Cuba	0	18	0	0	5.3%	0.0%
Djibouti	0	18	0	0	5.3%	0.0%

All Countries (By Voting Coincidence Percentage) (Cont'd)

COUNTRY	IDENTICAL VOTES	OPPOSITE VOTES	ABSTEN-TIONS	ABSENCES	VOTING COINCIDENCE INCLUDING CONSENSUS	VOTES ONLY
DPR of Korea	0	18	0	0	5.3%	0.0%
Dominica	0	17	0	1	5.3%	0.0%
Ecuador	0	18	0	0	5.3%	0.0%
Egypt	0	18	0	0	5.3%	0.0%
Eritrea	0	17	0	1	5.3%	0.0%
Gabon	0	18	0	0	5.3%	0.0%
Ghana	0	18	0	0	5.3%	0.0%
Guinea-Bissau	0	17	0	1	5.3%	0.0%
Guyana	0	18	0	0	5.3%	0.0%
Indonesia	0	18	0	0	5.3%	0.0%
Iran	0	18	0	0	5.3%	0.0%
Jamaica	0	18	0	0	5.3%	0.0%
Jordan	0	18	0	0	5.3%	0.0%
Kuwait	0	18	0	0	5.3%	0.0%
Kyrgyzstan	0	16	0	2	5.3%	0.0%
Laos	0	18	0	0	5.3%	0.0%
Lebanon	0	18	0	0	5.3%	0.0%
Lesotho	0	18	0	0	5.3%	0.0%
Libya	0	18	0	0	5.3%	0.0%
Madagascar	0	18	0	0	5.3%	0.0%
Malaysia	0	18	0	0	5.3%	0.0%
Maldives	0	18	0	0	5.3%	0.0%
Mali	0	18	0	0	5.3%	0.0%
Morocco	0	18	0	0	5.3%	0.0%
Mozambique	0	17	0	1	5.3%	0.0%
Myanmar (Burma)	0	18	0	0	5.3%	0.0%
Namibia	0	18	0	0	5.3%	0.0%
Nepal	0	18	0	0	5.3%	0.0%
Nigeria	0	18	0	0	5.3%	0.0%
Oman	0	18	0	0	5.3%	0.0%
Paraguay	0	18	0	0	5.3%	0.0%
Qatar	0	18	0	0	5.3%	0.0%
Saint Lucia	0	18	0	0	5.3%	0.0%
Saudi Arabia	0	18	0	0	5.3%	0.0%
Senegal	0	18	0	0	5.3%	0.0%
Seychelles	0	16	0	2	5.3%	0.0%
Sierra Leone	0	18	0	0	5.3%	0.0%
Singapore	0	18	0	0	5.3%	0.0%
Somalia	0	18	0	0	5.3%	0.0%
South Africa	0	18	0	0	5.3%	0.0%
Sri Lanka	0	18	0	0	5.3%	0.0%

All Countries (By Voting Coincidence Percentage) (Cont'd)

COUNTRY	IDENTICAL VOTES	OPPOSITE VOTES	ABSTEN-TIONS	ABSENCES	VOTING COINCIDENCE INCLUDING CONSENSUS	VOTES ONLY
Sudan	0	18	0	0	5.3%	0.0%
Suriname	0	18	0	0	5.3%	0.0%
Swaziland	0	9	0	9	5.3%	0.0%
Syria	0	18	0	0	5.3%	0.0%
Tajikistan	0	17	0	1	5.3%	0.0%
Togo	0	18	0	0	5.3%	0.0%
Tunisia	0	18	0	0	5.3%	0.0%
Turkey	0	18	0	0	5.3%	0.0%
Turkmenistan	0	18	0	0	5.3%	0.0%
UR Tanzania	0	18	0	0	5.3%	0.0%
United Arab Emirates	0	18	0	0	5.3%	0.0%
Venezuela	0	18	0	0	5.3%	0.0%
Vietnam	0	18	0	0	5.3%	0.0%
Yemen	0	18	0	0	5.3%	0.0%
Zambia	0	18	0	0	5.3%	0.0%
Zimbabwe	0	18	0	0	5.3%	0.0%
Iraq	0	17	0	1	5.0%	0.0%
Chad	0	2	0	16	4.8%	0.0%
Dem. Rep. Congo	0	2	0	16	4.8%	0.0%
Gambia	0	10	0	8	4.8%	0.0%
Liberia	0	11	0	7	4.8%	0.0%
Malawi	0	4	0	14	4.8%	0.0%
Niger	0	11	0	7	4.8%	0.0%
Rwanda	0	1	0	17	4.8%	0.0%
Kiribati	0	0	0	18	**	**
St. Kitts and Nevis	0	0	0	18	**	**
Average	0.5	13.8	2.4	1.2	9.6%	3.6%